Stories, Streets, and Saints

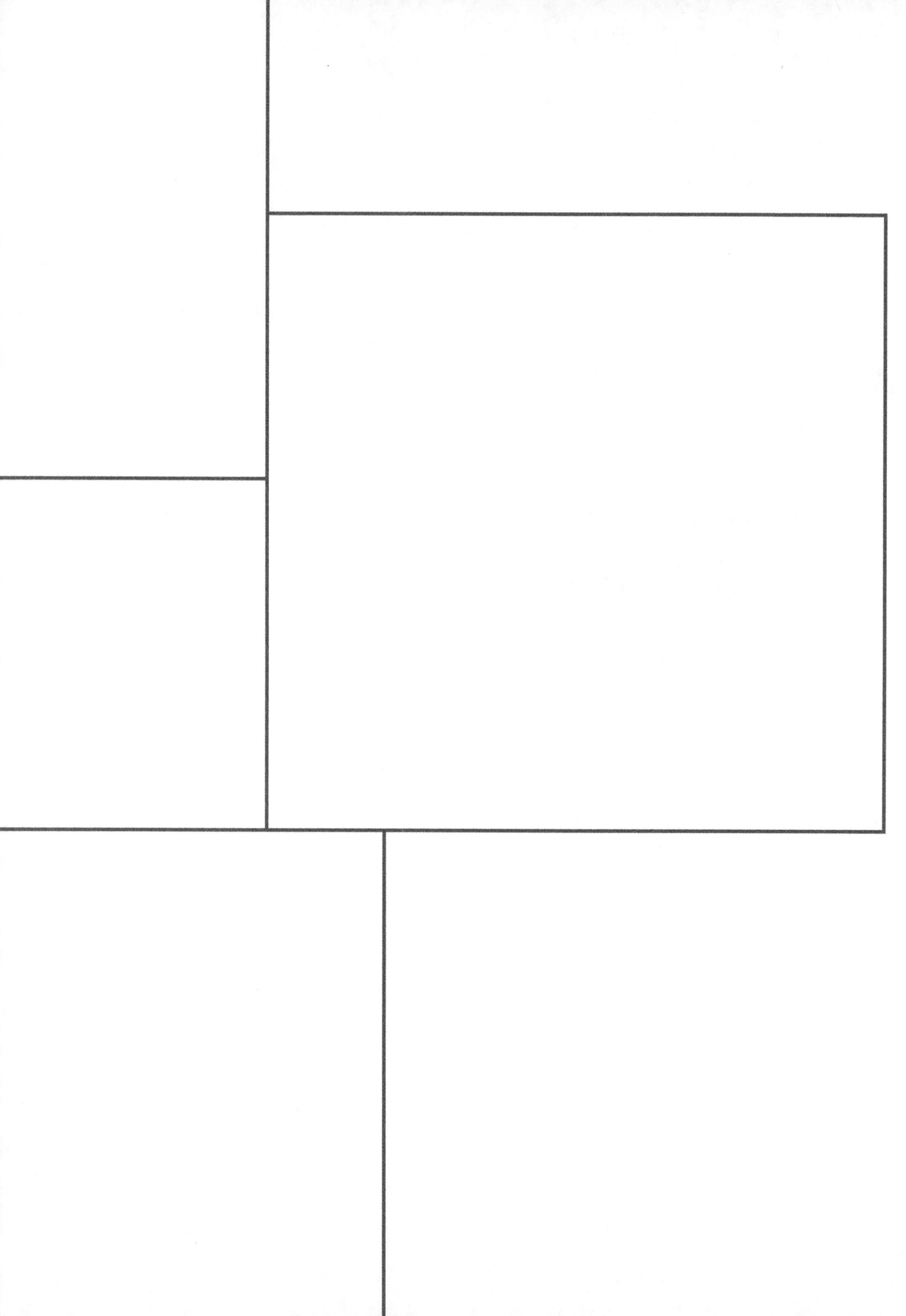

Stories, Streets, and Saints

Photographs and Oral Histories
from Boston's North End

Anthony V. Riccio

Foreword by Nicholas Dello Russo
Epilogue by James S. Pasto

EXCELSIOR
EDITIONS

Cover: Photographs by Anthony V. Riccio. TOP LEFT: Feast of Saint Anthony, 1981. TOP RIGHT: Feast of San Rocco, 1981. BOTTOM: J&N Market at 130 Salem Street, 1981.

Published by STATE UNIVERSITY OF NEW YORK PRESS
© 2022 Anthony V. Riccio. *All rights reserved*

Printed in the United States of America

No part of this book may be used or reproduced in any manner whatsoever without written permission. No part of this book may be stored in a retrieval system or transmitted in any form or by any means including electronic, electrostatic, magnetic tape, mechanical, photocopying, recording, or otherwise without the prior permission in writing of the publisher.

EXCELSIOR EDITIONS is an imprint of STATE UNIVERSITY OF NEW YORK PRESS
For information, contact STATE UNIVERSITY OF NEW YORK PRESS, Albany, NY
www.sunypress.edu

Library of Congress Cataloging-in-Publication Data
Names: Riccio, Anthony V., author.
Title: Stories, streets, and saints : photographs and oral histories from Boston's North End / Anthony V. Riccio.
Other titles: Photographs and oral histories from Boston's North End
Description: Albany : State University of New York Press, [2022] | Series: Excelsior editions | Includes bibliographical references and index.
Identifiers: LCCN 2022000152 | ISBN 9781438490083 (paperback) | ISBN 9781438490090 (ebook)
Subjects: LCSH: North End (Boston, Mass.)—History. | North End (Boston, Mass.)—History—Pictorial works. | Little Italies—Massachusetts—Boston—History. | Little Italies—Massachusetts—Boston—History—Pictorial works. | Immigrants—Massachusetts—Boston—Biography—Pictorial works. | Italian Americans—Massachusetts—Boston—History. | Italian Americans—Massachusetts—Boston—Biography. | Boston (Mass.)—Ethnic relations—History—Pictorial works. | Boston (Mass.)—Social life and customs—Pictorial works.
Classification: LCC F73.68.N65 R535 2022 | DDC 974.4/61—dc23/eng/20220128
LC record available at https://lccn.loc.gov/2022000152

10 9 8 7 6 5 4 3 2 1

To the people of the North End
who welcomed me into their homes
and trusted me with their legacies.

Contents

Acknowledgments — ix
In Memory of My Friend, Anthony Riccio: 1952–2022 — xi
  TOMMY DAMIGELLA
Foreword — xv
  NICHOLAS DELLO RUSSO

1 Life in Southern Italy at the Turn of the Century — 1
2 Leaving Italy for the Promise of America — 27
3 The Journey to Boston — 35
4 A New Life in the North End — 41
5 Becoming an American Citizen — 65
6 The Italian Mother — 71
7 The Italian Father — 83
8 The Oral Tradition: Family Stories, Dialects, Folktales, and Prayers — 95
9 Italy and the North End in World War I — 107
10 Garlic Necklaces, Camphor Bags, and Shots of Anisette:
   The Spanish Flu Pandemic in the North End — 113
11 The Molasses Explosion — 119
12 Italian American Street Life — 129
13 Going to School — 151
14 Justice Denied: Sacco and Vanzetti — 163
15 The Depression in the North End — 169
16 Seamstresses and Factory Workers: Italian American Women at Work — 181
17 Making It in the North End: Italian American Men at Work — 199

18 Making Wine, Drinking Wine — 217
19 Life in the Tenements — 225
20 Sicilian Fishermen in the North End — 237
21 Miracles, Societies, and Processions — 249
22 Christmas in the North End — 263
23 Irish and Italians — 271
24 Refugees in the North End: West Enders Tell Their Stories — 279
25 Local Politics — 287
26 Gangsters and Racketeers — 299
27 Life in a Cold-Water Flat — 305
28 The Changing North End — 311
29 The Old Waterfront and the New Boston — 333
30 Poor Tenant, Poor Landlord — 351
31 Meglio Pane e Cipolla, e Sola — 359

Epilogue: Anthony's Gift to Us — 379
    JAMES S. PASTO

Notes — 399

Acknowledgments

This book would not have been possible without the generosity of Lena Albanese, Rose Amato, Joe Anastasi, Joe Arigo, Nick Argiro, Tom Bardetti, Eugene Belmonte, Mary Beninati, Salvatore Bernardo, Rosa Birra, Josie Bosco, Josie Bossio, Fred Bourne, Rose Bradenese, Jimmy Brovaco, Bernadine Cacciola, Santa Cacciola, Anna Caffarelli, Pasquale Capone, Marguerite Carbone, Joe Cataloni, Maria Chiarenza, Maria Chiucchiolo, Vladimir Ciani, Ann Ciriello, Mary Colantonio, Frances Zanfani Corolla, Frank Corolla, Francesca Corrao, Teresa Costanzo, Antonio Crugnale, Philomena Crugnale, Theresa D'Alelio, Phil D'Alessandro, Marianna D'Antonio, Dr. Nicholas Dello Russo, Joe DiCenso, Nunzio DiMarino, Elvira DiMattia, Frank Favazza, Liberatore Federico, Giuseppe Freni, Rose Giampaola, Paul Grande, Anita LaRocca, Robert LaRocca, Frances Lauro, Marguerite Locchiato, Helen Luongo, Antonia Luzzo, Alice Manaro, Michelina Manfra, Angie Marinella, Eddie Marino, Louis Marrotta, Maria Missiano, Mary Molinari, Al Mostone, Mary Nastasi, Theresa Paglia, Arpito Pagliuca, Mary Pagliuca, Mary Pasquale, Mariano Penissi, Sam Perrelli, Rose Pesce, Joe Petringa, Lucia Petringa, Viola Pettinelli, Diego Picadacci, Josie Picadacci, Grace Pinelli, Charlie Polcari, Dominic Rosso, Angelo Sardo, Alberto Sorrentino, Crocefissa Summa, Leslie Surrette, Idolo Taglieri, Antonio Tarantino, Joe Troisi, Lena Troisi, Josie Tranquillo, Mary Arigo Ventola, Francesco Ventresca, Maria Virginio, and Josie Zizza.

Many North Enders made invaluable contributions to the book. I am grateful to Dr. Nicholas Dello Russo, a lifelong North Ender who generously contributed his knowledge, providing many missing pieces to the neighborhood mosaic that would have been lost to history.

I am also greatly indebted to my friend Dr. James Pasto for sharing his encyclopedic knowledge of the North End and providing his expertise at every step of the way. I would also like to thank Vito Aluia, a local historian who generously shared his firsthand knowledge and photographs of the North End. I would also like to thank Betty Panza, Richard and Bennett Molinari, and Sal DiMasi for their important contributions. Many thanks go to Andrea Palermo and Sebastiana Miano of the Biblioteca Comunale of Licodea Eubea in Sicily for their assistance. A special thanks goes to Tommy Damigella for his infectious enthusiasm for the book project and his passion to keep our Italian American history alive.

I was fortunate to meet Loreto Giovannone, an independent researcher who contacted me from Italy and generously shared his important research and documentation to uncover the hidden story of the Unification (Risorgimento). I also want to thank the Italian scholar Freedom Pentimalli, who deciphered and translated Maria Missiano's poem from her Calabrese dialect.

Words cannot describe the contribution of Damiano Saputo of Cinisi, Sicily, who dedicated countless hours helping to translate oral histories in nearly forgotten Sicilian dialects in my recordings from 1979 through 1982. Damiano's sincere commitment to the project's success often left me sitting in amazement at my computer late into the night. I want to thank Ned Scigliano, the great-nephew of George Scigliano, for sharing his knowledge of the life and times of his great-uncle. I also want to thank Eugene Mirabelli for contributing his mother's memoir of the North End and Keith Favazza for sharing the stories of his grandfather Frank and thus preserving the history of Sicilian fishermen that would have been lost to history.

Since 1980, the words of my dear friend and lifelong North Ender Mary Molinari resonated within me: "Anthony, I hope you make something out of all this; I hope you make a book so people won't forget."

Because of the contributions of many North Enders, both past and present, who graciously shared their life experiences, I sincerely believe this book belongs to them more than me. It is my hope that I have given their legacies the respect and honor they deserve.

In Memory of My Friend, Anthony Riccio

1952–2022   TOMMY DAMIGELLA

I will always remember how Anthony Riccio and I first became friends. It had to do with my reading his first book *Portrait of an Italian-American Neighborhood: The North End of Boston*. While it came out in 1998, I only first saw it about fifteen years ago when the title caught my eye as I was browsing in a bookstore. I read the preface right then and there, and as soon as I did, I realized I had found a compadre. Anthony's story of how he came to work in the North End and how he had traveled to Italy to the towns of his grandparents resonated with me because that was my story as well. I moved to the North End back in the 1970s and I, too, had gone to Sicily and visited my mother's hometown and met my relatives just as Anthony had done.

    I had gone to live in the North End because I had connections there. My mother lived there when she first arrived from Italy in 1925. She was just seven years old, and she had come to join members of her family who had been there since 1914. And while my father lived in East Boston when he arrived in the United States, his father owned a bakery on Clark Street in the 1920s. So, the North End was always home to me.

    When I saw an advertisement that Anthony was doing a presentation on his next book *From Italy to the North End: Photographs, 1972–1982*, published in 2015, and that it was at the New North Bennet Street School, I knew I had to meet him. I wrote to him and told him who I was, that I was planning to attend his presentation, and that I was looking forward to meeting him. Well, when we first saw each other, he knew me right away, and like good Italians we greeted each other with a hug.

That was the beginning of our very special friendship. I became engulfed in his devotion to tell "our" Italian American stories, and it took no effort on his part to pull me into the book you now hold. I worked with him closely as we researched stories together and as I shared my own personal family stories that went back to the 1900s. I understood how he became devoted to recording the stories of the *Anziani* (the Italian elders) who immigrated here at the turn of the century. He got to know them as he provided services for them at the Senior Drop-in Center. At the same time, he put his photo skills to use and now has over two thousand photos from that period of 1980s in his incredible collection.

What is amazing about Anthony is that he knew in his soul, at that time he was there, that he was watching the neighborhood begin to gentrify, and he surmised that the neighborhood people and businesses he was documenting—and falling in love with—would eventually disappear. He was right. Over the past several years, as he was completing his book, he would make his trips up from New Haven to the North End and meet with Jimmy Pasto and me so we could walk the streets together and he could shoot his before-and-after-photos for his book. Those were great days for Anthony because it served to invigorate him even more to tell these stories in a new book, the one you now hold. The three of us decided that we had to create an Italian American museum to become a permanent home for his collection of stories. Anthony had said it was up to us to make it happen, and a plan is in place to see it come to fruition.

In 2019, Rita and I had the opportunity to visit Anthony and his wife, Bunny, in New Haven for a special convention at which he was speaking, in the very neighborhood in which he had grown up. He had also become the Italian storyteller in New Haven, documenting the lives of Italian Americans there and in other parts of the state of Connecticut. My wife Rita and I immediately fell in love with Bunny as well. I also spoke later with one of Anthony's coworkers at Yale where Anthony worked in the library for twenty-two years. From the way his coworker spoke, I could see Anthony's enthusiasm for everything he did was infectious. Later, when Anthony met my family, and stayed for dinner at our home, and stayed for the night, he made his interest in my family's lives and their work apparent to me. That's just who Anthony was. They were my children, he was my dear friend, so my family mattered to him too. It was just another way we shared so much from our own hearts with each other.

In the past four years when Anthony made many PowerPoint presentations, he became the unofficial storyteller of the North End and was beloved by all who met him. His absolute sincerity and devotion toward our Italian American heritage had such an authenticity that it moved people to tears when he made his presentations, as he touched the memories of their families. In fact, during the COVID-19 epidemic, since he could not travel to Boston from New Haven, he began posting his many photos of the Italian elders on Facebook, which immediately stirred up a surge of sentimental emotions for the children and grandchildren as they saw pictures of their Nonne and Nonni. He was in constant communication with everyone as they shared and added to his storytelling.

In the meantime, Anthony was in continual contact with Jimmy Pasto, me, and another great North End storyteller Nick Dello Russo for collaboration as he completed this book. COVID-19 delayed the publication. Finally, in December 2021, he got the call, and the deal was made to move forward with the book. Anthony called me that same day and we shared this joy together. Thank goodness he knew this then, because four weeks later he had his fatal heart attack. His friends, along with Bunny, have stepped up to bring his final work to the public, with SUNY Press' absolute commitment to publish it, both because of its obvious importance but also because of their admiration for Anthony.

When Anthony made his wonderful PowerPoint presentations, he would always end them with a delightful photo of his father smiling sweetly as he was making a pot of espresso. Anthony would quote his father by repeating what his dad said to him: "Anthony, when I am gone, if you continue to talk about me and remember me, then I will always be with you."

Anthony, I pledge we will continue to talk about you, and so you will always be with us. Thank you for your lasting, wondrous gifts that you have left for us all.

—<i>Tommy Damigella</i>
MARCH 21, 2022

Foreword

NICHOLAS DELLO RUSSO

L'America

The White Star Line steamship *Canopic* was tied securely to the dock at the quay in Naples on a beautiful day in May 1899. The sun twinkled on the waves, small fishing boats darted around the harbor, and the old city looked serene under the early morning mist. The *Canopic* was a fairly new ship with a deep black hull, one funnel, two masts, and twin screw propellors. Her twin coal-fired engines could propel her at over fifteen knots and she could make the transatlantic crossing in little over a week during the fair-weather months.

The parade of immigrants began at the railroad station, the Stazione di Napoli Centrale, and slowly wound its way toward the Piazza Giuseppe Garibaldi. It was the same scene almost every day of the week. Rustic country people arrived, dressed in hand-spun woolens and carrying a motley assortment of valises and trunks. Men hoisted large trunks on their backs, women held children tightly to their thick skirts, and all the while the Neapolitan street toughs, the *guaglioni*, danced around ridiculing their country clothes, calling them the derogatory term *terroni*, and trying to entice the young girls to join them. It was only a short distance from the terminal down the Via Garibaldi to the docks, where several steamships were tied up awaiting their wretched cargo.

The scene on the dock was one of barely controlled chaos. Midship, the first- and second-class passengers were ushered aboard on a dedicated gangplank by the courtly and courteous bursar. The ship had room for five hundred first- and second-class passengers and eight hundred in steerage. The steerage passengers, almost all southern Italians, were herded aboard like cattle near the stern. They came from the desperately poor hill towns surrounding Naples and Avelino, from Calabria, and from near the city of Matera in Basilicata. There was also a large group of noisy Sicilians dressed in their colorful costumes and jostling each other good-naturedly.

Southern Italy and Sicily were emptying out. It had been forty years since Italy was unified, and the Risorgimento (Unification) had brought prosperity to the North, but the South, the Mezzogiorno, was stuck in a medieval kind of serfdom like an insect preserved in amber. The Normans introduced feudalism to Italy in the eleventh century and it remained in place for over eight hundred years. Even when the Bourbons supposedly abolished feudalism in 1806, the ownership of land passed, not to the tenants, but to the local aristocracy and foreign investors. It seemed as though there were scores of *nobili—baroni, marchesi, conti*, and even *principi*—who owned the fertile land and extracted excessive rents from the serfs. The typical southern Italian farmer, or *contadino*, may have owned a rough stone house without water or sanitation but worked on large, industrial-style farms where at least half of all harvests went to the absentee owner. The *paesano* would arise before dawn, walk an hour or more to the farm, work until sunset, and finally walk home exhausted. He did this seven days a week, all year round. No wonder they called life in the southern Italian villages *la miseria*. Malaria and yellow fever were endemic in the swampy marshlands and early death was an ever-present reality. Superstition abounded and every village had a patron saint to protect the people. Miracles were passionately requested by prayers and sacrifices. Many young men and women wore magical amulets made from red coral around their necks to ward off the ever-lurking *malocchio*, or evil eye.

As late as 1935 the Torinese doctor, artist, and intellectual Carlo Levi was arrested on the order of Benito Mussolini because of his anti-Fascist writings. Instead of sentencing Levi to jail, the Fascists imposed an even worse punishment on the sophisticated northerner. They banished him to live for a year in Lucania, now called Basilicata, in the far South, where he wrote a journal of his life in the villages of Grassano and Gagliano, which he published in 1945. He called the book *Cristo si è fermato a Eboli*, which was a common local expression meaning "Christ stopped at Eboli." The town of Eboli was the terminus of the railway line from the North. Beyond that point travel was difficult, and the region was isolated from the rest of Italy and from civilization. The people of those hill towns felt abandoned, certainly by the politicians in

Rome and even by their revered Catholic Church. Northern Italians considered southerners a different race of people, more like animals than humans, and called them terroni, "people of the land."

Levi was not confined to his house or restricted in his movements around the towns. Local officials were pleased to have such a famous intellectual from Turin in their midst and tried to ingratiate themselves with him. Levi, however, refused all invitations from the local leaders and instead aligned himself with the *paesani*, whom he grew to like and even admire for their inner strength, determination, and resilience.

There is an apocryphal story of an important minister from Rome who visited a small southern Italian village just before the turn of the twentieth century. The government was considering building a public works project for the town and he had come to inspect the area and meet the local residents. The mayor gave him a tour of the town, which seemed strangely quiet to the minister. There were a few elderly people sitting in front of their houses and some children playing in the dusty streets but no young men. The minister assumed the men of the town were off in the fields working the land and asked the mayor when they would return. "Ah," said the mayor, "if you want to meet the young men of the town, Excellency, you will have to travel to Boston or New York. They've all left."

∼

Among the passengers boarding the *Canopic* on that day in May were two teenagers from the hill town of Chiusano di San Domenico, outside Avellino. Carmela, a slight, fifteen-year-old girl with a turned-up nose, was traveling with family and friends to Boston. Nicola, the shy boy who stared at her in church, didn't have a ticket but somehow had sneaked aboard as a stowaway. Carmela was promised to him; he believed they were *promessi sposi*, betrothed ones. Nicola was also running from the police, because of an unfortunate incident concerning a dead priest, so escaping to America was of vital importance to him.

The spring passage was rough and many of those in steerage were constantly seasick. There was the smell of vomit, the unrelenting thrum of the engines, and the odor of hundreds of unwashed bodies to contend with. The screams of frightened country people, most of whom had never seen the ocean, made the trip resemble a scene from Dante's *Inferno*. Steerage passengers were allowed on deck only once a day, while the first- and second-class passengers were eating, so as not to be seen by the upper classes. They were limited to the aft deck at the stern of the vessel, where they were enveloped by coal smoke from the enormous funnel, but even that was better than the horrors of steerage. Sometimes steerage passengers refused to go back to the bowels of the ship and sailors had to beat them with wooden clubs to force them back down.

The mortality rate for steerage passengers was upward of 10 percent, and those who died en route were unceremoniously buried at sea. My great uncle, Alessandro Onesti, who owned the Hotel Rome in North Square, died on a return trip from Italy. He was wrapped in a canvas shroud and buried at sea, without a priest to bless his body and missing his diamond pinky ring.

When the *Canopic* landed in New York Harbor, the upper-class passengers quickly disembarked while those in steerage were transferred to smaller ferries, which brought them to Ellis Island for processing. From the deck of the ferry they stared in amazement at the great city with buildings that seemed to touch the sky. L'America was truly a wondrous place.

As they passed by Ellis Island, Carmela and Nicola surely would have noticed the enormous bronze statue of a woman holding a torch in her right hand and asked other passengers about it. Some probably thought it was a lighthouse guiding ships into the harbor. Others may have said it was the statue of a powerful American saint named Santa America, who would protect them. Whoever it was, they would be happy to see this mighty saint and would have made the sign of the cross to ask for her blessing and protection.

On the ferry the immigrants could breathe fresh air for the first time and thought their nightmare journey was almost over, but the indignities of Ellis Island lay ahead. On some days over ten thousand immigrants landed on Ellis Island, and Nicola, the stowaway, somehow managed to slip into that great crush of humanity. The immigrants were lined up, poked and prodded, and their eyelids jerked up with sharp hooks looking for trachoma, which, if discovered, resulted in immediate deportation back to Italy. Italians called Ellis Island *l'isola delle lagrime*, the isle of tears, because so many hopeful immigrants were refused entry and sent back to their home countries.

From New York Carmela and Nicola made their way to Boston, where they had friends and relatives. The train was expensive and they most likely took the coastal side-wheel steamship that left New York daily for Rowes Wharf in Boston. From there they could carry their trunks to the North End and finally begin their new life in l'America. The date of their arrival was May 25, 1899.

At that time, North Square was the center of the Italian North End. The house of the patriot Paul Revere was located there but, much to the chagrin of the Yankee Puritans, it was used as an Italian grocery store and cigar-manufacturing company. The young couple discovered that the North End was very similar to their Italian village, Chiusano di San Domenico. Italian was the language of everyday conversation, although they had a difficult time understanding some of the other regional dialects. There were grocery stores, butchers, cheese and wine shops, and all manner of other small shops that catered to the needs of the nascent Italian community. It was almost like being back in Italy but much more crowded and chaotic. There were also hardships to be endured. The newly arrived Italian immigrants were exploited by the owners of the factories where they worked; by the police and other city officials, who demanded payments for the most trivial considerations; and even by the *padrone* (bosses), their own countrymen, who loaned them money and then sold them into virtual slavery to pay it back.

The Boston Brahmins (Yankee Americans) were repulsed by the immigrants from southern Europe and Russia, particularly Italians and Jews. They considered Italians to be criminals and anarchists and Jews to be union organizers and Bolsheviks. The Eugenics Society of America was founded and supported by two Boston Brahmins, Henry Cabot Lodge, the junior senator from Massachusetts, and Joseph Lee, a wealthy Beacon Hill Brahmin. They excoriated and dehumanized these immigrants in their writings and grotesque cartoon caricatures published in newspapers owned by the anti-immigrant publisher William Randolph Hearst. In 1924, they finally succeeded in passing the Immigration Restriction Act, which severely limited immigrants from southern and eastern Europe (basically Italians and Jews) and favored those from what they considered the more refined and acceptable northern European and Nordic countries. This blatantly racist act remained in effect until 1965.

∼

Nicola and Carmela found a shared room in a tenement building on the North Square, which was owned by *paesani* (fellow Italians) from their town. Rooms were rented by the week, the day, or the hour. There was no privacy and only one toilet per floor, which had to be shared by several tenants. The couple were married in Sacred Heart Church and Nicola worked as a day laborer—"pick and shovel"—as they used to say, and as a longshoreman unloading coal from the barges that brought it to the Lincoln Wharf power station. By 1920 they had their own tiny, cold-water flat at 20 Moon Street and were raising a family, which eventually numbered ten children. They then moved to South Medford like so many other North End Italians and were able to send four of their six sons to college and one even to medical school. Once they graduated from high school, the girls were expected to help raise the younger children or get married as was the custom in Italian peasant families.

Carmela and Nicola's story has been told millions of times about immigrants of all nationalities and is still being told today. The early immigrants asked for little, expected nothing, and received even less. All they wanted was a chance to work, earn a living, feed their families, and educate their children. The only safety net they had was the strength of their backs and the love of their families. There was no welfare, no Medicaid or Medicare, no unemployment benefits, no food stamps or rent subsidies, nothing. Yet in spite of all the obstacles and prejudices, they refused to surrender. They relied on peasant skills and instincts developed and honed over millennia of enduring suffering and oppression. They were tough, resilient, clever, and yes, stubborn, and they survived and thrived. Their children and grandchildren benefited greatly from their sufferings and helped make America the great country it is today.

~

I was born in the North End of Boston one month before World War II ended and have lived there ever since. The North End of my youth and young adulthood was an Italian village. In many ways it was the quintessential Italian American immigrant neighborhood. Separated from the rest of Boston, first by blocks of semiabandoned warehouses and manufacturing buildings and then by the Central Artery roadway, which replaced them, the North End remained physically isolated from the rest of the city. It was also separated culturally and socioeconomically by being Italian and having a strong ethnic identity. Outsiders came to eat at the many Italian restaurants and in the summer tourists would walk on the Freedom Trail, but the North End remained an insular, Italian neighborhood well into the last years of the twentieth century.

Southern Italians weren't the first immigrant group to settle in the North End. Before the Civil War, the Irish came escaping the potato famine. The North End at that time was still made up of wooden buildings left over from the colonial era and the Irish crowded into these wretched hovels. Around 1880, eastern European Jews arrived fleeing the tsar's pogroms. Their quarter centered on Salem Street, where they had dry-goods shops, kosher butchers, synagogues, and schools. The Italians began arriving in the 1890s, and what began as a trickle soon became a tidal wave. Like all ethnic groups they re-created what was familiar, and by the early twentieth century the North End resembled an Italian village. Almost every street had a butcher, a bakery, a greengrocer, and a *salumeria* (deli), where Italian groceries were available. There were Italian social clubs and saint's societies that organized street festivals every summer. Settlement houses and Italian churches helped acclimate newly arrived immigrants to the oftentimes confusing social and cultural norms of the new country. The tenement buildings of the North End helped tens of thousands of immigrants gain a foothold in America. Most used them as a steppingstone to a suburban house with a garden, but some, like my family, stayed on and watched the North End change.

The single most important thing the North End had to offer the immigrants was the opportunity to work. From the 1860s onward, America was expanding and industrializing, and low-paid workers were needed to do the heavy lifting. The North End and surrounding neighborhoods had thousands of jobs in the wholesale meat, produce, and fishing industries. There were warehouses, restaurants, taverns, and coffee shops, all within a short walk or trolley ride. We had everything we needed right outside our front doors. My mother and grandmother would shop for food daily at their favorite shops. There they could speak in Italian and catch up on local news and gossip. As children, my parents, aunts, and uncles worked in typical blue-collar North End jobs, as a seamstress, candy dipper, salesclerk, secretary, bar tender, undertaker, auto mechanic, and bookie. Every morning Nonna would make a big pot of coffee accompanied by toasted Italian bread or fried polenta left over from the night before. When they returned from work in the evening supper, would be ready: chicken soup with a bitter green salad, fried veal cutlets, home made pasta, or maybe chicken cacciatore. After supper the men would go to their clubs to play cards and socialize. The women would attend classes at one of the settlement houses or go to a novena or mission at one of the four Catholic churches. On payday the girls would turn over their money to Nonna, who would give them a weekly allowance and save the rest in a metal coffee can over the sink. The boys got to keep their own money but had to contribute to household expenses. It was a wonderful way of life that was enveloped in love, family, and tradition.

∼

They say that history is the story of great men doing great things, but Anthony Riccio has taken a different approach in this book and has honored the quotidian. He has chosen to profile the ordinary lives of the thousands of Italians who settled in the North End. Anthony arrived in the North End in 1978, fresh out of graduate school in Florence, Italy. He came from an Italian American community in New Haven, Connecticut, so it was natural for him to accept a job as coordinator of the North End Senior Citizen Center. There he became friendly with the residents from my parents' and grandparents' generation, who were some of the last people to have experienced inner-city tenement life. Many of those elderly people were in their nineties and had immigrated to Boston during the great Italian diaspora of the late nineteenth and early twentieth centuries. Anthony quickly realized that their stories were about to be lost in the fog of time so he decided to record their memories. He visited them in their cold-water flats, looked at old photographs they had tucked away in boxes, and marveled at the memories they shared. Southern Italians who immigrated to America were poorly educated and their cultural traditions were passed from generation to generation by the spoken word, through stories and allegorical tales. This book is a record of those accounts, which are stories that come *di cuore*, from the heart.

The North End has changed, but like all great neighborhoods it is reinventing itself in a new and unexpected way. Italian families have mostly moved on to the streetcar suburbs and beyond. They are being replaced by young professionals who work in the financial district. Gentrification has made its inexorable changes and a once poor, working-class neighborhood has suddenly become posh. The neighborhood still retains a veneer of Italian culture but continues to evolve according to the needs and desires of the times. This book pays homage to those Italian families and to the millions of poor Italians who came to America seeking a better life. Because of their blood, sweat, and tears we have prospered, and we owe them our eternal gratitude.

—*North End*

Boston, Massachusetts, August 2020 Addendum

Anthony Riccio died a few weeks after submitting this book to his publishers. His passion was preserving the voices and stories of the early Southern Italian immigrants to America and his passing is a tremendous loss to the Italian/American community. While we mourn his passing, we celebrate his great achievement. This book will serve as a living memorial to Anthony's love for his Italian heritage.

Riposa in pace, caro amico, che la terra ti sia lieve.
Rest in peace, dear friend, may the earth rest gently upon you.

—*Nicholas M Dello Russo*

Life in Southern Italy at the Turn of the Century

> I had nothing in Montefalcione—if you didn't work you didn't eat.
> —NUNZIO DIMARINO

"Brigandone! Ma che vai trovando [You big brigand! What are looking for]?" There in the hallway stood my diminutive immigrant grandmother, whose daily routine on the first floor had been disrupted by my rumble down the stairs. Hands on hips and with a familiar grin across her dark olive face, her charcoal eyes danced with delight as they did whenever she caught her mischievous grandson misbehaving. She mildly protested my youthful transgression, playfully calling me a brigandone. Growing up in the late 1950s as a third-generation Italian American, I had no understanding what my nickname signified in Italian history or the volumes it spoke about the resistance to the northern military campaign to crush the South.

The commotion I had caused triggered my grandmother's memories of the briganti—bands of resistance fighters comprised of draft dodgers, deserters, ex-soldiers of the Bourbons, escapees, poor farmers, day laborers, carpenters, blacksmiths, coal miners, tailors, tinsmiths, porters, bricklayers, shepherds, coffee makers, a lawyer, a judge. All had fought against the invading Piedmontese army, which attacked towns like my grandmother's with merciless violence.[1]

Women fighters, known as *brigantesse*, also joined the insurrection. Descending from desolate mountain hideaways to wage surprise attacks, female soldiers rode on horseback and fired guns, often demonstrating more audacity in battle than their male counterparts.[2] They cut their hair and many dressed as men in battle to show allegiance to their band and to the insurgency. After skirmishes with the enemy, they changed into peasant outfits with an air of nonchalance, becoming valuable informants and message-carriers. As country nurses, they administered home remedies to the wounded. Risking certain death, they gathered critical information about enemy troop movements as spies and played important roles in planning acts of defiance with their male counterparts.[3] When arrested as outlaws, women were often granted leniency based on the patriarchal view that women are weak.

From the time of the Risorgimento (Unification) in 1861, government victors wrote Italy's history, portraying the South as an uncivilized and culturally backward territory. Italian Americans, many of whom are descendants of the southern peasantry, inherited an incomplete picture of Italian history from grandparents who told stories of poverty and "*la miseria.*" From its inception in 1815, the Kingdom of the Two Sicilies had actually been a thriving cultural and economic entity. Prior to the northern invasion in the 1860s, the kingdom's booming steel and iron factories produced the materials to construct the first suspension bridge, railway tunnel, and gaslight in Italy and also supplied the metals to build the second largest merchant fleet in Europe. Textile mills and silk factories proliferated throughout the South, employing over one hundred thousand women. Unemployment was unknown and the thought of emigration was foreign.

The banking system loaned money to support businesses at low interest and issued the first bank checks in history. The South gave far more toward the creation of a national treasury than the north, whose banks were in financial trouble with their banking overlords, the Masons of England. Learned teachers taught in a free public school system at every level and universities in Avellino and Salerno offered advanced degrees in medicine, theology, and law. The kingdom's population had the lowest infant mortality rate in Italy and nursing homes and hospitals proliferated, staffed by nine thousand doctors. Italy's first railroad line between Naples and Portici was created in 1839. The first electric telegraph was established in 1852. The kingdom created the first Seismic Observatory in the world as well as botanical gardens and a museum of archeology. The arts flourished in an era when sculptors, painters, music teachers, and craftsmen were often in demand. San Carlo Theatre, the first of its kind, was built in Naples in just two hundred seventy days.[4]

The causes of *brigantaggio*, the civilian uprising against the Piedmontese army's slaughter of unarmed civilians and looting of villages, was officially covered up as recently as 2010, when the Italian government spent €4 billion (roughly $4.5 billion) to celebrate the 150th anniversary of the Unification. Streets and piazzas are named for generals who ordered the shooting of unarmed women and children in Avigliano, Gioia del Colle, Pontelandolfo, Casaldini, Venosa, patria d'Orazio, Barile, Monteverde, S. Marco, Rignano, Spinelli, Carbonara, and Auletta, which were sacked and burned.[5] Montefalcione, whose many emigrants settled in the North End, suffered the same fate.

In Sicily, the town of Bronte was burned to the ground; Randazzo, Castiglione, Regalbuto and Centorbi were looted and destroyed. In 1863, when the Piedmontese government recognized that the counterinsurgency could not be suppressed, it enacted draconian laws for mass deportations and imprisonment of anyone suspected of brigantaggio, being a relative of one, or engaging in any perceived act of providing help to them. Entire families were sent to internment camps all over northern Italy, some to the islands of the Tuscan archipelago. Some were sentenced to horrible jails, others to forced labor camps in tobacco fields or salt and mineral mines and on private farms.[6]

In Sulmona, Abruzzo, the hometown of many North Enders, citizens were rounded up, given trials, and sent away to forced labor camps.[7] Because of the relentless efforts to uncover forgotten official documents in public and private archives, Loreto Giovannone and Miriam Compagnino (*Italiani Deportati 1863*), Antonio Ciano (*I Savoia e il massacro del Sud*), and Nicola Zitara (*L'invenzione del Mezzogiorno*), among others, have written the true story of the Risorgimento.[8]

Unification caused the South to pay a high price: the closing of its schools; the looting of its banks and treasuries; the disproportionate raising of taxes on the overburdened poor; the enactment of conscription; the dismantling of its iron, steel, and textile industries; the loss of farmers' government-sanctioned land; and the indiscriminate murder and plundering of its people by the Piedmontese army. Many of the deported (*deportati*) never returned to their small villages, further decimating the social fabric and economic vitality of the South. Under the guise of patriotism and national unity as a means to justify the colonization of southern Italy for its economic benefit, the Piedmontese government created the dire conditions that caused millions like my grandmother to leave. For those who immigrated to Boston's North End, the promise of America offered a future that their own country could not.

FIGURE 1. Nicola Argiro, 1981.

Nick Argiro Nicola Argiro talked about the nature of love: "When I say I love a you, eh no talk with the mouth *che* [that] I kiss a you, *ma* [but] with the heart, *con sango* [with blood]."

From the Earthquake in Messina to the Italo-Turkish War

I was in the *maremoto* [earthquake and subsequent tsunami] in Messina in 1908. My father was a lieutenant in the Italian Coast Guard. A captain said to me one day, "Argiro, now your father has been in this job, why don't you sign up? At least you'll make five years." I said, "I already have three years, Captain." So I let him sign me up for two more years. I was [a] policeman at the time, and we had to save the people in Reggio and Messina, and after the maremoto was over we built barracks and houses for the people. Then I got drafted for the 1911 Italo-Turkish War and we fought in Turkey for ten months. I signed up for five years and you couldn't go home when you were in the service at that time in Italy, it was under Vittorio Emanuelle III. He ran everything by himself, he was the head one, he was the king. I signed up because my father was an officer in the police. He was a big boss for the Barone Casalino, who was Senatore Delle Camere [Senator in the House of Deputies] in Rome.

It [the war] was lousy, black, stink[ing], ooh it was terrible. We had lice so big we could throw [them] at you, they'd bite you; we couldn't change our clothes—it was bad. We took the boat from Naples; it took fourteen, fifteen hours—it went like a fish—landed in Tripoli, we were in Ben-Ghazi, Tobruk, the police always had to go to the front. The Turks used to hide in the trees, and if you didn't watch they'd kill you when you passed through. Their bullets were thick (the Italians had smaller ones) and they'd do more damage—if you caught one of them, goodbye, you die. They put poison on them too; we called it *famusella*. I was wounded, I got shot twice. Sometimes we didn't eat for two days—we couldn't get supplies. We ate rotten potatoes.

We had this wise guy lieutenant from Palermo who told us, "Go ahead, go ahead!" I said, "Listen, if we go to their camp then we can fight, but not here—they're all on the tops of the trees. See those trees? They'll shoot us like fish." He said, "Oh, over there, over there …" I said, "Lieutenant, if you want to punish me, punish me, but it can't be—you can't take my squad over here and go over there, you have to command—go ahead, go where you like, I'm going here—report me!" He reported me. When he reported me, I couldn't do anything. They changed commanders and they sent him back to Italy.

The new commander was good. He said, "We gotta look out for each other, you watch for me, I watch for you, gotta watch one another." He split us up, no more two, three altogether, now one over here, one over there. The other commander wanted us like sheep all in one place—why you son of a bitch! I said in my mind; if I could I would have shot him in the head, I would have. The commander said to me, "Argiro, you know the commander who wanted to discipline you? He's dead. When he came back as [a] volunteer in the army his own squad knew all about him and they shot him." I said, "If I saw him here, I would kill him myself." He said, "Shhh! I won't put you in jail." I was a sergeant at nineteen. At my hearing the captain said, "Well, Argiro, he tried to do better. The lieutenant didn't know about the Turks in the trees, but Mr. Argiro told him that there were men up there and they would shoot us like fish because he was in the front. And he went to the back, alright, alright." And they gave me another stripe. I got more money and I, when I went home I brought three, four thousand lira. My father said to me, "Why did you sign up?" I was stupid to sign; I was young, I didn't care what they were doing at that time.

"We Were Like the FBI"

In 1911, I was an undercover policeman; we had to find the crooks, people who killed, it was a terrible job. It was like FBI here. We got seven lira a day, five lira was one dollar so I made a dollar twenty cents a day. A lot of other people were only making ten cents an hour. We called them the *Arditi* ["Daring Ones"] and we monitored and kept an eye on things. I signed up for five years. If they called you at night, you went; in the day, you went. You could never stay at one station, ten days in one town, five days in another, and if people saw you—we had to wear black masks, we carried hidden guns. You had to always keep moving so people wouldn't recognize you; the *gangisti* [gangsters] were very smart and they remembered the people who arrested them. We didn't arrest, we just watched, and we had a machine with [a] button you pushed to call. We'd say, "Yes, so and so and such a place, go and get them." The troops would go—twenty-five, thirty—and arrest them.

The most we ever stayed in one place was a week, then we'd go to another town to check it out, if it was quiet, if there were crooks. We'd ask from family to family. We didn't sleep in barracks because the bad guys would know the police were around, so we stayed with friends—the police would find a place for us. I knew where the gangs were, I had a good eye. I told my partner Vittorio, "Let's go inside there." He said, "No we can't go into that cantina, that bar, it's a regulation." But we went. He liked macaroni too much (laughing), so we went in and I ordered steak. And I watched as the gang over there played cards for money. We paid our bill and we left. Right away I called up and I said, "We have so and so over here." The troops arrived with machine guns, ten, fifteen carabinieri, and the lieutenant said, "Put them all in jail." They had a car, like a truck, and they put them all in there.

When World War I came, I knew they were going to send me to the front in Italy. A lawyer friend of my father told us, "There's a war coming; if you want to leave you better go now!" I came here in 1914 from Gioisa Ionica in Calabria. I lived in Brockton for six years, then I came to the North End in 1920. I came here because my father-in-law was here and I had a permit for one year from the government because I worked at the *deposito* [army base].

Michelina Manfra spoke about the nature of death, "Siamo sempre vicino la porta [We're always near the door]." Her remedy was "Si muore solo una volta [You only die once]."

Michelina Manfra

Christmas in Parolise at the Turn of the Century

Everything was outside, it didn't matter the weather. We gave gifts, but not like over here. Everything was nine, nine kinds of fruit, or nine types of *pasticcerie* [pastries], or nine kinds of nuts, or nine oranges. I don't know why it was always nine. I'm seventy-eight years old and I remember when I was three, four years old, they always did like that. My mother liked *mostaccioli* [a sweet pastry]. When I was little kid, when we had a party—chi ti le deva i soldi [who was going to give you the money]? Who had a penny in Italy when we were kids? Never! So I went to sell the grass to people who had horses, they'd give me a penny. So when Christmas came, they sold pastries and my mother loved mostaccioli, so we went to the store and we bought one each and we brought it to my mother on Christmas Eve. On Christmas Day everybody wanted to be the first one in church. When we went, my mother cooked, she didn't care for how many people. First, she cooked manicotti, cooked rabbit in the oven, made bread, then made the panettone—she made beautiful bread. All the family came—the grandfather, grandmother, my mother, my sisters, the son-in-law, nephews—they all came for my mother. My mother never came to my house. Christmas Day my father, my mother my grandfather, his mother, his brother, everyone—they went to church. When they got home, we had supper. Nobody moved from that table. Everybody kissed my father's hand.

Every town celebrated La Befana [the visit of the Christmas Witch] different. We had a beautiful ceremony. We had twelve small children and one who was the angel. There was a woman who went house to house to collect gold; they didn't give it, they lent it to dress up the *bambino*. We had the big bambino, the Christ child, everybody dressed him. On the morning of La Befana, they had the procession with music, the members of the *società* [society], and everyone would be crying. Then they would go get the bambino from the church and one of the twelve children would come out with the bambino. They took the bambino's clothes and these children, five, six years old, dressed him up in new clothes, and brought him back to the church. After the priest would get the little boy, bless the bambino with holy water,

FIGURE 2. Salvatore Bernardo, 1980.

give out bread, and they donated all the clothes, the stockings, the shoes, the underwear, the little hat, like a Santa Claus hat, to charity. When they finished the ceremony in church, on the side of the church on a big table, the nuns fed the thirteen children.

Salvatore Bernardo

Salvatore Bernardo spoke wistfully about his life as an elder: "Now I just hang around like a strange dog without its owner. No friends. Today you know who your friends are? The pockets! If you have money, then you have friends."

Life in Siracusa

When I was young in Siracusa—I was born in Canicattini Bagni in Sicily—I didn't run a hell of a lot, hanging around, working here, working there, doing different jobs. I'd work whenever we had a chance, building stone walls. I went to work when I was nine years old, I left school. I started work and I worked till I was seventeen years old. Once in a while we'd have to change with different masons because I was working with the masons, and each one has their own style, another one way, another had another way. Monday would come to Saturday night, and we'd do all kinds of work, but no money. I carried stone on my shoulders all the time, back and forth; we used to build dry wall, we used to put it on our shoulders and carry it and bring it [to] the mezzanine. No cement; that's just what we called dry wall in Siracusa.

Then we worked outside the city [roadwork] making holes, digging the ground, plugging holes, that's [what] we used to do. Money was pretty scarce. One day I was working and my father said, "Did you want to go down to America and see your brother?" I said, "Yeah, sure, I want to, I want to see my older brother." He asked me because my father was in the United States twice and he figured I'd have a better life. So two days later we went up to the city council in Canicattini Bagni, we started to make up the papers. The first thing you know, the eighteenth of March the passports came in and they gave me my passport. I left and I never saw my mother again. All my friends got killed in World War I. I got off the boat, the *Cretic,* in Charlestown in April 1913. It was one o'clock in the afternoon, that's when we got off the boat.

FIGURE 3. Frances Lauro, 1909.

Frances Lauro

Sciacca in 1909

I was born on North Street in the North End in 1903. My mother died when I was six and my father couldn't afford it here, and he took us back to his town, Sciacca, in Sicily; he had his mother there, so my grandmother could take care of me and my brother. My father left us and went back to the United States and got remarried. I was growing and I hadn't even gone to school yet, and my grandmother got sick and she was in bed—"Get me this, get me that"—and I did the best I could. I had to take care of her. Then my grandmother died. I can remember me and my brother alone. We sat in front of the doorway and she was in the house dead in the bed. So late at night a neighbor came over and took us in their house for the night. We slept on the stone floor. The rooms used to be all made of stone. The next day they took my grandmother, they put her on their shoulders like they did in Italy in those days—the casket, they took it and buried her. So we remained with the neighbor, the poor lady took us in. My brother was four years older than me, and they put him out to watch the sheep. The neighbor used to shave my hair close so I wouldn't get any bugs. Maybe that's why my hair grew so thick later! Then one of the women who was coming to America took us back to my father. He was already married with two children.

Giuseppe DiCenso

Giuseppe (Joe) DiCenso chafed at the bureaucracy in Italy, like waiting in lines to exchange money at the local bank. After one long wait, a man with more social status jumped ahead—"Ah onorevole [Oh your honor]," and he came first. Joe took his hundred dollars and left in disgust.

Sharecropping in Sulmona

When I was over there [mid-1910s], you go to work, they give you forty cents. Forty cents a day—you gotta get in at five, six o'clock in the morning, working the land, from five, six in the morning till the sun goes down, when it's dark. They give you forty cents for the day. Can you live with forty cents? You never got steady work. Somebody who owned a farm would say, "I'd like you to come in and help me tomorrow, alright I'll give you one pay." And the next day, when there was nothing to do, he'd say, "Well, I don't need you." What are you gonna do on a farm?

Marguerite Locchiato

"Girls Couldn't Learn to Read and Write on the Farm"

My mother and father never had the desire to go back, and I asked my mother why. She said because she had it bad in Italy. She said, "Times were so bad in Italy, and when I came here I was fortunate enough to get a good man, I had a good life here, and regardless of some of the people I know who weren't as fortunate as I was, they were even better off here than they were in Italy." [That was] in my mother's days. My father never spoke too much about Italy; I don't think he knew too much about Italy, he came so young. My mother had a really hard time in Italy: she had to work hard on the farm with the donkeys and all that. But it was strange how the father—she resented it a little bit—made her brothers learn how to read and write and not the girls. The father felt as though the girls would get married, [so] they wouldn't know, they wouldn't need that. Of course, that was them times and they were ignorant probably in them days.

Frank Favazza

Seventy-eight-year-old Frank Favazza was the oldest of eleven children and the only one to stay in the North End.

Life in Terrasini

I was born on North Street in a family of eleven children. My father was a fisherman from [the] province of Palermo, from a small town called Terrasini. His father was a fisherman. It was so poor in that town that my father, when they didn't have bread, he used to go to the chicken coops of the ones that had a loaf a bread—they were all poor then—and steal the bread from the chickens, clean it up—the scraps they liked to feed the chickens, that's how poor—and take it home.

Tom Bardetti

"You Had to Own"

My father came here in 1905 because he couldn't make a living in Italy. Necessity brought him here. In Italy nobody could make it. In those days if you stayed in Italy, you wasn't going nowhere. If you wanted to get anywhere, wanted to do anything, you'd have to get out of Italy; you'd have to go to either England, Germany, or Australia or some other country where you'd have the chance to advance. If you stayed in Italy, you couldn't advance because there was no chance there and that's why they immigrated to America as laborers. My father kept his farm in southern Italy. He came here two or three times.

He came here because you couldn't make a living in Italy. In Italy, if you didn't have [own] your own farm to work—you'd be [a] farmer, like, and you'd work your own property, your own farm, you'd get your crops, you use it for yourself and your family. And if you had any extra, anymore or a lot more, you could sell it, see? And like that, you could live. But if you didn't have a farm of your own you couldn't live in Italy at that time, in 1905, when he came here. He had a pair of oxen on the farm, and when you had a pair of oxen you was pretty good to have them because a lot people didn't have the money to buy the oxen. Then you had to feed them and everything and keep them. He inherited them from his family—he had the place.

Antonio Crugnale

"I Couldn't Have a Wife in Sulmona"

I started to work as a carpenter with my older brother when I was six years old in Italy. That's the way it was in Italy. We had our shop and we still own it. All the young boys in those days had to work. Almost as soon as you were born in those days, when you were five, six, seven years old, they would send you out to the fields as shepherds to tend the little sheep. I didn't have to do that, but I had to do something just like the rest of the boys. Luckily, I didn't have to become a shepherd, and I could work under my brother in his lumber mill and learned my trade, my *mestiere* [craft] as a carpenter, which is what I did.

I went to school up to the fifth grade that was run by a priest who lived near my house, where there was a church in our *contrada* [region] outside of Sulmona. This priest ran a school for the boys in our neighborhood. At the end of the fifth grade they took me to the city of Sulmona to take and pass an exam, because in those days, in 1926, you mostly only went up to the *terzo elementario* [third grade]. But I went there because this priest wanted me to become a priest because I was a good student. But he told my mother I couldn't have a wife. When I asked him why I couldn't have a wife, he gave me such a beating on the head, he left me bleeding quite a bit. Just for saying that! They had to take me to the hospital because the bleeding was so bad, and after that I got better and everything healed.

Michelina Manfra

Michelina Manfra was a solidly built woman with large hands who lived alone in a cold-water flat. Her father liked having Michelina around because she could do as much farmwork as any man. *Translated from Italian*.

Daily Farm Life in Parolise in 1913

Working on the farm in Parolise was beautiful. In the beginning you no like, *ma* [but] after, that's a your job, you work on the farm. In the morning you get, when it started to be [a] little light out, you get up and go to work and you be joyful every day, beautiful. My mother, seven-thirty, take a the breakfast, when my mother come on the farm we had a lot of chickens, my mother just a call, "Quee, quee, quee," and all a the chickens run a to my mother; she'd say, "Ma coming with the food." After she come, she cook at twelve o'clock make a the dinner. So this was our life. At noon she'd come and bring us food to eat. There were nine of us in our family and we never starved, we never was a millionaire. We never goin' a beg. My mother always gave us something because we always had it, we all had food. We didn't have a business, but we had wine—do you know how much wine my father sold? Aye, hundreds of quintale [1 quintale = 220 pounds]. Sunday morning on the farm I go to church, after church my mother made rabbit with *tagliatelle a mano* [homemade noodles], and after we ate, I take off a my shoes, my stockings, I go on the farm—to the vineyard and grapes—and I worked through October, November, December, with no shoes, no stockings, no nothing. Only once a week, on Sundays. Here in America, with two dollars I'm a go buy a pair shoes; over there how you gonna buy a pair of shoes? We enjoyed it; I had a wonderful father, I remember my father—how much I miss him! He wasn't too tall a fellow, he had a mustache, and he had blond hair, light skin, and blue eyes. He loved his family—he loved us! If you could have been in my family, you could hear him sing out, "I'm a rich man! Look at what I have! I got a beautiful daughter. I got a beautiful family!" He was a happy man and everybody loved him.

My father used to take me by horse and wagon to go shopping at the market in Atripalda or Avellino. They would call out to him by his nickname, "Hey, Misdeo!" I had one brother they called *Pecorella* [a little sheep], another *Cacciatore* [the hunter]. He used to sell his wine there. If we were there right now it would be *primavera* [the spring], it would be time to plant the seeds, *seminamo le rabe* [broccoli rabe], *li pasconi*, it's a green that grows during the winter and then by the spring it's already big, you have to *zappà* [till the soil], and put them under. Then the *grano* [wheat], was already planted. By October, would be when we picked the olives, the grapes in the vineyard. If it rained or if it was damp, you couldn't pick the olives because the tree would dry out. I always went with my father and my brother to pick the grapes. We were very busy. All the chestnuts! Oooh boy! Oooh! If I have a dream about chestnuts, I won't sleep! Oh boy! Too much work!

Now during *la vendemmia* [the harvest], you picked the grapes and my father didn't believe in the donkey, so we filled up the baskets to the brim and then we had to carry them on our heads to the town. When we were there after we dropped off the grapes, we carried all the leftover stalks and stems out in the country, one carried the baskets with the other, one with the other, we went back and forth. When night came, you think you went to bed? Oh, no! Then it was time to crush the grapes in big tubs. Now you do it with a machine in America, but all the men crushed the grapes in big tubs with their feet. Then we would climb up the ladder with our pails on our heads, we'd empty them into huge, tall barrels, they held a good hundred quintale of *ò musto*, we called the grapes before they fermented. Then the grapes would start to ferment, [and] the men would stir the grapes with long forks. We would stomp the grapes with our feet, that was our custom. When we were finally finished stomping the grapes around eleven or midnight, my mother would come around with kettles of warm water for the men to wash up and change their clothes. Then we'd sit and eat *baccalà* [dried cod], hot peppers with homemade wine vinegar, and drink our wine. At four the next morning we'd get up and start all over again. *Translated from the dialect of Parolise.*

FIGURE 4. Angelo Sardo.

Angelo Sardo

Life in the Province of Caltanisetta

The old days in Sicily were the days of *miseria nera* [the black misery], I remember there was nothing! If you wanted a salad you had to go looking for it out in the countryside. It's not like today, you can find greens or food to eat anywhere you want. That's the way it was in those days. There was no gas or electricity to prepare your food. Forget that! I had to go into the countryside to search for firewood to bring to my mother so she could use it to cook in her *fornellino* [little oven], made of brick. You had to start the fire underneath—pfff-pfff—and you had to keep fanning it, and you'd get tired and get more hungry with all that work you did even before you sat down to eat! There were no conveniences like today. Before, big families all lived together in one room or two rooms in Sicily. How could they all sleep in one place like that? If they didn't have a bed, they used the *cavaletto*, which in our homes we called a *trispida*. They used *i cavaletti di legno* [wooden boards], or sometimes they were made of iron, and they made mattresses out of leaves of corn stalks or with grass. They could never use wool to make mattress covers because it was too expensive for them. And they'd put the mattresses over the boards to sleep at night. In the morning they would break everything down and put everything in a corner of the house and put … *la buffetta* [the dinner table] back where it was. But you didn't do like you do today.

Today, for example, you have a refrigerator and buy enough for a week and then put it in the refrigerator. You couldn't even buy for one day! For sure! There were no bakeries like today where you could buy a sandwich or get mortadella, things like that. What the heck! To even have coffee at my house! Because being poor for us was shameful. As a young boy, along with the other boys, I used to go out looking for wheat in the fields with a little sack. They used to cut down the wheat with sickles and not with machines like they do today. And there was always some ears of wheat left behind to be found. That's what the boys did in those days, go out in search of wheat left on the ground, and we would bring [it] home to our mothers. They would bring them to the miller, who would grind them into flour to make bread. Then they'd bring it to the *forno* [bakery] oven—they used to pay *un soldo, due soldi* [one or two pennies] in those days, and they would make pasta, macaroni, bread—whatever the women made—for them.

Women were born to get married and they knew they had to guarantee a family, had to guarantee the husband to cook, wash, iron, raise the children, and there was no division of labor between men and women like today. Women's work was like this: What are you doing? Heh, nothing, I have children, that's all! A woman was nothing but *una fabbrica di figli* [a baby factory] in those days, ten, fifteen, twenty children. The firstborn, who would become the oldest, had to take care of his sister and brother. And that's how they survived. Because each child had an obligation to go and out and find something to do, to try something. We all had to do that. But we all ate. But we didn't eat like they eat meat, mortadella, this and that today, forget it! What we ate in those days was limited to bread and sardines, bread and onions, bread and olives. It was like a holiday when you had a piece of bread. And how good it tasted! Bread was all natural. You were never sick. We were all in good health in my family. Because in those days the fruit you ate was all natural, the mandarins, the oranges there, they never used that medicine, that poison on the fruits. That's where the sickness, the cancer comes from, that poison they put on them, from the chemicals you eat, it ruins your stomach, your ears, your nose. In those times, no.

Going to School

At six years old I went to school. But I went to school, not like now, a young boy, six, seven years old, what do you want? In those days it wasn't like it is now where school is enforced until you're eighteen. There, nothing! You were going to school and one day you didn't show up. The *professore* would tell you, "You didn't come to school yesterday?" "Eh, no." So you made up an excuse like "My mother was sick, I had to …" and then the professore would tell you, "Eh, the less students, the better we are!" And then (sarcastic voice), "What are you coming here to do? Become a lawyer? An engineer? Stay home. Better if you don't come anymore." The professore did this on purpose, with the intention of giving more instruction to *i figli di papa* [the children of the well-to-do], whose parents controlled everything in town; the *farmacista* [the pharmacist]; *il prete* [the priest]; *il sindaco* [the mayor]; *e qualche capo esponente della citta* [the bosses who controlled the jobs in town]. They were in control of everything—they were the mafiosi, they were the mafia.

That was the mafia because they had the people of the town *sotto i piedi* [under their feet], under their total control. The people used to go to work. They got up at four o'clock in the morning, and as long as there was light, they had to keep working for little wages, for a few pennies. It was *una vita disgraziata* [a terrible, unlucky life] they lived in those days in Sicily. Especially when someone went looking for work and the bosses tried to exploit them. The bosses would try to take advantage of the situation if you had a daughter or a wife they wanted or found attractive. So what would happen? A *capo esponente di lavoro* [foreman] used to go to the home of a poor family and check out the young daughter or the pretty wife, not in all cases, but in the majority cases they always tried to take advantage of those poor devils because they didn't have a lot of education and they didn't know even how to express themselves or fight back. At night three or four families used to gather and play cards or play bingo because there wasn't television or radio or any entertainments.

There were theaters but they had rudimentary films with subtitles. And the majority of people couldn't write or read so what were they going to do if they went to see a movie? I remember them saying, "What are going to see there, go and spend a half lira, eleven cents to see a movie?" So instead they'd all say, "What are we going to go there for? Hey, *facciamo quattro fave, quattro ceci* [let's cook some fava beans, some chickpea beans]." And they would boil ceci and fava beans and entertain themselves at night like that. And they would play card games for *centesimi, un soldo, due soldi* [a penny, two pennies], very little money. I remember that before 1922 in Sicily, it was a disaster. I was seven. Life was impossible. You were closed within four walls and a roof. Anyone who was intelligent could never take advantage of it because one could never leave your town very easily like you can today. It was like being a *prigioniero volontario* [voluntary prisoner]. And if one always stays in the same place, one never gains any experience. If you never learn a profession, what can you do? Nothing. Even if you had a good head on your shoulders, you could never develop into anything. That's because schools weren't obligatory then like they are now in Sicily. *Translated from Italian.*

I Camoristi

There were organized groups of people who were parasites, people who didn't want to work. They used to gather, go to someone's house, knock on the door, or sometimes they would go to the local bar where people were enjoying themselves. They would buy a half glass of wine, not a liter or a gallon like today, forget about that. So then two or three of their people would come into the bar. They'd announce, "We're playing cards for money, un soldo for each, go ahead. Now give us a half liter of wine!" And the owner would say, "And who are you?" They told him, "We are camoristi!" And if the owner didn't give them the money and wine they wanted they would beat him up.

In people's homes they did the same thing. I remember as a little boy, I was born in 1915, I used to listen all the time, "Oh, they killed that one over there!" And being a young boy like the others, I'd listen when all the women gathered together to talk, "Oh, the camoristi went into my cousin's house last night looking for money, he didn't have any, so they beat him up." Then you would hear another story from another woman, "*Sai cummari* [you know my friend], …"—you know how the women were in those days. There was no such thing as a meeting like here, nothing, there was nothing like that at all, I tell you it was real and true slavery. *Translated from Italian.*

Working in the Sulfur Mines

I remember those times very well, there was very little work. When I was seven, I was walking with my brother down the street on the way to work in the sulfur mine. We worked in the mines at that age, just like in the coal mines. Because we were small, we could work with the small shovels, and when we extracted the sulfur, we called it *i panotti*, like loaves of bread, but it was sulfur. So all the little boys did that kind of work [and] the older boys carried the sulfur on their backs to the brick furnaces. Sulfur is all mixed in with stone and other materials so it was brought to the furnaces and heated in a way that the sulfur separated from the impurities [stone] and fell off. What wasn't needed was thrown out. But you had to bake it to extract the sulfur, to make pieces as heavy as a hundred kilos. And then they were exported to other countries; it was a great trade industry.

So *i capi esponenti del lavoro* [the bosses] of the *miniere di zolfo* [sulfur mines], they took advantage of the families because the fathers would go out in search of work and they [bosses] would ask them, "Who are you? Where are you from? Do you have a family? Do have children?" And in those times in the families, you know they often had three, four, five, ten, fifteen children, twenty children. This one, twenty children! My grandmother, twenty-two. And another, "Hey, my wife, we have twenty-two!" At my house we were thirteen children. Then the bosses of the factories, there were no factories from where I was born [Caltanisetta], the only resource for the people to survive on was in the miniere di zolfo. There used to be seven hundred of them in Sicily, but now there's only three left.

In those days, the workers entered the mines on a Monday, and you wouldn't see them again until Saturday. And they used [to] come back home like mice. I remember because I worked in the mines, too. Because in those days you went to school a half day and a half day at work. I'd hear other stories.

You know how the women would say, "*Cummara* [Friend]!" In those days the women would get together and talk among themselves, "Mio marito non lavoro! [My husband has no work!] They don't want him in the mines because he's too old." Because when the men got too old they didn't want them in the mines anymore. "But the foreman says there may be hope for my husband, for my son, but hmmm, first he says one day he wants to come to the house and have a cup of coffee together." Then the other women said to her, "That's no good, you better watch out! He has gone to other houses like that looking at the daughter before he gives the husband a job—you got to watch out for people like this." I always used to hear things like this as a kid.

"He Shot *Capomastro* Macri"

So one of these foremen promised a man a job in the mines. But he went to this man's wife, and he said to her, "You know I promised your husband a job, but you know, I like you, and maybe we could arrange something and it won't hurt anybody." So the wife said to the capomastro, "OK, I'll think it over. I love my husband and I love my family and, you know, nothing has ever happened like this in my family and I don't like it." He said, "Look, if you want your husband to have a job, then you need to make me happy, too." She said, "I'll think about it." The woman was very embarrassed. Those times were different than now. Now it's enough just to look at a woman and say, "Let's go!" So this woman, when her husband got up early that morning, she asked him, "Where are you going?" He said, "You know where, I'm going to work, where he [capomastro Macri] promised me to work." She said, "Look, if you want to go to work, go to work, but I won't let you. I would rather die of hunger than you go to work." The husband said, "Why?" She said, "Eh (sighing), what capomastro Macri told me was that he was coming to see me here when you were at work. Why is he coming? To look at my face? He's coming here because he wants to screw me. That's why I would rather, my husband, that we die of hunger, go begging than to lose my honor for the job in the mine. This is no good." "Ah," her husband said, "That's OK It's good that you told me. It's all set, I know exactly what to do." He didn't do anything else but to leave with his pistol. Just as the capomastro was about to enter the mine, he emptied his pistol into the capomastro's back. He fell to the ground and lay there.

That day I went to work in the mine with my brother. I was seven and my brother was ten. We saw the capomastro on the ground. We said, "Ah, this one is drunk," and we gave him a kick in his backside. But he was dead, Cristo [Christ]! My brother, when we got home from work that night he said, "They killed capomastro Macri!" They all said, "Where was it?" We said, "On the street. O Cristo! We thought he was drunk, we tried to wake him up, but we couldn't because he was dead!" My brother was the type to get scared, but I was the stronger, I was never afraid of anyone. He was older than me, but he was thin and timid. So I went and told my mother and told her they killed capomastro Macri. My mother said, "Si! That no good." She said among all the women, between the cummari, "That lowdown no good *fetente* [stinker]!" The other women said, "Eh! Even with me! He said the same thing to me, he did the same thing to me and my daughter!" They put it all in the newspaper. He wasn't that young a man, the capomastro. But he caused so much trouble for so many people who didn't know what to do, and he took advantage of them because of the poverty of those times in Sicily. This is not just a story I'm recounting but it's something that happened during my lifetime. *Translated from Italian*.

Josie Tranquillo

Daily Life in Salemi in 1910

We had upstairs and a downstairs in our house. Downstairs my father used to have barrels of wine, barrels of olives; it was wonderful. Upstairs we had the dining room and the bedrooms were upstairs. Well, my father had a lot of land with grapes, plum trees, blackberry trees [bushes], and orange trees. Right near our door we had tomato plants, so beautiful. When I was young, in the morning I used to go with a little knife and pick [prickly] pears and eat as many as I could. Sometimes I used to get a little basket, take a little knife with me, and I used to go out to the grape vines, and I used to sit right under where the grapes—all nice and yellow—those were the ones I liked—and I'd sit and eat them. After I finished, I'd put [some] in the basket and [take] them to my mother.

In Italy, when we used to have rain showers in Sicily, on the roads, in the middle of the road after the showers we used to find *i babbalucci* [snails], so we'd get a basket and pick them—it was a wonderful place. We had an orange tree across the barn right near the house—my brothers and sisters used to send me to pick oranges for them and I used to go in the orange tree, I used to pick them and throw [the] oranges at them in the barn. In the winter when it used to get cold my mother used to get all the grapes and tie them and hang them over the beds in the rooms. I used to get a chair and climb on the bed and I used [to] take the grapes. Not only that, the figs—the fig trees—my mother used to cut them in halves and she used to dry them in the sun. When they dried, they'd get [become] all white sugar; oh were they good! My mother used to place them in a basket and place them on the bed nice for the winter for us to have. They used to be on a shelf over the bed. I was terrible, I used to climb on a chair and eat them, I shouldn't have done that but I used to (laughing); I was a devil when I was young. We used to call them *ficchi sicchi* [dry figs]. Oh, it was good, it was good, it was very good.

When I had nothing to do, I used to cut all [my] dolls dresses, sew and embroider them. I used to go down with my mother to wash her clothes in the river. We used to call it the *ciumalongo* [long river], and my mother used to go wash her clothes there. I used to go wash my little doll clothes there, and I used to hang them on the grass. And then I would embroider them. After I came to America in 1914 and got married, I used to cut my own children's clothes and embroider them, [and] I used to make my own clothes.

FIGURE 5. Mary "Carmela" Pagliuca.

With the help of elderly volunteers, Mary Pagliuca cooked meals for hundreds of elders who missed their traditional dishes. When she died in 1990 the elders hung a commemorative plaque over the kitchen door of the Senior Center in her honor.

Mary "Carmela" Pagliuca

"Sharing the Shoes"

In Italy I had seven brothers and seven sisters in my family. My father was a representative and he was always at city hall, my mother took care of all the children. My father was a big shot—he never worked on the farm. On the farm I used to carry the stuff, almost three hundred pounds on my head. What do you think, on my shoulders? I was a slave because my mother had too many kids. I raised pigs, goats, chickens, sheep—everything, I took them grazing. You had to make milk, cheese, if not, what were you gonna eat on the farm? We had four cows and I made milk and cheese; if you saw how much cheese I made in Italy, oooh, out of this world!

We had a lot of food on the table—milk; bread; once in a while kill a chicken, make chicken soup; once in a while kill the rabbits, make it with the macaroni. But not every day eat a meat, once a week. I ate beans and macaroni every day. My mother made fried eggs, make a big *frittata* [omelet] with onions, peppers, and cheese, and give a piece each to the children. Sometimes *scarola* [escarole] with beans. She got a fourteen a people, what are you gonna do? And no shoes, no *zoccole* [sandals]; I only had one pair of shoes for two sisters, every two girls had a pair of shoes.

To go to church on Sunday my sister came back and gave me her shoes so I could go to church, go to Mass. And when I got back, I'd take them off, clean up the shoes, and put them away. I couldn't use them on the farm because I only had one pair of shoes. My father couldn't support all the people; we had to work on the farm. To eat, not for a good time. If my sister didn't come back, I couldn't go to church. Lots of times I'd miss my Mass because my sister would start talking with her girlfriends, she no come a home early and I couldn't go to church because the Mass was already done. I'm a cry like a baby and my mother she say, "What are you cry for?" "I want to go to church!" "*Vai* [go] next Sunday, no worry about it, the priest a no give a you a piece of bread, what a you cry for? You cry because you lost a piece of bread? You go next Sunday!"

Leaving Italy for the Promise of America   2

> They did not hear what I heard, nor see what I saw. It was the call, the mighty call of the sea, the undying call for the larger life. And it was that call that in a not far-distant day was to lead me to America, there to find the opportunity for a true unfolding.
> —CONSTANTINE MARIA PANUNZIO, *The Soul of an Immigrant*

The Unification worsened the cycle of poverty for many families like the Capones in Montefalcione. When the last remnants of King Francesco II's Bourbon army fell at the fortress of Gaeta on February 13, 1861, this marked the start of the decades of economic inequities between North and South known as "the southern question." The new government levied taxes on the South's basic staples—salt, olive oil, vineyards, wheat, and mules. In a feudalistic economy where a small class of wealthy southern landowners (*latifondisti*) rented land to the peasantry, the people acquiesced to the new government's policies. To raise more money for northern coffers, farm properties were mortgaged by the government, which forced tenant-farming families like the Capones further down the social ladder, making them lowly *braccianti* (day laborers).

The new government repossessed church property and the *demani universali*, common areas traditionally granted for public farming and grazing. Representatives in the House of Deputies for towns like Montefalcione, near Avellino, were absentee landlords who lived as aristocrats in the north. By 1881, 65 percent of the Naples-Avellino population found itself without food or work.[1] Because of literacy and landowning requirements, farmers and craftsmen had no political voice and could not vote until 1912. Women could not vote until 1945.

On a sweltering summer evening in 1914, the squarely built, fifteen year-old Pasquale Capone took his place at the dinner table, a welcome respite after another long day of hard labor in the fields. He described the usual fare at dinner: "We eat just a bread, that's all, macaroni maybe once a week, meat maybe a couple a time a year, we can't buy, we have a no money to buy." Though young, Pasquale recognized the hopelessness of farmers trapped in the lower rungs of Italian society, and like many of his generation, he looked to America as the alternative to a future of unfair taxes, deadly earthquakes, malaria and cholera epidemics, and the vagaries of nature. High taxes levied by the northern government and increased demands of absentee landlords for up to 90 percent of their crops for rent had made farming life unsustainable for families like the Capones.

That night, hoping to receive his father's blessing to leave, Pasquale knew the centuries-old aphorism against change: "Non si lassà 'a via vecchia pe' a via nuova, sapé che tenn, nun sapé che trùva'" (One never leaves the old ways for the new; one knows what one has, but never knows what one will find). Pasquale's youthful aspiration to leave the confines of his village challenged the *via vecchia's* (old way's) cardinal rule, which families rarely broke. But despite his father's initial disapproval, Pasquale persisted: "Papa, let me try. I'll go to America, make some money and come back and buy a farm." His plea echoed the voices of many hopeful southern farmers, laborers, and craftsmen who ventured to the New World: "Let us try—let us go to America to seek our fortunes with steady jobs; we'll earn enough money to come back and buy our own land instead of being landless sharecroppers." That same year Pasquale joined the millions who left while the government stood by and watched the largest outsourcing of any labor force in Europe.[2]

Few in the great migration could have imagined what the promise of America demanded of those wishing to enter the working class. Shipping agents and coal-mining, railroad, and factory representatives recruited young men for backbreaking jobs in dangerous mines, laying trackbeds for railroads, digging underground foundations in bitter cold, laboring on fast-paced production lines in unhealthy conditions, and laying pipe in ditches. In return for their labor, however, the meager weekly wages provided a steady cash flow, which they had never experienced as farmers.[3]

Moreover, corrupt *padrones* (bosses) awaited the steady stream of countrymen who were inexperienced in American ways, offering them the "peek and shuvle" jobs described by Constantine Panunzio in *The Soul of an*

FIGURE 6. Teresa Costanzo.

Immigrant.[4] Among the tenant farmers and day laborers (*braccianti*) swelling the North End's Italian population from twenty thousand to thirty-three thousand between 1904 and 1914, there were barbers, carpenters, cobblers, bricklayers, masons, tailors, bakers, fishermen, small business owners, and entrepreneurs. When Pasquale arrived in 1914, his Avellinese countrymen represented the largest regional group in the North End.[5] Pasquale weighed the long-term benefits of steady wages, the opportunity to advance in the workplace, and the possibility of saving enough money to buy property. Like the majority of immigrants in urban neighborhoods across the United States, Pasquale decided the North End was a better place to live than his former home in Italy.[6]

Teresa Costanzo

Waving her withered hands as she wove stories in the dialect of Riposto, a town on the eastern coast of Sicily, Teresa Costanzo often ended her sentences with "*a matri*," a Sicilian term of endearment from a mother to a son, which is sometimes extended to a nonrelative.

"Onesta e Pulita"

Who thinks of it anymore, how long ago I came here? A long time ago! Ah … ah (laughing) … I came to America on board a ship and I can't remember exactly when it was. I had a daughter Jenna, a son Mario, a daughter Maria, another daughter. Then I had another *tri simenzi* [three children] in Italy, two boys and a girl, you see? We came back to America a second time on a ship too. See how long I've been here? But now I don't understand anything. Nuting! Because I don't associate with anyone, so I don't understand. I used to talk a lot with my husband.

But thanks to that good soul, my husband, we arrived here safe and relieved, thank God. It was a long time on board the ship. At the first sight of New York, my husband said, "I'll get in front." So I said, "No, no Gesù"—in Italy we call it *fidanzata* [to be engaged]. You see? He wanted a fidanzata. So he wanted to find a *picciotta* [a young girl from Sicily], who had a good upbringing and was honest. So his father came looking for me—that good soul, my father-in-law, I wish him a hundred years! He came with his friend Saruzzu Miceli, and he said to me, "You know my son, Angelo … we know who you are … that you are a *pulita e onesta* [woman who has good morals and is honest]." Then he said to himself (whispering voice), "Now I'm going to send my son Angelo to you!" Why? Because my father-in-law said, "Teresa Costanzo is a good woman." My father-in-law was still in Riposto [and] Angelo was still in Boston waiting for a good woman. So he [wrote] to his father, "Look, my father, I'll do what you tell me; I believe what you say about Teresa, but I want to be sure she likes me." Isn't it right like that? O blessed one! (In a lamenting voice): Oh may God bless his [Angelo's] soul that he wanted to make sure his son would like me! So I wrote a few lines to Angelo, "I am very happy your father came [to Riposto], that good soul my father-in-law!" But I had never met this *cristiano* [this person Angelo].

Two years went by. But when he [Angelo] got to Italy and when he saw me for the first time—right up to now—he was happy about my good upbringing and about my family. I said to him, "Are you just passing through, are you going to move on?" He told me, "No, no, I came here to marry you." We got engaged and were married in twenty-eight days, blessed be all the saints and the blessed ones! Then we left for America. I think of it right up to this minute. *Translated form the Sicilian dialect of Riposto.*

FIGURE 7. Francesco Ventresca and wife, Anna Ventresca, 1980.

Francesco and Anna Ventresca

Francesco Ventresca, a squarely built eighty-two-year-old man from Pettorano in Abruzzi, labored in the quarries of Maine before World War I and drilled stones by hand with his friend Gabriele Federico, who "held while I drilled—ding-dong-ding-dong—for twenty cents an hour."

Landing Alone at Ellis Island in 1915

I came to America alone in 1915 with one hundred lire in my pocket. It was just after the war began. The man who accompanied me during the voyage, as soon as we reached New York, looked at me and said, "Beh, questo è l'America, ognuno per se, Dio per tutti [Well, this is America—everyone for himself and God for everyone]." And then he left me to go to Maine. I had to go to Ohio and I started to cry. So a man came along and he said, "What's the matter with you?" I told him, "Mi ha lasciato [This guy left me]." The man spoke Italian: "Don't worry I'll take care of you." But then I remembered my father warning me, "Quella in America ci stevano i bum, ti rubavano [In America they have bums that rob you]." So I said to him, "Ma tu sei un bum [Are you a bum]?" He said to me, "Sonco bum? Che ti credi, ma a ruba i piddocchi e porto all'Italia [I'm a bum? What do you think I'm gonna steal, the bugs in your hair and take them to Italy]?" Then he said, "Non ha paura [Don't be afraid]," and showed me his badge with his number on it. He showed me to a smaller boat to take it to New Jersey.

But I was still scared and so I said to him, "Mi porta all'Italia con questo vapore [Is this boat taking me back to Italy]?" He said, "Ma no! No ha paura [But, no! Don't be afraid]!" So I took the boat to New Jersey, then to the Erie Railroad. The guy who took me to the train, he told the conductor, "This one has to go to Ohio—you take care of him." The conductor said, "OK, OK." So I said to him, "Ma quest qua non parla l'Italiano [But this guy doesn't speak Italian]." He said, "Ma questo qua ti capisce, tu parli Italiano, qualcuno Italiano vicino a te [He'll understand you, you'll find someone on the way who will speak Italian]."

So I got on the train—ting-a-tong, ting-a-tong—after two stations I grabbed my suitcase. The conductor said, "Where are you going?" Then, showing me his fingers, he said, "One, two, three." Then I met a Greek family on the train and the wife spoke Italian well. This Greek woman was born in America but lived in Italy and now she was coming back with two young children. So I asked her and she told me how long the trip was going to take, "Tu devi stare oggi, stanotte dormi, domani, e dopo domani arriva [You'll be here today, sleep tonight, then tomorrow, and you'll get there the day after tomorrow]." "Mannaggia ... O Padre [Damn ... O God]," I said to myself.

Tink-a-tong, tink-a-tong—we got to Baltimore and I was so hungry like it was just now [I can feel it now]. I had five lira in my pocket, one dollar. In New York I had a bag of food, but I ate it. I bought some sandwiches for four cents and switched trains in Baltimore—tick, tuk, tuk—all day and night, and the next day I made it to Columbus, Ohio, on March 11, 1915, to meet my uncle to work in the quarries. I made seventeen cents an hour, six days a week, ten hours a day. I made thirty-four dollars a month. If it didn't rain you were lucky; come two, three days of rain, you don't get no more thirty-four dollars, you would only get twenty-six, twenty-seven. After I paid my board—I was young man—what could you make? In 1922, I went back to Ellis Island to build dormitories for the immigrants. *Translated from Abruzzese dialect of Sulmona.*

The Journey to Boston   3

> There were some great fish with amazing strength chasing us in a race, jumping out of the water, diving, then quickly resurfacing with their backs showing until they disappeared into the distance.
> —ADOLFO ROSSI aboard the *Canada* in 1879, *Un Italiano in America*

Giuseppe Freni grew up on the family farm in Itala, near Messina in Sicily. After serving in the Italian infantry during World War I, he returned and told his parents he was going to America for two years to earn a *pocu di mili-una di lire* (a few million lira) and then would return to Sicily. After a day of tending lemon and orange trees, Giuseppe met his childhood friend Damiano, who confided that he wanted to go to America for the same reason. Like Constantine Panunzio and his boyhood friend described in *The Soul of an Immigrant*, the young adventurers, inspired by fanciful stories from returnees and letters with exaggerated claims of easy money and quick success, sailed to Boston. Like many immigrants, they had no idea of the dangers of transatlantic travel, the long hours of hard labor they would endure to survive, or the discrimination they would face in the New World.

Poor Italian immigrants were crammed below water level in steerage class, often packed into one large compartment with up to three hundred people living in close quarters with no privacy. Seasickness and infections spread like wildfire and lasted the entire trip. Families lived in small cubicles with a berth that served as a bed and storage space.[1] In many cases, young males left the ports of Genoa, Naples, and Palermo planning to send for wives and family members after securing jobs and saving enough money for their trip. Some promised to send for their wives and children but never returned, creating the class of women in Italy known as "white widows" (*vedove bianche*); their husbands had not died so they could not dress in black.

If letters did arrive with passage money, young wives who had never ventured beyond the confines of their villages gathered children and whatever possessions they could carry, bid tearful farewells to loved ones, and departed for the transatlantic journey into the unknown. During the voyage, children often succumbed to fatal diseases while grief-stricken mothers stood by helplessly and watched their burials at sea.

Those who came directly to Boston witnessed a booming maritime city, its harbor bustling with steamships transporting imported goods from foreign ports and others leaving with food, raw materials, and manufactured goods. Longshoremen loaded and unloaded cargoes on the busy piers jutting into the harbor from the North End, Charlestown, and East Boston.[2] Italians also caught their first glimpse of American naval might, passing battleships at the Charlestown Navy Yard. Unlike New York Harbor, where migrants were barged to Ellis Island, Boston's Commonwealth Pier provided ample room for examinations of new arrivals.[3]

Passenger ships docked at different points, with the White Star Line and the Hamburg-American Lines at South Boston's Commonwealth Pier No. 5 and the Cunard Line at Cunard Wharf at the East Boston Immigration Station, at Jeffrey's Point.[4] Other points of disembarkation were the United States Immigration Station on Long Wharf, which had a detainment facility at the foot of State Street until the late 1910s, and the Hoosac Terminal, adjacent to the Charlestown Navy Yard. The poor and downtrodden were not always welcomed with open arms on arrival.

Eleven-year-old Diego Picadacci left Riesi in Sicily to join his father's successful fruit and vegetable business on Charter Street in the North End. Traveling alone on the *Romanic*, he had been so sick that he had to be hospitalized for the entire twelve-day trip. Crocefissa Summa left Salemi in Sicily with two young children, landed in New York, and then sailed to Charlestown, thus ending a nightmarish journey that lasted seventeen days, where passengers received small meals in little jars, without dishes or utensils. She found work as a seamstress for a dollar and twenty cents a day and raised four children with her husband. At ninety, she summed up her life of self-reliance and economic independence: "We did alright; we never had to ask anyone for five dollars."

Some migrants never realized the promise of America and, unable to earn enough money to make ends meet, they returned home. For others, years of breathing toxic fumes without seeing the light of day in dangerous coal mines, working backbreaking jobs building roads and railroads, and toxic factory conditions took their toll, causing many to leave because of sickness, injuries, or disease.[5]

In 1913, seventeen-year-old Salvatore Bernardo, a laborer from Cannicatini Bagni in Sicily, left his home to live with his older brother. The landing at Charlestown left such an impression on him that he remembered the moment for the rest of his life. When the two young Sicilians from Italy landed at the Cunard Wharf in East Boston in 1922, health inspectors from the boat, the *Marietta,* boarded the ship to check the documentation of passengers and conduct medical examinations. After passing the inspection, Giuseppe Freni was about to disembark when an immigration official detained his friend Damiano and sent him for a medical examination at the East Boston Immigration Station on Marginal Street. When doctors found trachoma in both eyes, he became one of many tragic figures in immigration history who was sent back to Italy.

FIGURE 8. Josie Tranquillo, 1980.

Josie Tranquillo
Josie Tranquillo was seventy-five at the time of our interview in 1980.

Threading Needles on the *Canopic* in 1914

I came here with my mother in 1914; we left on May 20 and we landed in Charlestown on June 1. My mother came first and my father had to sell his property and land in Italy. I came on the *Canopic*; we came on the White Star Line. My mother was a wonderful dressmaker. She took me to America with her because she was forty-five and her vision wasn't good so she took me along to thread her needles. I was eight years old. All I saw was ocean and blue skies and blue water, that's all. It's a good thing we didn't stay too long. We started from Italy on the twentieth of May and we got here the first of June. It wasn't too long. But my mother was always sick; it was hard on the boat. And I used to go play with the kids—I was only eight years old. Once we saw a big fish coming up [to] the boat—it was coming up almost on the boat and everybody was screaming, "The fish! The fish!" It must have been a whale, a big whale. Oh, we were scared because it made all the water come all over the boat. I don't understand how it did that! We all got all wet—the fish came so high it made the water come all over the boat.

As young as I was, we used to get our food—we used to have coffee, that Italian roast coffee. I could never drink it, it was too strong. And no milk they gave you, it was all plain black coffee. Everybody got sick on the boat, everybody threw up; it was hard, miserable. I don't want to go back to Italy because I feel, oh God, all I used to see was sky and water, the blue sky and the blue water, the boat all alone in the middle … no I couldn't do that; I could never go back to Italy, not even on a plane, [and] it left me with a bad impression.

Diego Picadacci
Diego Picadacci was a resident on Charter Street from 1911 to 1978.

"We Landed in Charlestown"

I came here when I was eleven years old on the *Romanic*; it took twelve days in 1911. It wasn't too bad only I got seasick, that's all. They put me in the hospital until the boat reached over here. And then I was all right. We didn't go to New York—over here in Charlestown we landed. There was a navy yard in Charlestown, there were battleships going in and out; it was big place. Now there's nothing, they took it out. My father was here; I didn't come with my family. He'd been here for three years and then he sent for me. And we landed in Charlestown, with the *Romanic*; it was an English boat. At that time there were horses over here [and] there were electric [street] cars. I reached the fourth grade and I had to go to work and I quit. I was sixteen and I worked in the foundry in South Boston where they make all kinds of tools and machines, forty-eight hours a week for ten dollars a week. My father was in the fruit and vegetable business all his life on the corner of Hanover and Charter Street, on 396 Hanover Street. So after two years at the foundry I went into business with my father, I worked for him. Being your own boss was all right; yeah, it was all right. Charter Street was very busy—there were butchers, bakeries, and all the stores there were over here. There was fifteen stores. Now there's nothing, but at that time in 1916 up to 1950 there were all stores over there. They moved away because people moved away and the buildings went to hell, and everybody closed their places and went somewhere else. There were no condominiums then. There used to be a lot of Sicilians there were over here, always Sicilians, now there's nobody, only Abruzzese over here now, that's all. You used to go to work—we had the pushcarts on Hanover Street selling bananas, selling fruit; the people used to buy it and go to work. They were friendly people, but there were lots of killings sometimes. They used to go gambling and they used to get mad at one another, or playing for wine—that was terrible, oh yeah. People used to get nasty like, and they used to fight on account of gambling. Oh yeah.

Anna Caffarelli

Anna Caffarelli's mother always wished to die in her sleep. One night when Anna returned from a movie, her mother greeted her, saying, "I'm so glad you came home—I waited for you all night." Anna answered, "Ma, let's go to bed." Her mother died in her sleep that night.

From L'Aquila to Commercial Pier in 1905

My mother came from L'Aquila in Abruzzo in 1905. She was dying to come to America; she didn't like Italy because she heard so much about America. When she got here she said to me, "Quando sono venuta in America, mi credo che trovavo lu tesoro [When I came to America I thought I would find riches]." I said, "Perche Ma [Why did you think that, Ma]?" She said, "Oh, I'd rather go back to Italy anytime." My father said, "When are you going, next week?" My mother said, "Never!"

When my mother came to America the boats were so bad that my mother was eighteen days in the hospital, and my brother was four years old and he used to run around the boat; everybody had the kid. She was alone with my brother at the time. The conditions onboard were so bad that she made the entire voyage without eating once. Because the smells on the boat were so bad, she couldn't keep anything down. When my mother came out and my father met her in South Boston, at the Battery—she was [a] big, tall woman, and husky—she lost so much weight. So when my father came to pick her up in South Boston, he got scared—he thought she was going to die. He didn't even recognize her at first because she lost so much weight. She couldn't even walk when she landed—they had to take her in the car—and she swore she'd never go back. She came home [and] she had to call the doctor; she didn't eat anything, everything she ate she threw up. He said to her, "What happened to you?" She said, "Oh please! I was sick through the whole trip." And the little boy, my brother Gerald, everybody says to my mother, "And how did you keep him on the boat?" She said, "Everybody used to take care of him."

My mother would never go back to Italy after that because she got sick on the boat. In those days, fifteen, sixteen days on a boat—my poor mother. One time I was going on vacation, I was going by boat, [and] my mother said, "Oh no, Anna, please don't go on the boat, you're gonna get sick."

A New Life in the North End 4

> Here was a congestion the like of which I had never seen before. Within the narrow limits of one-half square mile were crowded together thirty-five thousand people, living tier upon tier, huddled together until the very heavens seemed to be shut out.
> —CONSTANTINE MARIA PANUNZIO, *The Soul of an Immigrant*

> Figlio mio, ogni paese è un compare, ogni territorio è un pagliàro (My son, in every town you'll find a friend, in every land you'll make your little home).
> —ANTONIA TONZILLO

Italians left the village *campanile* (bell tower) and left *campanilismo* (pride of one's birthplace) behind as well when they settled into beehive tenements near the steeple of the Old North Church. That Georgian steeple and its round-topped window were monuments to the night of April 18, 1775, when American patriots anxiously watched for signs of the invading British army. Old North's bell tower stood as a landmark to the American experiment of freedom and self-government, which the local Sons of Liberty were willing to fight and die for.[1] How would established American ideals mesh with the wave of immigration that was washing into Boston in the early twentieth century? Italians would find out.

When Charlie Polcari's family left Montefalcione in 1904, they joined the surge that changed the North End's ethnic composition to nearly half Italian, along with twenty-five other ethnicities, including Irish, Portuguese, Greeks, Polish, and Russian Jews. The original Genoese settlers, who were uncomfortable with the sounds and sights of southern Italians, were moving to the suburbs.[2] The Irish settlement on Commercial Street was giving way to Sicilians and Russian Jews around Salem Street were moving to Roxbury, Dorchester, and Hyde Park.

By 1920, forty thousand Italians had transformed the North End into a miniature southern Italy. To an outsider unfamiliar with southern dialects, the Italian heard in the streets sounded like exotic tongues. Italians on Sheafe Street, Hanover Street, Prince Street, and Hull Street spoke variations of Neapolitan dialect, with Greek, Arabic, French, and Spanish influences. Sicilians from Terrasini, Caltanisetta, Sciacca, Messina, Salemi, Riesi, and Riposto on North and Commercial Streets spoke different dialects of Sicilian, reflecting Greek, Arabic, French, Catalan, and Spanish influences. Dialects of Calabria were spoken on North Street and Abruzzese on Endicott and North Margin Streets.

Constantine Panunzio described the neighborhood's physical characteristics in 1914, "with narrow, alley-like streets massed with litter, air laden with soot and dirt, children with no playgrounds, and housing conditions with thirty-five thousand people crowded together, living tier to tier."[3] Alarmed by the neighborhood's high mortality rate and poor conditions, the city built the North End Park (1893), North End Beach (1893), and Copp's Hill Terraces and the Prince Street Playground (between 1897 and 1901) .

The new country welcomed the Italians with a handshake but held them at arm's length. Conditioned by centuries of foreign invasions and the ruthless exploitation by the ruling class, Italians turned to inner strength and to the family to nurture and protect them during hard times. They expected nothing from America, and in exchange for hard work, they hoped for a better future for their children. Decades before workman's compensation and social security, many *mutuo soccorso* (mutual aid) societies continued the Italian tradition of self-reliance, helping one another in the absence of government aid. Immigrants mingled with altruists and scoundrels, from social reformers who provided job training and taught home economics at the North Bennet Street School and the North End Union to ruthless padrones (bosses) and unregulated bankers who exploited them.

Charles Ponzi operated his infamous Ponzi scheme from his Hanover Street office, bilking many out of their hard-earned life savings. A group of *prominenti*—prominent people including lawyers, politicians, doctors, and businessmen—concerned with neighborhood improvement established the tradition of community advocacy. One of the first was George Scigliano, a beloved figure born to a Neapolitan father (Naples) and Genoese mother

(Chiavare, the birthplace of Columbus), who became the first Italian American to serve on the Boston Common Council in 1900 and the second to serve in the Massachusetts Legislature in 1903. Before his untimely death in June 1906, he supported the rights of workers to join the American Federation of Labor and enacted laws to end abuses by unscrupulous padrones and grifter bankers.[4] The editors of James Donnaruma's local newspaper, *La Gazzetta del Massachusetts*, wrote articles warning of the dangers of unregulated banks and offered a lawyer to those who had fallen prey to dishonest bankers. Other community advocates concerned with fairness were women. Rosa Maria Finnochietti was born in 1878 on Hull Street to Genoese immigrants. As the self-proclaimed first Italian American suffragist in Massachusetts, she joined the National American Woman Suffrage Association (NAWSA) in the sale of Liberty Bonds and in programs for food conservation during World War 1 and for the Americanization of Italian immigrants.

Immigrants found other advocates in Italian newspapers. Emanuel LoPresti, who emigrated from Licodia Eubea in Sicily (in 1910), began to publish *La Notizia*, a socialist publication that advocated for the rights of the workers, on Fleet Street (32–34 Battery Street around 1914).

With the same entrepreneurial spirit and willingness to work long hours that characterized the earlier German and Irish immigrants, Charlie Polcari and his compatriots pursued the promise of America. Pushcart vendors opened fruit and vegetable stores, barbers and shoemakers became proprietors of storefront businesses, *parrucchieri* (hair stylists) opened salons, and common laborers launched construction companies. Giuseppe Parziale sold the first pizza from his bakery on 78 Prince Street in 1908. Entrepreneurs opened three macaroni factories, the Maravigna Macaroni Company, the Boston Macaroni Company, and the Prince Company. Many worked their way out of airless, overcrowded tenements to the open air of suburban towns.

Placido Amaru immigrated to the North End in 1900 from Pietraperzia, Sicily. While he worked as a clerk in the local variety store, the owner noticed the young man's natural entrepreneurial spirit and his ability to read and write both Italian and English. When the owner sold him the building on 5 Prince Street, Placido expanded the store into an emporium. With "Libreria Del Popolo" (the People's Bookstore) inlaid into the tiled floor of the entrance, he sold books, tobacco, pipes, cigarettes, firearms, record players, sheet music, Italian newspapers, guitars, mandolins, and pianola and piano rolls.

By 1913, now the owner of a thriving business with "two cash registers that rang all day," Placido opened the P. Amarù Co. bank on the corner of Prince and Hanover Streets, which included a steamship agency where immigrants booked tickets on the White Line. On Sundays, his busy photography studio on 333 Hanover Street attracted "Italians in their new-bought suits from Filene's basement, with gold watches and chains showing on their vests, who had their pictures taken to send to the Old Country."[5] In 1913, Placido moved his wife, Maria, and their nine children, first to Malden, and finally to the affluent town of Lexington.

Seven-year-old Ann Mazzarino would realize the American dream in a different way when she immigrated to 284 Hanover Street from Licodia Eubea, Sicily, in 1925. After her marriage to Thomas Damigella in 1939, the two entrepreneurs introduced Earl Tupper to the Tupperware Home Parties concept, which helped launch his Tupperware Home Party Company in 1951. After Thomas told Tupper, "You have an excellent product, but it's dying on the shelves—it has to be demonstrated," they hosted parties in the homes of many friends and family with such success that Damigella Distributors became the first and oldest Tupperware franchise in the world up until 2016, when the family retired their business.

Other North Enders could claim success stories: both the Pastene Company and the Prince Macaroni Company began in the North End from humble beginnings, and John Ciardi, the august poet and translator of Dante's *Divine Comedy*, was born on Sheafe Street and lived his first six years in the neighborhood. And Tony DeMarco, born Leonardo Liotta to Sicilian immigrants from Sciacca, became the World Welterweight Champion in 1955. Public schools offered the children of Italian immigrants the means to break the centuries-old cycle of poverty that their parents had experienced in Italy. The American meritocracy offered some second-generation North Enders the chance for higher education, and professional careers with middle class affluence such as their parents could have hardly imagined.

In 1981, ninety-one-year-old Charlie Polcari reflected on his life as an immigrant who had lived the American dream. He had been one of the Bartel's Shoe Company's most productive and highly paid employees during the 1920s, and he proudly recalled owning the first motorcycle in the North End.

Viola Pettinelli

Viola Pettinelli was seventy-five and living alone. She paused to reflect during her story and then continued, smiling.

"All They Brought Was Their Knapsack on Their Back"

My father came from Abruzzi in Italy because as my father used to say, "There's bread and butter to be eaten here," and like he always said, "I'm still eating bread and butter, which I didn't have there." As a matter of fact, my father wouldn't eat anything but white bread since he came to this country, like sometimes we'd like the whole wheat or we'd like the corn bread. My father wouldn't touch it. He said he had it all his life in Italy and he didn't want to eat it in this country. So we would have our whole wheat or our corn muffin and my father would stick to his Italian white bread (laughing). They had nothing, just what they brought, the few things, the knapsack, you know, on their back—their clothes.

When they came here, they weren't looking for a handout. All they wanted was a job. And that's what they did. They went to work the next day—they couldn't speak English—with sign language they got their jobs. They didn't have jobs like you have now where you get up every morning and go to the same job. They went at the corner [North Square] and somebody needs a man, and if you qualify, you get the job and maybe you work a day or two, it all depends, and when that was gone, well you go out to the corner early in the morning and these men [padrones] used to go around picking up the men who wanted to work, and they'd come down the corner and they had these wagons with horses, and they'd say "Well, we need so many men to do such and such work at such a place." So whoever was qualified would get on the truck and they'd take them to the job. And that's how they started here in the North End. There were no handouts. Those immigrants didn't want anything—they just wanted to work.

Al Mostone

Al Mostone spoke on children growing up and leaving: "When you're born, we each have a candle—some are short, some are long, and then nature takes over."

"They Used to Barter [Bargain]"

Stuff here was not very plentiful when my mother got married, but it was more than they had on the other side. Here they had more freedom—they could barter. Most of the clothing people and the shops here in the North End were owned by Jewish people, who were the majority in the North End of Boston at that particular time. Because for two hundred years the English were in the majority, then of course during the Irish Potato Famine that took place in 1840 in Ireland the Irish came here, and shortly after the Jewish people came here. And the Jewish people, being a business-minded people, they started opening up clothing stores down here, they had grocery stores down here, they had meat markets down here—and some of the big stores today like Gilchrist's and people like the Vorenbergs originated here on Salem Street. And of course, where they were in business, small business, retail business, and our mothers didn't have too much money to spend, they used to barter with one another for clothing or food or whatever.
For instance, Wolf's Clothier used to be on the corner of Washington Street and Hanover Street. My father would take me in there (I was six or seven years old), and the salesman would say—they knew him by name—"Well, Christy, that suit costs five dollars." My father would say, "No, I don't want it, I'll give you three dollars." And he'd say, "Oh my God, I can't, I'm losing money at three dollars, it cost me three dollars." Well then my father would start walking out of the store and he'd say, "Hey, wait a minute, don't walk out, come over here," and he'd say, "Give me four dollars." And my father said, "No, I'll give ya three fifty," and they'd probably settle for around three dollars and seventy-five cents for a suit for a boy that's only about seven years old, and this is the way it was. And the shoes, it was the same way, you used to barter with them. It was an old European custom they had, see? Never to give them the first price.

The only thing they didn't barter for was if they went to the bake shop. If the bread was three cents for a certain type of a loaf, well, they'd pay the three cents. Now we had bake shops here in the North End. On Prince Street, right next door to Saint Leonard's Church there was a bake shop (Louis and Merry Bakery) there where they used to bake breads, pies, cakes, and all. And we'd wait till it was two days old, then we'd go in and buy a great big bag of mixed cakes or whatever for about twelve cents and the whole family would eat their breakfast just on that. Then we used to go on Sundays and buy baked beans, they used to bake the beans there, and we used to go down with a crock or stone pitcher, buy baked beans according to the size of your family. We'd pay, ten, fifteen cents. And the milk—you didn't get quarts, we used to bring our pitchers and they had ice chests and they'd used to put a dipper down into the chest, into the tin that was in the chest and ice, they'd pick it up, they'd pour it into your pitcher and that was three cents for a quart.

Rose Arigo Amato

"He Matched My Parents in the North End"

My mother came here and her father matched her up with my father, that was a match. She really was going with a different fella, but he didn't like the idea, her father. And my father was eleven years older than her. They're both from the same part of Messina in Sicily. But they got married here in America, in North Square [Sacred Heart]. My mother's father had come here first and he brought her here. Then my father came over. And he matched them. But she liked, loved, somebody else, but you know how it is. Them days, they listened to the fathers. But we had a good father, he was really good to us. My mother came very young, she got married in Sacred Heart. She moved to Endicott Street and that's where she stayed—we were all born on Endicott Street. And she died in the same house. She always loved Endicott Street; she wouldn't move anyplace else. Once my father moved her to North Street and she cried so much she went back to the same house—he had to bring her back.

She was the only Italian; there was Greeks, Polish, and Irish. She was the only Italian and then they all came; there were a lot of Sicilians on that street before. Then a lot moved to Medford and the people from around Montefalcione, Napoletani, and Abruzzese moved in. They all loved my mother; they used to say, "Hey, Donna Maria." My mother was a quiet woman; she used to sit on the steps with all of us, and they used to come by and say, "Hello, Donna Maria." She was a pretty woman, a dressmaker.

Mary Pasquale

As a young girl, Mary Pasquale acted as an interpreter between Italian mothers and doctors on the Boston Floating Hospital during whooping cough epidemics in the North End.

"Go Back Home If You Don't Like It Here"

My father was from Trevico, province of Avellino. My parents came here to better themselves. My mother got married in Italy, [and] after she got married my grandparents came here, my mother's side. After they came here they said, "Look it, why don't we send to get Antonetta [my mother], so that we'll have a family here." We were close-knit, with grandmothers and grandfathers. My mother and father became citizens, and they loved it. And they were never on welfare. My father was a gardener; he worked for the Forbes family in Milton, they were millionaire people. They had horses and they also had an Abraham Lincoln house [perhaps an old slave quarters]. My father was a caretaker—a gardener in the summertime and in the winter he'd take care of the steam, the furnace, and take out the barrels and everything.

My father was educated; my mother didn't know how to read and write. The only thing she knew was the one-dollar bill, the two-dollar bill, and the five. Anything more than that she didn't know. So my father used to buy the Italian paper, *La Notizia* or the *Progresso,* and he used to read it. And right across from my house there was a coffee shop that sold cigars, cigarettes, lemonade, or milk or any emergency things—not really a grocery store. And in the morning because it was cold out they'd all sit around a round barrel stove; they'd open up the front, put a few sticks in there, and they'd sit around and buy cigars so that they wouldn't be thrown out for hanging around. With my father, they would say nothing to him because they knew he bought the paper, he read it, and the whole conversation was what was going on in the papers. Some of them agreed on the news, [and] some of them says, "Oh, America is not like Italy. Italy is different." My father would say, "Look it, nobody is keeping you here, if you don't like it, get out. Go back home."

Charlie Polcari

At ninety-one, Charlie Polcari spoke with a sense of accomplishment, having fulfilled his dreams and saying, "I feel perfect." When I arrived the next day to continue hearing his story, his nephew met me at the door to say Charlie had died in his sleep that night.

The North End in 1904

I come over here in 1904 because I had to come; I came with my father because my family was here. It was good in [Montefalcione] but people were starving. There was nothing you could do. The people making a living there they had to go pick and shovel, or if some of them had land, had to struggle on the land, but there were a few people that had businesses in the *paese* [town], and they were making a little—the shoemaker, the tailor, barbers, that's all they had over there. But they wouldn't hire anybody, it would be all in the family. I had three brothers, [and at] that time it was a big trade to be a barber. They had a place on Endicott Street and then one went uptown. What the hell did I know, I was a kid, twelve years old, but I cursed the day I came over here. I didn't know nobody over here; I had a lot of fun in the Old Country, we were a bunch of kids. We had fun here too, we used to play on Endicott Street.

When I was a kid, when I came over here at twelve, thirteen years old, what do you think I was doing? I was going around the streets to find wood, coal, anything I could find in the street. One time the people had a load of wood on the sidewalk [and] they told me, "You want it, go ahead take it." They used to be a good-hearted people. They used to go downstairs, get some coal and wood, my mother used to carry it to the fifth floor upstairs, a pail of coal. And they used to go downstairs to chop the wood too. That's the way they were slaving—today, chrissakes, that's all they're doing, cleaning their fingernails!

One time I went down [to] the market; over there I saw five, six boxes of cantaloupe. So I see one of them was kinda ripe. I says to the owner, "Hey give me one of those cantaloupes, you're gonna throw them away anyway." He said, "Well, if I got to throw them away, take the box, put it on your shoulder and take it home." See, because my brother-in-law used to work down there I could get any goddamned thing I wanted. That son of a gun, I used to do a lot of work for him. I used to get up at five o'clock in the morning to

FIGURE 9. Alberto Sorrentino, 1981. A. Riccio.

go feed the horse—that's a hard job get up at five in the morning. He used to carry the fruit from Charlestown, take it to the market there. He used to make money, with the horse. And I done that for quite a while. And I never got a nickel outta him.

Alberto Sorrentino

Alberto Sorrentino played a few songs on his harmonica while telling his story (1981).

"Drei Cents a Funt"

I got tired of working for somebody for nothing in Mirabella, Italy, in 1912. I was a working boy, making four cents a day. I made twenty-four cents a week. Then I married the daughter of the owner. I came here in 1913 and I got into business. What do you want to do, work for somebody all day? I worked in wholesale, with the pushcart. Italy, the hell with Italy, I don't want anybody tell me Italy—who the hell wants Italy! I don't care, I've been there seven times, [and] every time I run away. There was no steady work. In 1913 I worked construction for two dollars a day for ten hours and I got fired, too. It was hard work. People were working on farms, ten hours a day, for a dollar a day. By 1920 I had three trucks, I had a horse and wagon, I had ten guys. When I went down Blue Hill Avenue, down Dorchester, they're all Jewish over there. "Drei cents a funt [three cents a pound]!" You come along, well like, girls mostly buy, women, you come along, say "Five funt for ten cents." What do you mean? Three funt per ten cents, three cents a pound! I learned Jewish [Yiddish] [and] I sell to Jews. I liked to sell them cucumbers, finf cents a shtikl [five cents apiece]. I used to sell in the West End too, near the Massachusetts General Hospital; some of the old Jewish people would be walking with young girls and the elders would come and see, and I'd say to them, "Cinque soldi allo pund, finf cents al funt, five cents a pound!" Sometimes they'd say, "Five pounds for ten cents," and I'd say, "No," [and] sometime I'd say, "Take a hike—Gen aroys!" And the little girl, seven or eight years old, would say, "Hey, don't tell my mother to take a hike!"

Tom Bardetti

Tom Bardetti was in poor health at the time of our interview but came alive when he described his father's self-reliance and goodwill to others.

"They Were Healthy and Strong"

A lot of the immigrants had the handicap of not being able to speak the language. So although they were healthy and strong, they used to give them pick and shovel jobs digging, digging—you didn't have to know how to speak the language to do that. He didn't know how to speak the language; you're in a foreign country, what could you do? You couldn't do nothing but labor, see? When my father first came here, they had to boarder, like if there was a family that had an extra room, they'd take in a boarder. Some used to have two or three boarders in the house. And the husband and the kids and the mother had to wash the clothes, bring them up on the roof on the clothesline. They had to do the rinsing, the cooking. He paid so much a month and they'd make arrangements if they wanted to feed him and take care of his laundry, and it would be in the month's rent, which was about ten dollars a month or fifteen dollars, but I think it was more ten than fifteen. That way there you didn't have to go and eat in a restaurant, you could eat what they eat, and being Italian with Italians, that food would agree with you. And it was all right. They had black stoves, iron stoves, you put wood in them, and coal. And you could boil anything, [and] if you wanted to cook anything, you'd have the oven too.

Rose Giampaolo

Rose Giampaolo described how chain migration led to chain occupation by friends and relatives who found jobs for the newly arrived.

"Someone Gave Them a Chance"

When the first generation came here from Italy, they came with just the clothes on their backs, and some of them had ten dollars, some had less than ten. And they had to make their life in a new world with no friends, no money, hoping that whoever was here before them would make it possible for them to get a start.

I remember my father, when he first came from Italy, and when he came here in 1899, he was a young man of twenty-four, and he sent for my mother a year later and then he sent for his brother. As soon as he saved a few dollars, naturally he would send for his brother, his brother-in-law, and they came here. And in those days—what I mean by boarders is either a brother or a brother-in-law—they put them up in their apartment as small as it was, give them a bed and food until they got a job. And then once they got settled, they would get their own apartment and live on their own. But in the meantime, they were given a break, like people like my father in those days and my mother, and this is how the Italian people kept coming over. It was someone that came before them that would give them a chance and make sure they got a job. People of my generation—I was born in 1909—most of them worked in factories, whether it was a candy factory or a clothing factory of some kind. Very few worked in offices because during my time not too many had a high school education, and college education was very far in between [few and far between] in my days, although the third generation, like, say, my children, lots of them have been able to go to college because it wasn't as hard for us to make that possible like it was for the first generation.

Lena Albanese

"Why Don't You Come over Here?"

My father came from Montefredane and my mother from Candida, near Avellino. My mother was twenty-six when she came to America and she brought a baby of six months over here, my oldest sister. They didn't like to stay over there and she had her parents over here, her family. And they always used to send and say, "Why don't you come over here? Your husband is here—you come over." Because my father had come over to America to work. And it happened that's why he left her with the small baby over there. So then when my uncle, God rest his soul, told my father, "Send and get your wife," so one day finally he got him to say yes to send for her. And my mother came here and she's been here ever since. When I was born in 1900 and when my mother first came to America, she got a place on Endicott Street, near Capodilupo's Bakery. There were a lot of Jewish people, a lot of American people living in the cellars down low like some of them are now today, see?

Of course we traveled—we went to Rockingham, Vermont, to North Walpole, New Hampshire—because my father was working on the railroad and wherever they used to send him—they made him a foreman—they had work, and he had to take his men with him and work over there, and at times he wouldn't come home nights to my mother. He was only making six dollars a week. He would leave at six o'clock in the morning and come back at six at night. I don't know what the workers were getting because I was too young to ask my father—we were too young—what they were paying. We would never think of such a thing. So finally then he got work in Boston when I was twelve, in 1912, but instead of the North End they shipped him over to East Boston, and Mother said, "No, you can go to East Boston, but I'm not coming this time, I'm staying here with the family." And in the wintertime, God rest his soul, you should have seen him, when he was coming from East Boston, his mustache had icicles hanging from it that it was so cold.

FIGURE 10. Mary Arigo Ventolo.

Mary Arigo Ventolo

Mary Arigo Ventola spoke of the kindness of her mother-in-law, who owned an eight-family house on Foster Street: "After she died, when I went to collect the rent: 'Your mother-in-law paid my electric bill.' Go to the next floor: 'Your mother in-law used to take two dollars, three dollars when I had it.'"

Donna Maria

My parents never told us anything about the trip or why they came from Italy—my mother was too busy sewing for us (laughing)! They usually came, they used to land on North Street, half of them, when they used to come from Italy. I mean a lot of Sicilian people lived down there. Well, they had cousins. They lived with somebody till they got on their feet, see, they get a job, and they go on their own. One of my uncles came over—my mother sent and called for him—and he put up a store on North Street—Anastasi Bros.—and he took his daughter over; she died very young. Well she went to work as a dressmaker, the best dressmaker going on Endicott Street! She sewed. They go on their own when they come here, they do better than we do. Are you kiddin'? They do! They're hard workers!

A lot of them used to go first to New York and then they'd land here. And the boats used to be way down Atlantic Avenue, the boats used to come in. Yeah, because I remember I think it was my mother used to go get my uncle down [at] South Boston Navy Yard or down [at] the army base or Atlantic Avenue. My father was a fruit dealer and he came from Messina, in Sicily. He used to have a store in East Boston—there was no name, it was just a fruit store, it was like a little basement like you know, he used to sell fruit. And I got eight sisters and one brother—oh brother, it was good!—in four rooms. And we were all in one bed, all right! Today they have a baby and they gotta have a baby's room (laughing)!

We were eight girls and one brother and then my mother used to send for [her] brothers in Italy to come to America, from Messina. She had to have papers to send for them. They couldn't stay here. Some of them were American citizens but none them could stay here because they had a wife in Italy. They're all dead now, but my mother used to make all the papers out you know, they became American citizens and they stayed here. My mother was responsible for bringing them here. I don't know too much about my father because we mingled in more with my mother's side than we did my father. But we had cousins with my father's side, but we didn't mingle that much with them. But my mother's brother, I have a cousin, they left the business to them, they're on North Street—bananas—Anastasi. Marie Anastasi is my cousin. Her grandfather is my mother's brother and they're all in the banana business because I go down [to] the store all the time. I had about four aunts; they lived next door to us on Endicott Street. We had a big, big family there. Years back they were more strict, they were more at home, the old people. These girls of today are out. They don't care about the kids, where they are, where they ain't.

Our mothers worried about them. I know my mother did. You know who I'd run to if I had a problem? Well, I'd go to my aunts, that's where you'd run to your family, your aunts, sure. My mother used to go on Salem Street and buy her meat; my father used to bring the fruit. We had big meals every day. The mornings she used to give us a soft-boiled egg, my mother. She used to give us cocoa; she didn't give us coffee, but she'd have coffee for herself. And then she used to roast the bread in the oven—put it in there—instead of toast! The toast, we put it in the toaster—they didn't have them things in them days you know! They'd put it in the oven, they'd toast the bread, slice the bread in the oven. And they'd give it to you to eat. Then at dinnertime, they give it to you at dinner, at suppertime, they give to you at supper.

I tell you the truth, the Italian people used to make spaghetti three times a week; they don't make it no more now. No more like before. I know I used to do it, but I don't do it anymore now. They used to do beans and macaroni, lentils, *ceci* [beans], piece of meat—you gotta have a second dish! Potatoes and eggs (omelet), potato cakes, fish. That stuff. We ate pretty good though. There used to be a store that made the macaroni before—there was a store on Prince Street that sold macaroni, that was years ago—she used to go there, the closest place. Because she didn't have much time. Are you kidding? By foot. Are you kidding, cars? Millionaires at that time had a car! Today everybody's got a car. Even the kids they got a car today (laughing)!

Frances Lauro

From the Yarn Factory to the North End

I'm gonna be seventy-eight and I was born right here in the North End. My father took me over there because he thought maybe he could get a job over there better. Those days were Depression time, you know. He wasn't making much money, so he had people over there, relatives, in fact my stepmother had relatives. See my mother died when I was a baby, I don't remember her at all. So my father took us all over there, to Pennsylvania where her people were. So he got the job there and was working there at the time. My mother and father were from Sicily, they call it Sciacca. He was a laborer. When he died, I wasn't even going to school, see? I was too young. I used to work in the yarn factory making yarn. In those days we started at fourteen. At school they weren't as strict as they are today. When we used to work, the truant officer used to come around you know, and I was so small, which I am still, and I used to have a stool to climb up to put the bobbins to work on the yarn, to spin. And, uh, that was that. No, they didn't say anything.

The only thing, I went to grammar school, I finished the grammar school. That's all. I couldn't, cause my stepmother wouldn't allow, I had to go to work those days. I had to work—where could I go? It was hard for us, a young girl like that, it was hard for us; we were all—most were young girls. Even at fourteen they used to put you to work those days, it wasn't like today. There was no age limit, at least at age fourteen or sixteen anyway in these days, but if you went out of grammar school they coulda gone to work, they couldn't stop you. The yarn factory, it was hard work, you betcha honey. It was very, very low, the money [pay], really, it was nothing. No union in those days. No strikes—we used to work and that was it. I worked at the time at fourteen, I was young. Sure because they put those bobbins stretched in the machine, you had to put those bobbins in, you had to fill them all up, you know. They used to empty it out, you used to get another bundle and put it in. A lot of people used to get hurt, they used to jam their fingers in the machine sometimes. But thank God, I mean I worked there until I was nineteen, twenty, and then we came to Boston back again. My father died and I had nobody over there in Pennsylvania after that so I had relatives over here. So I came over here, see? Came by myself. I had my people and I told them, I said,

FIGURE 11. Charles Ponzi on 135 Endicott Street, standing at center.

"Don't come down to the station, I'll take the train and I'll come myself and meet me down the station," which they did. "When you get here? Well, you fall in love, no? Yeah (laughing)." Then I got married here. Then I had the five children.

Helen Luongo

The Ponzi Scheme

He ran away with all the money at that time. My mother at the time skimped and scraped to get the money together to go [to the Ponzi office], and as she was going on Hanover Street, she met people who were coming back saying that he had failed. You used to deposit the money, you deposited it for one month and like, for instance, and he would give you 10, 12 percent and everybody went; well, the first one who deposited and took the money, well, it's all right. But the last ones. He ran off with the money! He was just a—like a, well, I'd call him a loan shark, I wouldn't call him a banker because he only had a store as an office. And my father lost money in another bank on the corner of Hanover and Washington Street. My father lost ten thousand dollars over there. That bank closed.

Vladimir Ciani

When I asked to interview eighty-eight-year-old Vladimir Ciani, he showed up the next day with a beautifully handwritten statement. He read the stories like an orator, rolling his r's and raising his voice when recounting important events as if delivering a speech to a large crowd.

Life in the North End in 1907

When I came to Boston in 1907, in those days, you could really call the North End a small city within a big city. Strutting through its streets was a pleasure, never fearing to be molested or bothered by anyone. In fact, Italian you could say was the official language—English was hardly used or understood. In those days the trolley cars were the only means of locomotion, coming and descending from Scollay Square, now known as Government Center. Buses and automobiles in those days were rarities.

For thirty-five dollars or less per month, you could have a six-room apartment in the best buildings of those days. The best meat—pure Chicago steer—thirty-five cents a pound, with the next best at twenty-five cents. Beans, three pounds for ten cents, all kinds of macaroni and spaghetti five cents a pound, imported olive oil, a dollar fifty per gallon. It was a great life in a way. But we must also consider the fact that weekly wages in those days were also pretty meager. One dollar a day was the average wage. A skilled artisan could command a trifle more. I also remember that our countrymen used to come from Italy, work during the spring and summer months, and then go back to the Old Country to their families for the winter months when cheap manual labor would slacken over here. They could very well commute quite easily because I distinctly remember that sometimes during wars of competition between transatlantic lines [they] would reduce passage rates to nine dollars per one-way trip. Can you imagine, nine dollars from Boston to Naples!

Paul Grande

Paul Grande and his younger brother Dominic ran Grande Barber Shop overlooking North Square, where they had been cutting hair since 1921. Paul recalled "Honey Fitz," John F. Kennedy's grandfather, giving fiery speeches to large crowds on North Square in the 1920s when he was the mayor.

"This Country Saved His Life"

When my father came here from Sicily in 1904 because he wanted a better living, he had nobody here, nobody he knew. Living conditions in Sicily weren't very good, so he came here without any relatives here—no brothers or cousins or sisters. Most of them (the first immigrants) had nobody here, no relatives at all. They had to start from scratch. The later immigrants had uncles, brothers, aunts, cousins—they had a job set up for them, an apartment. My father had to buy a secondhand stove, dishes, plates, silverware, a secondhand bed, everything secondhand. My father came alone, made a few dollars, made a hundred dollars in one year, and he sent for my mother a year later. He loved this country though, that's one thing.

He had his appendix out as soon as he got here. He had no family here, he was alone. My father always said this country saved his life because as soon as he got off the boat after three weeks, he had an appendicitis attack.

He didn't have a dime—it didn't cost him a dime—he had no money. He said, "I survived; if I was in Italy, I would have been dead." They took my father up to City Hospital and they took care of him—he was walking within two weeks. He said, "If I was home in Sicily, I wouldn't be living now." Because they didn't know what an appendix was in those days. He made it just in time—this country saved his life.

"Their Word Was Their Bond"

There was a closeness in those days, even when they borrowed money. When my father opened his first barbershop down the street in 1904, he had no money in those days. His next-door neighbor let him have three hundred dollars for a down payment. Two, three hundred dollars in those days was a lot of money for a down payment to buy the barber shop. No paper, no note—their word was their bond. They didn't have to sign papers, they didn't want no receipts, nothing. When they said something, they'd die for it. They would. They wouldn't back out of it, forget it. My father paid him back. Their word was their bond in those days. When they said something, they'd die for it. And, of course, my father paid him back. If you ever mentioned welfare to those people in those days, people would cry. If you ever mentioned welfare, it was a dishonor, a disgrace. Today they come in laughing, "Hey, I'm on welfare." If you ever mentioned welfare to those people in those days, they used to cry. Ever mention welfare they used to get sick, they didn't want to hear that word "welfare." They thought it was charity and they didn't want it.

Alessandrina Manaro

Alessandrina Manaro was a short, round-faced woman of seventy-seven, who often sang Neapolitan songs with gusto.

Working at Leopold Morse in 1921

My mother had fourteen children and there was little money. So I came to America in 1921 on the *Canopic*. Two days after I got to America, my sister said to me, "You gotta go to work because you gotta pay the money we sent you to come here." My brother-in-law took me there—it was where the Prince Macaroni building is, there was a shop in there. I was sewing, making sleeves on the jackets at the Leopold Morse factory, and that's where I met my husband—he was a tailor too. My first two days I made seventeen dollars. So I says to my sister, I'm gonna send the money back to my father and mother, you know, they had a big family. She said to me, "No, you gotta pay the board first and then whoever you marry pays for the trip when you came over here." So they took all my money from me, every week they took money from me—I had to pay board, and for the trip. Every Saturday, my brother-in-law used to take me to Jordan Marsh—he bought me clothes. I had long hair when I came from here, then I cut my hair. I didn't want to go out from 28 Sheafe Street, I was afraid. At night they had all chairs, they sit outta in front a door, they played cards.

My sister no allow me to go no place because I was seventeen years old, I was a beautiful girl when I came from Italy, now I'm old anyway. So when I put on the sleeves on the jackets, I put this a sleeves, I put over here because I never worked in Italy, because we had a small store, we were born into the business, we sold goods by the yard, salt, soap, oil, bread. So my boss came to me and said, "Che stai facendo [What are you doing]?" "Ho detto, sto mettendo le maniche [I'm putting on sleeves]," I said. He said, "Tu, le maniche, hai messo storto—questa manica addà i' qua [You put the sleeves on crooked, they're supposed to go like this]!" And I pushed him [and said], "Get the hell out of here!" I was afraid, I just got here from the Old Country and I didn't know much people here. So he did with his hands and said, "To hell with the Italiani." And I changed the sleeves and I started; every morning he's checking on me when I was putting on the sleeves. And a little bit at a time he fell in love with me. Later, we got married.

Cosimo Pietrangelo

Cosimo Pietrangelo made eleven trips back and forth to Italy to support his family.

Finding Work in 1922

I came to Boston in September 1922. I came with friends and we traveled together on the ship, and the first night we slept in the Webster House on Paul Revere Place. The next day we went all over Boston with someone who showed us, took us down the Boston Common, way up to the State House. Some friends here—they were all Italiani—we went to North Square to look for work. "Hey you, you want to work tomorrow?" they ask you. There was a lot of work at that time. And some bosses used to go around, "You working?"

We'd say no. "All right, come with me," and they take your name. And we kept on going like that. I worked forty-nine years in construction. My first job was with the Aberthaw Construction Company outside Boston. I got sixty-five cents an hour, a union job. Nonunion was sixty cents an hour. I lived in a shanty hut during the week for three months at a time. Stayed out in the woods all the time. Then we left the woods to come back to Boston, to North Street. We'd get laid off around Christmas and we'd come home to Boston. I'd leave my wife for four months at a time, go to Italy, come back to Boston, work, and go back.

Then I worked for a contractor, Frank Snow—we did a lot of electrical work all over Boston. In a ditch all the time. Then I went into construction work, shovel gravel, cement work, carrying brick, as a carpenter. I worked fifty hours a week and the pay was twenty-nine dollars a week, cash money, no check. The paymaster would come on the job, "Hey you, what's your number? Alright, sign here on this little slip." And he'd give you your money. It was a pretty good system, you know. We never get paid money like in the Old Country; there wasn't too much money around then because we had to work on the farms and wait to the end of the year to sell something.

Paul Grande

Paul Grande seldom left the North End. His only trip on his honeymoon to New York seemed far away. He marveled how his friends traveled to Florida "as if it were around the corner."

"The Banks Gave No Interest"

They used to land in Charlestown, at Charlestown bridge, the boats used to land there. And they'd come ashore. The first street they'd come to was Prince Street; they used to walk up Prince Street and end up in North Square. And they stayed here. There used to be five banks on North Square—this place used to be a bank, a bank across the street, Berradini, another one, Forte, two at the foot of the square, the Ferullo Bank and Stabile Bank. There was one bank on the corner of Prince and North Streets, and in the window they had a sign, "5 Dollars to Europe" with a big five. And a lot of people said, "Jesus, where am I gonna get five dollars to go?" They didn't have the five dollars to go back. This was 1906. All the banks had money in the windows, gold pieces right out there, right in the window full of gold pieces, money stacked up there, [and] nobody used to touch it. They used to close the bank at night and leave the money right in the window. Nobody touched it. Try to do that today! Jeez, those gold pieces were like a tray of pennies and nobody used to touch them. And the poor man would want a little interest, [but] the banker would say, "What interest? You're lucky I'm holding the money for you, so how the hell would you keep it if it wasn't for us?" Wouldn't pay them no interest. And North Square was always crowded with laborers waiting to get work in Maine, New Hampshire—wherever the jobs were. Those banks gave the people no interest on their money.

Becoming an American Citizen 5

> Judge: "What flies over the courtroom roof?" Mr. Ginnetti: "Pigeons."
> —CITIZENSHIP HEARING IN THE EARLY 1900S

On a sunny morning on June 19, 1943, a regally dressed woman walked between the grand columns of New Haven's stately courthouse and entered the main hearing room. Now that she was in middle age, Maria Grazia Santacqua's dream to become an American citizen had come true. Like many who emigrated from southern Italy in the early 1900s, Maria yearned for education, an opportunity denied to most girls like her in San Martino Valle Caudina, near Avellino.

In the patriarchal hierarchy of the South, the division of labor fell heaviest on young girls, who managed household chores, tended farms, raised livestock, and helped raise younger siblings. Maria was known as a strong farm worker, often helping exhausted relatives who could no longer lift heavy bushels, and carrying their loads on her head for miles without stopping. Having lived her adult life in New Haven since 1911, Maria marveled at the opportunities that America bestowed on its people. Eager to become a citizen, she attended immigration classes with her young daughter Elizabeth. She studied diligently to read and write English, memorized important events in American history, and repeated the answers to her children to improve her speaking skills. Under the watchful eye of her husband, Maria often practiced writing her name in anticipation of the day she would pass the literacy test at her citizenship hearing.

Among the pews in the palatial courtroom, Maria stood next to her husband, dressed in his Sunday suit, and her oldest children, Jenny and Frank.

As other immigrants raised their hands to take the citizenship oath, she recognized the familiar faces of Lithuanians, Poles, and Jews who had been in her immigration class. When the black-robed judge called her to come forward, the mellifluous sound of her name—Maria Grazia Santacqua—filled the room with music to the ears. With a confidence that surprised her family, she answered the judge's questions in the best English she could muster. When asked who the sixteenth president was, she answered, "President O Lincoln!" and enthusiastically volunteered, "Oh! And he freed the slaves!"

When asked why she wanted to become a citizen, her eyes filled with tears. In a voice loud enough for everyone to hear, she answered, "Because I love a this country. Italy was my country, I loved it, but I love this country because they send people to school."[1] Impressed with her answers, the judge smiled and said, "You got your citizenship papers." Maria carefully signed her name and received her citizenship certificate.

Maria Grazia Santacqua's appreciation for her new country echoed the sentiments of many immigrants who recognized the economic, educational, and social opportunities America granted its citizens. Their transatlantic voyage to American urban centers like Boston's North End signified the psychological journey from the despair of the Italian peasantry to the upward mobility the industrial working class provided them.

In the early days of emigration, approximately one of every three immigrants were young men who came alone for short stays to earn enough money to buy farmland when they returned home. Some people labeled them "birds of passage" for staying during work seasons and returning to their villages for prolonged stays when there was no work. But as time passed and their children were born in America, more decided to stay. Some never bothered to become citizens, comfortable in neighborhoods surrounded by *paesani* (compatriots) who spoke the same dialect. But for the many, like Maria, who had been born into Italy's caste system and seldom interacted with officials or had enough education to pass from voice to pen, they nevertheless overcame their limitations and became American citizens.[2] As Maria's daughter Elizabeth recalled, "My mother worshipped that piece of paper for the rest of her life."

FIGURE 12. Grande Barbershop, with Gaetano Grande and sons Paul and Dominic.

Paul Grande had a way of telling stories that catapulted the listener back in time. Sitting in an old-fashioned barber chair, he often smiled with pride when he talked about the good-heartedness and determination of the immigrants of his father's generation.

Paul Grande

"He Was So Enthused"

So when my father became a citizen after a few years he was here, and when he went up for his citizenship papers, it was funny. Italian he could read and write, but he couldn't read or write English so he couldn't answer any of the questions the judge asked him. He knew how to write his name, read and write it in Italian, but he didn't know who the mayor was, or the governor; he didn't know none of that stuff. He used to tell me the story [that] the judge scratched his head, he said, "Jesus, you're so enthused to become a citizen," and he gave him his citizenship papers without answering any questions, nothing. Because he was so anxious to get that paper and [the judge] gave it to him. He didn't know one question. He always spoke good about the country, that's all. And he said it, "If I was better off, I would have stayed there, what would I have come here for? I come here because I wasn't well off." He said, "I love this country, I want to stay here." And he never went back to Sicily.

FIGURE 13. Americanization Meeting, February 1921, at the Michelangelo Center.

Mary Pasquale — Born in Trevico, near Avellino, Mary Pasquale lived alone in a cold-water flat. She refused a subsidized, modern apartment because she liked how the old floors squeaked when she walked on them. Besides, she said, "Those homes for the elderly remind me of an infirmary."

Becoming an American Citizen

I remember when my mother became a citizen. My father failed twice, I don't know why. He was educated but he wasn't interested. In those days you brushed the hand of [paid] the fella that was a witness for you, he'd come for you, but they wouldn't lose a day's pay to come and be a witness, so my father failed twice.

My mother went to school at the North End Union, and after she learned her name, she used to print it and learned a few questions, [so] she was ready to go up with my father and several others. It was my mother's turn to go and be questioned. So the judge asked my mother, "How long have you been in America?" "Oh, a long a time," she answered him. "How many children you got?" She said, "I dunno, I gotta full house, I don't know—wait a minute, six girls and two boys." The judge then asked her, "Do you like this country?" "Yes," [she said], because she spoke broken English but enough to hold a conversation. Then he said to her, "Do you like Mussolini?" My mother says, "Mussolini? I don't know Mussolini, he's over there, I'm over here. I'm not interested in Mussolini. I gotta family here." And she became a citizen. When it came time for my father, they said, "You deserve a citizenship," and when they came back with a flag, honest and truly, my mother and father were so tickled, so tickled.

Marguerite Locchiato

"My Children Have to Become American Citizens"

They were really anarchists and they didn't believe in God; they were against the government and all that. When my father came here from Mirabella the first thing my grandmother said was, "My children have got to become American citizens," and she made them become citizens. My mother came from Chiusano and became an American citizen through my father, because when my father married my mother in 1903, if you married an alien, you automatically became a citizen. Then the following year the law changed. My father kinda feared them [the anarchists]; he was afraid, they were troublesome. My mother said one time they fired a shot in the building and that made my father really get out. That was maybe between 1912 and 1914.

The Italian Mother — 6

Chi tène' 'na mamma, non chiagnà
(Whoever has a mother, doesn't cry).
—LENA RICCIO

Deep in the hills of Avellino on the estate of Don Francesco, a farm girl received a long-awaited letter from America with a ticket to reunite her with her family in the North End. Al Mostone's mother had been indentured to the wealthy landowner as a "working girl," the name assigned to children of poor families who could no longer afford to take care of them. She had labored alongside other young girls, trapped in a dreary life of poverty and earning nothing but the shelter of small, primitive rooms and the meals to sustain them for the relentless toil in the fields.

When the young Cataldo girl landed on North Street wearing the linen dress her grandmother had made for her, she brought handmade sheets, bedspreads, and towels. In addition to the articles in her steam trunk, she transported a strong work ethic, the stamina to work from dawn to dusk, and the southern Italian code of righteous behavior, which she would teach her fifteen children. When she married a young man from the same village at St. Leonard's Church in 1902, they shared similar life experiences. Her husband had also been indentured to a farmer as an orphan and borrowed money when he was fifteen to sail on the *Canopic* to Boston.

The Mostones joined other immigrant families struggling to get an economic foothold in Boston. A keen observer of the inner workings of Italian families, their first child, Albert, became a local historian. After leaving school to support the family, he continued his studies by a kerosene lamp in the kitchen where he slept. As the eldest son, Albert was considered a second father by his fourteen siblings. The Mostones faced the same hardships as many poor families, living in cramped cold-water flats without adequate heating, bathtubs, indoor toilets, or hot water.

Although the father was the main breadwinner and authority figure, the Italian mother made sure the home was spotless, the children presentable, and the meals wholesome. Italian fathers worked in outdoor markets, constructed buildings, and built roads; Italian mothers built the family foundation in the kingdom of the home. With the help of the eldest daughter, the mother managed the younger children. In times of family conflict, she often acted as arbitrator, and when children misbehaved in school, she met with their teachers. She set strict curfews as a task master and doled out discipline, unafraid to spare the rod when the situation warranted it.

The Italian mother was the center of family life and set the example of righteous behavior, not only with words but also in her actions. She instilled empathy, teaching her children to imagine themselves in the shoes of the suffering so they could feel their pain. She entertained with folklore stories, sang lullabies and nursery rhymes, and recited proverbs, passing the wisdom of southern Italian culture to the next generation. Shopping in local stores and open markets, she was a fierce negotiator who never bought at the first price. She managed the family finances and found the time to help the family economy, sewing garments from local factories or taking in boarders. When the children were sick, she sometimes transformed into an exorcist, reciting secret *maluocchio* prayers and practicing the ancient rite of oil and water to dispel the *iannara*'s (witch's) spell of the evil eyes. Babies were delivered at home by trusted *levatrice* (midwives), usually from the same region in Italy.

The dynamic Italian mother was the quiet force behind the Italian American family, the glue that held everything together. Adhering to a tradition of welcoming the stranger as old as Homer's *Odyssey*, she always made room for one more at her table. Reflecting on his mother, Al described the ethos of Italian mothers, who led lives of selfless dedication yet wanted nothing in return:

> There isn't much you could say about your mother for the simple reason that she was all [about] you. She was at home. She did all the housework, all the cooking, the cleaning, made sure that your clothes were in good form. Her life was in three rooms, five rooms, four rooms. She would go to a movie once in a while and the son would take her or a daughter, but she asked for nothing. She'd go to church, had her own prayerbooks, her rosaries at home—they said it even in the daytime. She gave everything

up for what she had: her children. They would meet outside with other mothers, they would talk, or they'd go up to each other's houses and have a cup of coffee or a slice of bread or whatever they had, a cookie, but that's the way it was in those days, see?

The people who got fed first were the children; the mother very rarely sat down at the table with the father and the kids because she had to wait on them. And that was her kingdom, the home. And the children respected her for that; especially after they got married, they realized what it meant to be a mother in a home. And I can say my mother taught us all how to cook, we had to wash clothes in the tub with a scrubbing board, we had to do everything—boys and girls—so that when we got married we were able to carry on a home without any problems.

Many a times when we'd done things that wasn't right, they would cover for us, they wouldn't tell your father at night so that you'd get a wollopin—they would cover for you. If you were in trouble, you got in trouble in school, or whatever it was, she'd be the one to go up and listen to what they said, and then ball the daylights outta ya, but when your father came home at night—unless it was really serious, she wouldn't say a word to him. You see, it's something you could never—I can't put, I wouldn't know the words—she was there.[1]

Helen Luongo

"The Love of the Family"

I would rather have a Depression than what we have today. People were happy. You didn't have—my mother couldn't give us cocoa or coffee or milk. She'd buy the cocoa shells and make cocoa in the morning, she'd make a big pan. Then she'd get the bread and we'd all have—we couldn't have two or three slices of bread. One loaf of bread had to be enough for the whole family. We didn't have—but the happiness that we had, the closeness of the family! You don't find that today. You don't find that closeness of family now. I don't know, I can't understand it. That love of the family isn't there anymore. You wouldn't think of sitting down to eat, not unless the whole family was there. Everybody had to be at the table. And you had to sit until everybody was through. This is the way it was in my house.

FIGURE 14. Mary Pasquale.

Mary Pasquale

Mary Pasquale spoke wistfully about the responsibilities of being the oldest daughter in her family. Despite her hardships, she felt proud to have always done right.

Being the Oldest Daughter

Things were different when I was a young girl. I had to supervise the younger ones, bring them to the park and watch them and stay with them. Then when I matured to be around eighteen, nineteen, boyfriends, you know, would come around trying to ask me for a date. And the first thing I'd do was to tell my mother, Ma—" "Oh!" My mother would say, "You can't go, your father would kill you. You're the oldest one, you gotta go to work, you gotta bring a living for the rest of them. And look it, Marietta, you're the first one; if you go wrong, the others will follow you." And that pressed in my mind, that I had to be straight, on the level, which I was, right? I don't lie.

One day in my sewing class at the North Bennet Industrial School, after I finished a pattern, my teacher said, "Oh, you know Marie, your hip, one is higher than the other one." So I told my mother, I says, "Ma, you know what Miss Dunovan says? That one hip is higher than the other one." My mother said, "Oh sure! Too bad, too bad about her, she should have had your job!" Because, you know, when you're always carrying your little sister around in your arms I used to get tired, I used to put her on my hip and carry her there. So I got and I still have that condition from taking care of my sisters. It's a true story. I don't lie.

Helen Luongo

Helen Luongo knew an elderly couple who had lived near her on Salem Street for fifty-one years. When they were evicted, she went to the landlord: "I went to the landlord and asked them not to do it. They both died right after that."

"I Had the Responsibility of the Whole Family"

My mother died when I was fifteen years old, so at fifteen years old is the best part of your life that you can enjoy your mother. And I was left without a mother. And, of course, then at fifteen years old I had the responsibility of the whole family when my mother died. For entertainment we'd go to somebody's house, somebody had a player piano and we'd go, that's all. Then after my mother died, my father was even more strict. All we could go was to the Public Gardens, that's how far we'd get.

Viola Pettinelli

"Two Pennies Each"

My mother, well, she never went to work. There were seven children, but she stayed home. She took care of the house; my mother did all the cooking, all the sewing, all the patching—she was very good at patching, my mother. You could never find one of her patches sometimes! And wash by hand with the old washboard, you know? We had one Sunday dress, one Sunday outfit, the boys and the girls. And every Saturday night my mother would wash those Sunday clothes and press them and they were all hung up

FIGURE 15. Foster Street, 1905.

in the corner. Sunday morning, we'd get up, put on our best, and everybody went to Mass. At nine o'clock was the Children's Mass and we all had to go to Mass, and my father would give us two pennies each because that's what we put in the box. The priest would be glad to get the two pennies, so here was my father near the door, two pennies each, and we'd go off to church, go to Mass on Sundays.

Mary Pasquale

Mary Pasquale told folktales she learned as a child, half in English and half in Italian. Although she seemed tired and lonely, the conversation ended on an upbeat note, with us laughing together.

"My Mother Breastfed the Neighbor's Boy"

Mothers were mothers in those days. We were always around our mothers. You know, sometimes a mother would get so disgusted, get out, sit out in front of the door. But they were always close. But now, things have changed. I remember a time when my mother was sitting out in front of the steps, and she'd sit outside to get the air while the house had a wood fire in the kitchen in the summertime. So people would pass by and they would say, "Hello, Antoinette, how are you?" And they'd talk about how many children have you got, and all that stuff, and my mother would say, "I got seven." And the woman said to her, "Oh, seven. I've got two, I have one of them I can't even nurse." My mother said, "Oh, how come?" She said, "I don't know, I don't have any milk in my breasts." "Oh, don't worry," my mother said. "Look it, I feed my baby at twelve every day. I'll feed my child at eleven o'clock, if you can take your child in the house around one o'clock, they'll be enough of milk for both, for him."

This went on as long as it took for the boy to get off his breastfeeding. Those were the kind of mothers who were there at the time, and she wasn't the only one that was that type—a lot of them volunteered, nursing another [for a stranger] that gave you a hard-luck story. You don't find it now. Now if you drink out of a cup, they'll make sure it's sterilized before they drink out of it. It was motherly. And in those days, you know, if a baby was small, there was no Gerber's baby food. The mothers would take the food, chew it up in their mouth, take it with their fingers and put it in the baby's mouth, just like a little bird, a pigeon. There's where the love was.

Josie Zizza

Josie Zizza spoke with pride about caring for her mother at home until the end of her days. But recognizing the changes in the Italian family, she supported the North End Nursing Home in 1982.

"Taking Care of Our Mother"

We were good to my mother, that's why we took care of her. My mother died at home; she was sick for twelve years. The doctors advised us to put her in a nursing home,—we said no. She died at home. We were all there when she died. We used to take turns taking care of her every day. We all did our share. My mother lived until she was eighty-seven. We took care of her at home. Every day was somebody else's turn. They don't do that today, no they do not. My sisters, we took turns, we were eight girls. I had a sister that wasn't married and was living with my mother, and never had to stay home because we figured she needed—she used to stay nights with my mother during the night. But we thought she should work because she needed—and we used to take a turn, we all did our share. I worked four days a week, so Tuesday was my day. We took turns with my sisters. We all had a day each to care for my mother. Every day one of my sisters were there at seven-thirty in the morning till five at night. It worked out very well.

Frances Zanfani Corolla

"We Were like a Chain"

We didn't have washing machines then. That's how we were kept very busy. My mother would get that big pan and put it on the stove and boil the water. One night you'd soak them, one night you'd boil them, and another night you'd put them in bleach. It may sound ridiculous, but we enjoyed it. That's all we knew. But now they have modern dishwashers, washing machines and the dryers, but there isn't that closeness. If my sister was doing the stairs or if we couldn't go by the stairs, we'd be doing something else until she'd get through and then we'd do something else—we were always like a chain; we kept very busy, always very busy. That's why I miss my mother very much. She taught us what she knew. It's really sad. When young kids today come in, I don't know where do they get all that money, and they're paying it, but they're not clean like us. When I do my stairs in the hall or I clean [for] the young girl upstairs, she laughs. She says, "We're not used to that." I said to her, I've done this all my life. I'm used to cleanliness; you can't live in dirty—this is how we were brought up.

Josie Picadacci

Josie Picadacci was in her early sixties, and her face radiated a warm smile when she spoke about family closeness.

"We Walked Arm in Arm"

We had a very loving life. I only had one brother and he was beautiful, and when we went out, we used to walk arm in arm—you don't see that anymore. People used to tell my mother, "I saw your daughter with a boy. What's she walking around with a fella arm in arm?" It was my brother all the time. We all loved one another; there was so much love in the families. If I ever had a serious problem, not to burden my parents or to make them worry about me, I'd tell him. That was the family before. And everybody I knew was the same way. But I don't know what happened to the family. It's really a shame because it was so beautiful—it really was.

Rose Pesce, Josie Zizza

Elopement

Years ago in the North End, because they were so strict, they used to elope. If the mothers and fathers didn't want them to marry those people, they eloped! And, of course, it took a long time for the families to reconcile.

Josie Zizza

"She Eloped"

When my ex-sister-in-law got married, they were going to live in my mother's rooms across the street. Her mother was so narrow-minded, so old-fashioned, she wouldn't—she said to my mother, "You gotta come with me the next morning [after they're married]." My mother says, "I'm not going, I got eight daughters of my own!" She wouldn't let them go on their honeymoon. Honest to God, this is the truth. My mother wouldn't go. Today—one-night stands. That I don't believe in. My mother would always tell us the story of when she was working. There was a young girl. Her father used to bring her to work, pick her up at night, not to make any—so one day, eleven o'clock, she says to the boss, "I feel sick, can I go home?" So he said, "Well let me call your father." She said, "Well my father is working, I'll go home by myself." She eloped. Her father came and then waited for her near the factory, wait, wait, wait. She was gone. And he followed her. Years ago, that's what did it. My ex-sister-in-law, she couldn't go out with my brother alone. She couldn't!

Frances Zanfani Corolla

Frances Zanfani Corolla was sixty-eight and living alone. Her parents came from Genoa and Parma and were the first Italian settlers in the 1860s.

"I Have Room Thirteen, I Have Room for One More"

My mother came from a town near Parma and she taught us what she knew. And what she knew was the right thing because the old-timers—you can't take it away from them—when they put the law down, that was it. She had to be tough because she had eleven children to take care of. If she said something, we were afraid of my mother more than my father. She just spoke once. She used to say to us, "I'm the boss; if you don't like it here, get out." My mother was law. Law was law. We never worried about anything, always running, we had to go home to our mother and that was it. Nine o'clock eleven of us were in that house! Now to handle eleven children, she didn't want no help from anyone—no welfare. My mother worked and everyone helped out;

the older one would help the next one, the next younger down. She did it on her own because she knew how to manage that dollar.

We really had nothing those days, but we ate three good meals a day. See, I wasn't brought up with riches, I was brought up with love and affection, that's what my parents knew. They came when they were young and they figured they had nothing when they came here—they knew what it was to struggle.

We used to have E. Gray's, well they knew my mother come from a big family, they used to give us these big cartons of cookies for fifty cents—good cookies, but they were all broken up. Potatoes my mother would buy by the sacks—she couldn't buy a five-pound bag—everything by the sacks. And they knew my mother and father very well and they'd keep the stuff for them. We used to help my mother peel the potatoes. She would make what she called *la torta*—an onion and potato cake. You make your own dough, fold it, beat eggs and put [them] on top of it, bake it—it was very tasty and that's what we lived on. Plenty of polenta we ate, we ate plenty of macaroni, and plenty of greens. My mother wasn't too crazy about too much gravy (red sauce), she'd rather give us greens, all the main foods, you know, all the vitamins. We were never sick, all eleven of us.

We had a big, round, old-fashioned dining-room table, and we'd be all around the table, and my mother would put the big bowl in the middle of the table, and then we'd all help ourselves, and we'd all go for the bread, and the smell alone would make you eat. Then the neighbors would come in. My mother used to say, "I have room for thirteen, I have room for one more." Next door was Polish people, and say if we cooked Italian and they liked what we cooked, and if we liked what they cooked, we exchanged dishes. The windows were open and the aroma of the cooking, and "Oooh, I wonder who's cooking that?" Or somebody would come by, "Come on up, have a dish of spaghetti." You'd hear people [yell], "What are you cooking today? Is it something I like?" Whatever they were making, we'd swap dishes.

Theresa Paglia

"My Mother Taught Me"

So I used to get mad about it, you know my husband used to say, "Let's go see my mother," you know I was young. So I used to say, "all right." So I couldn't say the word ["right"] good and my mother-in-law used to tease me. And she used to say to me, "Tre', where does your mother come from"? I used to say "Montefregana [Mount don't give a damn]." So they used to laugh. You know, and I took and I took it, and so I used to get mad about it. Then my mother-in-law would say, "Mae, Tre', addó venne mameta [Mae, Teresa, where does your mother come from]?" I used to say "Montefregana." So finally I went to my mother and I said, "Ma where do we come from in Italy? Is it a bad place?" She said, "Why"? I said, "When I go to my mother-in-law's they wanna know where you come from and I tell them, and I say Montefr—" And she said, "Well how do you say it"? I said "Montefregana." She said, "Puozz! I could—no wonder they laugh at you!" I said to her, "Well, how must I say it?" So my mother taught me, she said, "Dici [you say] Montefredane." So I practiced it you know. So the next time my husband said, "Let's go to my mother's." So after supper, we clean up, and we go to my mother-in-law's. My mother-in-law, she says "Mae, Mae"—all my aunts from Italy, all the *cummariddi* [the little *cummare*—her friends] from the building were there, so my mother-in-law said, "Mae, Tre', addó venne mameta [Where is your mother from]?" I said [to myself] I'm gonna straighten them out tonight, boy! I took a deep breath, and I said, "Tu vuoi sape [You want to know]?" I used to cripple the Italian; but now I say it better—where my mother comes from, addó venne my mother? I took a deep breath and I said, "Montefredane!" And they all said (laughing), "Ahh! Si è imparata Teresa [Teresa learned]!" But all those towns, they have sayings. San Sossio (Baronia), "*Per l'osso, va a San Sossio* when you waste your time," or "San Sossio, *guaio nuosto*, our trouble," they say. Calabria, *capotuosto*, thick-headed. Then I used to say, a lot of times I'd look in my bag and she [my mother] used to say, "What is it?" And I'd say, "I can't find my chiavá [sexual intercourse]" instead of saying "*chiave* [keys]." But then I learned. My mother gave me lessons. My mother came here when she was a youngster, you know she talked a little bit. Then she got to say Filenes, and the Gild a Crist [Gilchrist's Department Store] (laughing). So then I learned.

The Italian Father 7

> I came to love the fathers too, many of whom were putting up a brave battle to make a living for their families.
> —CONSTANTINE MARIA PANUNZIO, *The Soul of an Immigrant*

From 1870 to 1910, 78 percent of Italian immigrants were young men in search of jobs. Denied the education for the necessary writing skills, few accounts of their working experiences survive. Constantino Panunzio's autobiography, *Soul of an Immigrant*, provides some observations at the time of mass immigration. As a Protestant minister intimately involved in the personal lives of the community, he described one Italian father "of fine sensibilities trying to provide for his five children, but whose heart was breaking beneath the load of difficult work."[1]

His description spoke volumes for many unskilled, illiterate immigrant fathers working long hours at manual labor jobs with miserable pay. At the same time, southern Italian men were portrayed as hot-tempered, vengeful, violent, mentally inferior, shiftless, and slovenly. For example, U.S. senator from Massachusetts Henry Cabot Lodge marginalized southern Italian men, declaring them dangerous to America compared to northern Italians, who he claimed were Teutonic and industrious.

Contrary to nativist stereotypes, most Italian men lived by the southern Italian code of manhood, which they displayed in every aspect of their lives. Some adhered to the Old World vendetta, sometimes solving disputes with a knife. The Italian father showed manliness by absolute loyalty to family, extended family, and closely held friends, who were usually from the same village. Critical to family survival, his role as the main breadwinner was unquestioned. In return, he demanded family order and expected clearly defined roles from his children. Eldest sons were often looked on as second fathers.

Giovanni Verga's *I Malavoglia* portrays *l'ordine della famiglia* (the family order) as one of the cornerstones of southern Italian culture. In one scene, the patriarchal grandfather, Master 'Ntoni, recites time-honored proverbs to reinforce the importance of family unity: "Per menare il remo bisogna che le cinque dita s'aiutino l'un l'altro" (To pull an oar, each finger has to help the other), and "Gli uomini son fatti come le dita della mano: il ditto grosso deve fare da dito grosso, e il dito piccolo deve fare da dito piccolo" (Men are made like the fingers of a hand: the thumb does like the thumb, the little finger does like a little finger).

Although he is the central authority figure, the Italian father usually counted on his wife to maintain control of the family, but sometimes he ruled with an iron fist. A staunch protector of family honor, he abided by the proverb, "Camina con una faccia pulita [walk with a clean face]," an aphorism warning off reckless behavior that could bring dishonor to the family name. His behavior was informed by a centuries-old ethos steeped in the values of "*la via vecchia*" (the old ways), which placed high value on dignity in actions and the ability to control emotions. He abided by the norms of *buon costume* (good manners) in his daily interactions, carrying himself with poise and self-control.

As protectors, men lived by the code of *omertà*, shielding their families from harm by silence. Following traditional matrimonial rites of the southern village, the Italian father often matched his children with a spouse from a trusted family from the same village or region. From 1909 to 1929, regional intermarriages in the North End reached nearly 80 percent.[2]

In married life, the roles between men and women were clearly defined yet mutually dependent. Drunkenness and law-breaking were viewed as juvenile impulses unworthy of manliness.[3] Men rarely divorced and desertions were rare.

At the turn of the century peasant families near Avellino faced high unemployment, the loss of sons due to conscription, crop-killing diseases, and crushing taxes on wheat, vineyards, and salt. In the wake of bread riots and near starvation, Angelo Luongo and many others left Montefalcione in 1902. North End small business owners often employed workers with good reputations from the same town or region. Hired by R. P. Pappas in the market, Angelo worked six twelve-hour days for three dollars a week, washing and cutting the ends of celery, pulling bad leaves off, and packing them into bushels.

One day in 1907, Mr. Pappas, who had five sons, and four employees with families of boys, decided to give Angelo a raise, but not for the usual reasons.

At a time when struggling families were dependent on each other for economic survival, Mr. Pappas wanted to celebrate the birth of his daughter Helen and awarded Angelo a weekly raise of fifty cents:

> And because he was so happy that finally he had a man that had a baby girl in his place, one of his workers had got a baby girl among them, so my father got a fifty cents raise a week. Imagine! And he thought he had a million dollars! Oh, my poor father, God have mercy on his soul. That's all my father used to say to me, "Solo per quello si stata fortunata, aggio pigliato cinquanta soldi alla settimana" (You were lucky only for that, that I got fifty-cents a week more).[4]

Tom Bardetti

"He Learned by Doing"

My father carried the hod, the bricks—you put the bricks in the hod and you lift them and put them on your back, you climb ladders with the hod on your back, you bring the bricks to the bricklayers up to the first floor, second floor, third floor, and that's the way he done it. He made cement—he could sand the cement with a pail of water; you put it in a pail when you made cement, and you'd bring it up to the bricklayers because they needed the cement between the bricks. He was no carpenter, he was no electrician, and he didn't get those jobs. He could speak only a little English and didn't go to school.

What he learned, he picked it up as he went along, he learned by doing, Italian and English. He used to read the Italian news and he knew what was going on in the world; he knew the different countries and the different states in the United States, he knew a lot of things. But all that there came by—was self-knowledge, see? He was self-educated. Well, he didn't have no education, but what little he had it was self-education and that was hard to do, yeah. My father told me that he learned how to read and write by himself; what he learned, he picked up himself. He picked it up as he went along. He learned by doing.

My father was a strong man. He had courage, he didn't have fear. But he had respect for people. He didn't have that crazy courage like to kill people or do things. He used to go out of his way to help people that needed whatever he could do. My father had a saw, he had a plane, and he used to fix things. He used to tap my shoes, give me haircuts when I was kid.

Josie Zizza

"The Thirteen Apostles"

When my father used to come up the house, he used to cough, we used to have to light a powder—he had asthma—when my father came in, we'd all be ready at the door. One had to take off his coat, one had to get his slippers, he'd sit down, one got him a glass of wine. My father never spoke, he never hit us. We knew just what we had to do. It was a regimen.

My mother had thirteen children, two in one year. We were the thirteen apostles.

FIGURE 16. Pinelli Family.

Grace Pinelli was seventy-five and lived alone.

Grace Pinelli

"Life Isn't Easy"

There was no fear in those days—you had protection all around you. My mother never had a key on her door or anyone in the North End, no doors were locked. That's how safe it was, it was neighbor helping neighbor; if a neighbor needed you, you'd be right there. Today you don't find that—I think life was better then, really. There was no such thing as welfare or any kind of state or federal aid; you had to work or you starved. If they didn't work, they'd go back to Italy. They'd go to North Square and wait for foremen from New Hampshire or further out and maybe get a group of men and take them back to work way out from civilization. And they'd live in tents. If you didn't find work here, you'd go there to North Square on a Sunday morning and these Italian foremen would pick whatever men they wanted. And they would have a woman, maybe the wife of the contractor or someone, who would cook, and they would pay them board for their meals and sleeping in a tent, but they were happy to do that to earn a few dollars. They didn't know the language, that was [a] barrier.

One time my father was working too hard, he knew he needed help at what he was doing as a laborer and he didn't know how to tell his foreman. So he said, "I want to go home," and that's all he learned. So he left his job, which he didn't want to lose, but he didn't know how to explain to him that he needed help, couldn't do it alone. See the barrier that was there in those days? My father had no skills, he made three dollars a week as a laborer. Life isn't easy. I met a young couple on the Waterfront recently, and I told them I try to know what the young people expect out of life, how they feel, how they think because I have grandchildren their age and I try to understand them, they're all good. You know what he said to me? "I want everything, and I want it now." I said, "Oooh, it doesn't work that way; you're in for a lot of disappointments because life isn't easy."

Al Mostone

Al Mostone served as the sexton at the Old North Church. He convinced Father Kellard, the minister, to stand in front of the Old North Church and ring the bell when Italian funeral and religious processions passed on Salem Street. Al said, "And from that day to this, we became one."

Being the Oldest Son

In the Italian home at that time the first son was considered a second father, you see. And the brothers and sisters sort of respected you for that. About seven years ago, my sisters were up [at] my mother's house and one of my sister's sons—he was grown up, he was married—they were raising Cain. What I mean by that was that they were talking out loud, so my mother was elderly [and] they were disturbing her a little bit. So I went in the room and said, "Hey, kids, that's it, no more." My nephew happened to be where they were, and all my sisters stopped arguing with themselves. It struck my nephew funny why they stopped because he couldn't believe his mother would stop. So when he went home, he asked his mother [my sister] why she stopped. He says "Ma, why did you let Uncle Al stop you from talking. He has no more right over you." My sister said, "As long as he's alive, he is my father. If he says stop, it means he has a good reason." My nephew said, "Boy, if he ever said that to me, he'd hear something from me that he probably wouldn't like." My sister said, "Louie, if you ever raised your hand [to him], you'd never walk in my house again." So this is the way we were, we were a closely knit family. And all the families, the majority, were like that.

Elvira DiMattia

"Everybody Sees Your Face"

If there were any medals to be pinned on anyone as a husband and as a father, I think my dad would take the gold one. Because he was strictly a family man. Outside of his church and work, my dad didn't know what it was to go into a club and have a game of cards with anyone. If he had a game of cards at all it would be at home with the family; one of my uncles would come, they'd sit around the table and enjoy themselves that way. Keeping up with our studies was a priority in our home. After supper my dad would come around and if he'd see one of us dawdling over, he'd say, "What's the matter, didn't you receive any homework?" So we'd have to get around the table, and even if we had to just read a book, but we had to show dad we were doing something. There was no going out after supper. We were home. These things sound corny now, but that's the way we grew up.

My mother had eight children. She lost the first baby. She raised seven of us, six sons and I was the only daughter. I don't think I was spoiled in any way. With seven children in the family you don't spoil anyone. Well, we were brought up in the love and fear of God, in those days there was no talking back to anybody. Respect originated in the home and we took that along with us in any field that we entered—school, church, work. And one of the things my dad always used to remind us—it may sound a little corny to some people. But it was his way of letting us know that everyone knows the characteristics of everyone—what we are—and he used to bring it out in this fashion: "If you can't afford a steak dinner, no one sees what you're going to fill your stomach with. But remember everybody sees your face."

Joe Petringa

Joe Petringa was sixty-seven and beginning to forget stories from his childhood because "there's no older people left in the family to keep my past alive."

"He Cooked on Sundays"

My father came from a town called Tuttora, provincia di Ragusa. He came alone in 1912, on his own, from Sicily after he served his time in the military as a *bersaglieri* [soldier of the Italian army]. He went to Lawrence, Massachusetts, to work in a wool mill. Then he settled in the North End, where he met my mother on Hanover Avenue. She was born in Riesi, provincia di Caltanisetta, in Sicily. She came here because she thought this country would be a better place to make a living. And they raised a family here in the North End, seven of us. I was born on Unity Court behind the Old North Church. My father always worked. He never believed a woman should go out for work in those days, they had too much to do. My mother was always at home. They didn't have the modern appliances. When times got tough, my mother had to make her own bread and macaroni—so how could a woman go out to work? She had more work to do at home.

My mother was the steadying influence in the home; my father used to enforce authority, either with respect or force because he was a strong man. My mother was the calming influence. But one thing I remember, every Sunday my father did all the cooking. He could make anything. And it was the best meal of the week. He used to make this chocolate pudding every once in a while—I still love it today.

Anita LaRocca

We Had to Speak Italian

The bakers [where my father worked] were downstairs in the building on Fleet Street and I lived on the top floor. They had a door so they could have some air from the hallway, and that's when my father would hear me coming down the stairs. Three of my siblings were born in Italy. We had to speak Italian at home with my father. He used to say, "Devi parlare Italiano quando tu stai in casa mia ma non in Inglese [Outside you speak English, but when you're in my house we speak Italian]." We had to speak Italian. And that's how I learned Italian. We were three little ones—we had to speak Italian. Later I tried to speak Italian to my kids, but my husband, Charlie, wanted it to be an English-speaking home; he said, "Anita, we're Americans, we speak English." But my father taught my son Robert how to count to a hundred in Italian, words like *forchetta* [fork], *tavolino* [table], and he loved everybody and he wanted everybody to speak Italian. He said, "When you speak another language, you are a richer person."

Fred Bourne

"Blood on the Sheet"

Italian fathers were very strict with their daughters. You'd take a girl out on a date and her father would say right out in front of her, "You be home at nine o'clock. You hear me? Nine o'clock." If you didn't bring her home at nine o'clock you got your head broken. Where can you go? First, you'd go to a movie, and you didn't smooch. Or you go parking on Memorial Drive, what the hell else could you do? If you were up [at] the house, you sat here, she sat over there. Even if you were engaged to be married. And you couldn't go to any hotel, you went to friend's house. I'm not kidding, I went through this. To make sure [that on the marriage night] there was blood on the sheet, that she was a virgin. And in the old days the doctors used to sew stitches for the ones that weren't virgins so that there would be blood on the sheet.

Lena Albanese

"Young Lady, I Got a Bone to Pick with You."

I went to work at fourteen years old because there was a place in Charlestown, the Charleston Cotton Mill, on Mystic Street, they would take fourteen-year-old girls to work in the cotton mill. So I used to go over there—there was me, a girl from Prince Street, another girl from Sheafe Street, and my mother. My brother was bigger then, he was beginning to go to kindergarten. That left me off that I could go to work. And one night we were coming home. And it happened that one of these girls was going with a boyfriend. And you know, before, years back, they had these open street cars with open sides, the conductors in the front. Well my uncle, God rest his soul, he was my mother's brother, he was standing in the back of the car and it was crowded with people. He saw us go by, but I didn't see him, but if I had I would have waved to him and said, "Don't say a word, I'll talk to you in the morning!" It was right on the corner of Kinney Square here.

So that morning when my father went into work, he said to my father, "Does your daughter go with a fella"? My father says, "No." My uncle says, "Well, last night she was with a fella." It wasn't me at all! It was this other girl, Florinda, that lived on Prince Street, that she was going with this boy. And you know how when there's two girls together, one girl stands on one side, the other girl on the other, the fella's in the middle? Well don't you think [my uncle] told my father. My father come in the bedroom in the morning, [and] he says to me, "Young lady, I got a bone to pick with you." I says, "What is it, Dad?" I says, "I didn't do anything." He says, "No, I don't think you did anything, but I'm gonna warn you." I said, "What is it?" He said, "Wasn't you with a man, with a boy last night going home from work"? I says, "Daddy, I was with him, but that girl [that] was on the side of me, on the inside, she's the one that was going with the boyfriend, not me. But we simply just walked together, the two girls and him." So he says, "Are you sure you're telling me the truth"? I says, "Yes daddy, I am." So he gives me a slap. I was still in bed you know, before he went to work, he came in the bedroom. I was still in bed and he whacked me on my behind and he said, "Don't let me catch you or hear anybody say that you're going with somebody." So I says, "But I wasn't going with him daddy." And I started to cry. See? Because I knew it was true! So he says to me, "Well, all right this [time] I'll let you go." But he didn't even hurt me. I said that after to my mother, "Why did he whack me? Because it didn't hurt at all (laughing)."

Josie Zizza

"You're Not Telling Me to Hurry Up!"

My mother was seventeen years old when she came to America, from Avellino. She came to work to better herself. She came here and she lived with her father. She used to go to work in a sewing factory. My father came here from Guardia Lombardia, near Avellino, and he came here to work, too. And I think my father was about twenty. They met here in the North End. My mother got married at eighteen. She had her wedding gown made at Jordan's. At that time Jordan Marsh was on Hanover Street. And my mother paid forty dollars at that time. Beautiful wedding gown, still have it.

So, they got married and my mother was nineteen when she had her first child. When my father started to work, he was twenty-four years old and he started to be a laborer. But my father was the type to work very independently. And my father was a construction worker. My father always told us the story, and that's why he always wanted the boys to go to school. He was working construction. In those days there was no union. And if you were good to the foreman, if you brought things to him, you know, you had to bribe the foreman … so he (the Italian foreman) says to my father one day, "Hurry up on the job!" digging the ditches. So my father says, "You're not tellin' me to hurry up!" He got the shovel and he banged it down and left. So he fired my father because my father said, "Don't tell me to hurry up!" And you could never answer back to a foreman in those days.

And with no money in those days, there was a police station on Hanover Street in those days, my father opened up a boot black shine (shop) for a nickel for a shine, men's shoes, women's shoes. My father made tremendous, he made so many friends. From then on, my father made a lot of friends, he shined shoes for five cents. So they got married, my mother had children, she had two children in one year! My mother had thirteen children, one died. But she worked in between sometimes to help. And my father made a lot of money and he bought two houses, this house (Cleveland Place) and that house across the street. And from then on—it was a struggle—but my father with twelve children.

Mary Pasquale

"They Came to Serenade Me"

I had a cousin of mine who was a very good banjo player, he used to play with the orchestras. But because he knew that I couldn't go anywhere, even to a social dance from the club like the North End Union, The Industrial School, The Michelangelo, you couldn't go. The North End Union had a social once a week in Hubbard Hall, you'd pay only a quarter, the boys and girls would pay a quarter, and they'd have an orchestra, my cousin used to play. Mr. Ganger ran a social at the Michelangelo. I went to the sewing class with Miss Dunovan, an old woman, but she was a beautiful teacher and had a millinery class at The Industrial School, but I couldn't go to the dance, no. So one night, because we lived in the stoop, we heard music outside. My father said, "I'd like to know who the heck is in the building at this time of the hour playing this music!" At that time by nine o'clock they were under the covers.

So, he fell sleep and he woke up again and it was about half past ten or eleven. He went out, sure enough it was my cousin with the banjo and two other guys, one with an accordion and one with a guitar. My father said, "What are you doing here? What are you doing"? My cousin said, "Oh uncle, I'm bringing a serenade to Marietta." My poor cousin was so embarrassed, my father chased them out. They just wanted me to know that there was somebody there that kinda liked me and he (the guitar player) wanted to serenade me. I liked it and so did my mother because we always confessed everything to our mothers. My mother would say, "What do you want from me"?

Mary Pasquale

Beating My Father's Curfew

You know the doors, well my father made metal contraption with a metal thing like that. At the end of it, he hung out a bell. So he lowered it down that if my brothers would come home late that bell would ring. Nobody had the key to the house, they were twenty-two years old, they never had the key to get in because they had to be in at a certain time. My mother knew he was being a little too strict, so she used to take the broom and push up the bell so that when they'd come in, the bell wouldn't ring. So my father would get up, he'd look around, and see the boys were there. My father says, "I was there at nine o'clock and he wasn't there, and now he's in, when did he get in?" My mother would say, "Oh, he was in at about a quarter past nine." And they came in about ten. Mothers always covered for their child.

The Oral Tradition

Family Stories, Dialects, Folktales, and Prayers

8

> Immigrants left tears and sweat, but no memories.
> —GIUSEPPE PREZZOLINI, *I trapiantati*

On a frigid New England morning in February 1980, Maria Missiano descended the creaky stairway from the third floor of her cold-water flat to brave the windswept streets. Dressed in a gray winter coat and shawl, she turned down Prince Street and headed for St. Leonard's parish hall. It was "Soup Day" at the North End Senior Drop-In Center, where Mary "Carmela" Pagliuca, an elder volunteer who cooked homemade lunches for the senior citizen community, had arrived early that morning to make minestrone soup.

Maria sat with her Calabrese and Sicilian *cummari* (friends), chatting and joking in their provincial dialect. When lunch ended, Maria surprised everyone. With a warm smile across her careworn face, she stood up, and politely asked if anyone wanted to hear *una story vecchia* (an old story). Everyone nodded in agreement. An unassuming woman from a small town near Catanzaro, she transformed into a raconteur, holding everyone spellbound with her story, pausing at dramatic moments, and shaking her head in disbelief over the fate of the poor man with ten children that she was recounting. On full display that day was the southern Italian oral tradition transported in viva voce.

Many illiterate immigrants like Maria had acquired the skill of memorization and recitation, which was the ancient method of transmitting folk stories, wisdom tales, and proverbs. Like Homer's *Odyssey*, an epic poem recorded from the oral tradition, Maria continued the ancient storytelling tradition, dating back to the Greeks who colonized southern Italy in the eighth century BC.

Because many North Enders had been needed on farms in Italy or spent years apprenticing to learn a trade with *un maestro* (a master) in the *bottega* (artisans') system, few other than the *prominenti* (elite) possessed the writing skills to challenge the Anglo-Saxon establishment's characterization of southern Italians as crude invaders who were culturally backward, mentally inferior, and genetically prone to criminality.

North Enders did not write their life histories but rather stored them in a collective memory bank. As witnesses to the Boston Molasses Disaster and Spanish flu epidemic, they preserved the cataclysmic events in their unique village idiom rather than official accounts recorded in public memory. Before the advent of the seductive power of television and the Internet, elder storytellers taught the next generation by reciting wisdom tales and proverbs. They entertained with fantastical tales of ghosts and spirits and kept family history alive by retelling the family stories. When elders spoke, children listened to learn rather than answer. The Italian American oral tradition began to fade when American-born children left the North End to pursue the American dream. With demanding professional careers, less free time, and family commitments in suburban towns, visits to Nonna's (Grandma's) house became less frequent. As elder voices were silenced by the passage of time, their stories gradually vanished in memory and the oral tradition was relegated to a cultural relic.

Quando il diavolo t'accarezza, l'anima va trovando
(When the devil hugs you, he's looking for your soul).
—LENA RICCIO

FIGURE 17. Lena Riccio, *maluocchio* session, 1999.

Mary Pagliuca

The Maluocchio Prayer

This is an *orazione* [a prayer] that the people from many generations ago, they used to talk with these priests, these monks, and they taught them this prayer, that when you do like this, it make the *maluocchio* [evil eyes] disappear. All the old Italians from the old days knew that, but the Americans don't believe in it. But it's real, it's true. My son-in-law, you have to see him, when he gets a headache, he goes to my granddaughter, "Laura, Laura, come here, come here, do the eyes, do the eyes! Right away!" If you want, I'll write it down for you—it's nice to have this. You get the dish and oil and put a drop of oil and if it gets big, then it means you have the eyes. If the oil doesn't spread, then it means you don't have the *maluocchio*. My mother tell a me to do "the eyes, *i maluocchio*" when you felt a little dizzy, when you had a headache, or if you went somewhere and had an upset stomach, and somebody put "the eyes" on you. So you, when you made the sign of the cross, you said this prayer:

> Fuggi occhi tristi,
> Prima della venuta di Cristo,
> Mo che Crist é nato,
> Occhi Crist se ne incantata,
> Santa Maria Maddalena scapigliata, Questo patto ricorreva,
> Questo occhio mal dicevo,
> Santo Cosimo e Damiano,
> I' te medico,
> e tu li sano.

> Run, sad eyes, run
> Before Christ arrived
> Now that Christ is born
> The eyes of Christ that bewitch, disheveled Saint Mary Magdalene,
> This covenant applied,
> This eye I would hex,
> Saints Cosimo and Damian If I treat you
> I will heal them.

FIGURE 18. Maria Missiano, 1980.

Eddie Marino recited a version of the prayer of the Madonna del Soccorso dating back to the turn of the century.

> The Prayer of the Madonna del Soccorso
> Maria Santissima di lu Succursu Ncurunata,
> Aviti la facci cchiu bedda di li rosi,
> Di li munacheddi di Sant'Austinu fustivu atturniata,
> Tutta china bedda d'oro ti visteru
> Di li marinara ncoddu fusti purtata,
> Surura chi nni iccasti di sintenza,
> Arrivannu a la chiazza di Sciacca chi ni cuncidissi na bedda razzia,
>   Viva Maria, viva!

> Holiest Maria of Mutual Help crowned
> Your face is more beautiful than a rose,
> Surrounded by the little nuns of Saint Augustine,
> Beautifully they covered you all in gold,
> On the shoulders of the fisherman you were carried,
> From their sweat you have given absolution,
> When you arrive in the town square of Sciacca, That you may grant
>   us a beautiful favor, Viva, Maria viva!

Maria Missiano

When Maria Missiano's brother returned from World War I, he brought her a copy of the widely circulated poem of Mastro Bruno Pelaggi, from his book, *Le poesie di Mastro Bruno*. As a young girl, she memorized a variation of the poem, "Ricorso al Padreterno" and recited it in Calabrese dialect for the rest of her life.

> Ricorso al Padreterno
> C'èra ùno chi tenìa dèci figli e u municìpiu no jutàva,
> e a li città e a Catanzàru no jutàva. Allùra scrivìu a lu re.
> U re u mmazzàru chid'ànnu
> e nisciùno li rispundìu.
> Allòra dìssi, mò li scrìvu a lu Pàtri Etèrnu
> e li ha dìtto così:
> Ti prègu, o Pàtri Etèrnu, lu mùndu m'u sdarrùpi, ca sìamu abitàti da
>   lùpi e piscicàni

e prièstu mìna li màni e vìdi còmu ha' mu fài e càccimi da sti guài, mannàja aguànnu! Non vìdi ca di fànnu morìri a pòcu a pòcu? Tu ti mentìsti di dòcu e stài mu guàrdi.
Tu sài mu lu bumbàrdi, non vòi l'artiglierìa,
ca dìci "Così sìa" ed è tùttu fàttu.
E ti priècu di nu fàttu, mu fài lu generàle
ca lu particulàre già l'avìmu dìssi a lu Signùri. Eguàli fa' lu destìnu, ca eguàli li crijàsti, eguàli
mu li guàsti, comu d'è giùstu.
Non mi nci dùni gùstu mi ndi dàssi qualchidùnu, sennò cu màstro Brunu hài chi mu sgràtti.
E si vùi u ci vidìmu, scìndi da ncùna vìa,
ca màtri mànda a mìa e ti dìcu tùttu.
Ca chìsta è la verità: èu mi ndi strafùttu,
àssami sta' pùru li scrìssi.
E non mi respundìu, ca l'hànnu assassinàtu.
Ti priècu cu li sànti mi lu mènti,
ca pe nu' àtr'i poverèddi facìsti lu destìnu
ca mu patìmu eternamènte.
E tu chi si Onnipotènte, Giùdici di giustìzia,
lu cchju per l'avarìzia mu nci pènzi.
Ha mu càcci sentènzi, mu trèma cièlu e tèrra,
mu li fa cunsèrva sti 'ssassìni,
cu chjòva spuntàti, màrtiri, etèrni guài.
È vèru ca tu lu sài, non vòi mparàtu,
ma se sapàrìssi chi mi fànnu a mìa
tu diciarìssi: "Cchju ndi mmeritànnu!"
E ti vògghju aguànnu chi lu pàni va càru,
lu bòvu di lavùru comu ngràna!
E prìma ca l'ànnu pàssa, pènsaci tu, o Signùri,
sennò cu li matùra, amàri nui?
Sài chi dìcu cchju? dissi, sta gràzija e nènti cchju: Tu li màndi a lu mpèrnu, ndi fài st'àtru pijacìri,
mu l'arrùsti còmu gghjìri alla gravìgghja
per nòmine sèculi seculòru, a lu Pàtri Etèrnu.

There was a man who had ten children. The town would not help him
And neither did the cities and Catanzaro. Therefore, he wrote to
the king.

The Oral Tradition

But that same year the king was killed
And nobody replied to him.
He thought: "I am going to write to God the Father." And this is what
    he wrote:
"Pray, God Almighty, destroy this world,
which is populated by wolves and sharks.
Take action, and see what you can do
To free me from my troubles, this goddamned year! Can't you see they
    are killing us bit by bit?
You withdrew and just sit watching.
You know how to strike, don't need big guns,
You only need to say 'So be it,' and it's done.
Above all, I pray you to take care of the generalities,
Since we are going to handle the particulars," he said to the Lord. "Make
    our destinies the same,
since you created us similar,
And similarly ruin us, as it is the right thing to do.
Don't please them by forgetting some,
And if you want us to see, with Master Bruno come down this way, So
    my mother can send me to tell you everything.
This is the truth: I don't give a damn,
Just leave me alone," he also wrote.
"The king did not write back because they killed him.
I pray you to include him among the saints,
Since we, poor folks, are meant
To suffer forever.
And you, being Almighty, Justice and Judge of all things, think mostly
    about avarice.
You must cause the earth and the sky to shake,
To torture these murderers,
with blunt nails, martyrdom and eternal pain.
But you know all this already, there is no point in telling you. Except that
    if you knew what they
are doing to me,
You would say: "They deserve much worse!"
Who knows what's goin' to happen this year, the bread is dear, And the
    fields may not yield enough!
And before the year ends, do something, O Lord,
Otherwise how are we going to grow?

I am also asking this and nothing more: Send them to hell, do us this other favor,
To make them roast like dormouse on a grill
In saecula saeculorum, my Lord."

Josie Picadacci

"The Dwarf"

One of my mother's *cummari* [friends] used to tell us stories, but it was a scary story. She told us when she was a young girl in Sicily and she was married and she was living in her mother's home, her husband used to go to work early in the morning, like three o'clock, four o'clock in the morning and it was still dark. She said one night she saw a beam of light; she saw a little dwarf and he picked up a chair, he put it near the bed and he climbed on the chair and he climbed on the bed. And he kept making fun of her—he was jumping on her and doing crazy things. So she got so scared, she didn't know what to say, she was going, "Get away! Get away!" but he wouldn't move. And then he told her, "I'm coming back tomorrow night." He did this for three nights, and the last night that he was there he said to her, "When your husband leaves, and your mother goes out, I want you to go and look in back of the stove and whatever you find there, it is yours." But she was afraid to tell her mother and she was afraid to go to the stove to see if there was anything there. And he told her, "I don't want you to tell anyone anything otherwise you'll never have any [good] luck and you'll have a lot of bad luck."

So, then this morning she said to her mother, "You know ma I saw this—" and told her what happened. So the mother said, "Well, come on we'll go look together." When they went and look over there they found a whole bag of coal. Now, they claim that would have been all money. But they found all coal. She wasn't supposed to tell anyone and she told her mother. So when [the dwarf] came the last night he said, "You didn't want any luck and now you'll never have any luck—you'll always have bad luck." I never forgot that story.

Now listen to what happened to her. She was married and her husband died; she got married again, her husband died; she got married three times, her husband died. One son, he was my brother's usher when he got married. They were, you know after they get married, they go around in the cars, they take a ride. The tire blew, he was fixing the tire and it blew up in his face, and he got all banged upon the face and everything. He went to the hospital—he was supposed to come home—[but] the son died.

"I Said No When I Was Supposed to Say Yes"

When I got married when I was seventeen and I didn't understand one word that my mother-in-law, my father-in-law said. My mother came from Messina. My in-laws came from Riesi and they talked altogether different—they sing when they talk, you know they have a certain dialect—I really didn't understand one word. And there I am, after I got married, you know how everybody comes to your house and visits you, right? And they would talk that way and I'd be looking at them, and they'd say something to me. I'd say, "Oh, yeah," and I was supposed to say no and I said yes! And they'd say to me, "What are you saying yes for if you're supposed to say no?" I didn't know what to say. And this went on and on and on. We were Sicilians but they came from a different part, altogether different. Their dialect was different—to me it was Chinese, that's how different it was. My mother talked one way, but as the years went on that I was married so long, and I got to talking their way, and now I could talk my mother's way and their way, and sometimes I'd get mixed up and use both ways. But then I got so good everybody was saying, "Gee we think you sound like a Riesana."

"I Used to Tell Them Stories"

When we didn't have any place to go at night, so we'd all sit down and tell stories. My mother-in-law was in the store for fifty years, so these kids, they had no one. So they used to be up [at] my house after I got married. And they actually grew up in my house. These were my sisters-in-law—I had seven of them. I had no sisters, but I had seven sisters-in-law. And they [their children] really lived up [at] my house. And I used to tell them all kinds of stories, and I would curl their hair with the curling iron, I did a lot for them at the time—I used to starch their clothes. And I used to tell them stories like this. Way before television, all we had was radio. And I used to love to, we used to sing. I'd get the kids all around just to keep them out of trouble and I'd say, "Let's have a singing contest." Or we'd play giant step. Or we'd play amateur hour, that's what we used to play. And then I'd have little gifts, and

I would wrap them up and I'd say, the best one is gonna get a gift, and they'd do their best, you know like they were really—it was cute. My sisters-in-law, sometimes, they think about it. I used to love to do that because this would keep the kids quiet and then especially when they knew they were gonna get a gift and I'd wrap it up and they'd say, "Oh, I'm gonna get a gift, what did you buy?" "Oh, it's a surprise!" And it was so cute because they did it like they were professionals, you know they wanted to do their best just so they would get the best prize. The kids of today, you couldn't compare. They never swore.

Italy and the North End in World War I 9

> My older brother, Arthur, died in the service. When they called my younger brother, Billy, he was on his way to South Station when peace was declared. The war was over and he kinda got mad because he couldn't go. But my mother said, "At least I have one at home"
> —MARGUERITE CARBONE

In 1914, when sixteen-year-old Francesco Ventresca left the countryside of Pettorano sul Gizio in Abruzzo to live in the United States, "per vivere, perche in Italia c'era sempre la povertà" (to live, because in Italy there was only poverty), he unwittingly avoided becoming a casualty of the Great War.[1] A few months after he left his five siblings and his parents, Italy entered that disastrous war in May 1915, which saw six hundred fifty thousand of its young men killed, more than 1 million seriously wounded, and its national debt increase from less than 16 billion lire to 85 billion lire in 1919.[2] Among the dead was Francesco's oldest brother, Giovanni.

Francesco's reason for leaving was not to avoid the war but rather to avoid the desperation of hard labor on the family's small farm. To conserve his only pair of shoes, he wore *i cioci* (cloth sandals), sometimes sewn together with strands of worn-out clothing. On Sundays he wore a suit "with pants in one style, the jacket another." He described the austere peasant diet as one "where I never knew what sweet stuff looked like, no coffee, no cake, but we made our own wine—all we had was wine."[3]

Luckily for Francesco, he arrived in the United States before the enactment of the 1917 Immigration Act, the brainchild of the nativist Senator Henry Cabot Lodge and the Immigration Restriction League of Boston. With literacy requirements, increased head taxes, and the expansion of "undesirable" categories, the new law severely limited the number of southern and eastern European immigrants entering the United States.

American isolationism kept the country out of the war until 1917, and the army ranked as only seventeenth in the world for readiness. Despite those who viewed Italians as unpatriotic and unworthy of American citizenship, the federal government appealed to them for help in the war effort. Like many of his countrymen in Boston, Francesco had been given the choice to join the Italian army or fight for the United States. He decided to register for the armed services: "They wanted to take me back in Italy, but I didn't want to go because of the war. If they took me over here it was better. In Italy, they didn't want any more soldiers because they needed food to eat."[4] Nevertheless, some Italians and Italian Americans, having been offered free passage, decided to return and fight for Italy. Of the 300,000 Italians and Italian Americans who joined the U.S. armed services, which numbered 4.5 million men, Italian-born enlistees were granted automatic citizenship.

By the time of the Great War, many Italian American neighborhoods like the North End were self-made communities, with little reliance on the federal government. The North End had its own newspapers, many self-help societies, social clubs, Italian churches, and many resident-owned businesses. World War I became the first crucible for Italians to demonstrate their loyalty to the United States. On August 16, 1915, two years before the United States entered the war, the *Boston Globe* reported a parade of three thousand Italian reservists and their friends marching down the principal streets of the North End "with Italian flags swung over their shoulders and at their head two men [who] carried two American flags between them," as they were "being cheered to the echo by those who thronged the sidewalks and adjoining homes."

On June 24, 1918, the *Globe* reported "that 5,000 Italians pledged $25,000 in War Savings Stamps" at North End Park, where soldiers, sailors, and over fifty societies gathered to show their patriotism. North Enders gave generously to Thrift Stamps, Liberty Loans, the Red Cross, and the Italian Red Cross, prompting the *Globe* to opine that "people are inclined to forget that the majority of our residents of foreign blood are faithful to the flag of their adopted country."[5]

Many Italians who enlisted in the American army were considered valuable additions because of their battle experiences in the Italo-Turkish War of 1911. One North Ender who had been in the Italian navy noticed an advertisement asking for volunteers outside the North Bennet Industrial School in of 1917. His expertise in building guns was put to use in the American army's arsenal.

Although Italian Americans constituted only 4 percent of the population, 10 percent of them gave their lives to the United States and Italian-born men won eighty-three Distinguished Services Crosses in the American army.[6]

Despite being wounded twice, Graziano Longarini of the 102nd Machine Gun Battalion returned and married Laura LoPresti, the daughter of *La Notizia* founder Emanuel LoPresti, and the two managed the newspaper after Emanuel's death in the Spanish flu epidemic. Ralph Palumbo, Graziano's fellow soldier from the same battalion, did not survive; on April 20, 1918, he became the first North Ender killed in France. On July 4, 1920, Cutillo Park at Stillman and Morton Street was named in honor of Vincent J. Cutillo and the square at the junction of North Margin Street and Thacher Street was named for Arthur J. Solari of the 101st Infantry Regiment, both of whom were killed in France.

Josie Tranquillo's twenty-five-year-old brother answered the call for volunteers and joined the army. When the family accompanied him to the Charlestown Navy Yard for a transport ship to France, he tried to reassure his worried Sicilian mother about the war, telling her confidently, "Mom, this is America—they'll send us home every month," but he never returned.

Josie Tranquillo

Lost in Action

On the ship to America in 1914 my brother sent [my mother] a letter saying, "Dear mother, do not take the trip anymore because in America it's very bad right now—Depression." There were no jobs; it was very hard to make a living. So as soon as my mother got this letter, she was sorry [that] she was on her way, but what could she do? Jobs were very hard to find so we moved back to the North End. Finally, one of my brothers, he was twenty-five—he used to go looking for jobs all the time and he could never find one. So finally, one day he decided to go make himself a volunteer in the army. So when he came home he told my mother, "Mother I signed up as a volunteer in the army." My mother said, "Oh my dear son, why did you do that for? Oh, now I won't see you anymore." He said, "Oh mother, don't feel like that. This is America, they'll send us home once a month to see our family."

But my brother went away and he never came back; there was no furlough for my brother. They took him straight to France. In the morning when he left, they left from Charlestown because there was a big, big boat, all soldiers.

The band was playing "Over there! Over there! Buy a bond, buy a bond, over there! We will march till it's over, over there." The flags were flying; we were on the North End pier—we used to have a beautiful pier, everybody used to go there to get air, but now they broke it down. Oh, a hundred, a thousand people on the pier watching their beloved ones going away to the army, what a sin, it looked like—today I feel it was manslaughter because they were all young boys. They were all saying goodbye, waving to their loved ones; the flags were waving and the boys were waving back to us and the band was playing. My brother went away and he never came back. I was eleven years old at the time, and he wrote a letter to my mother: "Dear mother, send me a newspaper from Boston, let me know how the war is going, what they're talking about and how far it's going."

So, my mother sent him the package. He never got the package—my brother was lost in action. They sent and tell us he was lost in action, and my mother said, "How could he be lost?" I used to go with my mother to the State House, the Italian Council, to get news of my brother from France; almost every day we used to go to see if they had any news because they couldn't find him. Finally, after six months they sent us a telegram that he was lost in action—he was dead, they couldn't find him.

After six months of all this, they wanted to send the body back to my mother but she said, "Gee, six months. You didn't know where he was? Lost in action, who are you going to send me now after six months?" So we didn't even take the body here so I don't know where he is buried. When the war ended all the whistles [were] going on, the war was over and somebody made like a clown, a man all stuffed with hay, and they were carrying him with music through the streets with the band playing. I don't know if it was supposed to be Joan of Arc or a Ku Klux Klan [member]. The war was over.

Frank Favazza

Frank Favazza thought recording stories was a great way to document a person's life. He asked, "Wouldn't it have been nice if at the time of Christ if he had left something like we're doing now? Wouldn't there have been more peace in the world, more believers in Christ?"

"We Waved to Them"

I was born in 1905 and when we were fishing out there we used to see troop ships. We all used to stop working, whatever we were doing, weather permitting. And we used to blow our foghorns and wave our hats at them, all the doughboys. We saw them going and we saw them when they came back when the war was over.

FIGURE 19. Giuseppe Freni in his rooftop garden in the North End

Giuseppe Freni

Giuseppe Freni joined the ranks of southern Italians, who were the mainstay of the Italian army. He survived the catastrophic Battle of Caporetto in October 1917, where forty thousand men were killed or wounded, three hundred thousand taken prisoner, and as many deserted.

Fighting in World War I

I was born on November 19, 1897, in the town of Itala right near [the town of] Messina, in the province of Messina in Sicily. We were pretty good, "un pezzo di pane, noi mangiavamo" ["so long as we had a piece of bread we ate and were satisfied"]—we ate all right. My father was a farmer; we owned our [farm] property [and] life wasn't too bad. As a boy I used to work out in the country, [and] I went to school. Then when I grew up, I went into the army. For four years I fought in the mountains during World War I. First I was in Monte Santo di Gorizia, then on Monte Cucco in Italy. Then I was sent to Brescia with the 136th infantry; I was in the Compagnia Mitragliere, the machine gun company of the 620th, and then from there I was in the Prima Reggimento Fanteria in the province of Udine. From there we fought at the Battle of Caporetto, and then we fought on Monte Tomba; then we went to Monte Sief and finally we stopped at the Conca di Lana. Then, while we were resting there, we took shelling from long-range artillery, and I was wounded in the leg and I was taken to the field hospital. There they gave me some injections for the infection.

[After being] wounded, I went to the hospital at Bordighera, in the province of Porto Maurizio, where they gave me forty days of convalescence, and it cost five dollars a day. After I got better, I went to the *deposito*, the army base of the Prima Fanteria; I was still serving as a soldier under the Prima Fanteria. They gave me my discharge to go home to my family. When I got back home to Sicily I went back to work [on the family farm] with my two siblings and my parents. Since I was wounded in the war, I got the Croce di Guerra [War Cross for Military Valor] and the Medaglia d'Oro [the gold medal for outstanding gallantry in war by junior officers and soldiers] as a Cavaliere di Vittorio Veneto [Knight of the Order of Vittorio Veneto]. The government gave all of us who fought in World War I a small pension.

Garlic Necklaces, Camphor Bags, and Shots of Anisette

The Spanish Flu Pandemic in the North End

They couldn't bury them; they had all the boxes outside in the street.
—JOSIE ZIZZA

The Spanish flu epidemic of 1918 killed an estimated fifty million people worldwide, with such dimensions that the *Times* of London reported, "Never since the Black Death has a plague swept over the face of the world."[1] North Enders had seen their share of death from natural disasters, epidemics, and disease in southern Italy. Nicola Argiro, who emigrated from Reggio Calabria in 1914, had been a sailor in the Italian Coast Guard and witnessed the 1908 earthquake of Messina, Sicily, which killed over one hundred thousand people.

In 1884 and 1911, deadly cholera outbreaks from polluted wells, an antiquated sewer system, and unplanned, unregulated building construction with substandard sanitation struck Naples and claimed the lives of thousands of its poor inhabitants. In 1911, cholera also struck Palermo, Sicily, and towns in the Campania, where thousands of victims died in excruciating pain without palliative medicine.

Since ancient times, Neapolitans living in the shadows of Mount Vesuvius and Sicilians near Mount Etna had lived with the constant threat of volcanoes, whose violent eruptions and fiery lava flows destroyed entire villages. Hillside deforestation caused rain runoff to settle into stagnant pools, breeding malaria-carrying mosquitoes, and the death toll from the disease reached 20,000 in southern Italy in 1904. Sudden mudslides often surprised the inhabitants of hillside villages, toppling houses and killing villagers in torrents of mud. Townspeople prayed to patron saints for miracles to change the course of lava flows or rain during droughts under the spell of the relentless Mediterranean sun.

On August 27, 1918, the United States Navy reported the first case of Spanish influenza from Boston's Commonwealth Pier, a major terminal for supplying men and materiel in World War I. As American forces raced to save France, the pier, which housed and fed thousands of the troops, had become overcrowded, providing an opportune environment for spreading the insidious pathogen, which had a remarkable ability to quickly spread through the respiratory system before the body could mobilize its defenses.

In the first weeks of September, the alarm was sounded at Fort Devens, which was thirty miles from the North End. There, army physicians noticed high numbers of robust young soldiers suddenly complaining of flu-like symptoms and dying within a few days. So many recruits died that the famous pathologist William Henry Welch, who was known as a "pillar of strength" and had witnessed every type of horrific disease, trembled at the sight of so many deaths. From September 1918 to June 1919, 675,000 Americans—both troops and civilians—died of the flu, more than the combined deaths of service members from World War I, World War II, the Korean War, and the Vietnam War.[2] When *La Spagnola*—what North Enders called the Pandemic—struck, the North End became one of many Italian American communities with the highest mortality rates.[3]

With the threat of the flu striking home and the specter of loved ones dying around them, North Enders applied home remedies that they had used in Italy to try to ward off the virus. Fathers gave their children shots of brandy and some school children wore garlands of garlic to school, alienating schoolmates with the strong odor. Teachers advised students to wear little bags of camphor around the neck.

Rose Arigo Amato, a lifelong North Ender who grew up on Endicott Street, lost her nine-month-old niece, and described a neighborhood in the midst of a catastrophe, "They couldn't get the undertaker, so the lady next door came over and dressed the baby on the table. They had to bury it right away because it was turning purple."[4]

As bodies piled in the streets, Mary Molinari, who grew up on Garden Court Street, described the hysterical screams for the dead, "Ooh, è morto figlima, è morto Giuanne, è morto chill àuto [Ooh, my daughter died, John died, the other one died]!" Notables like Emanuel LoPresti of *La Notizia* perished in the epidemic. He was given an Italian-style, open-air funeral, his coffin carried on the shoulders of his family—from his residence on 6 Prince Street to North Square—where eulogies were delivered by his associate editors, Ubaldo Guidi, Giovanni Amata, and Jerome Petitti.

So many parents perished that Father Antonio Sousa, the pastor of St. Leonard's Church, delivered sermons and wrote letters to mobilize the community for the care of orphaned children. He also organized a committee of local leaders that founded the Home for Italian Children in Jamaica Plain, which is still in operation today.

Mary Molinari

Garlic

My father held our family together, my three sisters and brother, and he made sure nothing would happen to us. There was the Spanish influenza at that time. I was the youngest of all of them and my dad was worried, and they used to put that stuff [camphor] around your neck. Oh, they were dying like flies in those days, they were crying, "Ooh, è morto figlima! E morto Giuanne! E morto chell àuto [Ooh, my daughter died! John died! The other one died]!" My mother put garlic all around, and camphor, we used to carry that; and my father had [a] bottle of Three Star brandy, and every morning he would give us a teaspoon, a little glass of that—he used to put it in an eyedropper for me—I used to feel a little drunk because I was a child, and I used to look for the brandy, where it was, because I liked it after. But my father was the type, he was afraid his children would get sick with the influenza. But we didn't have doctors, we couldn't afford it. So that's what we did. But thank God, none of us got it.

The garlic was to keep away the germs of the flu: maybe they thought it would help us, I don't know if it did or not. The teachers told us camphor. And then we'd have a string of pearls there with the garlic, and when we would go out: the place looked like the garden of garlic, [and] it stunk in the North End because everyone was wearing garlic. Sometimes, my mother, you know what she used to do? In our food, she would load us with garlic. I tell you, when I talked to anybody they would run away because I stunk of garlic.

Rose Arigo Amato

"My Sister Lost Her Baby"

The teachers told us to use camphor. We used just camphor in bags. My sister lost her nine-month-old baby. She was breastfeeding the baby and she didn't know she had the flu. She lived but the baby died. She was beautiful. And they couldn't get any undertaker so the woman across the street came over and dressed the baby on the table; they had to bury her right away because she was turning purple.

Josie Zizza

"Here's Your Glass"

When we had the Spanish influenza, my father bought camphor. He made it in small squares—we all had a bag—and every morning he'd give us a little glass of anisette, "Here's your glass, here's your glass"; none of us had a fever or a headache. Next door to me, on Cleveland Place, the mother-in-law and daughter-in-law died the same day. A lot of people, they couldn't bury them; Langone [Funeral Home] had plenty of deads. They couldn't bury them—they had all the boxes outside in the street. None of us had a headache, and every morning my father lined us up with a row of camphor; he used to break it up in pieces and tie it up with a string; and every week he'd change the camphor. My father always used to send me—the guy used to give me a tip—I used to make more money.

Marguerite Locchiato recalled the end of World War I on Sheafe Street: "We went beating the big washtubs and everything; we were kids and we weren't interested in wars."

Marguerite Locchiato

"People Were Dying"

I remember my father would come home at the time of the influenza. People were dying badly, and they would come and put some white stuff on a lot of the streets. And we'd have little sulfur bags pinned here, and my father would come home every morning with a pint of whiskey—I don't know if it was brandy or whiskey—we'd all have a little teaspoon so we shouldn't get sick. Just a pint every morning. But I remember people how they died. It was awful. There was a few people across from my house on Sheafe Street and they didn't know where to put them people, it was really, really awful. That was an awful epidemic.

Teresa Costanzo

"*Nustra Picciaridda* Maria"

I had him [my husband Angelo] make a gravesite when my daughter Maria died during the Spanish flu pandemic, and he put his name, Angelo Costanzo, on the gravestone. Do you know how many people died in those days because of the Spanish flu? So, so many! When he died I had them put my name on the gravestone, Teresa Costanzo, and they are still there. My *picciaridda* [little daughter] Maria died from it. I remember it cost two hundred dollars to bury her, and we put Angelo at a cost of five hundred dollars at the time to bury him over her. He died fourteen years ago and it seems just like yesterday, I'm telling you! My husband was always contented, and he always made sure I was happy, too. See if you can find someone like him! Today, *nfunnucunu* [lazy, uncaring]! You know what that word means? My children have a Mass said for him in our town of Riposto in the province of Catania where we're both from. It has a beach along the sea—what a beautiful place, I tell you!

My husband was a happy man, through and through. We came to America and we had children here, and we went back to Italy and had some other children, too. But *Il Signore* [God Almighty] took my husband and saved his soul. Now I thank God and I pray to all the saints that they don't abandon me and wait for me in High Heaven because I am sick now, and who will come and cure me? My son? Yesterday I had this rheumatic pain in my side. *Translated from the Sicilian dialect of Riposto.*

The Molasses Explosion   11

> We thought it was a firecracker.
> —HELEN LUONGO

On the morning of November 11, 1918, Marguerite Locchiato awoke to shrill whistles blowing on Sheafe Street. Roused out of bed by her older sister, she dressed quickly and followed the family to the celebration of Armistice Day, joining neighbors who went "out to the streets beating big washtubs."[1] But the euphoria for the war's end was tinged with sadness for the North End's fallen soldiers and concern for servicemen still in France. The community would dedicate the corner of Prince and Salem Streets as Ralph Palumbo Square and another on Richmond and North Streets as Gabriele Romano Square for North End men killed in Europe.

The Tranquillos would experience more months of sleepless nights before receiving official notice that their son's body had finally been recovered in France. The signing of the armistice had left the peace process unresolved, causing worldwide uneasiness about the prospects for peace. Still struggling with the effects of the Great Pandemic of 1918 as undertakers ran out of room in their funeral parlors, no one could have imagined the next tragedy that would strike the neighborhood.

During World War I, France and England's desperate need for explosives transformed the American munitions industry into a lucrative business, and molasses became a key product in this industry. Traditionally used for the production of rum, molasses was turned into industrial-grade alcohol to meet the demand for high explosives, which reaped record dividends.

In 1915, the U.S. Industrial Alcohol Company in East Cambridge appointed Arthur Jell, an ambitious man without technical or engineering experience, to build a holding tank in the North End. Eager to impress his bosses, Jell raced to complete the project before the shipment of roughly seven hundred thousand gallons of molasses arrived from the Caribbean. Sidestepping building permits to complete his mammoth tank in time to meet the deadline, Jell used substandard steel and tested the tank's strength with only six inches of water rather than full capacity.

The U.S. Industrial Alcohol Company's tank measured 50 feet high, 90 feet in diameter, and 240 feet in circumference, with eighteen huge steel plates secured with rivets, and it had the capacity to hold 2.3 million gallons of molasses. The massive tank on 529 Commercial Street was symbolic of the power of companies to place dangerous industries in poor, densely populated neighborhoods with little concern for public safety or fear of incrimination. Ignoring the warning signs of rivets oozing streams of molasses down its sides, which attracted neighborhood children, Jell ordered the tank caulked and painted gray to hide its faulty design. Knowing the project was near its end, Jell was devising an ingenious plan to convert the molasses into grain alcohol to sell to American breweries before the onset of Prohibition.

The morning of Wednesday, January 15, 1919, began like any other for "Donna Maria" Arigo, as she was known on Endicott Street. Following her usual routine on cold days, she awoke at dawn to fire up the wood-burning stove in the kitchen. Her daughters, Mary and Rose, found their usual breakfast of toasted bread from the oven, fried eggs, and hot cocoa waiting at the table. Rose left for a brisk walk to morning classes at the Eliot School on Tileston Street and her fifteen-year-old sister, Mary, who had recently been promoted to chocolate dipper on the first shift, headed to the busy factory floor of the Touraine Candy Factory on North Washington Street. It was a day the Arigo sisters would remember for the rest of their lives.

For other North Enders it was the same—a seemingly ordinary day that they would never forget. Carmella Lochiatto, with her children off to school and expecting a baby any day, returned to knead dough and bake bread for her children's lunch. Joe Cataloni sat at his desk in the fifth-grade classroom of the Eliot School, daydreaming of playing baseball again with his friends in the vacant lot next to the molasses tank on Commercial Street. Unknown to all of them, the unseasonably warm weather that day increased fermentation in the molasses tank, unleashing volatile gases under intense pressure with nowhere to escape.

On their way home for lunch, Helen Luongo and her younger siblings took advantage of the warm weather to gather firewood and ice along the Boston & Maine rail line on Commercial Street. Loading up their homemade wagon, the Luongo children were about to head home from Foster Street when they heard a loud crack that sounded like a firecracker. Just around the corner on Commercial Street, powerful gases caused the molasses tank to break apart, propelling chunks of steel two hundred feet long and fifty feet wide, which destroyed homes, smashed trestles of the Boston Elevated Railway, and unleashed a deadly fifteen foot wave of sticky, brown molasses, which engulfed and suffocated people and horses.

Luckily for the Luongos, they were far enough away from the tank to avoid the waves that killed ten-year-old Pasquale Iantosca and Maria Distasio, who had also been collecting firewood and were closer to the tank. Word of the explosion raced through the streets as fast as the thirty-five-mile-an-hour tsunami of molasses.

Rose Arigo Amato and her schoolmates heard the commotion in the streets as they left the Eliot School for lunch. Along with many others, they raced to Copps Hill to witness the scene of damaged homes and rescue crews frantically trying to save victims. Carmella Lochiatto heard the explosion, and with the Great War still fresh in her mind, she gathered her children to protect them from what she thought was an attack by German airplanes. That night the *Boston Evening Transcript* featured the molasses tank explosion on its front page, listing the dead and injured and noting the panic among the "foreign" population of the North End. Years later, North Enders who had witnessed the Molasses Disaster still recalled the cataclysmic event with sorrow, especially when they spoke of ten-year-old Pasquale Iantosca and Maria Distasio, who were connected to them in some way.

After the shock of the molasses explosion, North Enders turned their attention to public safety. In what had been an insular Italian enclave without a political voice, the community organized its first major advocacy campaign against potential environmental disasters caused by powerful business interests that used poor neighborhoods as dumping grounds for industrial pollutants.

On February 1, 1919, the *Gazzetta di Massachusetts* issued a clarion call on its front page—"Comizio di Protesta per Rimuovere la Gas Tank dal North End"—and announcing the formation of a committee to remove from Prince Street the dangerous Boston Consolidated Gas Company's Gasometer ("The Gassy" as it would be known), whose gas generator spewed out

FIGURE 20. Pinelli Family next to molasses tank.

a foul-smelling powder, making the adjacent homes uninhabitable. A petition filed by Attorney Vincent Brogna with the legislature containing thousands of signatures and organized protests ultimately forced the company to remove the tank and the area was eventually converted to a playground.

Joe Cataloni

Playing Baseball by the Molasses Tank

The North End Park, which is still there, that was our only solution for playing a little recreation, and you played ball. I was a catcher in them days, no mask, and I got hit here, here, three stitches, four stitches, trying to catch. So finally, some of the senior fellas that were around, they said, "Hey kid, you're crazy." We had courage, we wanted to play baseball; that's all we knew—there was nothing else.

We had the Boston Elevated [Railway] that used to run to Sullivan Square [and] that ran all the way down Atlantic Avenue, all the way down to South Station. Where the old fire station is down there, across the street from that they used to have a big molasses tank there. This was about fifty-five, sixty years ago, and they had an explosion there and that molasses—hundreds of thousands of gallons—ripped the structure. Molasses flooded all over the area, horse and wagon, that's all there was. A few people died—once you stuck in the molasses you were dead. And they had a helluva job cleaning that.

Angie Marinella

"My Friend Susie's Sister"

We lived on 60 Prince Street. I was born there. We were eight children—five brothers and three sisters in four rooms, a little toilet in the house though. My father used to go downstairs and chop the wood, and we had to lug it up. And then in the morning we had to go down and sift the coal before we'd go to school. And my older brothers would go picking up the wood early, and they used to get up at four in the morning; they used to go where the Boston

[and] Maine Railroad is, they used to pick up those chunks of wood. Then there was a shortage of coal. We used to go to Commercial Street and get the coal with the snow. Sixty cents a bag, a hundred pounds, I used to go with my brothers with the sled. And we used to get the hot cocoa on our lunch hour. That's the time that day the molasses tank exploded, and we were in school at the North Bennet Industrial School.

I came out of school and I went down there to see it. And what a sin I tell you, all the people that died, a couple of my girlfriends got caught. They lived across the way, they were going home for lunch at that time and they died, my friend Susie's sister died, another girl died, quite a few people died.

FIGURE 21. Molasses tank explosion aftermath, 1919.

Rose Arigo Amato

"There Was a Big Explosion"

I was in the sixth grade and the teacher says, "The school will be closed this afternoon." And so we all wondered, "What happened?" She says, "There was a big explosion." We said, "Where?" And they said, "Right up on Commercial Street." So we asked why. They said, "The molasses tank." So we all ran, and we stood at the park [Copp's Hill Terrace] and we watched. There was all molasses, horses dead. One house went up! Little house, exploded! They claim a lady was in there too that exploded. And there was a few deaths too, you know. It was wicked, really bad, really bad. And do you know in the summertime there was a whiff of that molasses, yeah, the smell of molasses yet. Yeah. It was even in the paper the other day, that there's a whiff, and that happened when I was in the sixth grade and I was twelve years old. It was a cold month, I think it was, but it was terrible, it was really wicked. All the molasses.

We had one of those big gas houses up Prince Street, but they took it out; people didn't like the idea of having it here [and] they have it in Dorchester now. Now there's a playground [The Gassy] there; that's where they made the Brink's movie.

Helen Luongo

Helen Luongo almost rose from her chair as she described her mother's fear for her children when she heard the explosion of the molasses tank.

"We Thought It Was a Firecracker"

The molasses tank that busted: we were down there picking up the coal and the ice for my mother because she couldn't afford to buy it. But we were happy. We thought it was a joke, going out, picking up the coal and the wood. We thought it was wonderful. In the morning the house was so cold! What a life. No, it was [a] hard life, but it was a very, very happy life. I wonder if they [today's generation] ever got on the floor and scrubbed floors on their knees without linoleum. I've done that in my life. The old days, the way we lived in the old days, it was a very, very happy life. Myself, my sister, and two brothers were on Foster Street when that thing busted.

My mother, oh God have mercy on her soul! She was wild! We had gone down because there used to be the trains on Commercial Street at the time, across the street from where the park is, and we'd go down Foster Street. And over there, we'd go down there and the trains would come and they'd throw coal out and ice. And we'd go down there with this little kitty-cart, go down and load up [the ice and coal]. And to Unity Street, that's where we had gone down. And the thing busted! My mother thought that all of us four kids had got caught in the eruption of the molasses tank. Did we hear the noise! But you know, kids, you don't—you know how many years ago that is? Yeah, I heard the noise, but I didn't make anything of it. I mean, we kids, we thought it was a firework or something. Now if I hear a noise, I'll make something of it! (laughing) I'll hear a firecracker and I jump.

Marguerite Locchiato

"The Germans Are Here!"

I remember when the molasses tanks blew up. That was in 1919. Well, we were home from school at the time and my mother was pregnant with my brother Peter. And it was just after World War I and we lived on 32 Sheafe Street. And it stays so much in my mind. We all had lunch and the girls were helping to clean up. My brother Joe was the oldest of the boys—there was two girls before him—he was sitting on the windowsill. And we heard this great explosion. And my mother got excited and she hollered, "Oh my God, we're being bombed, the Germans are here!" So she took us all, and she wanted to huddle us up, and my brother ran out to see what happened, and he went up the hill from Sheafe Street.

He went up the hill and I guess he saw what happened. My mother was so worried about him. Everybody thought the Germans had come, that there was a bombing there. But you know, from the end of Snow Hill Street we could see all the molasses and things there. But my older sisters, when they went down to see, they could remember; my sister Ester said that one of the girls she went to school with lost her little brother there—he was going home from school. Fortunate enough a lot of kids were still at home [and]; they weren't on their way to school [even though] there were a lot of people living on Commercial Street at the time. But ooh, I'll never forget [how] all the people start hollering, "The Germans are here, the Germans!" All the Italian people, oh gosh. My mother thought the Germans had bombed us. From Snow Hill Street we could see everything. We remembered—my sister especially—remembered how one of her schoolmates lost her little brother in the explosion. Fortunately, a lot of kids were home from school at the time on Commercial Street. But I'll never forget all the Italian people hollering, "The Germans are here, the Germans are here!"

Frank Favazza introduced himself saying, "My name Favazza means a large dark yellow bean in Italian."

Frank Favazza

The Smell of Molasses

I remember the molasses explosion in 1919 very well. I went down there. I was fourteen at the time. There was a large rumble from the tank, which held millions of gallons of molasses. The tank stood on the wharf near North End Park, minutes from where I lived. It was an unbelievable sight. The explosion was tremendous, creating a sea of rushing brown goo! At the time there were mostly horses, and many people were trapped and couldn't escape the suffocating goo and drowned. Many people died, twenty-one total. It was hard to flee from the rapid wave of disaster. I think if I still had the same shoes I still got—it was just the way the papers said. I remember it like today; I didn't hear the explosion, but I heard about it and I went down there that same day.

And I remember like yesterday a large player piano floating down Hanover Street in the—well it wasn't floating—well it was floating because the whole mass was going—nothing floats on molasses. That is my most vivid memory I have, I'll never forget that! Oh, it was high, feet high. Quite a few people died there, [though] not anybody I knew. That was in the North End Park. It took years before it really—because molasses, no matter if it rained or whatever weather—stays for a long while. Eventually, even when it evaporated, but that smell of molasses lingered on for months and months and months. For years the streets had that sticky residue. People were constantly washing down sidewalks and streets and firemen were always hosing them down. That sweet smell, the floor tracks in our houses, and the tacky doorknobs would remind us of that mild winter in January. But eventually, like everything else, it all disappeared.

Italian American Street Life 12

> People chopped wood for their stoves on the sidewalks because there were no cars, there was plenty of room to walk, and people often sat on the curbs with their feet dangling in the street; whoever who had a car in those days were considered millionaires.
> —FRANK FAVAZZA

In the early 1940s, Dominic Rosso, a drummer from a popular New York vaudeville troupe, toured Boston. After performing at the Old Howard Theatre and the Casino Burlesque House on Hanover Street, he fell in love with the city, which he described as "all together, not big and spread out like New York." After experiencing the embrace of the North End, with easy walking distance to the lively entertainment center of Scollay Square (which featured burlesque performers like Sally Keith, known as "The Queen of the Tassels," who originated the dance of twirling tassels at the Crawford House), he decided to make the North End his home. Dominic had grown up in New York's sprawling Little Italy, which he described as "going on for miles, East side and West side," so he found the intimacy and physical closeness of Boston's North End a better place to live.

Others felt the same attraction. The social activist and author Jane Jacobs visited Boston in 1959, a time when the city considered the North End the worst slum in the city. Despite having one of the highest concentrations of dwelling units in the country, antiquated buildings, and few parks for children, Jacobs found the streets "alive with children playing, people shopping, people strolling, people talking." She found the street atmosphere one of "buoyancy, friendliness and good health so infectious that I began asking directions of people just for the fun of getting in on some talk." In the widely read *The Death and Life of Great American Cities*, Jacobs defended the North End as the kind of vibrant community that challenged the misguided theories of city planners who were destroying old ethnic neighborhoods all over the United States.[1]

Although the Italians did not design the layout of the North End, they transformed the streets with the village lifestyle of southern Italy, changing the parks and corners into stage sets where friends conversed with animated Italian gestures in regional dialects. Replicating the pulse of the busy streets of Naples and the cacophony of shouts at Palermo's La Vucceria open-air market, colorfully named pushcart vendors roamed the neighborhood hawking their wares. Open-air markets and fruit stands doubled as meeting points where people handled vegetables, checking them for freshness while listening to the latest rumors flowing through the Italian American grapevine. Long before the invention of social media, the streets buzzed as the information highway to exchange neighborhood news. With a keen sense of wanting to protect each other, which had developed in native villages, North Enders kept their eyes on the street for *stranieri* (outsiders).

The cultural legacy of southern Italy was on display during religious processions, when the streets overflowed with the faithful and society members displaying religious banners marched to the music of the Roma Band. Celebrating the patron saint of their native village, North End families opened their doors to friends and relatives with sumptuous meals. The author Marc Fried described the strong bond of connectivity between the people of the West End, which applied equally to the North End: "You became part of one another, your friends were friends with one another, and everybody else knew everybody else." Social connectivity survived in the North End because the automobile failed to disrupt the lifestyle of people who walked to work and frequented stores, churches, social clubs, and settlement houses within the confines of a self-contained neighborhood.

Mary Arigo Ventolo, who was born in 1904, described a lifetime of walking: "Are you kidding? Cars? Everything was on foot, only millionaires had cars then. I couldn't even get in a car that I didn't get so sick, but I'm used to it now. My nephew used to take me to Dorchester on Saturdays, but he had to stop the car and let me get out because my stomach was so upset. I don't even know how to take a streetcar—I never traveled with streetcars."[2]

FIGURE 22. The Torrese Club, Endicott Street, 1981.

Frances Lauro

On North Street

My children were all born on North Street. We were one clique—all from the same town in Italy. At that time we were stupid; now they do this and they do that and they don't have any kids. I used to have one after another like a little rabbit. They all grew up at once—it was nice; at least they were all one family on North Street. They used to sit in the doorways, we used to sing, kids always used to play hopscotch, you know—beautiful! Now they don't believe in that no more—they got their boyfriends over there waiting on the corner.

Arpito Pagliuca

Arpito Pagliuca was the president of the Torrese Club.

Playing Cards with the Boys at the Torrese Club

I was born in 1897 and I came in 1921. I'm a member of Saint Anthony's since 1921. I'm seventy-nine, been here sixty-five years, before he was born (pointing to one card player). I've been a member of the Saint Anthony Society since 1921. These guys fight, call each other names playing cards, then the next minute it's over. I listen to you sometimes and sometimes you listen to me.

> CARDPLAYER 1: Cut 'em!
>
> CARDPLAYER 2: No! You're supposed to watch!
>
> CARDPLAYER 1: Come on, cut 'em what's the difference?
>
> CARDPLAYER 2: They're your cards! All right!
>
> CARDPLAYER 3: I wanted to know!
>
> CARDPLAYER 2: But I ain't supposed to tell ya! You're supposed to watch!
>
> CARDPLAYER 3: I wanna know because I wanted to see what kinda cards I gotta give this other thing.

CARDPLAYER 2: Yeah, but you're supposed to watch!

CARDPLAYER 3: I watch. I wanna make sure if anything—I watch.

CARDPLAYER 4: You don't see no families come over here no more. Forget about it. Those days are gone. Three or four kids. They don't come over here, the old days, right, was four, five, six kids. You don't see it no more. What do you see now? Outsiders. Fly-by-nighters. They come and go. Young kids, school kids, that's all you see. Hippies, what the hell—they come and go, you see yourself. Where they come from who the hell knows. There's no Italians coming back. They find their own homes; they don't return over here. The North End, right. It's all out-of-towners. They come from different states, even countries. You'll never see that; those days are gone. Big families coming back to the North End—forget about it. That's passé. A club like this we call a privilege, call it a pastime that's all it is, you wanna to go some place, kill an hour or two playing cards, have drink that's all. That's about it. But the old days are gone, the old times aren't coming back here no more; the large families, you don't see that no more. Let's face it, the North End is gone.

CARDPLAYER 2: When does he lose? What does he lose, you tell me?

CARDPLAYER 5: Two dollars, two dollars.

CARDPLAYER 6: When he loses, he loses. Now he's a win, he's on the top, he quits, that's all. He always does that.

CARDPLAYER 3 I do it? That's the first time I did it. And I'm gonna keep on doing it!

CARDPLAYER 2: I tell you what, you go to hell!

CARDPLAYER 5: That's good, he plays wise.

Arpito Pagliuca: He no wanna go to hell.

CARDPLAYER 3: They do it to me, I do it to them.

CARDPLAYER 6: Get outta here!

CARDPLAYER 2: You sweat too much!

CARDPLAYER 1: Hey! Hey! Stop!

Al Mostone

Al Mostone explained the important role Italian societies played as an independent source of community help before the advent of public assistance programs.

The Societies and the Columbus Day Parade

Each town from Italy would try to group their town people and they'd make a small society, like the Society of Maria Santissima Incoronata and so many different ones. My father was in seven of them. They'd pay seventy-five cents, a dollar a month. Well you see they had a benefit, those societies. If they were sick, they'd get seven dollars a week; they tried to build their treasury up so they would protect the members themselves. And then they would have what they called *à bicchierata* [a nice little party] for the families together, or they'd run a dance at Saint John's Hall and they'd sell tickets, and that money all went into the coffers of their own societies. And whenever there was a parade, like the Columbus Day Parade, it used to start in the North End Park years ago.

Every society would be out in full regalia. They'd have their badges over here and their hats on their head, and they'd go in the parade. The North End was quite popular in those days, the parades, and once a year they'd have a Mass said in whatever church they went to, whether it was Sacred Heart (Sicilian) or Saint Leonard's (Neapolitan) or Saint Stephan's or Saint Mary's, they'd have a Mass said and that's the feast, their patron saint. The Sicilians, the Calabrese, every one of the townspeople in Italy had that.

Once a month they'd have their regular meetings in there; they used to rent a hall on the corner of Snow Hill and Prince Street—there was one on the other end of Prince Street, there was one on Hanover Street, one on North Street—they used to rent these halls. One of their biggest things was to try to get a set of American flags and Italian flags all done in silk and embroidered in gold and silver or whatever colors they wanted. And they used to have a big time on the Baptism of the Flags. They would bring these flags to the church, and have the church bless them and baptize them. They called it *Il Battesimo delle Bandieri*; they used to say, "Quando battezzamo le bandieri [When we baptize the flags]." And they used to have a big time! Open the hall up to everybody, have all kinds of beer by the keg, peanuts and biscuits and sandwiches—you name it, they had everything.

Louis Marrotta

LouisChiusano di San Domenico from Montefalcione and his father came from Chiusano San Domenico. Born on North Street, he learned the art of making pastry from his uncle at the Cafe Vittorio.

"A Bunch of Fellas from Corner to Corner"

I've lived in the North End for sixty-five years. I like it over here. Everything is close by. Everything is alright. No trouble. Nice livin'. What else could you say? Everybody was so friendly years ago. Everybody used to walk in somebody's house, you know, coffee, sugar, whoever wants this, they used to give—but today a lot of strangers are coming down here. There was a gang of people, all kind of nationalities, from corner to corner a bunch of fellas, pool rooms, just having a lot of fun. But today you hang around the corner and there's no friends to talk to, all your friends, they moved out, married. There's only a few left, guys like us, Natale and me, that's about all. Don't forget Natale! Those were the days. Salem Street, North Street, Hanover Street, loaded. All kinds of nationalities, Jewish, Irish, Italians, Greeks, all friendly. Not too many children years ago. A few robbers. They never went in the house and steal, I mean they [never] ransacked the house, they never did that.

We were very strict with our fathers. You gotta be home at a certain time. If you go home one minute past nine you used to get a beating. We never stayed out late up until ten, eleven, twelve o'clock. Unless you were about twenty years old, twenty-one, twenty-two. There were cops on the beat, lot of cops on the beat over here at that time. Quite a few of them. They used to kick our ass to go home at nighttime. About eight, nine o'clock if we didn't go, he'd come up there and kick our ass: "Get out, go home, go home."

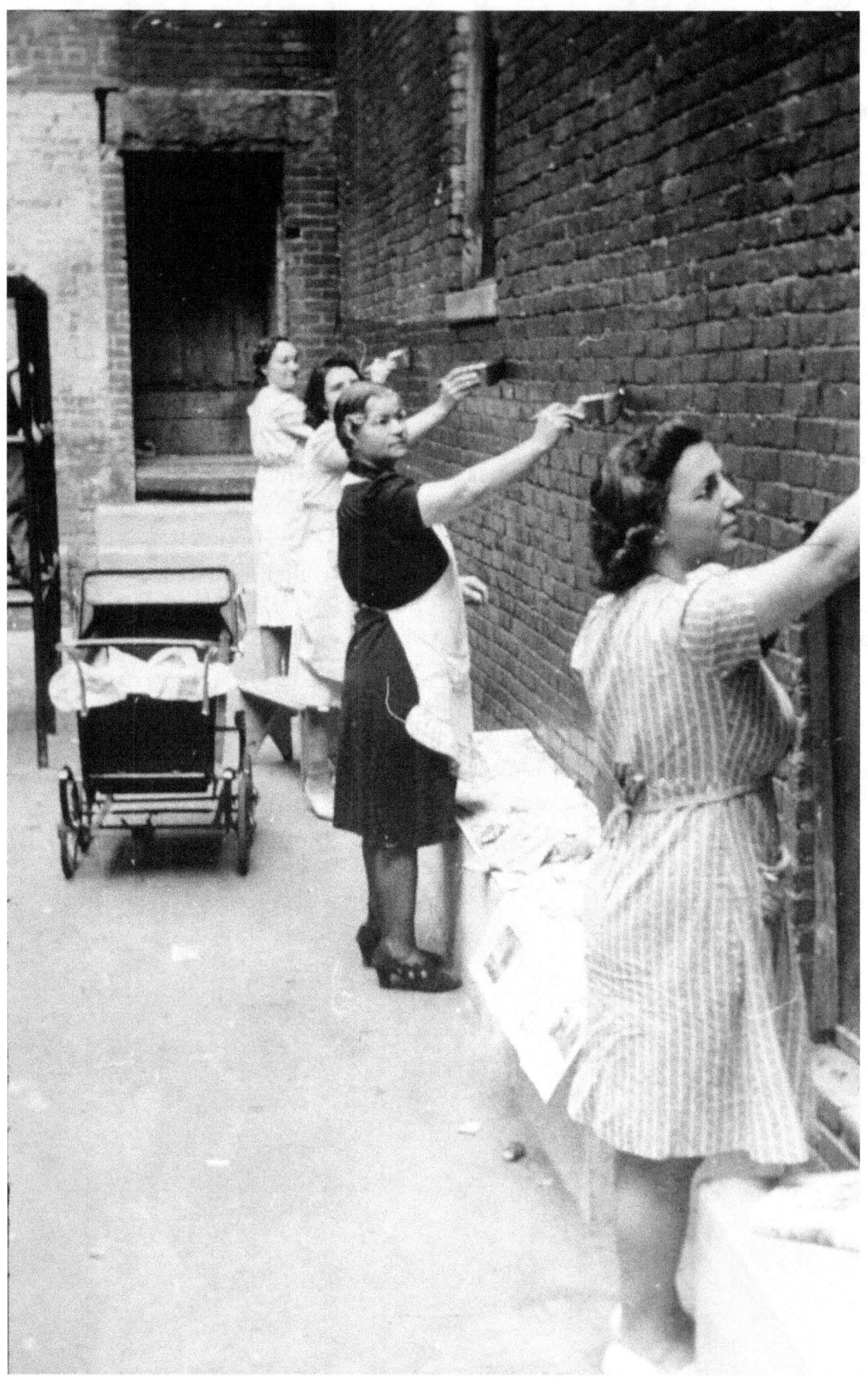

FIGURE 24. Neighborhood Cleanup Day, Cleveland Place, 1931; Josie Zizza, second from left.

Josie Zizza

Life on Cleveland Place

The street wasn't paved. And the buildings across the street weren't built, big buildings. And we used to go barefoot in the summer—it was hot in those days. After they paved, when it was a hot day my father would open the hydrants. And all the kids would bathe, they would put on their swimsuits, and all the women come out with brooms and would clean up the whole street. Once they called the police on my father [and] they came over. They couldn't do anything. He said, "Well I'm cleaning the streets for you, you know, the kids all love it." They used to beg my father, "Open it up!" Those hot days. We didn't have the pool [on the Waterfront]. We had the ocean down there. It was filthy. They used to beg my father, "Open up the hydrant," and the women used to come out, they'd bring their kids. They'd bathe. It was really nice. They threw down three small apartment houses [on Cleveland Place] so we made our own playground. And it was ground dirt so we, the neighbors, we all collected some money and we got somebody to pave. And then we bought our own paint, and we painted it all around, you know, the walls, to keep it clean. Then we had money [and] we had a jungle gym put there and a couple of slides to make the children play. They don't have that today, believe me. Those days, we did our own thing. They don't do it today. And we had a little bank account too. And a lot of children—that jungle gym was iron and a lot of kids were getting hurt—so they threw it down.

As far as I remember I lived here all my life. I don't know whether I was born here. See, I got married here and I lived downstairs when my mother took sick, and I had four sons. I bought the house from my mother years ago. I remember even where the Prado is, there was a candy place, that's where my oldest sister was born, and my brother. Where the Prado is now, there was a small alley. That's where they were born, "Candy Place." My mother took in boarders to help support. We used to stay out till two, three o'clock in the morning outside during the summer days. And we'd all get together and have coffee. We'd go over the roofs and we slept up [on] the roofs [and] the neighbors next door would bring coffee and cake. My mother had no one here. When she used to have her babies, my mother didn't have a sister or anybody here. When she used to have her babies the neighbors all came in. They'd make chicken soup with chickens and everything. They'd bring chickens.

It was wonderful in those days. We had no baths—there was an outside toilet—and two families lived here on each floor. And no heat. Bathtubs, sixty-four-dollar question. Radio: we didn't even have a radio; we used to crochet, get together, play cards. We didn't have TV those days. There was plenty to do. I never, never saw my mother take an aspirin. She never used to say, "I'm tired, I have a headache," never. She always kept busy. Then on top of that my mother had a few boarders too to keep the family income, you know. I had to go to work because my brother was going to college. Those days the girls had to go to work. I used to belong to the cooking club—Mrs. Dunn had the cooking class at the North Bennet Street School—we had the mothers club, we had places to go, but not at night. My father—we would never go out at night. If we come home at nine o'clock at night, we'd get it. There was no such thing. Now they go out at ten, eleven o'clock.

Frank Favazza

Carrying the Bread on Fleet Street

There was no such thing as going down to so-and-so's store to get me a loaf of Bond bread. My mother used to make the dough, make the bread, and put it in the oven sometimes and bake her own. But sometimes she didn't have time or for whatever reason, there used to be a bakery on Fleet Street where they used to make round breads. He just baked bread, he didn't sell anything else. Bread, bread, that's all. He'd say, "Come back in an hour or two." One, two, three, depending on how many she made, put it on a board on my head. And quite a few times those breads slipped on the sidewalk and I'd pick them up as best I could, clean 'em as best I could. But I'm tell ya, them breads tasted better. Of course, the streets weren't as dirty as they are now. And she'd say, "What's this dark thing here?" I'd say, "Well, the oven maybe cooked more on this side or something." But they knew, they knew it fell down or something.

> Rose Bradenese married at seventeen. She used to go to the Casino Burlesque Theatre on Hanover Street on Saturday nights to see the comedians but never to the Old Howard Theatre "because there were too many men" there.

Rose Bradenese

Midwives and Lighting the Stoves on Salem Street

I lived all my life on Salem Street. I'm going to be seventy-six next month. It was beautiful, all Jews. I used to go and light their stoves on top on a Friday and they'd give me ten cents because they couldn't light their fires on a Friday. And I used to go up on a Friday morning, light their stove, and that was their religion—it was their tradition; they couldn't light their stoves in their houses. They used to have all kids go up and do it for all the other people. They'd give them a nickel, a dime—it was a lot of money in those days. They were all Jews, very nice. Salem Street used to be a two-way street and we used to have a firehouse next door to us—they had the horses.

If you had a baby in the house by a midwife they'd bring chickens or eggs. My mother had all her children in the house and the people used to come with eggs and chickens or sugar. Yeah, they wouldn't bring money or gifts or dresses. It was good, real good. They never had their children in the hospital—they all had them at home. And they'd have the midwife come over and deliver the baby. And then after they had the dispensary up there on Hull Street, then they would call a doctor from up there when they had a baby.

> Joe Petringa enlisted in the Marines eight months before Pearl Harbor and fought in the third division on Guadalcanal. He said of the war, "I got wet between my toes, as the Louisiana boys used to say."

Joe Petringa

"The Jewish Merchants Spoke Italian"

I was born on Unity Court behind the Old North Church and then we moved to 57 Salem Street. There were a lot of Jewish businesspeople. Just around my time—I was born in 1918—they were starting to leave to go to the South End and Roxbury because that's where they ended up. But I remember all the Jewish fellas as the storekeepers, and they all spoke Italian. Because my

FIGURE 25. Procession on Sheafe Street, 1920s.

grandmother used to go shopping and I used to go with her and they used to speak Italian, the Jewish merchants. It really was something. The last fella I remember that was Jewish was Mister Clayman. He had a dry goods shop on Salem, right across from Parmenter Street. I remember one thing about him—he had a son who was a rabbi. In those days there was Will's Clothier on the lower end of Salem. Of course, they tore it down for the expressway. I got one of my first suits there—my grandmother bought it for me

Lena Albanese

Daily Life on Sheafe Street

My father found five rooms up on Sheafe Street because my mother had seven children at the time. Then she had the last boy, that's Louie. And we stayed there a good twenty-five years. We had a cake store underneath us, then there was another store where they filed the saws, sharpened them and sharpened scissors and knives and all that stuff. We lived up there on Sheafe Street for thirty-eight, thirty-nine years in one house. And then my mother moved. She took the flats across the street. Because there was less—my sisters started to get married and then who got married one way, who got married another, everybody left my mother, and my mother was living with my youngest sister [because] she was the last one to marry. And my mother said, "Well I'll stay with you." So, she did. And when she died, she was still with my sister, but I used to live not far from them on Sheafe Street because I got married and I lived on 6 Sheafe Street and they were on 20 Sheafe Street.

It was all Italians on Sheafe Street. People would stay out in the streets like they do now and talk with different ones when you meet them. They would ask you to go up their house. Or we'd sit down [at] the door. You could sit in front of the door and sleep all night and nobody would touch you. They wouldn't even say boo to you. My father had a chain going across the vest, the two pockets with a watch on. He never lost that; nobody ever took it away from him. He had a ring on his finger. A signet ring, which my mother gave to him for a birthday—they never took that off of him. Sittin' on the steps sleeping. You can't sleep today on the steps and people go by and not touch you! We used to sleep on the fire escape. All night until the morning. Nobody would say anything to us. We would fold the blankets, put them down on the fire escape, get a pillow for our heads and a sheet over us, and we'd sleep on there. Because we used to get warm days. We used to go up [on] the roof. Make a bed [on] up the roof with the blankets, the pillow. Oh, those were the happy days, not today.

We had nice days. We used to sing; we'd sit in the doorsteps, five or six girls. We had a guy across the street would play the guitar or the harmonica and us girls would sing, say, until eleven, twelve o'clock singing at night. And everybody would watch by the window. Everybody had their windows open a lot. Of course, who could stay up? Who couldn't because they had to get up earlier, and then they wouldn't stay, they'd just listen until about nine, ten o'clock and then they'd go. And no one would say, "Stop playing, stop singing." Nobody like they do today—today you can't even breathe and they tell you "Shut up!" We used to sing "The Butcher Boy." And talk. We'd probably have candy or a cookie. And somebody would bring down tonic [soda] or maybe a cup of coffee once in a while, whoever could afford it more I suppose. But there wasn't too much going on [in] the streets—just you do your shopping, you go up, and that was it for the day. And in the afternoon they had maybe a couple of hours, they'd come down to the door, they figured maybe they forgot something and they'd go out and buy and they'd go back home. And that was it. Like we do now. There's no difference of the streets. The only thing was it wasn't as filthy as this, and I always say it—they're letting the North End here go to the rocks. Because the government or whoever is in charge or the Board of Health don't go around.

Why do they put that dirt on a Saturday in front of the houses? Because the next day they know is a Sunday. Why? Why don't they get after the landlords? If they had to pay a fine, you'd see how quick they'd clean it! And they wouldn't put it out there. They'd warn the families in the buildings. We never did. I remember my brothers, they were eight or nine years old. They would go and look for boxes because we had wood fire and coal fire years back. We didn't have much gas. They used to go down to Dock Square where Quincy Market is now and the market. They would come back and bring a couple of boxes—they were wooden—they would chop them in front of our house on Sheafe Street and whatever splinters, or whatever dirt, paper, whatever was in the box, would be laid aside. They'd have to sweep it, pick it up, and bring it in [in] the barrel. The wood they would bring up [into] the house and we lit the fire with it. And then when my mother got the wood fixed good, when the fire was fixed good, she used to put the coal on top of it. So, you see, and that went through all night, the rest of the day until the next morning, when my mother used to get up and she would sift the ashes—not up [at] the house though—they had one of these tins. The stove was made with an opening and a pan fit in. We would pull the pan out because it would be cold and bring it downstairs and we would sift it. What coals were in there, when my mother made the new fire she would put those coals, they were half-used, on top of it. And it would keep it all night. So, you see, that's what we did. I used to go down when my father was working on the railroad; my father could take home the old railroad ties. They used to give them away. And my father used to get a team and take them home or if he knew somebody that had a pushcart or a horse and team, he would ask them if they would come and do him a favor, come and pick them up. My father would give them a few bucks, see? That was the only way we brought the family up. We had hard times before.

FIGURE 26. Arigo family on Endicott Street.

Mary Arigo Ventola

Life on Endicott Street

My parents came from Messina in Sicily. I'm seventy-five now. I was born on 160 Endicott Street in 1903, right near Saint Mary's Church. Do you know where Saint Mary's Church is, they threw it down? So, it's a couple of years now, but that's been there for years and years. I went to Saint Mary's School that belonged to the church. Now they knocked it down and they haven't built anything yet. Oh, it was good, going to school in those days! You were afraid of the nuns, not like today! Oh, God, today, they're not a scared a nobody! It was wonderful years back. Better than today. Kids had more respect—and better. Then from there I went to public school. The Catholic schools were more strict—you had to go to church and you had to say your prayers. And of course, the public schools you didn't have to. They were more strict than the public school.

Then from there I went to the Hancock School [and] the Cushman School. I lived down there about twenty-one years, then I got married and I moved to Commercial Street. But I didn't get married at Saint Mary's, I got married at Saint Leonard's Church—right here (tapping her finger)—because our mothers were all Italians—and they brought us to the Italian church. They had the wedding receptions in the house then, they didn't have no halls. When we got married, we had it in the house, we didn't have it in halls. They invited their own families like, you know.

But today they have big, big times. They go in halls, restaurants, halls. It's way different than before. The American people went there, Saint Mary's, and they came from Charlestown; Mayor Curley used to come there, oh yeah, Charlestown people, West End people. Mayor Curley, oh he was wonderful. I'm tellin' ya. Really, really nice. I used to sit behind my mother's window on Endicott Street and watch him come into Saint Mary's Church. He was really a wonderful man. These guys today! And that's how it went broke because they didn't come no more. Mayor Curley died, all the people passed away, and—so it went broke, the church.

FIGURE 27. Joe Troisi on Salem Street.

Joe Troisi

"They All Used to Come to Salem Street"

I was born and baptized in Italy. I was two years old when I come from Italy, provincia of Avellino; [my] father was from Campanarello [and] my mother was from Mirabella. I've been in the poultry line all my life, I've been slaughterin'. When I was a kid Fulton Street had a couple a slaughter houses there for poultry, Richmond Street had a big slaughterhouse there for poultry. Ferry Street had a couple of slaughterhouses in there. Then I went into business for myself. I put the poultry market right here in the North End on 135 Salem Street, the first store there with poultry and eggs. When I got in the poultry market, everybody opened up a poultry market after me. During the Second World War, I was the originator of the market in Boston. No meat, so I put up fresh poultry. I had a good business at that time. I was there about twenty years between the poultry line I had and fruit and vegetable. Well that business there that I was in, well we used to put about eighty, ninety hours a week.

You couldn't help it, that's fruit and vegetable, you hadda go and buy from the market. We used to go to the north market, the Quincy Market, that's the south market, all around there, and then sometimes we hadda go in the terminal and we hadda get up all kinda hours. Four o'clock in the morning was the earliest we ever got up. We hadda go and buy it, they'd take it down with express, we had to unload it, and then we'd put it up in the store and then fix the store all up. We used to work eighty, ninety hours a week and sometimes even more. Night and day. We never used to see the bed, very little. And I finished up there.

There were a lot of businesses on Salem Street. It was a good business section and we all done our business on Salem Street. And then it slacked off. The big markets started to come in. And the people, instead of coming in to Boston, they didn't come no more in Boston. They all went shoppin' around their communities where they lived. They all used to come from all over, right here in Boston and Salem Street. Well, everything changed. All new developments. Not here in the North End, you don't see it too much, but out of town everything is all new developments. There's big markets, small markets. And that changed Boston. Everything is coming to a big change here in Boston with the Quincy Market and Faneuil Hall. Maybe I won't live to see it; Boston will be all thrown down and built up new, that's what I really think. But not right now. It's a big change on Salem Street—it ain't no more like it used to be because the big markets outta town today took the business away from us people down here. And that's the reason I went off. I was in business here on Salem Street. Everything changed and a lot of them had to get out of business. It's a poor business now, poultry market, today it ain't worth nothin'. Everybody in the meat line, these stores all carry poultry and knocked us out. There's a big change in Boston. You see, these chain stores are taking over a lot of business—there's a big change in Boston in the food line. There's very, very little food stores left here; they all closed down.

Rose Arigo Amato

Life on Endicott Street

Oh, the North End was beautiful then. We used to sit in the doorway, hot weather, sing. It was so nice, I'm telling ya. You could leave our doors open and you know, we used to sleep sometimes up [on] the roof in the hot weather and leave the doors open, you didn't have to worry about nothing. And there was no trouble at that time. It was so beautiful. And the month of May was like the month of July years ago, and we used to have little slips [for] going out and we used to jump rope with the slips on. That's how hot the weather used to be at that time. And the snow in them days, you couldn't find yourself. Used to be deep, deep walking. Of course, we had a blizzard [the blizzard of 1978], but that blizzard was nothing compared to what we used to have. We had no school for weeks and weeks, them days. There used to be the man with the horse-driven water team, he used to water the streets. Then we had the ice man, he used to sell the ice by the hunks, fifteen cents', ten cents' worth. My mother used to buy it and she used to give the fella extra money because she used to feel bad they used to climb all them stairs—it was four flights up and she used to give him a quarter extra. Then we had the man with the slush, it was like an ice. And I remember when my mother used to get the milk, she used to go get it by the pitchers—they used to sell it by pitchers; she used to go in the store, she used to bring a pitcher and they used to fill it. There was a store where she used to buy hot baked beans and brown bread on Saturdays. She used to make a lot of her own baking too. Oh, she used to like to make leg of lamb in the oven. She used to like to make chickens all stuffed in the oven, stuffed peppers, eggplant, all that. She used to love to cook. She was a very good cook. With nine children, my mother and father were always busy. Always wash and iron.

"They're All God's Children"

They're [youth] not as polite, and that's number one. When an old lady used to go by, they'd take them under the arm and walk, pick them up you know. Now if they see an old lady go by, they make fun of them now, they make fun of ya, you know? It's different, altogether; they don't help you. They see you with bundles, they don't help you. I remember years ago, old ladies, when they used to have a lot of bundles a boy would go up to them and say, "Can I help you?" And they helped them. And they never answered back. They never made fun of old people; now you see an old person go by, and sometimes they make fun of them and everything. I've seen that with my own eyes. They've done it. They do it. They haven't got that respect, they haven't, no.

There's a lot of change. They answer you back, terrible. There is a difference; we didn't have all this crime going on. The North End isn't like it used to be, but I'll tell you one thing. You'll always get help from a neighbor. If you're sick or anything, the first thing they do, they run to your house and help you out. Cause they come over and they want to know what's wrong with you, you know, if they don't see you around or something, they want to know what's happened to you or they'll ask somebody, "I haven't seen so-and-so for a long time, what happened to them?" A certain party will know and say, "Well, this one, she's sick at home." She'll tap at your door and say, "What happened to you?" Or they'll see you on the street: "Why didn't you let me know that you were sick?" That's the way they express themselves, you know. No, that's one thing about them, they're not, uh—like if they see anything going wrong, they don't let anybody get away with it. They see a stranger or anybody doing anything there. You could never rape anybody in the North End and get away with it. They'll get after them!

The North End, that's one thing about them, they'll get after them. They don't like Black people here. They won't let a Black person come here. A couple of Black people tried to move here. They got right after them. Pushed them right out. Although I feel bad for them, too, just the same, I don't know. I feel bad for them, I don't know why, but I think they're God's children too. I feel bad too. Listen, the white ones are just as—ah huh-huh—I know that. Just as bad. I mean you know what's right is right—they're God's children; God put them in the world too, you know what I mean?

Rose Giampaolo

Salem Street

But there was a lot of discrimination in those days. In the North End especially, we had a lot of Polish people and we had Jewish people. And the Jewish people discriminated against the Irish in those days [when] the Irish began to settle in the North End. The Jews came first. The Irish were abused. The Italian people came after the Irish and Italian people were abused by the Irish, and so this is the way it was. And I remember those days, I do remember. We had quite a few Jewish people here. In fact, we had a Jewish synagogue on Salem Street between Cooper Street and Baldwin Place. And we had all these little Jewish men with the little black beanies on their head, and their wives would help them out with their businesses, and they'd have their clothing outside hanging on a line or maybe they'd have a rack. And then they'd call you in. And the Italian people all patronized the Jewish people, they really did, because there were all Jewish businesses in those days.

Viola Pettinelli

Viola Pettinelli was born on North Square in 1906 next door to the Paul Revere House.

Walking Barefoot on North Square

And I can remember the teams of horses and in the wintertime, we had the horse-drawn sleds. We used to jump in the back to get a ride. We were never allowed to go barefooted—never. And I always wanted to go barefooted because we had some neighbors, well I don't know if it was financial, but they were allowed to go barefooted. And, oh, my mother and father didn't agree, even if it was a sandal; we used to wear a lot of sandals, they were like fifty cents a pair, like the monks wear. But we had to wear shoes. So, one day I had to go to the store. My mother gave me ten cents to buy a loaf of bread down on North Street.

In the meantime she had company and she was busy talking with the company, and I says to myself, here's a good chance for me to go out barefooted! So, I took my shoes off and I went down the stairs. I get across the street and it was a summer's day, and the sun! Oh, the sun is burning my feet! I didn't realize I was a tender foot and, oh, I didn't know what to do. I took a few steps, and I couldn't go forward to get the bread because the sun was burning my feet, that hot pavement. And I couldn't come back because I was in the middle. Well I was in agony. I was afraid my mother would be looking out the window and see me without shoes. So, well, I took a chance. I came back. And I tip-toed in the house and I put my shoes on, and I went and get the bread. To this day my mother never knew that I snuck out without my shoes. Never again! Oh, I never went out barefooted again. We all like to do what we're not supposed to do.

Idolo Taglieri and an Elderly North End Woman

Life on Prince Street

ELDERLY NORTH END WOMAN: I had to wait a whole week for the shopping van because they didn't want to come around the North End. Yours came to Saint Leonard's.

IDOLO TAGLIERI: No, I had to wait. I had to wait a day.

ELDERLY WOMAN: They go to other places first and then—

IDOLO TAGLIERI: Yeah, it's the last stop.

ELDERLY WOMAN: Yeah, it's the last stop because they hate to come around the North End.

IDOLO TAGLIERI: You know why? It isn't because of the people.

ELDERLY WOMAN: It's a good thing my son is here—I put some of my things in his freezer.

IDOLO TAGLIERI: It's too congested, that's why; it's worse now than it ever was.

ELDERLY WOMAN: I know it. Yeah, your truck, the car can't even—

IDOLO TAGLIERI: The cars going by, they're knocking me out, they're killing me slow but sure.

ELDERLY WOMAN: You have a tooth pulled? Oh, I thought you had a tooth pulled.

IDOLO TAGLIERI: Me? (laughing) I got no teeth!

ELDERLY WOMAN: They can't even park over here, they don't bother. They come the last minute, they don't give a damn from the North End.

IDOLO TAGLIERI: You're right, honey.

ELDERLY WOMAN: And if you tell them to move they'll give you a punch in the mouth if you tell them to move.

IDOLO TAGLIERI: You're right, honey.

Going to School

13

> Italy was my country; I loved it, but I love this country
> because they send people to school.
> —MARIA GRAZIA SANTACQUA

During the Unification, the northern government unleashed *i nuovi pirati* (the new pirates) on the South's institutions, looting banks, stealing masterpieces from its artistic patrimony, and gutting its school system.[1] In 1867, 92 percent of the southern population was illiterate, with schools under the direction of northern upper-class interests, and new laws that guaranteed children three years of public education were never enforced. For the lower classes, who were in the throes of poverty, the added weight of increased taxes to enrich the North required more hands-on subsistence farms, making school further out of reach.

The status of *ben istruito* (obtaining knowledge from books and going to school) had been a right reserved for children of the privileged on their way to professional careers as teachers, lawyers, and doctors. Accordingly, poorer southerners associated schools with the entitled class of elites, while teachers looked on southerners with distain. Southern immigrants took this attitude with them to the United States and entered North End schools with an inherited sense of inferiority.

In 1924, the D'Alelio family received a long-awaited letter from the North End. Relatives had located an apartment so their growing family could leave Pittsburgh and start a new life in Boston. Like many of her generation, Signora D'Alelio carried bitter memories of Montefalcione, especially when her businessman father forbade her to attend school, telling her, "If you go to school, you'll meet a guy and get married."[2]

When she married the young man her father approved of, they decided to immigrate to America, which liberated her from a future on the family farm where "she had to work like a horse, tending walnut trees and baking bread for the hired hands on her father's farm."[3] In Boston, one of her first official acts was to enroll her children in the North End schools. Her oldest daughter, Theresa, found a high-quality school system "because when we went to school, we learned, and they said Boston was the best place for the speaking of English, it was very good here."[4]

The classrooms of the Eliot, Paul Revere, Charlotte Cushman, and Hancock Schools became the intersection where the cultural values of southern Italy met the Anglo-Saxon value system. School teachers believed Italian immigrants should conform to the Protestant ethic of the dominant culture. Discouraging Italian language and customs, they believed schools were necessary institutions to convert Italians into righteous, orderly Americans. Teachers emphasized education as the key to individual advancement, in stark contrast to the Italian belief in economic advancement of the family. They sometimes met with non-English-speaking parents to persuade them not to take their talented American-born children out of grammar schools. Other educators and social reformers believed Italians lacked intellectual curiosity, and because of their slow assimilation and failure to learn English, recommended courses in manual labor for them because "they were good with their hands."

In response to the major influx of immigrants to Boston, the social reformer Thomas Mann founded the common school to provide vocational skills and Robert Woods proposed manual training for "slower" immigrants to restore work values in industrial schools. The social reformer and philanthropist Pauline Aggiz Shaw founded the North Bennet Industrial School in the North End, the first vocational school of its kind, where immigrant children were instructed in printmaking, woodworking, electrical wiring, and sheet metal skills, though the staff had little understanding of "the social background of the people in their native background."[5]

But not all educators failed to understand the values of southern Italian culture. John F. McGrath, the principal of the Eliot School, expressed a view that differed from those who believed Italian students were unteachable: "After ten years' experience teaching them, going into their homes, eating and sleeping with them, I have discovered that we have much to learn from them, which would benefit us. We are looking at the immigrant from our viewpoint. We want to make him over to suit us."6

Some Italians arrived with already formed ideas about the importance of education. For example, Alfonsa Emilia Mazzarino LoPresti hailed from a well-educated family from Licodea Eublea in Sicily. In 1920, when her future son-in-law, Graziano Longorini, asked for her daughter Laura's hand in marriage, she told him, "No sheepskin, no marriage."7

Much to the dismay of her parents, Theresa D'Alelio chose to leave school to work in a local clothing factory. Many young people, like Lena Albanese, wished to continue with school but had to withdraw. Despite the pleadings of Miss Bigelow, a sympathetic teacher who met with Lena's non-English-speaking mother to try to convince her to keep her gifted daughter in the seventh grade, Lena had to leave to take care of her brother while her mother worked on a farm in Arlington. A few years later, Lena had a second chance for an education. While quarantined with pneumonia for three months at the Peter Brigham Hospital, she decided to "make myself useful" by caring for the patients on her floor, "bringing plates in and out and removing bedpans." Impressed with the young girl's intelligence, and willingness to learn, the head nurse, Miss Doak, selected her for the nursing program at the hospital.

Lena's mother supported her career dream, but her father disapproved, relegating her to a life of menial jobs in factories. Years later, when Lena was caring for her bedridden mother, she stood by helplessly, mindful of the medical knowledge she would have attained as a nurse, and with deep regret said, "See Ma, if you [had] let me be a nurse I could help you now."

Josie Zizza

"One Extra Piece"

In those days my father didn't believe, they didn't believe the girls should go to school, only the boys. My oldest brother was going to Tufts Medical; he graduated English High. Then my father figured—my oldest sister went to work, she didn't care too much for school. But I did. But I couldn't go because my parents said I had to go to work. I come from a very large family—my mother had twelve children; I have seven sisters and four brothers and I was the third oldest. So we had to go to work. I loved school—I wanted to go to school very badly. I was always on the honor roll. I was good at figures. I only finished the eighth grade. I was denied the opportunity to go; I wanted to go to high school, but I come from a large family and I was forced to go to work because in those days the boys had to go to school. They said the boys—the women had families [so] they didn't have to go to work, which was very, very wrong.

So I had a couple of brothers and my father insisted they go to school; I had my oldest brother, and he entered Tufts Medical School, but he didn't complete it. So we had to go to work to support them to go to school. But then I insisted later—I was the third oldest—I insisted that my youngest sisters should go to high school and I worked on them and they went. But my mother and father got together—they figured I should go to work and help with my brother [as] he was going to college. But they [my parents] were determined. In those days they used to say the girls had to go to work, they get married, they stay home and have babies. I was mad within myself because I really wanted an education. I was mad, I was very mad at my family too. My father had a lot of property and he lost it in the Depression with Ponzi. So I used to make the deals for my father; I'd go with him to the lawyers and everything, and my father used to say, "You should have been a lawyer." I used to do my brothers' homework. Because by then, my [oldest] brother didn't finish school. And then in those days they used to say, "Well, go nights." There were no night schools, and you had to take a streetcar, and we were kept strict, you know. Where could you go nights? The boys had to go to school and learn something.

But in those days we had to go to continuation school. We worked when you were fourteen. And for two years you had to go to continuation school a half a day a week. That was a law. I was fourteen and I only weighed seventy-six pounds. But you had to weigh ninety pounds in those days to go to work. So I went to school, and the teachers were very upset that I had to leave school. I'll never forget, Miss Bigelow was our principal, and she told my father, "What a sin to take her out." But they were determined. So I went to get on the scale to get my working certificate and I only weighed seventy-six pounds. And the limit then was ninety pounds. So my parents kept me home for a whole year on a home permit. My mother went to work for my brother's college. So they kept me home, made me do nothing; they made me drink a quart of milk a day, eggnog. At the end of the year I still weighed seventy-six pounds.

By this time my father and mother were determined that I had to go to work, I should go to work. So my father brings me to the shoe store on Salem

Street and buys me a pair of oxfords. They were a half a size larger than what I usually wore. And my father had a lot of round things, they looked like fifty-cents, made of lead. So they filled my shoes up and they put a diaper around me because I was very scrawny and very thin, and they put lead in there. So they took me to the medical school there and I tipped the scale at ninety-one pounds. So that's how they gave me the permit to work. But the doctor still wouldn't give his permission. So my mother said, "No, she still has to go to work, she has to help." But after much debating they gave it to me, but I had to go every week and get weighed because if I lost one pound they were going to stop me from working. So every week my father put an extra piece in to make sure that I didn't lose weight, because they said if I lost any weight I had to stop working. But I didn't. When I started working I started getting taller; I was always on the skinny side but I gained more weight.

Lena Albanese

In the teens, Lena Albanese and her mother worked at Loose-Wiles Biscuit Company on Causeway Street, which later became Sunshine Biscuits.

"But She Likes to Learn School"

I went to school but I couldn't graduate or anything. I left in the sixth grade. I was just promoted into the seventh and I went from September to October, and I didn't learn too much because I didn't have enough time to learn. My mother took me out because she had the other small baby and I had to take care of my brother—that was the youngest brother—and my mother went to work, see, instead of having me go to work, because in those times you had to have a school certificate. You had to go a half day to school. There were some people that had factories or stores, they didn't want to leave a half day to give to you. So I kept on for about a year like that. In fact, before that, when I left school, Miss Bigelow asked for my mother. So my mother said, "Well, I have to go up to school. I don't understand them or anything." She said to me, "You talk and you tell them why."

So, I told Miss Bigelow, she was the head one, the supervisor from the school. And Miss Bigelow said, "Gee, that's a shame your mother has to take you out because you want to learn, you're a good kid, and I hate to give you a leave of absence from school because you can't come to school anymore." I said, "No, I wouldn't be able to, Miss Bigelow, because I have to take care of my brother. And he's on a bottle. And you got to feed him. And you got to change him and everything and I can't very well do that." So she said to me, "Well all right, I'll discharge you." But my mother had to come up to school the next day after I had spoken to her. And Miss Bigelow said to my mother, "I don't see why you want to take your daughter out of school. She loves to learn. She gets one hundreds in arithmetic all the time. It's too bad." She wanted to hear from her, what she had to say! So my mother told her the same thing but only she told her in Italian and then I had to translate it to her in English. And she said, "But she likes to learn school and I'm sorry because she can't graduate. She's only got another year after this." Because in those days there was only eight grades. Not too long after that they started with the ninth grade.

My mother said, "Well, I feel bad because I have to take her out, but I cannot keep her in school any longer because she has to take care of the baby and I gotta go to work." I really cried that day because I really wanted to go to school because I wanted to continue to become a nurse. My mother went to work on a farm in Arlington for two summers. She had to be up [at] the North Station here, where you go up the stairs to get the Elevated [Railway], at half-past five in the morning in order for her to get to the job at six o'clock. And I would take care of the kids—they were smaller. When I came back from school, I'd go up, pick them up, give them their bottles, make them eat, and bring them back to the lady that was taking care of them for those few hours while I was in school. And my mother used to get home at seven o'clock at night from the farm. Oh, we went through a lot, though. We worked. My other sisters not too much.

My oldest sister was my mother's pet because [my mother] said she was skinny and she didn't have the strength to do a lot things, so she used to pick on me a lot, "Do this, mama, do this for me." And I would go and do it. And they would say, "No, I can't do it, ma I can't do it, I don't know how to do it." And my mother would say to me, "All right, you go, see what you can do." I'd go in the market or go in any grocery store and I could figure it out in my mind how much I would spend before the man would even make the account out. I loved arithmetic. She would get seven or eight dollars for the week. But no taking home nothing! No vegetables, nothing. If they ever took anything they had to ask the boss, you know the foreman, whoever owned the land there. Now if he felt like giving it to them, he'd give it. And if he didn't, he'd say, "No I can't give it to you" if he had a certain amount to make the boxes or the bushels, whatever the stuff was, see? After that she went to work at Loose-Wiles, a factory on Causeway Street—they used to make all the cakes and crackers.

Marguerite Locchiato spoke about the holidays and her parents: "They never left their house; everyone had to go to them on holidays."

Marguerite Locchiato

"They Took Interest in Their Children"

We had obligations; we had chores to do in our house. We had to be home at a certain time. Now I went to school, I had to be home no later than twenty minutes to four. I had to give an account to my mother. My mother was home to see that we were there; once we were there, we had to tell her where we went. But we had to report home. No way, if we stayed after school, we'd have to tell her why we stayed after school and get a lickin' on top of it. There was no way the teacher was ever wrong, not in my house anyway, never wrong; even if they were wrong, they were never wrong. You could rest assure[d] of that.

And you talk to some of these kids, I don't know sometimes I listen to them talk—what I had in the sixth grade, in the seventh grade, in the eight[h] grade, they haven't even got it in high school now. What are they teaching them? Is it me or is it them? And when I went to school there were forty pupils in that room. Now they have assistants, they have counselors. Where's our money going to, to them big people? Our teachers had to correct our papers—there were no promotions if we didn't get promoted. I'll give you an instance. There was this girl Madeline—she came from a big family too—and she said, "I'll never forget, I didn't get promoted one year. So when I went home, my father asked us if we got promoted and I told him I didn't get promoted and he wanted to know why." So she said to her father there was no more seats in the sixth grade. Well the father went up in the air: "I'm a taxpayer and there's no seats in the sixth grade!" So she said, "I thought by [the] time September came he would forget about it." Well by cracky he didn't. Because September when she went to school he was right there to find out. And he was giving the teacher an argument: "You mean to tell me I'm a taxpayer and there's no room for my daughter in the next grade?" The teacher said, "No! Your daughter didn't pass; she didn't get promoted because she failed." She said, "Margaret, I got two beatings instead of one."

You see how interested our people were; even though my mother was an illiterate, she could not read or write, my father could, but my mother wasn't stupid or ignorant. Some of them people were illiterates—they couldn't read or write—but nonetheless they were interested in the welfare of their children and they took interest in them. As illiterate as they were, and some of them were ignorant, but nonetheless that makes a difference I think. That's the changing world. When we were kids, any of us that went to school, there was no way we could hook [cut] school. Now you see the kids in the street, their mothers don't know whether they're there or not. The teachers would get in touch with our mothers. They say I come from the Stone Ages—what Stone Ages?

Mary Beninati

Jewish, Irish, and Italian Girls

I was born on Charter Street. There was a school on Charter Street, a six-room house, the Eliot School, and I went there to the third grade. Then I went to the Hancock from the fourth to the ninth and I graduated from the Hancock School. Then I went to work. There was no high schools in them days. But I wish I did have the opportunity, I loved school. Not that I'm proud—I was A's, B's, I was always on the honor roll. I loved school, oh! But I couldn't keep it up. Well I went to nine grades, which was wonderful, you know? But yeah, they, I remember all my teachers; we were happy, they were wonderful. We were all Jewish girls, Irish girls, Italian girls, it was beautiful, beautiful. We all enjoyed each other. After I graduated, we all went to work. Hardly anybody in them days went to high school, so the ninth grade, that was the first high. But I loved it; I had good marks and I enjoyed it. I had the Italian teacher that taught me Italian. In the seventh, eighth, and ninth grades they taught us Italian. Well, Miss Collarton, this teacher, she taught us Italian. Well I'm not bragging, but I read and write fluently; I love the Italian language. See, I learned it at home, not the way you write it, but she taught us the Italian, it was really wonderful. I spoke Italian at home with my mother and father at the time, but they speak their style; the Sicilian people don't talk like real—you know, you learned it in school really—[I] loved it. I wish I could have gone to school and taught Italian, that's how much I loved it.

Viola Pettinelli

"You Had to Learn English"

When I went to public school, and I enjoyed it, but when I went to school, I couldn't speak English, I spoke only Italian because my parents both spoke Italian; they had just come here, my friends and neighbors—90 percent were Italians—we had a few Jewish, a few Irish, one or two English, but it was predominately Italian, so that when I went to school I couldn't say a word in English, so I had to learn English and not as we do today, bilingual, no. There was no such a thing as bilingual, not until you got until the fifth or sixth grade. You had to learn English. And believe me, there were seven of us, and we all learned our English right. We didn't have any problem. My mother and father always believed we had to go to the library. Here's another thing my mother had: if we didn't come home with home lessons [homework], come weekends, my mother and father would say, "No home lessons? No books to read? What's the matter with your teacher, she doesn't give you any homework?" If we didn't have any homework or we didn't have anything to do, "Well, go to the library, get a book!" So if we didn't have any work at home, don't ever be idle, you had to go to the library. So when we went to the library it was very, very quiet; you couldn't even whisper, everything was silence. Then when we got to the fifth or sixth grade, we had to take a foreign language. Then my folks thought I should take Italian.

"Your Teacher Is Your Mother"

We had nice teachers in those days. Our teachers were dedicated. If they got married, they couldn't work, they couldn't be teachers. We had a lot of unmarried teachers, we had elderly teachers. Well in those days, they went to Radcliffe, Wellesley, and Simmons and they were terrific. I really miss those teachers. They taught us beautifully—they were beautiful teachers. I liked them all very much. But the teacher was always right there. When I was in the third grade, we had one girl who was fresh, and the teacher seemed to be having trouble with her. The teacher was a lovely teacher, Miss Bibby, an older teacher with beautiful white hair, and she had red and white skin, she had a pretty, chubby face. She asked this girl to take her mother in and the girl never told her mother.

So one day the teacher sent another girl to the house to tell the mother that she wanted to speak to her. So this woman, a nice, tall woman, came to school with a baby in her arms, I'll never forget. So she comes in there and the teacher calls another pupil to interpret for her. This was the second or third grade. When the mother hears whatever was told to her [about her daughter], she took the baby out of her arms [and] she put the baby on the front desk there. Her daughter was standing nearby. Well, she slapped that girl's face. Oh, the girl was highly embarrassed. We were all embarrassed for her. We all got our slaps, but right in the classroom in front of all the kids! And the teacher just looked there. Then the mother picked up the baby and said to the teacher, "Ah righta, ah righta (in broken English), if she gives you any more trouble—" and she left. We weren't supposed to give any teachers or priests or nuns any trouble. No back talk. My mother, when we went to school, she said, "When you're in school, the teacher is your mother"—that's the way we were brought up. That's the truth; these are true stories. You couldn't go home and say "So-and-so hit me." My parents would ask, "And why did she hit you?" "She hit me for nothing," we'd say. So every time you'd say you did nothing, you'd get a whack in the face. "You stayed after school? Well, why, what did you do?" "I did nothing." Bang! "What did you do?" "Nothing!" You'd get another bang! Until you had to tell what you did. Because no mother in those days would believe that the teacher was going to keep you after school for nothing. You must have done something. So what are you going to do?

Continuation School in the North End

In 1919, fourteen-year-old Viola Pettinelli left the eighth grade and began a forty-eight-hour workweek in a book bindery, which she found fascinating. Being underage, she had to attend continuation school on North Bennet Street until she was sixteen. She earned ten dollars a week and considered herself lucky.

I went as far as the eighth grade. Then after that I went to work. And I got a job at the Vermont building right down here on North Margin Street, and I was working forty-eight hours and I was making ten dollars a week in 1920, and everybody envied me because very few people could work forty-four hours and get ten dollars. And then not only that. In those days we had to go to what they called continuation school because we were underage and I wasn't sixteen, so I had to go to continuation school until I was sixteen years old, and the continuation school was right here on North Bennet Street. So we had to go there four hours a week, so my day was Monday mornings from eight to twelve, but I still made my ten dollars, where some boys and girls had to go to continuation school [but] their bosses didn't pay them for that four hours, so that's why everybody thought I was lucky. This was bindery work. It was very fascinating. I liked it very much even though I was fourteen years old. I liked the job and I think the boss liked me too because he used to let me do mostly something a little more delicate.

We had to do a lot of reading and writing because everything was printed, especially when he had bank jobs to do. He seemed to call on me more often. I really liked it. I was there quite a few years. It was a Canadian firm, it was a branch, and then right before the Depression—we didn't know a depression was coming—then I lost my job there because it closed up, so one by one we lost our jobs. Then for a while I went to work in Waltham at the Waltham Press and then a combination of the Porter Press and the Waltham Press. But I didn't like it because I had to get a ride to get down there.

Justice Denied   14

Sacco and Vanzetti

> The belief is likewise widespread that in the trial of these men there was a confusion of issues, as between their guilt or innocence of the crime charged, on one hand, and the acknowledged radicalism on the other.
> —ROGER BALDWIN, *New York News*, 1927

> I wish in this last hour of agony ... that our case and fate may be understood and serve as a tremendous lesson to the forces of freedom so that our suffering and death were not in vain.
> —BARTOLOMEO VANZETTI in letter to Nicola Sacco's son

Fred Bourne graduated from Brown University with a degree in journalism and became a sportswriter in the early 1920s for the *Boston Post*. Soon after, he married "an Italian girl," Ester Vanelli, from the North End and became a lifelong resident of 12 Unity Street. Though Jewish, he assimilated into Italian American culture with such ease that the neighbors thought him Italian. Fred's observations reflected the objectivity of a trained journalist and the intimate knowledge of a local historian.

As a North Ender who followed the twists and turns of the seven-year trial of Sacco and Vanzetti, he went to the Charlestown Prison the night of their execution on August 22, 1927, and reported one of the most consequential moments in American judicial history. Fred recalled the moment when the horrified crowd outside howled in disbelief as electrical charges coursed through the bodies of Sacco and Vanzetti, dimming the lights in the prison windows.

Nicolo Sacco and Bartolomeo Vanzetti, two anarchist immigrants who had openly supported worker causes and protest strikes and had written articles in Luigi Galleani's anarchist newspaper, *Cronaca Sovversiva*, were sent to the electric chair for the murder of a paymaster and a guard of a shoe company in South Braintree, Massachusetts. During the seven years between their arrest, trial, and execution, the presiding judge, Webster Thayer, suppressed key witness testimonies in their defense and dismissed conflicting evidence that would have cast doubts on the merits of the case. In a moment of blatant prejudice, after Thayer had denied a motion by the defense in 1924, he bragged, "Did you see what I did to those anarchist bastards the other day?" The trial and execution raised troubling questions about the fairness of the American judicial system.

Beyond the controversy over Sacco and Vanzetti's innocence or guilt, the decision challenged American democratic principles: could individuals in a free, liberal, and modern society express radical views and diverse cultural practices without fear of persecution?[1] Many North Enders viewed Sacco and Vanzetti as innocent victims caught in an unjust American legal system in search of a culprit. In May 1920, Aldino Felicani established the Sacco-Vanzetti Defense Committee in the La Notizia Italian Newspaper building on 32-34 Battery Street (256 Hanover Street was in 1925) in the North End. He echoed the sentiment of the neighborhood, quoting the Italian ambassador Rolando Ricci in *La Notizia*: "The conviction of Sacco and Vanzetti has as much to do with their being Italian as with being anarchists." *La Gazzetta di Massachusetts,* the largest Italian American weekly newspaper in New England, remained neutral throughout the case, avoiding any comments in support of the men. The editors adhered to James V. Donnaruma's business plan, which aligned with elite Boston Republicans and the powerful Lodge family, who bought advertisements in the paper.[2] The execution of Sacco and Vanzetti provoked outcries and mass demonstrations around the world from workers who saw their own fates in dramatic replica in Massachusetts.

In an atmosphere of Red Scare politics, most Americans were preoccupied with the Bolshevik Revolution and the Wall Street bombing, which was attributed to Italian anarchists, agreed with the outcome of the trial. For the majority, justice had been served and the executions were justified. The Sacco and Vanzetti case remained vivid in the minds of many North Enders, who remembered the trial proceedings, the protest marches on the pair's behalf, and the large crowds along the funeral procession. They recalled the undertaker who waited outside the prison to bring the bodies to the Joseph A. Langone Funeral Chapel on 383 Hanover Street, where, William Langone said, "Three days and three nights, people came in droves. The coffins were open."[3]

In 1977, Governor Michael Dukakis reviewed the case and determined that the men had not received a fair trial. He later declared August 23 of that year as Sacco and Vanzetti Memorial Day, and during the event he read a proclamation that resonated in the minds and hearts of many Italian Americans who believed the two were innocent: "That any stigma or disgrace should be forever removed from Nicola Sacco and Bartolomeo Vanzetti, from their families and descendants, and so, from the name of the Commonwealth of Massachusetts." Issuing the proclamation in English and Italian, Dukakis called on everyone "to reflect upon these tragic events, and draw from their historic lessons the resolve to prevent the forces of intolerance, fear, and hatred from ever again uniting to overcome the rationality, wisdom, and fairness to which our legal system aspires."[4]

In 1997, the Dante Alighieri Society of Massachusetts commissioned a memorial bas relief by Gutzon Borglum, the sculptor who created Mount Rushmore with Luigi Del Bianco, for the presentation of the Sacco and Vanzetti. On the seventieth anniversary of the execution of Sacco and Vanzetti, the plaster casting was formally accepted by Boston mayor Thomas Menino after earlier governors of Massachusetts and mayors of Boston had refused memorial committees in 1937, 1947, and 1957. Mayor Menino commented at the time, "The city's acceptance of this piece of artwork ... is intended to remind us of the dangers of miscarried justice, and the right we all have to a fair trial."[5]

Fred Bourne

Fred Bourne evoked the sense of horror and injustice at the Charlestown Prison when Sacco and Vanzetti were executed.

"The Lights Went Dim in Charlestown"

Like all the young people at the time in 1927, we were all very curious and we went to Charlestown and stood outside the prison walls. It was crowded with people from the North End, because when they threw the switch, the lights would dim the whole prison. So when the lights went drrring!—everybody let up a howl. They were standing outside the gates by the hundreds. You know, electrified. But you could see inside the prison where the cells were. They would go dim. You'd see them go dim once, go dim twice, go dim—they probably give you four or five shots. They [Sacco and Vanzetti] maintained their innocence, and people became very vehement because they claimed the Italians were being picked on like the Irish were being picked on in 1898. [The people felt] they were using them as an example. In the opinion of I'd say even 95 percent of the Italian people, they were innocent. However, they did go to the chair. They were howling against the execution! There were demonstrations. There were appeals. Nobody paid any attention. They just put 'em in the chair and pulled the switch, that's all. And even today, there's still controversy whether or not they were guilty because they were actually convicted on the word of another man. They weren't identified by the people who were held up and shot. They were identified by some bum who went back to Italy, I don't know if he's still alive; he was in the Charles Street Jail and I guess he was implicated and to save himself he became the stool pigeon. Of course, Sacco was a very inoffensive-looking man, and I remember the pictures of him very well, and Vanzetti was a big, husky, mustachioed guy. And this other bum [the stool pigeon] looked like a weasel, which he was. It created—even today amongst the Italians it's quite a controversial subject and it's been years since they were executed. But I did see them dim the lights in Charlestown. And of course, there hasn't been anyone electrocuted in Massachusetts for years, and a lot of them should have been but they aren't.

Phil D'Allesandro

Phil D'Allesandro felt that people of the modern era "don't even have the time to bless themselves and to say thank God for the day."

The Sacco and Vanzetti Procession

When Sacco and Vanzetti were electrocuted at the prison in 1927, the two men were at Langone's on Hanover Street because no undertaker would take them, so Freddy Langone's grandfather [was an undertaker] and he took care of the procession that started on Hanover Street all the way up Tremont Street. The mounted police dispersed the crowds—there were thousands. There were no automobiles in those days, and everything was horse and team and wagon, although the funeral cars were automobiles—I don't know where they got them, but they had them. August 1927 was one of the greatest events in the North End. Of course they didn't believe in our form of government we had here, so they were electrocuted. Governor Fuller was the governor at the time. As we went up towards Boston Commons, they dispersed the crowds, and they continued to the crematorium in Forrest Hills.

Angelo Sardo

"They Couldn't Defend Themselves"

In the early days of immigration here in the North End, it was a difficult life for them. They left the chain around their feet in Italy and here they put it around their necks, the poor devils. Why was this? Because they didn't know how to read or write. So they didn't know how to defend themselves. And that's exactly what happened to Sacco and Vanzetti. Because anyone coming from Europe is considered *istruito* [educated], because intelligence and education is double. So anyone educated, anyone who finished high school, knew how to read and write. The first mafiosi were those here who took advantage of those poor devils who couldn't read or write. Just like they throw people in jail without proof. Maybe it's just based on, "Do this work for me!" "Ah, I'm tired." "Put this one here in prison then." But today, little by little, these people have become educated, they have evolved. *Translated from Italian.*

The Depression in the North End — 15

Guagliò, ci sta 'a leggierà (Young boy, times are tough).
—LOUISE BOMBACE SAVO

On a cold winter morning in 1931, Josie Piccadaci heard a loud knock. Concerned by the sound of an unfamiliar voice, she cautiously opened the door to find a man from the gas company in a khaki uniform and bow tie checking the list of nonpayers. In the wake of the stock market crash, Josie's husband had lost his job as a truck driver, and the meager welfare checks forced them to decide whether to feed their two little children or pay the monthly gas bill. The man struck a polite tone and said, "Lady, I'll have to shut off your gas."

Faced with the prospect of a freezing cold-water flat, Josie answered with a sense of resignation, "Well, if you have to, shut it. I don't have any money." Hearing children's voices in the background caused the man to pause, and he said, "Look, you know what? I think you need it more than they do," and left the gas on.

Many struggling families like the Piccadacis survived the Depression, not only through unexpected acts of kindness from outsiders but also because of the strong neighborhood network, which was based on mutual assistance. Josie described how the North End dealt with the Depression: "Anybody who had anything, shared it. We were close because we were all the same position."[1]

The stock market crash in 1929 unleashed shock waves from Wall Street to the brokerage houses on Devonshire Street. As stockbrokers, speculators, and wealthy investors wailed over their losses, working-class families in poor neighborhoods like the North End were hit the hardest. In 1934, 43 percent of North Enders were unemployed, far more than the overall percentage in the city of 30 percent.[2] Manufacturing occupations suffered the most: in 1930 there were eight thousand people in the shoe and leather industry, a number that was cut in half by 1940; the forty-two hundred workers in the textile industry were diminished by 25 percent; and the clothing industry discharged 30 percent of its workers.[3] North End fishermen had already seen the price of fish decline prior to 1930.

Marguerite Carbone recalled the Depression's negative effect on married women, who were required to leave their jobs.[4] Facing dire economic conditions, North Enders applied time-honored survival skills from southern Italy, where deprivation and limited resources had been a way of life. Over centuries, ingenious women in Italy with limited resources invented what is now called the Mediterranean diet, feeding large families with farm-to-table ingredients. During the Depression, North End women continued the southern Italian tradition of *le cucine della povera gente* (the kitchens of the poor), preparing affordable, healthy meals that sometimes meant the difference between sustenance and hunger.

Although reformist social workers and sociologists believed the North Enders lacked social organization, they overlooked the neighborhood's practice of reciprocal obligation, an ethos transported from ancestral villages that helped them overcome the Depression. For North Enders, helping someone in need reflected the southern code of behavior, expressed as *fare 'na crejanza* (to do a good act). Receiving an act of kindness required the individual to return the act at a later time. In Italian American society, to be considered *ben istruito* (well educated), did not mean advanced degrees but rather being well-mannered, and treating friends and neighbors with civility, kindness, and courtly manners.

William F. Whyte documented the sense of loyalty between the American-born generation of North Enders during the Depression in *Street Corner Society*. He noted the difference between the individualism of the "college boy," who was seeking upwardly mobility and eager to pursue a career outside the neighborhood, and the "corner boy," who sought advancement in terms of personal relations and fidelity to the community rather than in profit and loss.[5]

In 1980, Josie Picadacci, a lifelong North Ender, compared how people helped one another during the Depression to the individualism of the "New Boston."

You don't see people like that anymore. They were really beautiful people, that's all I can say. A lot of the people during the Depression, people were close [in the North End] because everybody was in the same position, no one had more than the other one. So naturally, they were close together; if they could help one another, they would. I know that one time I had a girlfriend that she couldn't even afford an ice cream for her kids, and I would take my kids and her kids to Burden's Drug Store on Hanover Street and buy an ice cream for her kids and my two kids. Maybe I had a little more than her—I knew she couldn't afford it, so I could never buy it for my kids and not for hers, I'd buy it for all of us—and this is how it everybody was. Anybody who had anything would share it. That was so good, that was beautiful. That was the North End at that time.[6]

Marguerite Locchiato

"They Were Really Hungry"

I know people found it hard during the Depression, but if you should ask me, in my house it wasn't. Thank God, I was lucky enough. Like some of us were lucky enough and some of us weren't. During the Depression there were people out of work and they would go out wherever they could get a job, they would go chopping the snow off. I know my brother-in-law did. I don't know what they would pay them, but they'd be around, people that really wanted to work. And they'd go out and make sure that they did work. They weren't like now that these—they go to welfare, they don't care if they work or not because it's coming in. At that time there was no money coming in and people did really suffer. With me, we didn't. But you'd get some people, they did, and they were really hungry, they really did go hungry.

I remember I chummed with a girl and she didn't even have a piece of bread that morning, which was kind of pitiful because it was Depression; she was the oldest, her father wasn't working, and she was about my age and her father had little bits of kids. Her father used to try to do the best he could to go out to try to get most anything to do—they didn't have. A lot of them after that went to the WPA [Works Progress Administration] and all that, and people just would do most anything to get on them projects so that a few dollars would come in so they could eat.

Fred Bourne

Having lived in the North End for many years, Fred Bourne said with a grin, "Nobody hates Italians like Italians."

"She Fed Three-Quarters of Unity Street"

To go through the Depression you had to become a comedian. Not necessarily a thief so to speak, but you had to cut the law a little bit in this respect. College graduates were working on the WPA for thirteen dollars and ninety-five cents a week. In those days the rent in the North [End] was anywhere from twelve to twenty-one dollars, which was a lot of money when you were only getting thirteen dollars and ninety-five cents and you had three or four kids. Now I was in the cab business. Now I'm gonna say this frankly because it is as it is, so you listen. You couldn't get anybody to take a cab. So it was Prohibition, so you sold pints and you took guys to whorehouses because there was three-dollar places and they gave the cab driver a dollar for every guy they brought up, and I had to stand in Scollay Square. So I used to take ten, fifteen sailors a night, and I was making a hundred or better a week when guys were working at thirteen dollars and ninety-five cents. My wife used to feed three-quarters of Unity Street because in those days on welfare you only got six dollars a week. And you had two kids. What could you do with six bucks a week, twenty-four bucks a month, you're paying twelve dollars a month rent and you only had twelve dollars to live on?

Josie Zizza

"Nobody Gave Us Anything during the Depression"

My father lost eighteen thousand dollars during the Depression, he accumulated that much. He had given loan money for mortgages for land. My father had a lot property. And in fact, I didn't know he had willed me forty lots. I lost it. I never paid taxes [and] I lost it. They built that highway in Revere. He had land in Wilmington, Arlington, but he lost it all, eighteen thousand dollars; my father was sick over it. In fact, we were the ones who boosted the money because he used to work hard. And nobody gave us anything. All we had was what my mother and father had, and we worked for it. I got a job with my sister in a paper box factory. And I worked there, I was on piecework there and I was getting a little more money—the hourly wages was thirty-five cents an hour. But it was the same thing, forty-eight hours and I was on piecework. I was an operator of a machine to make paper boxes. It was a little better than the candy place, but I had to work hard to make my dollar. Then I got married and my husband was working—he was making fifteen dollars a week; he was in the Trimont machine company. He was a machinist on a milling machine; they made screws and all that in the machine shop. That's all the men made, fifteen dollars a week. He made very poor pay. And then the factory closed up and he had no benefits, nothing. No one had benefits in those days, nobody. We paid doctor bills as they were, as they came along.

Then my husband got a job as a porter, as a maintenance man in a building on Tremont Street. It wasn't enough for the family, of course not. And I left my baby—he was nine months old, my mother was upstairs and she took care of him—and I went back to work. I had furniture to pay, we got married, we had no money—of course the rent that time, my mother owned the house [so] I only paid fifteen dollars a month rent. But we had to buy coal. It was expensive for us at that time, but we survived. Food was much cheaper. But we didn't have much. We never went anywhere. We didn't have a car. Then I made fifteen, sixteen dollars a week; we used to combine our pay and pay our bills, but we hardly had any money left over. We never went out. In the end I made more money than my husband at Colonial Packing because we had a union there.

Mary Pagliuca

Life during the Depression

I was born January 1914. I emigrated in 1934 from Avellino. My husband take a me over here. He came to Italy, marry me. When I come in to Boston I took a my baby [Linda], nine months old. And after I put my baby to board I went to work. In 1935 I started to work. I was twenty years old. I went to work in the factory, the Pick a Lilly, pack a the fruit in the box. I started at twenty-five cents an hour. I make nine dollars eighty cents a week, I pay a dollar twenty cents carfare. I pay four dollars a week to take care of my baby—my *paesana* [woman from town] took care of my baby—to feed my baby, to buy the milk, make cook *pastina*, eggs, give a piece a meat, give a meatball, she took care, and so all I made was five dollars a week. I go to work for five dollar an[d] eighty cents. Very hard life. You know why? Have to wash a the clothes by hands, I no have a no gas, I have the stove with the coal, light a the stove. I no have a the coal, too much a high, bag a coal, twenty-five cents, so I use wood in the stove. It's a very high at the time. The rent was eight dollars a month. Way down on top of Giro's Restaurant on the corner of Hanover Street and Commercial. Three rooms. No baths, no hot water. And no heat, nothing. I had the bathroom in the hallway, use a two family. I was there almost seventeen years. And no jobs. Everybody work with the welfare, they call the WPA, they take [earn] thirteen dollar a week; the poor people make three days a week and they have thirteen dollars. Three days, thirteen dollars. My daughter, husband, and I lived in three rooms—no heat, no bathroom, no hot water—for eight dollars a month. I used to go down [to] the market and buy potatoes cheap—twenty-five cents for fifty pounds—and carry them home on my head.

My husband worked pick and shovel for thirty-five cents an hour. Everyone was working on the WPA—go in line and get milk and the WPA give a three quart a milk, some bread, some fruit to the poor people. From 1934 to 1936, no money over here, nobody work, everybody go with the welfare. Buy the macaroni, three pounds for ten cents, day-old bread five cents, loaf of bread ten cents, the best pork chops or meat fourteen cents a pound, lamb chops twenty-five cents a pound, but who had money! To buy a leg of lamb would cost me a dollar fifty. I work all week for a dollar fifty and I spend it on that? No, I make macaroni and beans. Every day. Sometimes I used to cook three pounds of spaghetti at night and eat it the next few days because I had no gas. Couldn't buy coal—no money. My husband would look for lumber when the ocean would bring it in. Then we'd use it in the stove.

Giuseppe DiCenso

Giuseppe DiCenso was seventy-nine at the time of our interview. He said so many poor elders were on fixed incomes because there was no social security when they were young workers.

"I Didn't See My Wife for Seven Years"

In 1930, in the Depression, a lot of people with the family here took their family back to Italy; they couldn't support them, there was no work, there was suffering over here. They at least had a house over there, they had a little land, they went back over there. I owned a lot of land there but what are you gonna do working the land? Over here the pay went higher when the war came; over there's no money in the land. In the small towns, they almost all worked on the farm around Sulmona in Abruzzi. Farm work you just make a living, that's all you can make; you can't get no money out of it. You gotta plant the stuff and then take five, six months before you have enough to sell anything, and you just make a living—that's all you can do. We used to eat, we don't suffer too much, but you couldn't buy meat like you do over here— maybe you buy it once every six months—you never had any meat. I like this country because the pay is more high, you make a better living.

See, everybody worked on the farm, and on the farm you'd plant everything and have to wait six months before you'd have any crops to sell, and you'd make just enough to live. And you'd have to work from sunrise to sundown for forty cents a day; the work wasn't steady—they'd call you only when they needed you. All we could do was eat. I used to go back and forth because I had a wife there, stay two or three years, and then come back here for three or four years and go back there. In 1933 I went from a laborer to the engineers union; I was lucky to get in the union and I learned how to run machinery. In 1933 the pay was sixty-five, seventy-five cents an hour. In 1929 we dropped to thirty-five cents an hour! And it was hard to get a job too. From seventy-five cents you drop to thirty-five cents an hour, what the hell are you—can you make with thirty-five cents an hour, with eighteen, nineteen dollars a week? That's all you could bring home. It was tough. The stuff was cheap to eat, but you didn't get any money. When you're young you spend the money, so when you don't get it, where could you spend it? In 1939 I came back here, the war broke out and I couldn't go back to Italy. I didn't see my wife for seven years.

FIGURE 28. Frank Corolla at his shoeshine shop at 347-A Hanover Street, 1981.

Frank Corolla

Frank Corolla was sixty-eight at the time and ran a small shoeshine store on Hanover Street.

Unloading the Freight Cars

I used to unload the semolina sacks for Prince Macaroni; they had fifty-ton freight cars that pulled right into the building. I used to work two or three hours all alone in the car, picking up hundred-pound bags, putting them on a conveyor belt that used to go upstairs. There'd be two men that used to take them off. Then sometimes they'd have bags that used to come in two hundred pounds. I used to be all alone in there—fifty, seventy-five, hundred pounds in the freight car; I used to pick up the two hundred–pound bags like that, carry them the length of the freight car—thirty, twenty, feet, put it on a belt—two men upstairs couldn't keep up with me. Two hundred–pound bags, pick 'em up (laughs). I'd get three dollars to unload a fifty-ton freight car.

Well, three men, we used to split ten dollars, three dollars apiece, two men upstairs; we used to take turns in the freight car, one night apiece. I was working for the WPA, that was extra, and I used to work that on the side. Sometimes we'd get two freight cars, boy, six dollars was a lot of money! After all the years that I worked, you'd think I should be able to take a trip, but I can't because I raised my kids. I gave them the best of everything, you know, well, the best that I could, shoes, whatever I got for them was nothing but the best. I remember my wife, she used to stay up till two, three in the morning ironing their dresses for school the next morning. Now they go with dungarees.

In those days, they didn't have diapers like today. We used to take them, put them on the old scrub boards, wash them by hand, take the clothes, hang them up on the roof so they could get the nice fresh air. Today now we get these, what do you call 'em, Pampers? Put them on, they throw them out the window! Them days there if you didn't scrub the old diapers and put 'em back on—my poor wife, no washing machine, all on the scrub board with six kids, all by hand. The oldest was eight years old; we had twins too. It ain't like today, you buy the milk already in the bottle and you give it to the kid. She used to have to boil and sterilize thirty-two bottles every time she used them, thirty-two bottles a day to feed them. Today everything they feed from jars. Thirty-two bottles every day! She worked hard around those kids.

Frances Lauro

Frances Lauro often baked bread, leaving round loaves on my desk at the senior center.

"Oh, Those Days Were Tough"

My husband used to work in the Necco Confectionary Company—he was a candy cutter. He worked there all his life, for thirty-five years, the poor guy. And what the hell, the time he worked during the Depression, people buy candy? They don't buy no candy, naturally. Forty dollars a week. And I had five small kids in the house I couldn't string along. The poor guy used to tell me, "What do you want me to do? I gave you the check." And that was that. Everything had to come out of that check.

I had no washing machine—I used to wash everything by hand. I had to buy the coal for the stove, which was cold. Couldn't pay the rent, although the rent was low, it was fifteen dollars, of course those days I had two rooms, but oh, I had it tough. I really had it tough. Is that enough to feed five children? It's better now because things are really changing; they get a little more money, [a] little security you know. But in that time, there wasn't. I had the kids, I had no heat, no nothing; we used to have cold stoves. My neighbor told me, "Go to the welfare, they gotta give you something cause you got five small children."

So, me like a dummy I went up there. I said, "Do you know I got five children, all small you know, I can't—at least I need a little coal." "Where is your husband working?" "Oh, he works in Necco Confectionary." So what do they do? Honest to God! They got the phone and they connected to where my husband was working, and they told the person that they'd help when school started. So in other words, they didn't want to give me nothing. And she turned around and said, "Well he's—" I said, "I'm not looking for money, at least give me a little coal to heat the house. You don't want to believe me, come down the house, investigate the condition of the house," I even told them. They didn't come down. But they didn't give me no coal and no money. They said, "Now your husband is still working and soon it'll pick up."

You know, honey, I'm telling you like I'm telling my own children. I went home and I cried all afternoon and I told this woman [my neighbor], "Don't ever tell me to go anyplace!" That day I said I don't want to go no place no more. I had to manage. And I struggled all by myself. God gave me the strength to raise the kids and that was that. They refused me!

A lot of people, they used to get something out of it. Why? Because they used to give [bribe] them with a gallon of wine, or this and that. The old days—this was the old times, Depression times. I didn't get nothing. I went home and don't ever tell me to go anyplace. I managed.

You know what I had to do? I had a little insurance, twenty-five cents insurance. So I owed the boss, the landlord, [he] was very, very nice to me. So he used to come up (raps the table) for the rent money, say, "Frances." Well I'd say, "Gee, right now, you know—" Right away, he used to go away cause I used to know the people so good. You know what I used to do? I used to go up and get the insurance book; I used to call him, and say, "You wanna come with me?" He would say, "All right." I used to cash the check and I used to pay him the three months I owed him. So I used to cash in my insurance check to pay the rent. Sometimes I owed the landlord three months' rent. The insurance wasn't much because it was only twenty-five cents, but it helped me pay the rent.

I used to buy a big bag of flour to make our own bread. I still do it today. I'd fry potatoes and eggs and feed them like that. My husband used to go down [to] the market, and I'm not even ashamed to say it, on Saturday night, and buy the cheapest meat he could find to feed the kids. Nobody died. But they were nice and healthy, I tell you the truth. We were still here. And that's how I used to struggle with my kids. But I mean to say I really struggled. I had no help from nobody, nobody. It was terrible. Oh, those days were tough.

Michelina Manfra

Every month Michelina Manfra divided her meager social security money into piles on her bed, "One for the rent, one for her other bills, and a twenty-five cents for Nino, the *ubriacò* (drunkard) who lived downstairs."

"I Made Clothes from Flour Sacks"

The men were seven months with no work and five months a goin' to work. The work was forty-five cents an hour. You know, with two dollars you buy some meat. We managed. We never go on the city [welfare]. We never go borrow five dollars from somebody else. Make a *pasta e fasule* [macaroni and beans], I make bread in the oven in the morning, and the kids eat. I buy the sack of flour and make a the bloomers for kids, make a the slips, the shirts for my son, yeah, all by hand.

Seamstresses and Factory Workers

Italian American Women at Work

16

> Cu sapiri arripizzari, mai ò munnu poviru pari
> (One who knows how to mend clothes never looks
> poor to the world).
> —ANTOINETTE TOMMASI MAZZOTTA

Although women were traditionally responsible for managing households and raising children, they proved themselves able breadwinners working outside the home to help the family economy. North End women joined production lines in low-paying, labor-intensive work as floor girls, chocolate dippers, and packers in candy factories; separating cotton as pickers in the local mill; food processors in sprawling plants; and seamstresses in the garment industry. A small percentage of professional women filled the upper ranks. Luisa Leveroni and Rose Jannini, the first women doctors in New England, lived in the North End. And Elvira Leveroni and Louise Badaracco achieved international status singing in the San Carlo Opera in Naples and Metropolitan Opera in the United States.[1]

Marguerite Carbone's aunt, a well-known, French-trained modiste, owned a fashion studio on Temple Place and created stylish outfits for her wealthy clients. When she married a prominent hairdresser from the neighborhood, the two became affluent enough to hire local dressmakers for their children's clothes and a milliner who came to their house to fit them for hats.

Garment factory owners benefited from a readily trained workforce of Italian women with prior sewing experience in Italy and some with professional skill as *sarte* (tailors) who designed and finished garments. In 1905, Francesca Corrao, age fifteen, immigrated to Boston from Sciacca on Sicily's southwest coast and worked as a seamstress. Rising at dawn, she left her tenement on Moon Street, turned right on Fleet Street, and headed down Commercial Street to Lewis Wharf, beneath the rumble of passing the Elevated Railway trolleys. Amid the waiting crowd she met her beloved aunt and the two paid a penny to board the "Penny Ferry" to cross the harbor to Lewis Street in East Boston, where they worked in a clothing factory she called "a causuna" (pants). As a seamstress doing piecework, she earned five cents for each finished pair of pants. Francesca described the factory's fast-paced task system, which was introduced by eastern Europeans, in which men and women worked in teams as sewing machine operators, bastors, pressers, finishers and helpers during the various stages of pants production:

> Lu machinista facia li gambe, e mi li dava a mmia. E io ci ncimava tutta la cinta, mittia kempsi—cucia—e ci li dava arreri a lu machinista. Lu machinista li passava a la machina li cucia a la macina, dopu chi li passava a la macina, e mi li passava e mi li dava nautra vota a mmia e io mittia la laina, li buttuna 'cca 'nta pilicedda, tannu c'eranu li tiranti, sai? E mittiva li tiranti 'nta la fly i buttuna 'nta la fly, buttuna di cani e ci li arreri a lu mchinista dava nautra vota o machinista, iddu li passava, nice, tutta finuti E mi li dava nautra vota, c'avia fari li barri sutta, Colchi barri a li vota ora e lisci, si? E chiesti erano li causuna asina chi finia, passava quattru voti 'nta li manu mei.

> The sewing machine operator did the legs and then he handed it me. And I started to sew the whole waist, made the outline, tracing it with kemps—coarse wool—then I handed it back to the sewing machine operator. Then the operator sewed it on the machine, and after he passed it through, he gave it back to me again. Then I sewed the lining, sewed the buttons (on the fly—this was before zippers), then the trouser snaps (for suspenders), oh, there were a lot of those snaps, you know? Then I handed it back to the operator. Then he passed it through the machine, and it came out all finished and nice. Then he passed it back to me again, and I had to sew the hems, and that was your finished pair of pants. It went back and forth from me to the operator four times before it was finished!

Like many North End women, when Francesca "mi maritavi, e accumminciai a accattari figghi" (married and had children), she stayed home to raise the children, but she brought *causi* (pants) from the factory and finished them at home, "a la casa e cusia dintra, mi purtava quattro o cinque para di causi e li cusia, e ci li purtava finuti" (I brought four or five pair of pants to sew at home, and I finished them there).[2]

Mary Pasquale

"Sapissi Qualche Guagliotta?"
(Might You Know of Any Young Girl?)

There was about five or six chocolate factories in the North End; Daggetts was one. I was a chocolate dipper at Liggetts and Schraffts and Lovell and Covel. When I had anemia, I took time off from Schraffts. It was right before the bridge [on the corner on Kinney Square] and they had a beautiful factory with a hospital. And I was sitting in the doorway on Prince Street where I used to live. Down come this man that owned a candy factory on Snow Hill Street and his name was Angelo Cataldo, they lived in Medford. He says to my mother, "I'm looking for girls to dip, and uh, sapissi qualche guagliotta [might you know of any young girl]?" My mother says, "Eh a mama," my mother says—that's how she used to talk—"Eh a mama, figliama è malatta qua, tenne na malattia, ma essa sape tutti chillo che addà' fa [my daughter is sick right here, but she knows how to do everything]." I said to my mother, "Ma, but why did you tell him that?" She says, "Well so he'll know you can go." So he [Cataldo] said, "Even if she comes three hours a day. I'll give anybody a bonus if they can get me one girl to work."

So [I] lived here at the end of Snow Hill—all I had to go was across the street, up three buildings and there was the factory inside his own building. My sister says to me, "Marie you can dip a little, why can't you go?" I says, "I don't want to go." I went there and I stayed four months. He got rid of the forelady and I was forelady for eleven years. [Then] we moved from there—he got a place up on Fulton Street and he opened a big factory, Liberty Chocolate, around the First World War, and I was seventeen or eighteen and I was the forelady there. But the girls used to like me. If you're a forelady, you got to treat the girls right.

Josie Tranquillo

The Candy Factory in 1914

I was only nine years old in 1914; I used to scrub wooden floors on my hands and knees, scrub my own clothes, never forgot. I used to go to the second grade and I only had one dress to wear—I used to wash it at night, wear it the next morning. I went to work with my mother when I was twelve years old. She took me to the candy factory on the corner of Endicott Street and Causeway Street. It is where Polcari's is now, and there used to be a candy factory; I got four-fifty a week, for five days and a half. And we worked until twelve o'clock on Saturday. I used to get the dates on a big board, open them up, roll them up, and throw them in the sugar. Then they used to put them in boxes.

Marguerite Locchiato

"Differentials, Bonuses, and Orchestras at Schraffts"

In 1924, when I was fourteen, they took me out of school and I went to work at Schraffts, right over the bridge on North Washington Street. I was a floor girl and was getting eight dollars and eighty cents a week. I worked from eight o'clock in the morning till twelve o'clock, I'd come home for dinner, I'd go back and start at one o'clock till five o'clock. Then I'd have to go a half a day to continuation school because I wasn't sixteen years old. You weren't allowed to go on a machine, anywhere near a machine, until you were sixteen years old. It was a good place to work—it was nice benefits there and it was very clean. When we were fourteen years old in Schraffts they used to have an orchestra, the people who worked there played instruments, and during lunch hour they had a stage and a great big dining room that faced the water, the ocean. They'd play from twelve to one o'clock and they'd dance if they wanted to dance. They would give us cocoa and coffee, you could have that for nothing. Of course, us kids we'd have fifteen extra minutes of dancing—we'd have a ball. At Christmas time they would have that stage decorated beautiful with all kinds of boxes—they'd have them on display—like "The Gold Chest" and "The Rose" and "The Miniatures." And it would make such a beautiful display, and you could get the best box for fifty cents a pound. Then when I was sixteen years old, I got another job; I would start from eight o'clock till five o'clock, but we had to work Saturdays until a quarter to one— we worked about forty-six hours.

When I was sixteen [1926], I got nine-thirty-five. We worked on a bonus and a differential. You would give them a certain amount of work and over that you would get a bonus. The bonus was for the quality and the differential was for the production if you gave them a little more. The girls used to dip and they would put it in a cooler, and it would take just so much time to dry. And I would just slip [the candies] out and put them in trays, pack it in trays, put my number on it, and then I would load it on the truck, label the truck and it would go out. That truck would be checked, and it would go into the packing room, and they would pack it in from there. And say if I made sixteen dollars, I would get three dollars differential, that was nineteen dollars, and three or four dollars bonus, and at that time that was a lot of money, you know, in Schraffts—it would bring me up to twenty-three, twenty-four dollars a week.

We got paid for every holiday. After five years you'd get two weeks' paid vacation; if you worked there two years, you'd get a week. And our vacation would be the first two weeks of July, it would be a shutdown—it was always like that. We stayed there until 1928, and then they moved to Sullivan Square; they built their own plant there and I was one of the first to go there. And I stayed there for fifty-one years. That was the only job I had, from fourteen to sixty-five, from 1924 to 1965.

Mary Pagliuca

One of Mary Pagliuca's favorite sayings was "Uno Dio, uno marito" (One God, one husband).

"I Only Saw Him Once a Week"

I used to get up at five in the morning [and] make lunch for me, my husband, and my daughter. My husband worked for Stop and Shop. I left at six-forty in the morning for Everett—work began at seven-thirty at Hoods Milk (formerly Dolly Madison), and I was a forelady on salary for thirty-four years. So I'd come home from Everett by five-fifteen at night—I'd go upstairs, eat a little. My husband worked nights, so I would only see him on Sundays. For twenty years I saw my husband once a week, on Sundays. How do you like that? I make a money, ma [but] I sweat a blood! Once a week, every Sunday.

Can you believe what a life I had, this country? When he wanted to tell me something, he'd write a little note and leave it on the table. When I came home in between jobs I'd read his letters he would leave for me: "I did this for you today," I paid the bill or I cashed the check, "I went shopping for you, I put it in the refrigerator." Then he'd write, "If you need anything, before you leave, put it down in a note for me." So in the mornings, before I left for work, I used to write back, "Dear Tony, please do this for me," or "Tony, please buy me a loaf of bread." And he'd buy it for me. He would just be coming home at seven in the morning and I'd leave at six-forty. He'd sleep till eleven, get up and go shopping for me, rest up, and go back to work. When I'd see him on Sunday, poor man, he'd be so glad to see me—he'd hug and kiss me.

Mary Pasquale

Mary Pasquale's father started the Society of San Euplio, the patron saint of Trevico.

Stitching at Leopold Morse

The First World War I knew how to run my machine, my home machine, the machine that you run with your feet like that, but not an electric one. So my girlfriend, she knew how to run a power machine and she me got a job at Leopold Morse down in the South End to make uniforms. She said, "Marie, don't worry, I'll be sitting near you and I'll supervise you." I got the knack of it, the foot control, but I didn't know you had to wind the bobbin while you were working. I stopped working and I was winding the bobbin. Lo and behold the inspector came in, he looked around, he says, "What are you doing girlie?" I says, "I'm winding my bobbin." "Oh," he says, "How long have you been running a power machine?" "To tell you the truth," I says, "I didn't. My girlfriend told me to fake it, that she will [supervise me] and she'll teach me how." He says, "You sound like an honest girl—can you sew by hand?" I says, "Yes." I says, "I'll tell you why I know. I'm a very good stitcher because when I used to go to the sisters' school, you had to make a sample. They gave you a cloth, make a sample—back stitch, running stitch, chain stitch, feather stitch, button-hole stitch. So I got number one." So he says, "The girl will teach you how to finish the lining and the sleeves and the lining on the bottom of the uniform." When he looked at it he gave me a puncher, a tape measure, and a pencil [and] I had to take care of all those Greek and Sicilian people that used to sew by hand. And I became an inspector and a forelady.

Theresa D'Alelio

Theresa D'Alelio described Hull Street as "the Beacon Street of the North End; when the Jews lived there and Italians could not. As the Jews moved out, it became home to the Genoese, known as the Italian Jews."

"Sometimes We'd Go on Strike at Boston-Made Dress"

I went to the first year of high school, then I left when I was sixteen and went to work for eight dollars a week. I gave my mother something [and] I'd buy my own clothes. I felt I wanted to go to work. I was sorry I left—I could have gone to school. But my parents were angry I left. I went to work as an inspector of dresses in a dress place. The bosses were nice but sometimes we'd go out on strike. We used to like that (laughing). They'd call you up on a holiday and say, "Come in, we're busy." One Thanksgiving, I'll never forget, the boss came right down, he says, "Oh I need—some work has to go out, some dresses have to go out, please come in." My father was there, he said, "What do you mean taking my—!"

The boss said, "No, no, this is a holiday, they can't come in, but I need them." So we felt bad for him and we went in for a couple of hours. I used to be on the floor of the Boston-Made Dress [factory]; it was on Kneeland Street near Chinatown. We worked there about five, six years, but then on account of the strike, they tried to beat the union. So they moved to Waltham, near the railroad tracks, but they [the union] followed us there and got in there. I got up to eighteen dollars a week when we got the union. I used to enjoy going to work. I was in charge of all the girls; I'd give out the work in bundles and the girls wanted piecework but I wasn't [doing that]. I was giving out the work mostly out of the office, making up timecards. And they'd come to me for the work. They made good money, but I was on salary—I could only make so much a week. He wouldn't put me on piecework because I used to inspect the work.

Josie Tranquillo

"I Brought My Work Home"

I used to get up at five o'clock in the morning when I lived on the top floor on 28 Fleet Street; the sun would rise and come right in my bed. So I'd sit on the bed and start embroidering stockings. I used to make arrows on stockings—they had this style in 1921 when I got married. I used to embroider, I used to have a plastic egg in the silk stocking and stretch it, make the stem first, go up in the middle with the stem, and sometimes we had to make two colors—ten stitches one color, go back with the other color of thread, ten stitches of another color—and then we'd have to make the arrow on the top, then we had to make an edge like a tree at the bottom. I used to make a penny a minute, sixty cents an hour. Nobody used to make sixty cents an hour at the time. My husband used to make less there than I even did. A young girl, imagine that, so much money, hurray! I did that until I was seven months along with my baby, after all what can I do? (laughing) I didn't want to stop working. That's why I went to the factory—Massachusetts Knitting Mills on 1000 Washington Street, I used to work for—I used to go there, bring my homework home, and I used to do it and I used to bring it back to the factory. I worked as far as seven months along—that's all—no more after that.

Lena Albanese

A Floor Girl at Starr Confectionary

I went over to a candy place on Fulton Street, the Starr Confectionary, a small place, but at least he [the owner] got along [and] he paid his people—the dippers and all. And once in a while when I had nothing to do I go down there to see how they dipped the candy. And I was saying, "Oh, you do it like this, like that, and you put it on the board, take the boards off, and pile them up about twenty high, fifteen high." And I liked it all right, I liked the forelady who was there and the owner, he was always with us. In there we worked from eight to five, and when we started to work everything was all ready and all we had to do was start working. I was a floor girl, and anytime I didn't have anything to do on the floor I'd do other things like pack the five-pound candy boxes or the fancy boxes, put [in] a piece of each one [kind]. And that's what we did all the time.

We used to bring the boards to the dippers. They were in another room. Or either if they were in the same room with us—because the five-pound packers were there with the fancy packers on that side of the building, and on this other side we had all the girls that were dipping. And we'd take the boards and bring them to them. But we had to clean the boards out, put the clean paper on, and give them to the ladies. And they would dip their candy and put them on there. See? That's what we were doing.

Lena Albanese

When Lena Albanese's husband proposed marriage, her only stipulation was "that I stay in the North End."

Working in a Cotton Mill in Charleston

I went to work at fourteen years old in 1914 because there was a place in Charlestown, on Mystic Street, they would take fourteen-year-old girls to work in the cotton mill. So I used to go over there; we used to go on foot, we never used to take the bus—all we had to pay was five cents but we never took it. We walked past the Charlestown Bridge, go into Charlestown, and go down Mystic Street. And there was the factory. We used to have a lot of fun though. They had a lot of this yellow stuff in one pile in Charlestown. Well that was the factory right there in Charleston, right on the side of it. Even if you went by streetcar, you'd see that pile and you'd say, "Well, that's the cotton factory." There was four girls of us, three came from Prince Street, and me from Sheafe Street, and my mother. My brother was bigger then; he was beginning to go to kindergarten. That left me off that I could go to work.

We had to be to work at seven o'clock up until five o'clock at night. We had an hour for lunch and that was it. I was working on the press. We would fill up the baskets of cotton and we'd throw it on the press and they would make bales out of it, to a certain amount. The fellas used to be downstairs, and that's what we were doing all day long. And the ladies were picking the cotton, all different kinds of cotton. They'd put each one separate, and if there was any straw or anything that wasn't supposed to be in with the cotton they would take it out. And that's what we did all day. On a Saturday we worked a half day, and we worked five eight-hour days and a half. In the afternoon we would come home and do our shopping, my mother and I, because I was the second oldest. We made four dollars and fifty cents a week for forty-four hours. So you see that wasn't much. We went to school a half day at the continuation school on Legrange Street here in town and they would take off that half day from our pay. So we used to come home with three dollars or less a week. They weren't paying much at that time. I worked in the cotton factory until I was sixteen years old.

Mary Arigo Ventola

Mary Arigo Ventola was born in 1903 and noted, "Everyone had midwives in those days—there were two on Endicott Street."

Life in the Candy Factories

We had to go to work, fourteen years old, take you right out of school and go to work! My first job was candy. Oh, I remember the molasses tank broke that time—I was working—I was just starting to work at that time! Oh, I musta been fifteen, sixteen years old then. Believe me, we hadda work, not like the kids of today, they handle all that money! My two grandchildren yesterday had five dollars in their hand! We never had it. My kids never had it! Look at the toys they buy, these kids today. Sixty-five dollars! My kids didn't even have a ball! They're spoiled today, really, really spoiled. That's all the jobs we had. I was stupid—I had to go to the candy factory! I didn't get a chance to finish my education in school, no.

My first job was at Touraine's at Community Square. My sister was the forelady and she took me in there. I worked in a candy factory. At the beginning, we made thirteen dollars a week, eight hours a day, five days a week. Dippers and all, everybody made that. Now try to get dippers! No dippers. They got machines, you know the machines? And they put the candy on the machines. And the chocolate drips on it. And there's a thing that makes the mark [swirl]. Where you gonna get dippers today? All the old people were dippers, and then who is going in a candy factory today? Nobody. They don't know how. It was cheap. Well that was it. I had to stop working. I wish I could still work, not for the money, just to be with the people. It's so depressing to be alone.

I worked at Liggett's. It's not there no more. It's a storage house on North Street now. Then Theroux. Then I got married and I had stay home for the kids. Then I went back to work. Most of the people in the North End worked in the candy factories. My last job was with Howard Johnson; I was making forty, fifty dollars a week about nine years ago, now they're making over a hundred dollars in the candy places. Now they have a factory in Quincy out there, but they were in Boston.

Rose Pesce

Working at Deran's

I worked in a candy place here in the North End for fourteen, fifteen years. I really liked it. The pay really wasn't that much. At the time it wasn't bad considering the time cause this was thirty-five years ago [mid-1940s]; the pay wasn't that great but it wasn't bad either. It was eight to five, and we'd go in a half a day on Saturdays. They supposedly paid overtime, but how many times it got to the point when the forelady asked and we felt it wasn't worth it. Yes, they paid you overtime, but when you figured it out, what they took out of your income tax, we said, "We're coming in for four hours, what are we getting out of it?" It was four hours. What they took away from you for the income tax, it wasn't worth it, so we—she used to come, the forelady, she was Italian—and ask us—she knew. So [she] used to come by us on a Friday night, "Do you want to work?" We used to say, "We don't want to work no more on Saturdays, it doesn't pay." I told her, "For me, forget about it, I don't want to work no more—it doesn't pay!" For the income tax, it was like we worked for nothing that Saturday. It was a dollar, a dollar and a quarter an hour; you couldn't make less than the minimum. We worked and we used to ask for a raise. And Madonna mi! We'd get together, you know—we had a Jewish boss.

To get a raise was like pulling teeth. And we used to say, "We're going to quit." And then he would give us, say, "Well, I'll give you a penny raise." And of course, not that we were satisfied—we figured that's it, and that was it. Every time we'd ask for a raise he'd give us about a couple of pennies' raise, you know, two cents more. It was hard work. We felt we didn't get what we deserved for the work we put out in this place in the North End. The place was nice, we enjoyed ourselves—the people, we were like one family—but as far as the work, even up to today when we talk about it, we go, "He took our blood," we say, like in other words, we worked like dogs and we got peanuts for the way we worked.

It was packing candy, chocolates, but we produced a lot of work! But he didn't give us the wages he should have given us. No union, [so] they get away with it. We wanted to join the union; we used to have, like, not arguments, but the girls, the workers, we'd get together and say, "We want—we'll ge—" but then before you know it, they'd back out. And how could you do?

They must have been afraid, don't ask me. How many times we'd get together and say, "Let's walk out, he needs the workers." But, yeah, yeah, yeah, we do all the talking, in other words, not fighting, but we'd be—"As long as we say what we're gonna do—you're gonna be behind us?" But come to find out, "Well gee, I can't do it." And "I can't afford to do it, what if he lays us off for a couple of days? I can't afford to lose a day." And it would never work out. But if he had a union of course he would have had to pay, like Daggett's did at the time, a dollar thirty-five.

This candy place, Deran's, it was a small place and we were like one family, a hundred or so, on Medford Street, right on North Washington Street. Our wages in Deran's, the Medford Street candy factory, were nowhere near that. It wasn't much. We used to argue—we were mostly Italians, maybe a couple of Jewish workers, a couple of American or whatever you want to say, even the men who worked in the candy room, Tony and this Joe, they were Italian. His two nephews worked with him [the boss] in the office—they did the shipping. No Italian immigrants—they were born here but our mothers and fathers were born in Italy, girls like that. A few Italian women too, but there weren't that many at that time; there weren't that many immigrants as come as today, not that many. We'd argue but then it would be all over. There was no discrimination, nothing like he's making more than me or I'm making more than you, no, no. Because we didn't have no union anyway. This place had no union.

Josie Zizza

Generosa "Josie" Zizza was the president of a senior citizen organization and often represented the North End as an elderly advocate at meetings around the Boston area.

Working in a Chocolate Factory in 1928

I went to work in a candy factory, D'Orlando Chocolate on Portland Street. It was an Italian company. And I did hard work—I was a floor girl, what else could I do? I didn't have any education. I started working when I was fourteen years old. I was a floor girl in a candy factory. It was my job to bring boards to the ladies who dipped chocolates by hand, you know, whatever they wanted. It was hard work. In those days, we got thirty cents an hour. We used to work all day Saturdays too. There was no such thing as time and a half on a Saturday. No, no. No such thing. We worked forty-eight hours a week. There was no such thing—you couldn't ask for a raise, are you kidding? Unless the boss really liked you and you had to work a long time. There was a lot of piecework. The dippers were all on piecework. How many boards of chocolate they dipped, they'd get so much. Everything was piecework in those days. There were no unions. There were no strikes; we just worked the way we had to. They worked us to death, believe me.

Josie Picadacci

"No Woman Is Worth One Hundred Twenty-Five Dollars a Week"

After I was married, my kids were old enough, and I—well, I used to tell my kids, "I'm gonna get a job." They didn't care if I worked or not because my kids were older now. And my husband wasn't working. So why can't I help, you know? But the thing was, they thought, where would I get a job? And I'd tell my husband, "I'm going for a job." And they'd all laugh at me: "You're going for a job? What are you gonna do?" He'd say, "Well, you know, what are you going to do?" I said, "I don't know but I'm going for a job." But I fooled them.

So I just happened to pick up the paper and I saw a job on North Washington Street, packing all kinds of stuff like nails and hooks and hangers and things like that. When I got home I said, "I got a job!" They were all laughing, "You got a job? Doing what?" And I told them. I said, "OK, you said I wouldn't get a job." I went to work and worked there for three years, and finally I used to teach them, that's how good I was at it. Then I said—well, I wanted a raise. They were giving me a dollar an hour. So I wanted a raise and they said, "Oh no, we can't give you a raise." So I says, "Well I'm going for another job." So like I say, I never wanted to stitch, but I said, "Well, let me go looking for another job and see what I can do, if I can't get another one I can always go back this way." So at twelve o'clock instead of going to lunch, I went looking for this other job on the other side, the Hoffman building, just before the Charlestown bridge.

Well anyway, I went to this place and I started stitching. First, I started taking threads out, that's the first thing we start. And then we started to stitch.

And we made the baby clothes, the baby sleepers, you know the sleepers with the zippers, things like that. Well that's what we started to make. Well, then they got a machine, and the forelady and I got so friendly, like I knew her for years, you know, you just get acquainted so easy and so fast. She was very good to me. And finally there was this big machine for making slippers. So she says, "Jo, why don't you try it?" I say, "No," I says, "a big machine like that, three spools of thread"—I got so scared, I said no.

So anyway she convinced me, she said, "No, try it." So I tried it. And I loved it. And I caught on to it fast, you know, that I was making a lot of money. And at that time, a hundred and twenty-five dollars was a lot of money! So that's what I was making, and we did that for a while; there were two of us doing it. And we made that kind of money for a few months. But then the Jewish boss says, "No, that's too much money for women. No, no, you can't make that kind of pay." Even though we were putting out the work. They didn't want to know, they just didn't care.

Well, finally, they told us they were going to discontinue it. So they would get some girls and do it on a Saturday because I wouldn't go in on a Saturday [so I could be with my children]. And they would get these girls to work on a Saturday [and] they did such a terrible job that they just had to stop doing it because they had to throw them away. See, there was a knack to doing it. It just so happened that I caught on fast, you know some things you just can and some things you can't. So they tried to, you know, they wanted me to show them, [and] the boss says to me, "Show me how you do it, tell me what you're doing." And I said, "I can't tell you, well I mean you have to watch me." So he would watch me, but it didn't do any good because they couldn't do it. It was just something that just was—it was funny, but that's the way it was.

Mary Pagliuca

Mary Pagliuca recalled the immigrants believing the streets in America were paved with gold. Describing the stamina required in labor-intensive production jobs in the 1930s and 1940s, she wiped her brow and exclaimed, "I sweated blood to make a dollar."

Working Day and Night

When I first came from Italy in 1933 there were no jobs. My first job was with the Dolly Madison Company, and I went to work for twenty-five cents an hour. I worked a half day on Saturday for eleven dollars a week. I used to pack raspberry pie, mincemeat pie, apple pie, and pie fillings. During the war we packed for the government. Even though sugar was rationed, we used to have all we needed. Five hundred pounds of meat I used to boil in a thousand-pound kettle and grind it in a big machine—I'd put in raisins, apples, sugar, a little vinegar, and pack it into ten-pound cans and send it overseas. I used to send peaches, marmalade, apricots, prunes, strawberry jam—we used to send four, five hundred cases at once. First I'd put in one hundred pounds of sugar in the kettle, then ten gallons of vinegar, ten gallons of honey, for every hundred pounds of meat. The machine would mix it up and the cans were cleaned by machine and filled up with a hose connected to the hopper on the kettle. Then the women would put them in cases. My boss liked me because I could weigh the grease, the raisins, the brown sugar, honey—I used to be able to stay on my feet.

FIGURE 29. Mary Pagliuca at the Hood factory, 1938.

Working at Night

While I worked my day job, I worked the night shift from six in the morning to two in the afternoon at the Boston Sausage Provision Company. There were three shifts going all the time in 1945, 1946, and there were about seven hundred people working. I worked in the skinless meat department for two dollars and seventy-five cents an hour. I had to take the skin off the frankfurters, cut the skin off with a little knife, put my name on the box, close the box, put my number on it, send it down the belt, the girl take a my number and put it in a box. She'd [the forelady] watch her watch—"It's nine o'clock! Stop the belt!" Then they called all the numbers out by the box numbers, "Thirteen! Fourteen! Fifteen! Number seven, you're four boxes short!" So when you get a the pay, less money. I had to make a hundred pounds an hour. I had to make ten boxes an hour or they'd take it out of your pay. Sometimes I'd make fourteen or fifteen an hour and I'd give my extras to some of the slower women—sometimes they fell asleep during the night shift.

When my foreman, Nick Argiro, found out about it, he got mad at me and he told me, "Look, Maria, you work very hard—I want you to keep every box for yourself. And next week I'm giving you a ten-cent raise." At first, I didn't want the raise—it didn't look good getting more money than the other ones. Then one night the superintendent came to me and said, "Maria, I'm giving you a dollar seventy-five an hour—you're worth three dollars an hour—you do the work of four people." I was never a box short. I never fell asleep. I wanted to make money [and] I was young.

I retired crippled. During the day I worked in dampness [and] in the night I worked in the freezers with the frankfurters—I took care of the skin, it was all ice pipes. During the day I worked with Hood's Milk [Company] packing the fruit in the boxes—it was all water and steam and everything—all sweat, it was damp. Now I retired at fifty-four years old, all crippled, got arthritis, bum heart, everything.

Michelina Manfra

Michelina Manfra compared America to Italy, saying, "Quando piglia la checka, se tu il padrone [When you get your paycheck, you're the boss], but if you go to Italy without money you wouldn't even get *pasta e fasule* [beans and macaroni]! I would like to go back to my old church to hear the Mass, the music, but I wouldn't stay a minute longer."

Life as a Picker at Bay State Lobster

I was a picker for twenty-nine years at Bay State Lobster. La vita è tough la dinto [life was tough in there]. We used to work piecework, lotta time we work all day, lotta time we a two hours, lotta time you go in and you come out, it was a no busy. First I picked lobsters, then crabs, the shrimps, too. I rolled the lobster legs in a machine—you know who teach a me? Richie Perez, he was little boy working there. But I never wanna pack the fish. I wore boots like a man and rubber apron, oof! Now everything change, now they have breaks, an hour lunch and if it's busy, work stops at four. Before they gave you nothing. When you pick a the crabs, there was meat in there and you'd spend a lot of time, and I would make one pound and put it in the can. The other people would be jealous: "Hey, you made one pound!" But I wasted two hours! I made one pound for ten cents of meat. You pick crabs, in the can, one pound, ten a cents the boss pay you, ten a cents a pound, that's all. If the crab was a big, a little better. I say the truth—I like a work nice eh quiet, nice eh gentle, not be rough, no be put the shells in, take a my time. I no make a too much, lotta time I make a one pound in one hour. They asked, "What you make, how much you make?" I used to make three, four, five dollars a week. One time I make a ten dollars, and they gave me the ten dollars, and with the ten dollars in my hand and all the way down [to] the market, "I make a ten dollars! I make a ten dollars!" Ten dollars, you know, you buy a lotta stuff. I went right to the meat store on North Street where the Madonna del Soccorso is, and with three, four dollars I bought so much meat, put it in a basket, put in on my head. We had no refrigerator, no icebox, no nothing; in the wintertime we put it in a box on the fire escape.

Making It in the North End
Italian American Men at Work

17

> Binidici Signuri sta jurnata
> Falla léggia comu 'na passiata
> Guida li me pinsera mentri travagghiu
> Pigliami' ntempu prima ca sbagliu
> Tenimi luntanu dalla lagnusia
> Dammi rispetto ppi ccu sia
> Calma li me nervi e dammi paci
> quannu iè fari soccu nun mi piaci
> Bless this day, Lord
> Make it easy as taking a walk
> Guide my thoughts as I work
> Intercede in time before I make a mistake
> Keep me away from laziness
> Make me respect others
> Calm my nerves and give me peace
> When I have to do something I don't like.
> —ANONYMOUS, Sicilian worker's prayer

In 1910, 65 percent of Italian men in the North End were listed as unskilled.[1] Chain migration, and the chain of housing that resulted from relatives who found work for the immigrants, supplied the labor force of stonemasons, ditch diggers, hod carriers, mortar mixers, bricklayers, and craftsmen to fill the growing need for road construction and erecting buildings and for cheap labor on the production lines of shoe, leather, and textile factories. Some with marketable skills resettled in other cities as stone cutters, garment workers, shoemakers, stonemasons, and quarrymen.[2] Many transported a formidable work ethic rooted in centuries of hard manual labor.

In *Conversazioni,* the authoritative sociologist Danilo Dolci asked a Sicilian laborer what he considered a good worker. He answered, "Se un uomo non lavora non puo portare mai da mangiare alla famiglia" (If a man doesn't work, he can't feed his family). When asked if there were any other reason to work, he said, "Anche per la dignità, un uomo è lavoratore" (A man works also for dignity).[3]

Once a young shepherd, Angelo Santomaggio had tended the family's flock of sheep, often moving his herd *a pascià* (to graze) at the foot of Monte Velino near his home in Avezzano in Abruzzo. He described the philosophy of work for the southern man: "Nella vita ci sono solo tre cose: rispetto, onore, e la nobilità di lavoro" (In life there are only three things: respect, honor, and the nobility of work).[4]

As pick and shovelers, Italians soon discovered the economic and social reality of the New World when building the streets they thought had been paved in gold. In *Christ in Concrete,* Pietro DiDonato's authentic narrative of the working man captures the ethos of Italian American bricklayers. Based on his working experiences, DiDonato invites the outsider to enter the unrewarded world of rugged workers whose grit and determination under terrible conditions helped build America, earning them the respect of their peers as protectors and good family providers. When the scaffold breaks, plunging Geremio to his death, his mind immediately turns to his children and he cries in agony: "Brothers, what have we done? Ahhh-h, the children of ours!"[5]

Many Italians traded the pastoral rhythms of the Old Country for the factory whistle of the industrialized city, where honor and the nobility of work could only go so far. They would quickly learn how to navigate and survive in the new society, which had its share of schemers like Charles Ponzi, unscrupulous *padrone*s (bosses) who cheated them out of wages; real estate agents, insurance agents, and slumlords who exploited them; and bankers who pilfered their savings accounts.

Nicholas Dello Russo, a lifelong North Ender whose grandfather immigrated in 1896, described the neighborhood's shadow economy as a necessary alternative to survive:

> The immigrants quickly learned that they were on their own. They could maybe trust a few close friends or family, but everybody else was out to

exploit them. Money was tight because America was on the gold standard, which kept a limit on the amount of cash in circulation. When North Enders could not make ends meet because of sickness or loss of paychecks from gambling, money lenders were always ready to lend cash, at a price. People lived day to day and needed cash to pay the weekly rent, buy food and clothes for the family. If a man got sick, or lost his paycheck gambling, his wife would have to somehow come up with the cash needed for day to day life. She couldn't go to a bank. Family and relatives could and did help as much as they could.[6]

Jane Jacobs reported the reluctance of bankers to issue loans for housing rehabilitation because they considered the North End a slum. In response, the neighborhood devised its own solution: upgrades were subsidized by local businesses and housing earnings and the skilled work for renovations was bartered between residents and relatives.[7] To make ends meet, some booked numbers or sold bootleg liquor and women bartered for food and clothing.

Nicola Dello Russo arrived alone from Chiusano di San Domenico, near Avellino in 1896, and like many found the only work available for the unskilled as a day laborer. In the rough-and-tumble Waterfront section on Lewis Street, Nicola met a tavern owner nicknamed Zachero who took a liking to the ambitious young man and allowed him to sleep on the floor in exchange for doing odd jobs and keeping the place clean. In 1919, he sold the tavern to Nicola, who with his wife, Carmela, had ten children by the mid-1920s. Since the small tavern and restaurant, which seated only twenty people, could not support the family, Nicola relied on his North End street smarts to survive. Besides some bootlegging, the most profitable venture made was moneylending. Loaning money to his friends and business associates resulted in a return stream of income from their restaurants, food shops, and construction companies.

From his profitable business in the North End's shadow economy, Nicola bought a two-family house in Medford on a double lot, thus propelling his family into the middle class. Retaining the agrarian lifestyle of the Old Country, he set aside a half acre for Carmela to plant a small truck farm, with a greenhouse for planting seedlings in the winter. In a setting reminiscent of the Italian countryside, Carmela and Nicola planted apple, fig, and peach trees; built an extensive grape arbor, chicken coop, and rabbit hutch; and tended a flock of ducks that roamed the property. Nicola Dello Russo, who had arrived penniless and homeless to the North End, realized the American dream for his sons, not only sending them to college and one to medical school, but also backing them with capital to start their own businesses.

FIGURE 30. Al Mostone giving a tour of the Old North Church, 1981.

Al Mostone

"We Didn't Have Unemployment"

Laborers could only work from the month of April to December. On construction work, once the snow came down, all outside construction work stopped—it isn't like today, they continue on today, but in those days, it stopped, came right to a dead stop. We had no welfare. We couldn't apply for anything like that. We had no unemployment so it was their objective to make sure that they saved enough to carry the rents through the wintertime; they'd have the coal in the cellar, and they'd buy a barrel of flour, a sack of beans, and whatever else could be kept in the house. Almost every construction family would do that where the husband worked in construction work.

So, say the husband died in the house and they had four or five kids—they'd never go for welfare. And if my mother had something in the house, she'd say, "Al, take this over to Mrs. so-and-so's house and give her that," [and] somebody else would give her something else, until she was able to go out and get something for herself. See, but she was never left alone because in the tenement houses we'd have six, seven—the house I lived on North Street had twelve families living in one building—and we were practically one family. And if you needed any assistance or if we even thought you needed any assistance, it was given to you. What little we could, you got it. I don't know why in those days they were that close, I can't figure it out. Today they're not that way—you don't know the people up on the second floor.

FIGURE 31. Nunzio DiMarino, 1980.

Nunzio DiMarino owned a successful tomato business on Commercial Street on the Waterfront but lost it when the Boston Redevelopment Authority took his property during redevelopment.

Nunzio DiMarino

Laying Bricks, Paying off Mayor Curley

I came to Boston by myself in 1919 on the *Madonna*, the French line, when I was seventeen; it took twenty-eight days to get here and I went right to work. I was [a] bricklayer and you had to work ten hours a day. You had to! What are you gonna do? You take it or leave it and they send you home, it ain't like today [when] you can go to collect the money. At that time you couldn't go collect. There was nothing; if you were a loafer, you had nothing, that was it. I worked in Boston for six, seven months, then I went to work in construction for five years with the Ferullo Company. At that time in the 1920s there was all hourly prices, thirty-five, forty, fifty cents an hour; sixty cents was the top man, but you had to be really good to get sixty cents. You had to be a good man to get forty, fifty cents.

They [Ferullo Company] had an office on North Square; they did a lot of pipe laying, sewer work. We never used to stay in one spot all the time—we used to go to Vermont, New Bedford, Providence, to Connecticut, Vermont, Maine—we used to go all around. We used to hire a house and we used to cook ourselves. You could get the job easy. Then I got married in 1925 and I didn't want to go out of town. Then I started working here in construction in Boston, and my first job was building the dormitories at Harvard College. Then I went to work for Caputo and we worked in Quincy, built all the concrete strips for Wollaston Beach. It was a lot of work. Then we went to work at Hyde Park High School for eighteen months in 1927, and I became the foreman for nine years—I had seventy-five, eighty guys working for me—and I was young too. Then we worked on Wellesley College for a couple of years, the Woodland Hospital; we done the high school in Roslindale.

See, the contractor came from the same town I come from in Italy, Mirabella, see? And he blew it, he blew all the money he made over there. Because he was stupid. You see sometimes a guy gets rich and you can't talk to him no more, see? That's what happened to him. He went broke after that, all right? See, when he got the job, [Malcolm] Nichols was the mayor—he was a Republican. When we were building the high school and we were almost all through, we had the election and [James] Curley came in. So when Curley came in he wanted (whistles) the money, he says, "Hey you done the job, you have to give me some." He [my boss] says, "You didn't give me the job." I told the contractor, I says, "Look, he wants twenty-five thousand, give it to him." What are you gonna do, that's what was going on. So I says, "Give it him." He didn't want to give it him, so he got a lawyer; it cost him sixty thousand dollars for a lawyer—Mansfield—he lost the case and he went broke. And he couldn't even get jobs anymore.

Fred Bourne

"Tough Tony"

They used to hire them [immigrant laborers] by the day; fifty or sixty guys used to line up on Unity Street every morning and they'd pick ten or twelve out of them to go to work on construction jobs. Ninety percent of the laborers were pick-and-shovel or some kind of construction work. And they used to work six days a week, ten hours a day for twelve bucks a week. They used to have to pay a tribute. There was a fella—"Tough Tony"—that every week he came over and you gave him two dollars. If you didn't give it to him, you got your legs broken. In fact one guy that lived in the apartment behind mine, married fella, twenty-three, from Italy, refused to pay the tribute in those days so they shot him right on Unity Street—they killed him—which in a sense put fear into all the others, so that if you made twelve bucks a week you knew that two dollars went to the boys."

Charlie Polcari

Working in a Shoe Factory in 1909

I got my first job, a shoe factory. I used to take the electric car every morning at six o'clock to go to Revere, to the Bartel Shoe factory. Morning and night, morning and night for more than five or six years. That's where I learned my trade. I done the worse goddamned job and I only weighed ninety pounds. What the hell, I was seventeen years old and I only weighed ninety pounds.

FIGURE 32. Charlie Polcari, 1980.

That kinda work never bothered me. My first job was to blacken edges on the shoes with black paint—the stain—you had to go around twice with a toothbrush, do it as fast as you could do it. That wasn't piecework. We were getting six dollars a week, ten hours from seven to six, Saturdays seven to four!

We built this country, I don't give a goddamn what people say—we put the hours in, we put the time in. And we built this country and these people today are getting the benefit out of it and they don't appreciate it. You don't know what we went through for seven, eight dollars a week, working ten hours a day. That's where I learned my trade. I learned how to do everything in the shoe factory. The first one gets the first case—if you finished ahead, you get the first case.

But you had to do seventy-two pair of shoes for three cents. You wouldn't think of that. You had to square the nails under the heels for three cents a case; you had to stamp the bottom of the shoes with the machine for three cents a case; laminate, polish, buff all the bottom of the shoes for three cents a case. You buff the whole damn shoe for five cents a case. A case and not a pair! A case! A case is seventy-two pair! You had to handle one hundred and forty-four shoes before you got three cents. We had a machine with three sides—the first, the second, and then we had to brush them for three cents a case.

Well, I got along; I was glad that I got a job anyway. I said what the hell, I didn't like to go to school and I made good for the shoe factory. You wouldn't believe it, there was a LaBiano fella over there working in the factory where I was working. He was the fastest son of a bitch you ever seen in your life. So I seen him; "Jesus," I says, "Look at that guy the way, how fast he's working"— he used to vvvff! vvvff! vvvff! I said, "You wait"—I didn't tell him, I said it to myself; I never told anybody, I never said anything to them anyway because you know they would feel offended. (laughs) I says, "There will come a time when I'm gonna beat the shit outta you"—and I did. And he said, "Son of a bitch! There was never a man who could beat me and you come over here and beat me." He lived six months and [then] he died.

There was nobody in the world who could beat me, any kind of job that is, in the finishing room. I didn't know anything about stitching, I didn't go down there. But in my room nobody could beat me—stamp, laminate, buffing, bottom finish, polish—anything you could imagine—blacken. There were two fellas—one was a fighter too, a big fighter—and he was doing the same kinda work I was doing but he was a kinda slow fella, different. There were Sicilian fellas working on the other side of the factory, they were shining shoes on the bottom. So they had a lot of work behind them, see? It made me laugh (laughing).

So the boss said, "Go ahead, there's machine over there, help this guy to get the work out." So I went over there and they didn't know who I was; they thought I was a Jew. They started to work and I see they started to talk Italian: "Hey, let's hurry up, we don't let the boss fire us." I was laughing; I didn't say nothing. And I started to work and they followed after me; they worked like hell and we got through with the work like nobody's business. They said, "Let's work or he's gonna get us get fired, he's gonna tell the boss." And then when I told them I was Italian, the son of a bitches laughed like this [imitates the laugh].

When they put me on piecework, that's when I started to make money. I was a kid for, chrissakes, sixteen, seventeen years old. One week I made forty-five dollars—you know what forty-five dollars means? It means a lot of money. And I used to make that much money. They offered me eighty dollars a week in 1923, 1924! All the factories used to come and call me—they wanted me to go back to work. I had friends, foremen—for chrissakes, they were crazy—they come up the house to call me! They offered me everything.

Elvira DiMattia

"My Dad the Street Sweeper"

My dad came here in 1892. He came here to work just as a young lad. When he first came here he did odd jobs, anything he could lay his hands on. Then he went back to Italy and decided he wanted to get married, about twenty-two years old and he married my mother from the same town, a little town about four miles from the city of Avellino. About four or five years later my grandparents came and they all settled in the North End. He went to work in Mount Auburn Cemetery taking care of all the lots there, cutting the grass, and then he became the section foreman over there. He could have really gone on his own as a landscape gardener, he knew that much about it, but he went to another cemetery digging graves manually. In those days that's how they used to dig them. Then they went on strike and were never called back. He had an application to work for the city of Boston and he went up to find out about it, and he was pretty high up on the list at the time, and he told them he was out of a job and told them he had a family, seven children, his parents living with us. He went to work sweeping the streets with a broom, not getting on a truck—one man used to work on one side of the street, one man on the other, manually—they used to sweep the streets at night.

They used to have welfare workers who used to receive welfare from the city at the time. That was before the state took it over. And they would be assigned to one of the more experienced workers. Working that way would be in lieu of the welfare money that the city paid them. His route was always around the business area, State Street, Congress Street, Portland, and so forth. In the wintertime when they couldn't sweep the streets because there was snow and ice they would be assigned where the catch basins were to make sure that there was an opening where the melting of the snow could find its way into the sewer, into that catch basin. And if the elements warranted it, my dad had to shovel to make those passageways for crosswalks. Sorry to say they don't do it now. We had pretty big snowstorms when I remember, when I was a child, but getting out was very easy because we knew that we could always cross from one street to the other because the city felt it had the obligation to create those passageways for us. Of course, if it froze, they couldn't very well shovel it—they used to take a pick and break it.

Helen Luongo

Helen Luongo sewed custom drapes at home and said, "I sell most of my drapes to people out of town."

"My Father's Candy Store"

He used to make fudge, taffy apples; he also sold corn in the summertime on Unity Street where the fountain [Prado] is now. Right at the corner, it used to be Webster Avenue, and our house was right at the corner of Unity Street and Webster Avenue. And you go through Webster Avenue and you face Saint Stephen's Church; we had Saint Stephen's Church in the back of the house and we had the Old North Church in the front of the house. The back garden where the Old North Church is now, that garden they have in the back, that used to be 19 and 17 Unity Street. And over there that's missing, there was 18, 20, and 22 on Unity Street; they threw down those three houses and the passageway, Webster Avenue, to make the Prado. And then in there, there was a candy place, Unity Place, right up through. And one candy place, from Webster Avenue used to come out where the Eliot school is now on Charter Street. So when you'd go up Webster Avenue from Unity Street, you could either go out left on Webster Avenue or you could go right.

FIGURE 33. Salvatore Palmerozzo, 1981.

FIGURE 34. North Square, 1890.

Salvatore Palmerozzo

Salvatore Palmerozzo was eighty-three at the time of our interview.

"It Was a Crooked Business"

I ran away from Italy when I was seventeen—the First World War started. My first job when I came here from the Old Country in 1914 was a "lousy" boy. We had to work, they take a me in the woods by [the Elevated Railway] electric car, to Bay State Road; we sleep in a shanty all summer, and in the winter we no do nothing. And you had to buy all your food from the company, you go buy stuff in the shanty over there. Fifty cents an hour, ten hours a day. I found work at South Braintree—that was crooked business—they were in North Square and they [the bosses] made the people go to the shanty, send them all out, to Maine or New Hampshire, and they'd take a percentage of their wages as their *padrone* [boss]—it was a crooked business. And sometimes they'd say, "Give me a dollar, I'll give you a job," took the money, and went away. Lotta crooked business. It was a pretty tough before. After coming over here after World War I started, not even for five or six months, people were saying, "Let's go back to the Old Country." I said, "Screw you."

Tom Bardetti

Puffing on a cigarette, Tom Bardetti described the power of the boss. His voice became gruff recounting workplace conditions without protections in the 1930s.

"The Boss Was Law and Order"

And in them days, around 1930, the boss done as he seen fit, what he done was done. Right or wrong, nothing said—he was the law and order, see? If he didn't like your looks or he didn't like your ways, or he didn't like the way you worked, or you didn't work enough, or you fooled around—you were slow or anything—he could fire you for any of those things. If he wasn't satisfied, he'd get rid of you, he'd hire somebody else. And it made no difference how long you worked in there, see? Now if I was workin' for you for about two or three years—that didn't mean anything to him, to you. If you had a friend, you fire me and hire him, just like that, see? You could lay me off and tell him to come in the morning to take my job. And what could I do? Nothing. I couldn't do anything about it. If I went to the law, they'd give you [the boss] [the] right anyway. You're the boss—you've got the right to do anything you want. If you're not satisfied with anybody who's working for you, lay him off and hire somebody else. He had the right to do that. That's the way it was, see?

There was no forty hours; anytime you worked more than forty hours you got straight time—there was no overtime. Today you got a lot of protection—the unions, the laws came in, and they got grievances, shop stewards. If you have a problem, you bring it up and you have a union committee in the shop to consider your case, and if they think you have good case, they take it to arbitration. At least now the person that works, he's got a defense and he can bring charges against the boss; he can do it through the shop steward and the grievance—they put it into the committee, and they have a hearing on it.

Working in a Shoe Factory

I always did factory work in South Boston. I had no training. I didn't go to school for a trade, I didn't go to trade school—all I got is a grammar school education, that's all I got. I ain't got no trade. Some things I can do, some things I can't, that's all. That's it.

I worked in a cut-sole factory on the soles of the shoes. Big, big bends, big slices of rawhides, the backbone and everything of the cattle—they used to skin the cattle. When they killed the bull, they'd skin 'em for his hide. Then they had a tannery in Cincinnati where the people worked—they tanned those hides in chemical stuff, and they'd take all the fur off, and it leaves the leather skin. And they used to cut the skin and they used to make a bale with a rope, rope them up in about a hundred or two hundred pound bale with a hook and put it on a truck. They got a block like on a machine and the press—they step on the thing and a heavy iron comes down—boom! You put the leather on the block and you put the die—size eight, size nine, size ten, or whatever it was, and you step on it; you take one sole off, and you take another one, and then another one, and another one. They make all soles outta them leather strips.

I used to get laid off because it was seasonal work like in the candy factories. They'd make Christmas candies in the summertime and then around Christmas they're laid off. That's the way it was. In the shoe factories, when they got orders to make shoes, see, they'd buy the leather.

Joe Petringa

"He Was Good with Horses in the North End"

My father was a livery stable owner when I was young. He was a teamster—horse-and-wagon operation. He had a stable—he used to keep fifty horses and up to a hundred on North Margin Street, Endicott Street. Then he had a stable in Charlestown on Miller Street, which is not there anymore. I was just growing up [mid-1920s] then. He was a great trainer of horses—my father was very good at keeping horses. If they were ill, in two or three weeks' time they'd be back in very good condition. He took care of them—he would clean them off, feed them the right food, and he was always with them.

In those days the barn was next to the home, like a farmer would have. In the city you'd be living next to it. Of course, the North End had stables all over in those days. There's two buildings now that were primarily stables—there were two on North Margin Street, one on Endicott Street. My father used to rent out the horses to businesses, and those who owned their own horses would board them just like a garage. Every once in a while you'd have to shear the horses, and I used to help him do that up until I was seventeen years old. Some fella would want a favor done, he knew my father was handy on it and he was really good with horses.

Petringa's Trucking Company

We started our own trucking business, Petringa's Trucking Company, in December 1934. We ran until 1955 when we discontinued the trucking business. In the 1930s the trucking business was in its growing stages, and it was very interesting in those days. That was the best way to ship goods immediately, by truck. I went all over New England—primarily Connecticut from Boston, that was my run. When we first started, the hours were good, from six to four o'clock; Saturdays were always a half day. Then when we got larger some of us would start at two-thirty in the morning, get through at eight at night, but we were always two men, you know.

But the average day was seven to five [and] the average week was fifty, fifty-five hours. Of course, it was a slower pace in those days. Oh, there was pressure on you then because the demand for service was greater than now.

Always was. So you had to be really aggressive in those days. But today with everything being unionized, the pace is slower. That's the way it was. I mean when I say slower, the vehicles were slower; instead of going sixty, seventy miles an hour in those days.

I remember I was driving my first truck in 1936 when I was eighteen, go thirty-five miles an hour with a truck, that was high speed, Buddy Boy. That was high speed. And you could get stopped by a state trooper by going thirty-five miles an hour on Route 28, going to Lawrence and coming back. But today it's different. Well even in 1950 was different, you were to go fifty, fifty-five, sixty miles an hour, the early fifties. I used to anyway. Sometimes seventy-five miles an hour. But in 1935, thirty-five was top speed, I mean it. Gas was six, seven, eight gallons for a dollar, yes sir.

Making Wine, Drinking Wine   18

> L'acqua fa male, ma il vino fa cantare (Drinking water makes you feel bad, but wine makes you sing).
> —JOSEPH RICCIO

North Enders used their living spaces to maintain Old-World traditions. In the asphalt-covered urban village without backyards, some created rooftop gardens. In cellars below busy streets, they continued the ancient rite of wine making. The season began in September at the loading docks in Chelsea, where old-timers competed to be the first in line to pick the best-looking zinfandel and moscato grapes from California. Before the age of ready-pureed grapes, the process began with mincing grapes in an electric grinder and then squeezing them by hand with a *stringitura*, a long pipe attached to the wine press, to extract every last drop. The grape juice, known as *ò must*, was placed in wooden barrels to ferment for a certain amount of time, based on the sugar level of the grape.

Wine was considered a natural part of each meal in Italian American households and was respected for its medicinal qualities. One elderly North Ender adhered to the proverb, "L'acqua infracèta i bastimenti a mare" (Water rots the ships at sea), and refused tap water, drinking only wine with meals. Others believed city water was tainted; as one said, "I only drink wine because city water rots the pipes." Children were given wine mixed with soft drinks at the dinner table. An unspoken rule in Italian American families forbade drunkenness and considered it shameful behavior.

At eighty-three, Pasquale Capone measured his life making wine like J. Alfred Prufrock measured his life in coffee spoons in T.S. Eliot's *Love Song of J. Alfred Prufrock.* Unlike the bored J. Alfred Prufrock, whose life was mired in the quotidian social ritual of drinking coffee, Pasquale measured his life in wine making, celebrating his journey from the penniless sixteen-year-old immigrant who survived on day-old donuts to the contented elder with enough money to raise and marry off four children and still buy crates of grapes for his red wine. While second- and third-generation Italian Americans measured their middle-class status by pointing to new cars and buying homes in the suburbs, Pasquale measured his successful life through sixty-one years of consecutive wine making. Sipping a glass of wine amid the aroma of fermenting grapes in the cellar, Pasquale put his house in order:

> I like all a my children and I don't want them to be mad at me, not a one of them, until I die. I don't care what a they do to me, I still like a my children, I got all a nice grandchildren, they all a like a me—everybody like a me, me and my wife. I don't want to stay mad at no one until my eyes a close. Then a when a my eyes no open anymore, that's a the time I be mad at a my kids, I'll be seven feet down! (laughing) All my four kids are good, my grandchildren—we all stick together, nice. To me, I couldn't stand one day not talk with my kids, the whole family in other words, wife and everything, I no can stand it. I don't want to stay mad until I die, that's all. I'm in this country sixty-seven years. I was never better than anybody, I never fight with anybody, I never argue with anybody, if somebody do something a wrong a to me, I took it, but no argument, I hate to argue with anybody—I wanna stay quiet, that's all. That's a my life.[1]

Tom Bardetti

Zinfandel, Muscatel, and Concord

My father used to know how to make the wine. The zinfandel wine you squeeze with the muscatel. See the muscatel is the white grapes and they're sweet. This zinfandel is another color; it makes good wine, it gives it color too. And they used the concord grapes—they didn't come in bushels—it came in baskets, like the baskets they sell the mushrooms [in] now, see? And they used to squeeze that in with that to give it color like—the concord grape is no good to drink, it's only for color, see, it gives it the color to make the wine. That's what he did. He knew how to buy it too. He used to go into the grape yard; he only used to buy fifty bushels. Fifty bushels makes two barrels. Now that's two barrels of squashed, crushed grapes makes one barrel when you squeeze it, see? And that's all he made—he didn't make it to sell. He didn't like—he had a family; there was my mother, my brother, and another brother that died. And he didn't want to sell wine—have guys come in the house, you sell them a bottle, they stay there drinking, they stay in the house all day, they're hollering, singing, and doing everything. My father was sensitive—he didn't like that. He never done that.

Like before they used to have gambling. So now the guys knew that if my father was living in here the way he was, they'd tell him, "We'll come to your house tonight and gamble." So all right, they'd come in and gamble and give you about ten dollars for being in here, but my father wouldn't do that. People used to make wine to sell, not only for the family use, but to sell it, too. But my father never cared to do that. It was against the law at that time to do that, see? My father never wanted to get in trouble because he was afraid they might deport him if he did that, see?

Fred Bourne

"Water Rusts Pipes"

In the old days, the old guys, everybody had a place in Revere, including my father-in-law, where they had grapevines and a bocce court. You don't see that anymore. Of course, there's a few old-timers who play bocce down [at] the park but that was a big thing years ago on a Sunday. I saw my father-in-law drink a gallon of wine for forty years and never saw him drunk. He never drank a glass of water to my knowledge and I never saw him drunk. They used to go to the icebox, there was a refrigerator in those days, and pour a glass of cold wine when they were thirsty. They didn't drink water. They used to say, "Water rusts pipes!" (laughing) It was a very interesting period. And it is a period that has faded.

FIGURE 35. Antonio Crugnale and wife, Philomena, in the cellar on Tileston Street, 1981.

Antonio and Philomena Crugnale

Making Wine with Philomena and Antonio

PHILOMENA: Oh, every year we do this work down here in the basement, from when we bought this house twenty years ago (grape juice dripping), in 1960 on Tileston Street. Before we used to do everything by hand, but then Antonio put a little motor [to mash the grapes] and made everything by electric. Wait a second while I wash off some of the [antifungal] spray left over on these grapes from the baskets. (Turns on the electric grape masher.)

ANTONIO: Some of the grapes are a little too hard, the bigger ones.

PHILOMENA: Some of them are a little too dirty—that's all! Ah, the grapes are beautiful! The grapes are good this year—they cost twelve dollars a bushel this year [1980]. They seem sweet this year, good.

ANTONIO: In Italy, it was different—we used to mash up the grapes stomping them with our feet!

PHILOMENA: And sometimes we used our boots! (laughing) Then we used *o tòrchio* [the wine press]. Tutto [Everything]!

ANTONIO: Now we've got everything electric!

ANTHONY Riccio: So you like making wine, right?

ANTONIO: Sure, it's all right, even you told me so!

PHILOMENA: Antò, and what did the author-writer say? Bevi vino [Drink wine]!

ANTONIO How do I know? Who knows? A glass of wine, you can have, but not a big glass! (machine mashing the grapes as we talk) See this machine? I made it myself! It turns and turns and mashes the grapes.

PHILOMENA: Now we put everything in the *stringitura e si stringe* [in the grinder]—you squeeze the grapes. Tutta finita [All done]! Let me put this in there—this year we didn't mix any *bianca* [white grape]; it's all *nera* [black] this time, We're making all red (dripping sounds from the liquid). Sometimes we mix a little white grape, but not this year.

ANTHONY Riccio: La signora è forte [your wife is strong] too, Antonio.

PHILOMENA: Eh, Tony, what can you do? The children don't have the time, the chance to come here because they're always so busy, so there's only me and Tony who have time to make it. They came last night after work or else they wouldn't have come at all because they always have work to do. They were supposed to come tonight to help but—oh, easy, easy with this (tosses grape juice into a jug, chuckling). *Translated from the Abruzzese dialect of Sulmona.*

Making Wine, Drinking Wine

Pasquale Capone

As another year of making wine passed, Pasquale Capone talked about the love of his family: "All a time I always think of my kids, all my life. My wife kept my house rich, she knew how to keep the house, save a dollar. We had nothing, we had all these good times."

"I Like a This Country"

It's a all right to make a glass wine homemade, but it's a lotta work. Oh yeah. Mo' nessuno piu vuole lavorare [people born today, they don't wanna do this]; they like to drink the water, that's a what wine they sell in the store! Because they no wanna do the work! That's a lotta work, this! You gotta go eh buy 'em, take it home, take it down a cella, then a you gotta squeeze 'em, you know, with a *stringitura* [machine] like that. Yeah, sixty years—this year it'll be sixty-one I've been making wine. Nineteen-twenty I made my first bottle of wine. I just got married. But when I was little kid in Italy, my father made me work on the farm. Eh, that's the life that used to be over there! That's why I come over here; I work three years, make a little money, come back a there, buy a farm. But once I come over here, I never went back. Cause I like a this a country.

A Lifetime of Wine Making

I came from Italy in 1914—no mother, no father, no sister, no money, and no job. I was sixteen years old. Nineteen-twenty was the first year I make the first bottle of wine. I make a only one barrel, I have a no money—could I make anymore? But now I make a three or four barrels for my family, my [grandchildren] like the wine, my daughter, and my son too. I'm eighty-three and I haven't stopped since. I don't know; if I don't make it, I feel lost. I make cause I no like the wine in the store. I no like the store wine. I'd rather drink a glass of beer than that. That's why I make it. The store wine, that's a no grape wine. Cause I been in California two times [and] my son take me to the place where they make a the wine, and over there, one barrel was vinegar barrel, thirty-three thousand gallons, was a bigger than my house! I dunno how many kind of wine they showed me that day. And I never liked a one! That's a chemical in there—that's a no wine the one you buy in the store, it's a chemical.

See, you gotta know the grape; not everyone make the same I make because I know the grape. I know the grape upside down. For sixty years. And when the people go over there, "I wanna buy grape, gimme thirty bushel of that grape." Some grape, you take a hold of the grape, soon as you touch a them, the stuff inside come a right out. When I buy 'em, the stuff, when you try a squeeze them, no commen out. And then when you put 'em in your mouth, they gotta crack a like a nuts. And it's gotta be a little dry—that's the time you make good grape. I know the grape upside down. The grape I used to buy four, five years ago is a no commen no more—I don't know why. Well, I pick the best I can do, that's all, that's all I can pick. They grape I used to buy years ago was outta this world. But no more. They don't come here anymore. But I get the best what I can get. I pay more price, that's all. But no get that grape like four or five years ago, forget about that. I dunno where they go, or they use a them down there, I dunno.

Last night we squeeze the grapes in an electric machine at my daughter-in-law's house. This stays maybe ten days, might stay twelve, might stay fifteen, depend a how much sugar it [the grapes] got. If there's a lot of sugar, it boil [ferment] a quick. This here, this year, no gotta much a sugar, that's all you can get. My niece gotta the thing to measure how much sugar. And this is what we make a last night. Take about fifteen minutes to squeeze, all done. Years ago, the machine was by hand. Years and years ago, before I come here, they used the feet—that's all they had, put on the boots. Everything is more clean now. I used to do it by hand, with a *stringitura* [manual grape squeezer]. See, I put all the juice out; see, when it comes up like this, when it starts to boil [fermentation], come up like that. And I come in [down to the cellar], every night and every morning. I got this long thing [pitchfork], and every day I come down and I push 'em [grapes in the barrels] down. Once a day. The next day I come down again and—zap! I push 'em down and then it stop a boil. When it stop a boil, I taste 'em; when it come out, the sweet gone, then I take it out a here, take the juice out and put them in the press, and I squeeze little by little. I no squeeze 'em all at once—give 'em four, five bang, let it go for ten minutes and sometimes you give another four or five bangs.

Life in the Tenements   19

> The neighbors came with their stools, chairs and benches. They slowly filled the sidewalks on both sides of the street, leaving little room for walking. On Friday and Saturday evenings, our street resembled a block party.
> —VITA ORLANDO SINOPOLI, *From My Bakery Perch*

Tenements in poor neighborhoods have historically been linked with disease, crime, and chronic poverty. They have also provided themes for winning political issues. Thus, after two failed mayoral campaigns, Richard C. Lee propelled himself to victory in 1953 by the condemnation of tenements in New Haven's Oak Street neighborhood and a plan to eradicate the slums. The new mayor's ambitious renewal project established New Haven as a "Model City," which other cities emulated, destroying ethnic, working-class neighborhoods across the country in the name of removing urban blight. The man directing the bulldozers in Connecticut was Richard Lee's economic development director, Ed Logue, who would later try his hand in Boston, a city with larger dimensions.

When the West End's tenements were razed, dispersing its residents, middle-class professionals took their place in fancy new high-rises. The North End's tenements survived the wrecking ball, but the stigma of shame attached to them by critics outside the neighborhood endured.

The reputation of the North End as a slum existed before the Italians, beginning in the 1840s when poor Irish immigrants poured into the area, replacing wealthy residents who fled to Beacon Hill. For decades, Boston's social reformers, bankers, nativists, and journalists continued to associate social ills with filthy, densely populated tenements. In 1871, the journalist Samuel Adam Drake blamed the North End's deteriorating, disease-ridden tenements on Italian immigrants. Offended by the aromas wafting from open kitchen windows, he combined his disdain for Italian cuisine with crowded tenement conditions: "Nowhere in Boston has Father Time wrought such ruthless changes, as in this highly respectable quarter, now swarming with Italians in every dirty nook and corner. In truth, it is hard to believe the evidence of our own senses, though the fumes of garlic are sufficiently convincing."[1]

At the turn of the century, most three-room apartments in the North End measured three hundred square feet and cost twelve dollars a month. In 1885, the average number of families in tenements was between four and fifteen, totaling sixty to seventy individuals.[2] Many shared the same bed, with kitchens often converted into sleeping areas. In some cases, over sixty members of nine families shared a bathroom in the cellar. Families often sublet to tenants, who paid a dollar a week, fifty cents for women. Cheap boardinghouses accommodated ten or twelve single working men crammed into one or two rooms at a cost of twenty-five to thirty cents a week.[3] Much to the dismay of the *prominenti*, a brothel opened on Hanover Street. Heaps of trash were often left to accumulate in piles, filling courtyards and blocking hallways. Apartments lacked ventilation and tenement dwellers on lower floors and in hallways and cellars seldom saw the light of day. In the late nineteenth century, the North End's mortality rate was twice that of healthier neighborhoods.[4]

Two decades later, the author and poet John Ciardi described Sheafe Street as a block of five-story walk-up tenements, with most floors divided into front and rear flats. He provided a picture of improved living conditions in a family's fifth-floor apartment, its large kitchen furnished with a simple table and chairs, a cast-iron range as the main source of heat, and a soapstone double sink with one basin to wash clothes and the other for dishes. Gas lamps with jets emitting a motionless blue flame illuminated the rooms.

Tenements teemed with life as generations of interrelated families interacted with each other often, visiting in apartments, passing on stairways, clustering on stoops, calling one another from open windows, sleeping on fire escapes, sitting on sidewalks on summer nights, and gathering on rooftops. North Enders coexisted in close quarters with neighbors from the same economic and social class, treating each other with the same informality that existed between common folk in Italian towns. Knowing the intimacies of each other's lives, they intervened in times of trouble, took care of each other's children, exchanged dishes of food, and celebrated holidays together.

Frances Zanfani Corolla's mother, an immigrant from Parma in northern Italy, raised eleven children in her small apartment. She assigned house chores to each one, teaching them compassion for the less fortunate. In *The Urban Villagers*, Herbert Gans identified the West End as "a community of struggling working-class people living in old tenements unconcerned with the status of address, the need for a manicured backyard, or residence in carefully zoned neighborhood, a place where people were judged on friendliness and moral qualities and not on the basis of housing."[5] The same description could have been written about the North End.

Nicholas Dello Russo, a lifelong resident who grew up in a Salem Street tenement, articulated what was lost when the neighborhood was changed by powerful political and economic interests:

The problem was, the city hated the tenement neighborhoods. They called our wonderful neighborhood a slum and were constantly coming up with urban renewal schemes to improve our lives. Of course, they never asked North End residents about this. The arrogance and condescension of the politicians was astounding. They told us we were poor, but we didn't feel poor. They said we were living in squalor, but our apartments were spotless. They wanted to improve our lives but all they did was encourage gentrification and force lower middle-class people out of the North End. The West End was the ugly paradigm of that kind of urban renewal, one that still resonates today. Tenement neighborhoods were a burden on the city because they used all the city services but didn't generate enough income in the form of taxes to pay for those services. The callous politicians asked themselves why should these lower-class Italians occupy prime real estate in the heart of Boston and not pay their fair share of property taxes? It came down to money against lives and money won.

FIGURE 37. Mary Molinari and husband, Louis, on 146 Richmond Street, with North Square in the background, 1950s.

Mary Molinari

Tenement Life on Garden Court Street

My parents came here in 1902. We had many affairs; many a time we'd have a wedding right in the house there on Garden Court Street. One of the girls would get married and we'd be invited. They [the women] worked for two weeks; they'd do the *muzzalette*—it was a biscotti, a cookie with molasses and nuts—and they would work all day; they had big picnic table full of cookies—they would cook day and night. There used to be a lady, her name was Carmella, she lived on the first floor and she would bake homemade bread, and you could smell it all over the street. Well she would come out with a loaf of bread and cut it all up nice and hot and everybody would have it.

Years ago, coming out of church, walking down the street, you could smell the sauce coming out of the kitchens for Sunday dinner. We used to enjoy that kind of living. Now when they cook, they've got fans to blow the air out of the kitchen—and all the smell goes out too. In our house we'd go down to see the people on the second and third floor. We'd visit each other, have coffee. I'd go up and down those stairs two or three times a day, and it was good exercise. Now I've moved to a condo [after being evicted]. But I still liked the old ways better. As you'd walk up, you'd see your neighbor on the different flights of stairs and we'd have coffee together. But today, these new homes for the elderly are like hotels—all tight and closed. It isn't like years ago. Now everyone watches television inside. Before, it was different; people would leave their doors open and no one was afraid of anything. Someone would always come by to see you—they'd tap on your door and come into your house. In the old building it was one big family. Now everyone locks their doors up, and they have to call before they come to see you. In the old building if they'd hear you going up or down the stairs, they'd come out of their doors and say "Hi, good morning," and talk to you so nice.

You know what I liked? We had the roof—we never had one of those terraces or anything, so we'd go up the roof. We used to go up the roof on summer nights, and my uncle had a guitar, and my father had a mandolin, and they'd play and sing all through the night, and it was beautiful. My mother had a little table—what table! It was a box! She'd put a tablecloth on it, cut up watermelon, peaches, and in a big pitcher would have wine and peaches all cut up; it was nice on hot summer nights, nice and cold. We used to buy a big piece of ice and my mother, with a pick she would cut some ice and put it in the pitcher. My mother would invite everybody from the building on Garden Court Street. You'd think it was a penthouse up there—the place was coming down on us, but we were happy. Out in the street in the summer, another person would come down with a big pitcher of lemonade or ice tea—they couldn't afford coffee—and we'd be sitting down, and this would go on all summer; it was a beautiful street, it was one big family.

Those same people, when I got married on Garden Court Street, I invited them all. They all came to the church, and when I came home from my honeymoon they were all looking out the window—they were all greeting me, calling me from here to there, but I didn't want to look at their faces because I was bashful. We loved one another; it seems people were different in those days—they were humble, they loved us. They were happy days. Today I don't see it. Today you know what you find? Who is better than the other—they want to keep up with the Joneses. I don't believe in that. I enjoy people's company, and I was brought up like that, and I'll die like that.

Josie Picadacci

Josie Picadacci was concerned about her elderly neighbors who were left alone to fend for themselves, and she often baked for them.

"Friendship Was Friendship"

I had one very, very good friend of mine. In fact, when I had my kids, we had them in the house at the time. And she used to be my nurse. And I used to be her nurse. This is how close we were, like sisters. And she was a widow for seven years; then she got married and she moved not too far away, but I mean she's not in the North End anymore. See, friendship was friendship. Whatever you could do for anybody, this is how we were. It didn't matter what it was. That's the way it was.

Rose Arigo Amato

"She Wanted the Sun on Endicott Street"

My mother was from Sicily, Messina, and oh, she said it was so beautiful there that they used to have, they used to pick the fruit right from the trees, she says, and the fig trees and oranges, any kind of fruit, you just had to pull right from the tree. She said it was so beautiful, and they had the ocean right there. I come from a family of nine, eight girls and one boy. Some of them say, we didn't have that, what they have today, but I can say we did. We had plenty of clothes, plenty of food.

My father was in the food business. He used to bring home fruit in cases; the house was always full of fruit. My mother was a dressmaker; she used to sew all our clothes and she was a really good dressmaker. She used to be a dressmaker in Italy for all the rich people, she was so good at it, you know. I was born on 160 Endicott Street in 1910, right near a beautiful church [Saint Mary's]; I lived right on the top floor. I was born there on the top floor; my mother never wanted to move from the top floor because it was so sunny there. She used to love it there; she says, that's where she wanted to pass away, and that's where—you couldn't move her from there. We once moved below, to another floor, and she cried so much, she wanted to move back upstairs because she said she wanted the sun. And that's where she really wanted to pass away she says.

It was nice, sunny. We had five rooms. We had our own bathroom. Of course, at the time, very seldom, you wouldn't have a bathroom, we had a place to go, like on North Bennet Street, to go to take baths. Years ago there wasn't baths in the buildings. My mother was the first one to have shutters outside. It was a new building when she moved in. See, they didn't put no bath in though, they had everything but a bathtub. But it was nice, sunny; she used to have that house painted every six months, I don't know why. Very clean, very, very clean. And people were amazed the way, with nine children all the cooking she used to do, that she was so clean. She was so immaculate. Sundays was a nice day because we used to gather all together; my married sisters would come, because I was the last one, I was the youngest. I had sisters that married fourteen, fifteen years old (laughing). I had one fifteen, another one sixteen. And it was nice; they used to come and gather around on a Sunday [and] we'd sit around the table.

Al Mostone

Respect for the Neighbors

Us kids were brought up to respect the old people. I could never come into your mother's house and say, "Aaye, Mary!" Oh no, I'd have to say Aunt Marie or *Donna Maria* (Lady Marie) or *Zia Maria* (Aunt Maria). And the same with the older person. Or if your mother was carrying a load of bundles in the street and if I saw her and didn't help her take it up [to] the house, my father would knock my block off. If I was in the Elevated [Railway] streetcar and there was a woman standing up and I was sitting down and I didn't give her my seat, I'd know about it. They had a tighter control on the kids in those days. And we lacked nothing—we enjoyed ourselves; we didn't have much money, we didn't have no radio, no television, we had nothing. But still we managed to enjoy ourselves. Church would run a dance, society run a dance, it wouldn't be only our crowd, it would be the whole North End.

FIGURE 38. Tenement stairway, 1979.

Viola Pettinelli

"Fifty-Six Steps"

I enjoyed my youth over here; I enjoyed it very, very much. Oh, I don't think I'd want to change it for something else. I can't explain—I really liked everything about it. Well, in those days, it was more togetherness. We talk about togetherness—no, we had more togetherness there. Families, oh, I don't know. There was no such a thing as being private, private to a certain extent. If my mother was sick, as soon as one of the neighbors would know, they'd come in, take over.

My mother would go upstairs. I'll never forget the time the woman upstairs took sick and she had two young girls at home. Well after my mother got us started, she would run up there every morning and get them started to go to school, you know? Today? Well, today they help you but not as much, so that if my mother was sick and the neighbor is cooking or whatever and she knows my mother isn't well enough to get up and cook, well, she'd send up a pot of whatever it was down, so there was no problem there. Today, well, we have it, but it's changed a little.

Of course, in those days we didn't have crime. You could have your windows open, your fire-escape window, nobody ever thought of going to bed and locking your fire-escape window. We lived on the third floor and I went up and down, I wouldn't know any other way. I'd get lost if I didn't have fifty-six steps to climb. The doctor counted them for us. One time he came to see my mother and he said, "You know how many stairs you got there?" I said, "No, I never counted them." He said, "Why you've got fifty-six steps!" I said, "Why? You counted them?" He said, "Oh yes, all my patients seem to be upstairs, no one is downstairs." But I don't mind them at all, no. We wash them, we keep them clean. I try to keep mine clean.

FIGURE 39. Prince Street, 1980.

Al Mostone

"We Had Our Wakes in the House"

In those days the wakes were always in the house. We never went to an undertaker or an undertaker's parlor. We'd stay up all night with the body. It was all by candles; there was no electricity. That's the way it was, all by candlelight. We were fifteen kids in a cold-water flat with three rooms.

Frances Zanfani Corolla

The Welcome Sign

I had to leave school the second year of high school because the money wasn't enough and my mother needed help. I was working for seven dollars a week. There were eleven of us. We had our chores. We had no time to run out and play. We had to do those chores, and that's how we never got into any mischief. If we had a lollipop, we were happy. We lived better then. We were happy. We were all one big family.

So if we knew a neighbor was sick, we'd all be there—we'd all run in. Whenever there was sickness, our door was always open—there was always that welcome sign without even knocking on the door. They'd see you with [the] door open and they'd say, "Come on in," in Italian; "Are you tired?" Or if we had wine, we'd give them a glass of wine or whatever we had on the table we shared—our tables were always full in those days. It was like a welcome sign—you didn't even have to put that welcome [sign] on the door because the door was opened. The old people always had that welcome sign—their arms were always open. I knew that if I came home from work late I wouldn't have to worry about my children—my neighbor would take care of them. And I never forgot that. And that's what I mean about closeness—the love was there. But today it's not so. I miss that; we don't have that today. Today we don't know what's going on or how or when or why.

Sicilian Fishermen in the North End   20

My father, like his father, was a fisherman, and
I also followed that way of life. It's in your blood.
—FRANK FAVAZZA

In the late 1800s, Giovanni Verga's novel, *I Malavoglia*, chronicled a poor fishing family in the town of Aci Trezza on the eastern coast of Sicily. Considered a masterpiece of Verismo (Realism), it was published at the same time Sicilian fishermen were dipping their oars into the waters of Boston harbor. 'Ntoni, the patriarch of the Malavoglia family, recites proverbs to underscore time-honored beliefs of fishermen from Riposto, Sciacca, Terrasini, and Acireale transported to the North End: "Fa il mestiere che sai, che non si arricchisci camperai. Contentati di quel che t'ha fatto tuo padre; se non altro non sarai un birbante" (Stick with your trade, you may not get rich but you'll get by. Be satisfied to be what your father made you, if nothing else you won't turn out a scoundrel).[1]

Italian fishermen lived in a society that considered them lowest on the social scale, beneath the poorest farmer. In Terrasini, society was divided into three separate socioeconomic groups—*buggisi cu buggisi, viddanu cu viddanu*, and *marinara cu marinara* (merchant with merchant, peasant with peasants, and fisherman with fisherman), who celebrated different saint's days, abided by different customs, and spoke their own dialects.[2] Antonia Luzzo recalled fishermen ascribing to the same social norm in the North End, where parents arranged marriages between fishing families, seldom intermarrying with those considered above them in social class: "S'aviano a maritari tra r'iddi, parenti e parenti" (They used to marry among each other, relatives to relatives).³ Protective Sicilian fathers disapproved of daughters working outside in factories, preferring to keep them close to home baiting fishing lines and repairing trawling nets on the tenement rooftops.

Rising before dawn, fishermen walked from North Street to T Wharf and Eastern Packet Pier, boarded leaky dories, and rowed into the harbor, unwinding long trawling lines with baited hooks from *cartiedde* (large baskets). Frank Favazza, who was descended from generations of fishermen from Terrasini, described sunrise on the water: "There is nothing in the world like the sight of the sun rising on the calm ocean water—u mari dorma" (the ocean is sleeping).

Sicilian fishermen plied their trade in the busiest fishing port in the western hemisphere, with a fleet of some five hundred vessels hauling tons of cod, flounder, and mackerel to the Waterfront's fish-freezing and storage plants, which were the largest in the world.⁴ Some locals worked lumping fish, a dirty, backbreaking job unloading the daily catch from the arriving boats. Cutters and pickers worked under such oppressive conditions at processing plants like the Globe Fish Company that in the 1950s and 1960s, mothers warned daughters who didn't like school, "You'll end up picking crabs down on Commercial Street!"

Though they were poor, North Enders respected the Sicilian fishermen for being honest, hardworking, and brave. As larger fishing boats replaced dories and motors replaced oars, fishing expeditions increased to three days, often to George's Bank, Jeffries Ledge, and Stellwagen Bank. The bigger boats went on expeditions that could last weeks, while the smaller "Guinea fleet" left early on Monday morning and returned on Wednesdays.⁵ Born into a fishing family in Favarotta, Sicily, Leonardo Favaloro was so in tune with the rhythms of marine life that his fellow fishermen said that "he knew where the fish lived." When returning to port, Frank Favazza often stood guard on the deck of his forty-foot boat the "*Saint Mary*," harpooning hungry sharks on the hunt for fish hooked to the *palangàri* (long lines) running from his boat. After three days of rough weather on the water and physical strain, often with little sleep or water to bathe, Frank would return so exhausted that he would crawl up the several flights of stairs to his apartment on his hands and knees.⁶

Fishermen who braved the waters, never knowing if they would return, sold the catch to dealers and fish brokers who paid them low prices and enjoyed high profits in the buying and selling. Mariano Pennisi was descended from a fishing family from the coastal town of Acireale. Born in 1889, he immigrated to the North End in 1913; he described the poverty of a fisherman's life due to the low value of fish: "Iava a piscari di quand'era piccolo e cca orai pisci ad una pezza o pondi e prima, menzu sordu; calamari, a menzu sordu; aricchi, a menzu sordu; baccalaru, a menzu sordu; e ora una pezza e menzu i calamari—e senza vuscari nenti!" (I was a fisherman since I was a young boy. Now fish are a dollar a pound, but then they were a half-cent, calamari, a half-cent a pound, cod, a half-cent a pound, dried cod, a half-cent a pound; now calamari is a dollar and a half—we couldn't make any money!).[7]

Sicilian fishermen adhered to the centuries-old techniques they had learned in the waters around Sicily. As ancient mariners in the New World, they navigated by dead reckoning, using the sun, moon, and stars as guides and plotting a course determined by the compass for a certain number of hours. To guide their ships in the darkness of night they gazed at familiar stars, steering toward a single star for a set number of hours. On cloudy days they relied on the compass, factoring in the wind and currents. They recognized fishing banks by the color of the water and the number of sea birds in flight. Before sonar technology, they threw sounding lines tipped with wax over the side to determine depth and the characteristics of the oceanic landscape fathoms below. A good fisherman knew a muddy bottom was often good for scallops; pebbly bottoms meant ground fish like cod or haddock. Some skilled captains could make a lot of money for the owner and the crew.[8]

When Frank Favazza returned home after days on the water in rough seas and unpredictable weather, he felt a sense of *paci* (peace). If the fishing was good, he would say, "*Pani é duci*" (money is sweet), not with a sense of greed but rather for the sweet peacefulness that came from providing for his family.

In the late 1960s the local fishing trade became a casualty of the "New Boston" when the city transformed the Waterfront into a high-priced community for upwardly mobile professionals. Old wharves, small businesses, and storage sheds were replaced with luxury condominiums and the massive Quincy Market Cold Storage building was cleared for a parking lot. When Boston's plan to renew the Waterfront included building Waterfront Park, sailboats replaced fishing boats, permanently displacing the Italian fleet from Eastern Packet Pier and T Wharf. Captains of small boats could not compete with fleets of mighty ships, some from foreign countries, transporting huge cargoes into the harbor. The era of Sicilian fishermen and the brotherhood they shared on the Waterfront was over.

Gone were the days when fishermen greeted one other with the fisherman's handshake, grabbing forearms rather than hands slippery from hours of gutting fish and baiting trawling lines. Voices of fishermen exchanging the latest news in Sicilian as they worked on their boats disappeared. Many moved to Gloucester to continue the fishing trade; others retired. Some

FIGURE 40. Teresa Costanzo. Costanzo family album. — 000

old-timers like Frank Favazza stayed behind in the North End, spending his days with old *cumpari* (friends) reminiscing of times when "the cigars were long and hand-cut, the espresso thick" on T Wharf. Inspired by the stories his beloved grandfather Frank often told, Keith Favazza wrote a poem dedicated to the Sicilian fishermen of the North End:

> When I look at the horizon, where the sky meets the sea I see the sun fresh & ablaze
> A new beginning,
> a glorious sight to behold in awe I stare speechless
> Overcome with the beauty before me brilliance in color
> Ocean waves silently crashing against the boat gulls diving and singing
> I am a fisherman as my father was as his father was[9]

Teresa Costanzo

A Fisherman's Wife

We came to Boston because my husband, Angelo, was a fisherman from when he was young. We lived on North Street. In those days everybody lived by their *mestiere* [trades]. He was a fisherman down by the water at the fishing piers on Commercial Street in the North End. You know how many fisherman used to be down there? And they all lived with that fisherman's trade. My father, good soul that he was, was a fisherman. My son, my father-in-law, they were all fishermen. My husband's trade was a fisherman his whole life. But thank God! He was the *patruni* [owner] of his ship, and he used to go out to fish the waters. He worked long hours for little money. He had expenses. He had all the *chi conzi* [long fishing lines for trawling].

In those days, do you know how much fish were worth? Two cents a pound. You know how many fish they used to throw back into the sea? Two cents a pound in those days. Do you know how many fishermen were down at the docks along Commercial Street? A lot! He never earned much money because fish was cheap. The people who could buy fish bought them. The people that couldn't buy fish didn't. What they couldn't sell, they'd throw away. See? See? But we didn't spend a lot—the cost of food was cheap too. Now everything is high.

We all lived on North Street. You know how it was—a person has to take the good with the bad, and we have more bad than good things, you understand me, *a matri*? Yeah? That's how it seems. Look, now I am old, understand, *a matri*? I don't visit or see anyone anymore. I just pray to all the saints the world doesn't forget about me! I am thankful to you, *a matri*! See if you can help get food stamps. The world has changed. Nothing is fair anymore. Do you understand me? It used to be nice, we had our *marketa* [market], everything, yeah, yeah, yeah. Things were cheap. Eh, eh, eh—things were fair, things were right. But now, no. What can you do?

FIGURE 41. Frank Favazza with long line and *cartedda* (basket) on the *Saint Mary*.

Everyone has their trade, their work. I feel discouraged, the way the world is now. You see this coat I'm wearing? I've had it since my husband Angelo, that good soul, was alive. It's going to be fifteen years, if not more. But I keep it clean, I keep everything clean. You see? You see? Angelo and I respected one another. My husband worked to help his family and I always knew how to take care of money. I thought we should put some money aside for our future gravestone here. Angelo has his now, all clean and well-kept. *Translated from the Sicilian dialect of Riposto.*

Frank Favazza

Frank Favazza was nicknamed "Captain Storm" by his fellow fishermen because of his willingness to venture out in rough weather.

"It's in the Blood"

In those days they didn't have to teach you how to be a fisherman. It's in the blood. You'd see your father do it and naturally, there was some pointers they had to give you, but in the windup, when I was sixteen, seventeen, eighteen years old—I graduated school at fourteen—I was telling my father, "Pa, you're not supposed to do this with the hooks and the strings and the trawls and whatever—do it this way." I learned it quick, in other words.

Then I learned how to run a boat [and] I bought my boat, a forty-footer. I learned the waters. I learned just before I gave up fishing at the end, how to chart a course, not expertly, satisfactorily. I could go and find, say, forty or fifty miles from Boston, going east all the time, a little spit of bottom, probably an acre wide—that's a pin needle when you can find it in the middle of the Atlantic Ocean—I used to find it more times than not. We used to hire them—we had a crew of six, five, six—depends, sometimes four, between four, five, and six. And when we used to go fishing, we never gave salaries—the catch. There's four hundred dollars. The owner used to take one share for the boat for any damage to the gear or the boat needs to be overhauled and whatnot, so many things. And he'd take one for me, one for the boat, is two, and the four men, one share each, they all divided equally except of course the owner of the boat had to get an extra share because he's supporting the boat. If he loses the boat, which we had no insurance, we couldn't even buy a piece of bread—things were so tough in them days.

No matter if you was better than me, we all—we figured this is the best this man can do, we all got a share; everybody got a share and if you happen to be sick and you couldn't come out or something we still gave him a share even though he stayed home. With my share, I just took it home, it was part of proceedings—if we made, say, thirty or forty dollars in them days for three days' work. One day to go out, one day to come back, and one day to sell the fish—encompasses three days—if we made thirty or forty dollars that was a big thing. And another thirty, forty dollars, the share of the boat, that would help a lot, but I'd have to keep it because you'd need repairs, you'd lose the gear—gear cost money; you know, when you lose your lines, gets hooked up on the bottom of the ocean, cold, and you can't go down there. And you pull, and it if slides off the rock and if not, it would break.

We used to sell the fish first to the local fish stores on Atlantic Avenue; it was only a few feet from where we docked the boat. Then they had the fish pier, the Boston fish pier in South Boston, and we used to go over there, and the buyers used to get in there like the stock market when they bid, "You so much—" And they'd keep bidding: "Six cents a pound! Who's the highest bidder? This is it! It! Sold to Harding Fish Company!" And whatever the prices were. We'd unload the fish there. Then we'd go to the exchange and they'd give you the money or a check. Then I used to take it down after we unloaded the fish. Then we used to share it up. One share for the boat, one for John, one for Jim, one for Tony, that's all.

One funny thing was when we used to share up. We were so dumb in them days. (laughing) You know that so much taken off, so many shares would equal so much each. We didn't do that. We'd start, we figured it all out—ten dollars, ten dollars, and make six piles—depends on how many piles—and keep going until you run out of money. It was fun. Then when I went to school, I said, "Pa, what are you doing, all that? How much did we get?" He said, "We stocked three hundred dollars," whatever. All right, three hundred by six, be, uh, six times six is three sixty, come down a little more, and I'd make it quick. But he'd be all day, especially if there was one-dollar bills, two-dollar bills, he'd be all day sharing up. (laughing) I loved fishing.

The Waterfront had two places where we'd tie up our boats. One was called Packet's Pier, and there was another, Big Wharf. And the wharf where we used to tie our boats up had at least fifty boats. We didn't know such a thing as [a] TV or an automobile. You know, we spent a lot of time on the water, even when we didn't go fishing. We had to prepare, do a lot before we went out. You had to do the new trawls; sometimes we used to go for clams, and there used to be thousands where Logan Airport is now, and we used them for bait. And there was another place we used to go for mussels and use them for bait in order to save some money, and by not buying the bait we used to make our own. And it was backbreaking, see—it took a lot of time. You had to dig the clams, then you had to shell them and put them on the hooks; it was a helluva job. I did it maybe because we didn't know any better. I don't know. Maybe it was for the best. Because nowadays the people are getting spoiled by luxury—if you have one television, I gotta get two. Your car—I'm gonna get a better one; see in them days we appreciated every little thing we got.

And we never ate unless my father gave the order, "In nome del Padre e Figghiu e Spiritu Santu [In the name of the Father and the Son and The Holy Spirit]," we never—God forbid you put your fork in there. You'd get a backhander. No, he never hit us. No, but we had to say the prayers.

Now I've been to places, I see people—the poor woman is still putting stuff on the table and they're starting to dig in. But things change. There was no such thing as hours. When the weather was good, we worked all the time. When it was bad weather, that's the time we rested, because if we took off time on good weather, what do we do, take off on good weather, and then the bad weather comes, what do you do, take some more time off? Who's gonna pay the rent? The weather commanded everything. Naturally if it was Easter or Christmas, big holidays. One thing—my father, he never went fishing on Saint Joseph's Day, the nineteenth of March. His name was Joseph, my father. "Pa, let's go out and make some money." "No, maybe tomorrow we go." His name was Joseph and he respected the saints! "No," he said, "We don't go out on that day."

Our day began with no set time. It depended where you had to go. If you had to go out far, you got up early. We'd hear the news down on the wharf through the *cumpari* [friends]. A lot of them had relatives who were fishermen. "Hey, John, hey *cumpari*, did you catch any fish over there?" And we'd gauge that way, where to go. But in those days, things were really tough. You had to sound the bottom to know how deep you were. We had to do it by hand with a leaden piece of weight with a line that touched the bottom. When it touched the bottom, then you'd measure—one, two, and so forth. In modern times they had depth finders—they had everything. As you were running along, you see it on the machine there, the depth of the boat. You had to do it by hand on those cold winter days; you had to go to the bow of the boat and throw out that lead overboard and pull it up, and your hands would numb. That's progress. But I tell you, we didn't make much when I was a youngster in the 1920s, [but] we always had plenty to eat on the table. We weren't rich, my parents weren't rich, in fact at the end we all had to chip in, but we were a happy family. My father was a saint; he was a good man [and] they called him the Abbott.

FIGURE 42. Frank Favazza (in the cabin) and son Joe on the *Saint Mary*.

Anna Caffarelli

Anna Caffarelli spoke about her Sicilian neighbors in 1980 with the same empathy she had had for them in the 1920s.

" Fisherman's Life in the 1910s

We lived on 282 North Street for thirty years. All Sicilians lived in our building, and we were no fisherman; we were the only Abruzzese family in the building, we were among all the Sicilians, and my mother used to say, "Quella terra bruciata [that cursed land]" [referring to Sicily]. But they liked my mother [and] they didn't know what else to bring her. Every day the fishermen would come over and bring loads of fish, whatever they caught—calamari, lobsters—to my mother, and she used to say to me, "Go and bring this to this one, go bring this to that one, chi si li mangia tutto queste pesce [who's going to eat all this fish]?" Everyone had three or four kids.

Those fishermen, in the wintertime, they didn't have nothing to eat most of the time—they couldn't make any money, they had to go on welfare most of them. They'd give them maybe a week five or ten dollars for the kids—they'd do it more for the kids—and the social worker would come around. They'd starve in the winter. The fishing boats cost them so much to keep up and they worked very hard. My mother would cook a *pasta e fasule* [macaroni and beans], and say to the woman next door, she had five or six kids, "Here Maria, give this to the kids." And that Sicilian woman Maria made me laugh—she didn't like the idea of my mother giving to the kids; she used to say, "Your mother is always giving [to] my kids." And I'd say, "What the hell, they eat it, don't they?" She had a kid almost every nine months—she died first with cancer, she was young, and her husband died and left; a fisherman's life is a tough life, they don't last long.

My building was big—every floor had five apartments and it was five stories high and everybody had three or four kids in three rooms, two rooms. We used to have a little boy next door to us, his name was Jimmy and every afternoon he used to say, "Angela, what are you having for dinner?" You'd think that he was her son. And my mother used to give him a dish, at night he'd come and my mother would give him some; so then it got so there were three or four brothers and sisters; and all the kids used to fight for the food so my mother had to send the pan of everything to them. But my mother wanted to adopt Jimmy but his mother wouldn't give him up. The mother never cooked for the kids—they used to eat sandwiches all the time. My mother said one day to the woman, "Maria, *fai una minestra buona* [make a good soup] or something." "Oh, no, ma [Oh, no, but]." All the fishermen in the building used to have *le feste* [the feasts] on North Street, and you should have seen the people—they'd didn't know what else to buy! They used to buy stuff by cases, crates of everything! My mother used to say, "Come hanno trovato li soldi per accattà' tutta questa roba ma [How come you found the money to buy all this stuff, but when the day of the week comes you don't have nothing to cook]?"

One thing about my mother, she always used to cook when we came home from school. "But the Sicilians—m'annoia [they annoy me]." My mother used to tell them all where to get off; my mother used to say, "Jettà a va Napule! Jettà alla casa [Get the hell out of here, go home]!" They always used to say, "We don't mind Angela because Angela is very good to the kids." My mother would always use to say, "Did you eat, Jimmy, did you eat, Anthony?" "Yeah my mother made a sandwich." My mother was like a mother to them—she would go all the way to cook for them. My mother used to love to hear the Sicilians talk; she used to get mad, she couldn't understand, they'd come, "Angela, you gotta *la avugghia*?" My mother would say, "Che dice questa la avugghia [What's this *avugghia*]?" And she used to call me because I talked Sicilian, "Vedi che vuole questa qua [See what this one wants]." You know what the *avugghia* is? It's a needle. Thread, sugar, salt, pans, the forks, the spoons—they never had anything and they used to come for everything you could think of.

They used to make their *cartedda* up on the roof in our house; they used to bring them home and the woman used to get a dollar seventy-five to fix those up. Sometimes we'd go up the roof; she'd say "Sit down, help me to do the *cartedda*," and I say, "Get outta here." The smell of fish was terrible. The *cartedda* they called it, it had all strings all around it and on top of it they had hooks and on the hooks they put bait and throw it in. Now they use a big net. Then the landlady told them she didn't want nobody to go up the roof and bring the smell in the building, so all the men used to go to the wharf. My mother always used to say, "*La limosina* [an act of charity] is better than being a millionaire because God helps you." That Jimmy, he's handsome, he's the healthiest one of the bunch, nice and healthy; he was healthy looking and he looked like a fighter. Even today when he sees me, I say, "God bless you, you still look nice and fat." He says, "Yeah your mother fed me!"

Paul Grande

After Paul Grande finished cutting his customer's hair, he sat in the barber chair while his brother Dominic stood and listened to the story.

"The Fisherman's Wife Breastfed Me"

In those days, everybody had their doors open. And whoever was sick in the building, everyone would come down, who brought you chicken soup, who cooked for you, clothes, who'd do your beds. Because the husbands all went to work and they couldn't stay home and take care of their wives, so all the neighbors used to take care of them, feed the kids, take them to school or clothe them or wash the clothes for them. When my mother died, I was young, a baby. In those days they didn't believe—they all breastfed. Used to see the women in the street breastfeeding their babies, they didn't think nothing; you'd see the women breastfeeding their babies and you'd think nothing; you'd go right by them in the street, see a woman breastfeeding a baby and you just keep on walking. And when my mother died, I was a baby and they didn't know how to bottle—they didn't have milk bottles or formula, they didn't have none of that stuff. And the next-door neighbor, the husband was a fisherman, she was a fisherman's wife, and she breastfed me for about a year and a half, two years. Her name was Vitale and I still know her sons. She used to love me; when I used to see her in the street she [would] say, "How many times I breastfed you."

Miracles, Societies, and Processions   21

> Quando passa lu santo, la festa è finita
> (Once the saint passes by, the feast is over).
> —LENA ALBANESE

At eighty, Ursula Baldassare still followed the same daily ritual she had followed as a young girl in Avellino. Rising at dawn to get ready for Morning Mass, she wore a black dress and a hand-embroidered black mantilla over her head as the traditional sign of respect of women entering the sanctity of the church. For Ursula and her elderly *commare* (friends) who attended Mass at Saint Leonard's at Prince and Hanover Streets, what occurred after the faithful left the church held the most significance.

Beset with loneliness from the dislocation of their families and suffering from the pains that come with advanced age, they turned to the saints, praying for divine intercession to end their troubles. To the right of the darkened main altar, a side chapel dedicated to the saints offered comfort. The Mass over, they made their way to the chapel, solemnly genuflected on the resting pew, and bowed their veiled heads, praying to their favorite saint in a moment of arrested silence. A cast-iron candelabra stood in front of the chapel, with rows of candles in wine-red jars emitting little flickering flames that illuminated their shawled figures against white walls of the unheated church. Snapping open black change purses, they dropped coins into the candelabra's donation slot, passing slender wicks to one another to *appiccià a lampa* (light a candle), giving thanks to the saints for granted favors and beseeching them as protectors in future times of need.

Ursula and the other elderly women attending Morning Mass represented the last generation of Italian Americans to practice an Old-World religious rite whose cultural antecedents preceded Christianity. Centuries before the birth of Christ and the building of parish churches and grand basilicas, the Greek settlers of Magna Grecia in southern Italy constructed magnificent temples to honor the gods. In the cella of the temple, the faithful brought votive objects—food, precious objects, and drink—before the statues of gods and goddesses. Pageants and religious festivals performed in their honor were the ancient forerunners of religious processions through the streets of the North End.

South of Avellino, in the region of Campania, one temple in Paestum was dedicated to Hera, goddess of marriage and childbirth. The Greek tradition of revering anthropomorphic gods was adopted by the Romans, who renamed them. In the Roman world, Hera became Juno and the race of gods and goddesses reappeared, subsumed and transformed into the figures of saints and Madonnas in Catholic churches. Just as the faithful participants of Magna Grecia in southern Italy believed fervently in the power of the gods, so the faithful of the North End believed in patron saints. Recalling the ancient ritual of honoring the gods in processions from the temple, North End societies carried their statues out of churches and parish halls in public presentations of appreciation, displaying the saints and Madonnas through the streets of the North End.

Jimmy Brovaco immigrated to the North End when he was eighteen. Compact and squarely built with powerful biceps in 1980 at age seventy-four, he still possessed the vitality of a younger man. As one of the last of his generation to participate in the summer feasts, he took delight in helping other societies as a bearer of patron saints during their processions. But his greatest joy came in July with the three-day feast of San Rocco, patron saint of his village near Avellino. The night before the feast began, he climbed to the second floor of the Saint Leonard's parish hall, where he unlocked the glass door of the niche holding the statue of San Rocco. Filled with desire to honor the saint, he carried the heavy stone statue down the flight of stairs with the help of a younger society member, a feat of Herculean strength for a man his age. There on the first floor, elder members of the San Rocco society—Tommasina Brovaco, Josie Bossio, and Mary Nastasi—awaited to dress and clean San Rocco. With great care, they affixed a golden halo over his head and replaced the staff in his arms in anticipation of the festivities at the intersection of Thacher and North Margin Streets. With blue eyes twinkling, Jimmy described his traditional role in the North End feasts: "San Rocco, allo ventisette, ventotto. Sono portato tutti i santi, e mo che aggio fatto vecch, non mi venn, no more. Solo San Aggripina non aggio tryato" (I've been carrying San Rocco since 1927. But now I'm getting old and I can't do it anymore. The only statue I never tried carrying was San Agrippina) (laughing).

As one of many old-timers who fervently believed in the power of the saints and the need to respect them, a bewildered Jimmy Brovaco could not understand why some of the feasts were changing into moneymaking ventures right before his eyes, their original religious meaning lost for the entertainment of tourists: "Tutt a munnèzza, no police a man, tutti ubriachi, Marònna, everybody mangiano come i porci, non posso sentire manca la musica" (It's filthy, there's no policemen, everybody gets drunk, Madonna! Everybody eats like pigs and I can't even hear the music).

As Ursula and Jimmy's generation faded, one member of the Roma Band who had played at the feasts for many years remarked on the changes: "Now these feasts I play at, I don't know, like, two people outta twenty thousand, really. That's the truth. All strange faces. I was fifteen years old, I remember playing these things, like you'd stop at everybody's yard, everybody's house, eat, drink, whatever you want. You never talked about money or how much you were gonna get, or how much the saint took in or whatever. Now it's all money."

FIGURE 43. Eddie Marino.

Miracles, Societies, and Processions

Eddie Marino

Eddie Marino was adopted from an Irish orphanage by Sicilians from the North End. Despite the look of Ireland on his face, he spoke in perfect Sciaccatani dialect.

The Miracles of the Madonna del Soccorso

I've been there in the society since I was a kid. My mother and father were the founders and the other old-timers of the Madonna del Soccorso Men's Society—my mother and my aunt Anna Sutera—were the founders of the Woman's Society. My father was from Sciacca, but he came here when he was six years old. My mother was born here, in New York on Elizabeth Street. My aunt was the president for about thirty years, for so many years she used to get the people together. For instance, *lu paisan* [person from the same town] of ours, and if you marry a stranger, she could join in because either the husband or the wife is our kind and we used to let them come in. They used to join our club just the same. Had to be Sicilian, yeah. Unless you married one of our kind, you couldn't join in. Well, they dissolved it; the mothers passed away, you know. This young generation—I'm the only one I think—very few that are interested in that.

Two hundred people carry her in Sciacca. I made a promise to her when I was on skid row and I turned to her. I got my power, I made up my mind, forget it, forget it, forget it, because I was in the drain, Anthony, I didn't know no friends, didn't know no family—I was gone. Everybody used to walk away from me, give me a nickel, give me a dime, give me a quarter. Just for what? For a drink. I turned to her and Sant Agrippina and I got my wish. I got the miracle and I got away from it.

One day she was coming out [in the procession] and I said, the exact words I said, "I'll never forget, dear Blessed Mother, if you're gonna let me lead this life either you change me or you take me right now, even if I go tonight." I should have said those words long ago—I've stopped for twenty-four, twenty-five years now without touching a drop. I make a promise to her every year, I give her something—it's like a wedding. Every time it's the feast I patronize her, give her something. Now when I got off of skid row, the first I made her that crown; I started on the crown then I went up, I was paying my mother five, ten dollars a month. On other years if my mother sees the Blessed Mother go by I'll give her my best thick rope chain I brought from Italy, when she was in from of my house I'd just hang it right on her; it was something—the people were crying their eyes out, they couldn't believe I gave it. It was like a wedding; every year I used to save my pennies, my nickels, my dimes, as long as I kept my promise. My sister, my brother helped me out a lot in here, and I used to make a promise—we used to put, they used to put so much apiece for me too. I did a lot of beautiful things for her [the Madonna] in memory of my mother and father. And every year as soon as she comes down, I have the honor of taking off the crown and put it back on her.

My nephew Joe Guarino used to carry her every year. My brother was on his dying bed, the last year—he carried her last August. Another time my nephew Joe Guarino was very sick, and I turned to her and I said, "Dear Blessed Mother, let him come home on Christmas." Before you know, on Christmas Eve, I get the call my nephew Joe could lead a normal life—he was home on Christmas. It's something unbelievable what's she's done for me.

My mother saw Sant Aggripina and the Blessed Mother on her dying bed—they appeared to her. She told me when she got better. She said, "I seen a beautiful blonde young lady dressed in blue—that was the Blessed Mother." She was devoted to the both of them and she seen them. Then when she took sick the last time, I had a framed picture of Sant Aggripina. That door—I slammed it, I shut it, it never fell. When my mother come out of her bedroom, that frame fell right in front of her feet. She made me understand my mother wasn't coming back, because I was devoted to her. And that happened in my life, I can't deny it. It's not imagination, it just happened.

I was present when that frame fell in front of her foot. I picked it up, she kissed it, and she went away. That frame fell, she fell, that was it—that was her death-knell that she had to go, that's all. Because we all have our destiny. Oh, I go crazy when she comes out [for the procession]—I can't help it. I just break down crying and crying when she gets out of that door because all my memories come back to me—my mother, my father, whatever she did for me. And I go after her and Sant Agrippina barefooted on the Sunday special day they're on the street in the procession—that's the vow I made as long as I live. Then I do the vigil Friday nights, I do it for her on Thursday when she comes back from the wharf, all night until morning, until they relieve me. I'm the only one that comes up here and patronizes her, lights, candles. When someone gives their time to the Blessed Mother, that's an honor for me to thank them.

FIGURE 44. Madonna del Soccorso Society, 1900.

Antonio Tarantino

The Legend of the Madonna d'Anzano

The story of the Madonna comes from the oral tradition, and the people of Anzano and my relatives from Scampitella all know the story. The Madonna was originally called "Santa Maria del Silice," but since she was found in Anzano, they gave her the name Santa Maria d'Anzano.

Anzano was once a thick forest, with only a few small dwellings where the herdsmen and shepherds brought their flocks and oxen in the evenings. Towns with any significant numbers of inhabitants were distant. Some farmers from Trevico, the ancient town and residence of the bishop of Zungoli, and farmers from the contrada of Scampata near the city of Contrada,

Scampitella, which was named because of its lack of trees, banded their herds to graze. An old mule trail traversed the forest, which was a paved roadway—the Via Romana Euclana, Ercoleo or Euclana—and they followed their herds into the woods. There in the thick woods of the forest, surrounded by brush, they saw in a cave a statue of a woman seated on a royal throne with arm rests. On her left knee she held a baby boy with a small globe in his right hand. The Madonna was surrounded by light and dressed in a royal blue gown sewn with stars. But the story that we knew, the story I heard the monsignor tell us when I was an altar boy, was that these shepherds grazing their herds in the woods for some time became tired and fell asleep. After two or three hours, as dusk approached, they suddenly awoke to find their animals gone. Overcome with desperation, they began searching for their animals, but night had fallen and they could not find them. As they were walking through the woods, to their right side a light attracted them, drawing them to it like the star that guided the three Magi from Jerusalem to Bethlehem when they found the baby Jesus. These shepherds were drawn to this light and what did they find? Cutting through the brush, they saw a statue inside a cave. With simple faith and love of the Madonna, the faithful reported what happened to the bishop of Trevico. Later he brought his clergymen and they tried to transport the beautiful, majestic, and heavy statue to Trevico on a farmer's wagon pulled by oxen. The wagon moved, but after a short distance down the road, at Macinan, where even today the devoted Trevicani pilgrims still make a yearly pilgrimage, the team stopped dead in its tracks.

Despite all the hard pushing and yelling from the herdsmen, they could not force the oxen and wagon to move on. They tried to bring the wagons with [the] statue down the Via Erculea to the town [of] Zungoli, without success. At one hundred meters, they tried again down the Via Erculea at a place which today is called Casino. The wagons stopped again and the oxen would not move. The third try towards Scampitella, the same thing happened. Wagons and oxen stood in their place. The men understood at that point the Madonna wished to stay where she had been found. They brought her back and they built a church that became a beacon of light for all the local good herdsmen, farmers, and shepherds.

Men, women, and children walked to the church and gathered in the evenings. They sang prayers in praise of their "Santa Maria of Silici," her name taken from the "Via Lastricata a Selce o Selciata [the Madonna of the Paved Road]," which comes from *silex-silicis* in Latin. *Translated from Italian.*

The Miracles of the Madonna d'Anzano

The Madonna d'Anzano Societa was founded on January 5, 1905, here in Boston by the first immigrants who came to the North End. My uncle, Giuseppe Luigi Paglia, was the first giudice di pace [justice of the peace, or president] of the society and he had his barbershop on Thacher Street where the laundry is now, and nearby was the society with over two hundred members. My brother Carlo was another founder, and he was president for many years; then there was Sebastiano Scapicchio, Pietro Di Sessa.

When we had parades, and Giuseppe Luigi Paglia made them wear uniforms with top hats, smoking was prohibited, and if someone failed to march erect, he fined them a dollar, two dollars. During our meetings we always had to conduct ourselves with decency. If we make any money, we put it in the bank account and we split it with our ladies' society and with the president, Concetta Giamba, who has been there since 1947. She has always been a very hard-working woman from Anzano and very supportive of the society all these years. She's old now and she's the honorary president for life.

But from its very beginnings they wanted the Madonna to become *la protettrice del North End* [the patron saint of the North End], but the priests—you know how it is, they didn't believe it was proper—because the Irish were here first and we had Saint Patrick, and that's the way it was. But we always wanted her to be the patron saint of the North End. In fact, so many people hold her in such high esteem, and they venerate the Madonna, because she is so miraculous.

There are episodes that occurred during droughts when there was no rain in the town for four or five months. I remember when I was the organist at the church. Monsignor Petriglia from Trevico came with a procession and there was no change—the air stayed still, and the people were asking for water, asking for rain. After the parish priest from Trevico finished his prayer of praise to the Madonna, the procession left the church to walk with the statue of the Madonna of Anzano not too far away from the church. The procession filed out with the little children first, then the young children who were making their First Communion, and just after they took a few steps past the monument of Anzano with the statue of the Madonna d'Anzano, it began to pour! It was a miracle!

There was another miracle another time; it was the day of the festival, the Madonna's feast day, and the bells were ringing not far from the statue of the Madonna. It was on this day the boys would go up the bell tower to ring the three bells, and they had a beautiful sound. In the square in front of the war monument to the fallen soldiers, a crowd of people were in the market; it had outdoor stalls where vendors were selling their wares—clothes, shoes. Somehow the part of the bell fell apart and the big clapper fell thirty meters down from [the] bell tower into the crowd in the piazza, miraculously not hitting anyone. An incredible thing! It was a huge piece, long and thick. One of those bells must have weighed close to a ton, mamma mia! And it fell to the ground right out in front of the church. It made the people cry to think that had it fallen on anyone it would have killed them instantly—it was a miracle of the Madonna.

Another time we had been waiting three, four days to have our procession because it had been raining very hard. The same monsignor who used to come every year from Trevico to preach recited a prayer in praise of the Madonna and then he said Mass, and the rain again started in a heavy downpour. The parish priest said, "We're still going out, even if it's still raining hard." As the procession left the church in the heavy rain, it suddenly began to turn into a fine, fine drizzle—it was beautiful—and it all became clear; even this was a miracle, no? *Translated from Italian.*

FIGURE 45. Feast of San Rocco, 1980.

Miracles, Societies, and Processions   257

Mary Nastasi	Mary Nastasi's two grandchildren came into the kitchen from playing outside. When they heard the story of San Rocco they sat on her lap and listened.

San Rocco and the North End

The feast of San Rocco began in 1921. I was five years old then; I was born in 1916. My parents and their people from the village of San Michele Baronia in the region of Avellino brought it here. We used to look forward to it; we used to get dressed up pretty, in our fineries, and they had their hall on the corner of Snow Hill and Prince Street. And after the procession all us kids would go there and have sandwiches and ice cream and they'd be dancing. We had company from all over; the cousins would come from all over, from Springfield, Connecticut—it was one happy family then. There was never any bickering—everyone was so happy, and money was scarce, but I tell you the saint used to collect more money then when money was—wages were low and everything else was cheaper. We used to have a ball; we used to look forward to it. Our mothers would cook from soup to nuts—this one was coming, that one was coming, they'd have everything on the table; it was a ball.

We always had it down here, on North Margin and Thacher, as long as I can remember. During World War II they stopped the feast; a lot of the boys were at war, so all we had was a procession. In 1949 they started up with feasts like this again and it's been going on ever since. We used to have it two days and one night, from Saturday to Sunday. In the old days only the *paesani* [people from the same village], the people of the society, used to do everything. Their children used to carry the flags, the ribbons, the flowers, and carry the saint, but no more. It's kinda hard now—just the men carry the saint down the stairs at the church and sometimes you can't even get them.

My cousin Josie dresses up the saint and puts all the gold on him. Then Josie and Jimmy Brovaco take turns with the vigil watching the saint overnight, and on Sunday I donate [for] the High Mass and the procession follows with the Roma Band. But the young generation doesn't bother with it anymore—I don't know why. They come down for the Mass, but they really don't take an interest in it. But, you know, I'm surprised that quite a few people from outside the North End call me. They're from the same town as my parents in Italy; they ask if their nephews and nieces could carry a flag or a ribbon in the procession. I say "Sure," and we let them take turns. It keeps the tradition alive. Up until ten years ago you had to bid to carry San Rocco or to carry the flowers, even the ribbons or the banner—they had to bid to carry them. The highest bidder carried it. I try to keep the feast as religious as possible. I don't know what's happened, but it's getting out of hand—prices have gone way up, the printer charges more, the band costs more, the cost of the food [for everyone in the procession]—it costs a lot. And the city won't help us pick up the trash bags left behind.

A Vow to Saint Rocco

You try to keep the tradition. Seventeen years ago, my daughter was born with hemangioma in her hand and they wanted to amputate the whole arm at the time. We wouldn't let them. And I made a vow after I came to my senses, that if they wouldn't touch her I would open my house for two days (during the feast) and I'd make a collection asking people for donations and that would be

FIGURE 46. Mary Nastasi walking barefoot, 1981.

Miracles, Societies, and Processions

my vow to the last day I lived—and I've been doing it for seventeen years now. I have open house and [at the feast]) I have my bird cages and I have the birds come out, balloons from the roof, and all that. I thought it was just something nice, very festive, the balloons and fireworks they shoot off in the school yard, the ticker tape. Booze, I don't go for it—I try to keep it as religious as I can. The younger generation doesn't bother, they don't take that much of an interest in it; I get very perturbed with them. I just vowed to give all the donations to the church and that I would walk barefoot during the procession until the last day I lived. And every year since that day my daughter and I walk the procession together. To this day [the doctors] haven't touched her.

I'm a great believer in miracles in more ways than one for everything. If somebody's having bad luck I say, don't worry, there's a God, he'll take care of you if you pray hard enough. Like a few things have happened to my cousins, the Brovacos, really bad things, and they came out with flying colors, so you know you say you pray to San Rocco, could it be or isn't it? And you have to wonder. So it has to be if you believe in it; you gotta believe in it real strong. Like I say, it's like everything else, you have to work for it, you have to earn it. It isn't just a fly-by-night thing, you know, you pray today and forget for a week and start all over again. You have to pray—you pray every day and every night.

Tommasina Brovaco   Tommasina Brovaco's voice rose in operatic fashion as she talked about the miracle of Saint Rocco.

The Dream of San Rocco

We believe that all the saints have miraculous powers, but Saint Rocco is very special to us—he's miraculous to us [and] our town holds him very dear. If you're sick and you ask for his help, he'll give it to you, and he did a lot of beautiful things for me and I can't forget him. And you have to believe in him. When it was time for my husband's heart operation, he was always crying with fear and he didn't want to have it done. The night before his operation, he had a dream of Saint Rocco. He told him, "Joe, have the operation and have no fear, I am here to watch over you." The next morning, after the operation was over, my husband told me the story of his dream: "Last night I dreamt of San Rocco, and he told me that he was watching over me." And he went through the operation in total peace. And that's why we hold Saint Rocco in such veneration!

San Rocco's Chain

My mother in Italy had a daughter who had *maluocchio* ["the eyes"—she was sick from a spell put on her by someone] all the time when she was young—she was sick. This was forty, fifty years ago in my town, Flumeri. My mother had this long gold chain and she gave it the statue of San Rocco. He's covered with them because of his miracles. So my mother gave her chain to San Rocco in thanks for granting her a favor to heal my sister. She always had a vow to San Rocco. I can never forget Sant Rocco, both here and in Italy. There was [a] young man in my town who was in love with a young girl and he was getting married, but he didn't have the money to buy a gift for his wife. He was the bell ringer of the church and he would go and ring the bells early in the morning when it was dark. So he thought to himself, I'll go into the sacristy and take one of the chains off San Rocco. Who will know? The next day he saw an old man behind the door with a cane. The old man said, "Good day." The young man said, "Who are you?" The old man said, "You don't know who I am? Yesterday you took my chain. Why did you take it? I want you to bring it back." The young man was so stunned he couldn't speak because he realized it was San Rocco. The young man died seven months later from the fear that struck him when San Rocco told him to bring the chain back. This is a true story. *Translated from Neapolitan dialect.*

Josephine Bossio

Josephine Bossio was the president of the San Rocco Society. She and her elderly society members dressed the statue of San Rocco and made all the preparations for the procession.

"San Rocco Healed Me"

When I was six years old in Flumeri, Italy, my sister and I had a terrible sickness. And the doctor told my mother that there was nothing that could be done to save us. In desperation that night my mother, who was very devoted to San Rocco, went up to our church of San Rocco at midnight to cry. Our church is on top of a small mountain; below was all farmland and small houses where the townspeople lived. And when the people heard my mother screaming, they didn't know who it was, so they went up to the church and they found my mother unconscious on the floor. But at that same moment, we started to get better and I began to drink again. San Rocco healed us.

The next day when the doctor came by to visit, he was expecting to hear us crying out, because in Italy when death comes, the people scream and cry. But he walked into our house and he didn't hear anything. He said, "This is a grace from—" And my mother said, "San Rocco has granted me *una grazia* [a favor]." My mother told us, "San Rocco has healed you." And that's why we've devoted ourselves to him for our whole lives, till we die. San Rocco is the patron saint of our territory in Italy.

"San Rocco Appeared"

When we had our earthquake about twenty years ago, there was a man there who came from another small town. He had a sack and he was going to get some salt. San Rocco was in the street and he asked the man who he was, and he said, "You're not going to get salt now—go to that town and wake everyone up." So the man asked him why, and he answered, "You'll see." As the man was walking towards the village, he asked, "Who are you?" He said, "My name is Rocco and I watch over this town." When the man got near the church of San Rocco, he saw flames and the sky had become red because the earthquake was coming. He began yelling to awaken and warn everyone and they were all saved. Then the people carried the statue to the convent because the earthquake had damaged the church. San Rocco always saves that town, always. *Translated from Neapolitan dialect.*

Christmas in the North End — 22

> Primma Natalè no famme e no friddo, dòppo Natalè famme e friddo (Before Christmas no hunger and no cold, after Christmas hunger and cold).
> —LENA RICCIO

Italian immigrants adapted to the American celebration of Christmas, switching the Italian holiday from January 6 to December 25. Italians had grown up knowing the biblical account of the Adoration of the Magi and the folk figure of La Befana, who followed the star to the Magi, leaving sweets in doorways on her way. Women performed in Christmas plays at the North End Union, reciting poetry in Italian to describe the brilliant star that guided the Three Kings to Bethlehem. In the early days of immigration, festive dried grapes tied with red ribbons brightened drab cold-water flats and bountiful suppers at the Christmas Eve table reflected the economic stability of steady work.

For some, like Angelo Luongo, the excitement for the Christmas season started before Thanksgiving with his search for the perfect Christmas tree. Equally important was the Christmas Eve banquet he cooked for his family and many visiting relatives. Before the era of Christmas toys, Annie Arigo could hardly wait for the special moment when her father gave her a Christmas stocking filled with her favorite treat of fresh chestnuts. Her sister, Mary Arigo Ventola, recalled in the late 1930s when "the guys down the corner from the social club on Foster Street" spread Christmas cheer to local children. Dressed as Santa Claus, Gabe Piemonte stood by the Christmas tree at the playground handing out gifts.[1]

As North Enders became rooted in the working class, Christmas trees once decorated with dried grapes tied with red ribbons, fruits, and candles were now trimmed with lead tinsel and strands of spun-glass angel hair and strung with colorful lights. La Befana, who brought small gifts to children, was replaced by the robust, red-cheeked Santa Claus, who left Tonka toys and Raggedy Ann dolls for the magic of Christmas morning.

During the Christmas season, the North End's normally vibrant streets buzzed with heightened activity. North Enders shopped for Christmas specialties on Salem Street: special cheeses, choice meats, grappa (Italian brandy), apertivi (aperitifs), and large chunks of torrone nougat. Voices from Giuffre's Fish Market hawked the traditional Christmas delicacy: "*Anguilla! Anguilla capitone!*" (Eels! Big eels!), which were squirming in a large metal tub.

Reminiscent of street vendors in Naples, Sam Natale yelled "Pizza, cauda, cauda!" offering fresh, hot pizza from his makeshift stand on the busy corner of Salem and Cross Streets. Some shops offered regular customers a glass of wine or a shot of special liquor to toast the holiday season. A group

FIGURE 47. Maria Chiarenza, 1981.

of *zampognari* in traditional peasant outfits roved the streets, serenading the neighborhood with Christmas songs on pastoral flutes, bagpipes, and clarinets. Friends and relatives exchanged holiday cheer on the street and returned home with a sense of satisfaction, anticipating the Christmas holiday they would enjoy with loved ones.

Maria Chiarenza

"I Was the Shepherd Girl"

I came from the province of Caltanisetta in Sicily, from Riesi, in 1924. I came with a baby fifteen days old, another child three and a half, and another four and a half years old. Then I had three more children here. I'm eighty-three now. My husband, too. We put on a play, "*Zappatore* [Tiller of the Soil]." We used to put on plays in Italian at Christmas at the Michelangelo School, and Mrs. Bloom was in charge at the time. Oh, how many the plays I've been in! I still have all the costumes for all the parts I played. We used put on our neighborhood plays at the North End Union, too. In one of them [about the birth of Jesus] I played the part of a little shepherd girl who wanted go along with the shepherds, but they told me, "Tu sei piccola [you're small]." I had to dress for the part of the little shepherd girl, with clothes made of goat skins, a little red shawl, and a little beret. In one scene I had to be asleep with a little lamb. I was supposed to be quiet as the shepherds were watching the little sheep. But just when it became light, I recited the following:

>"O che spendida notte
>Che bella notte
>L'aria pieno d'incanto
>Le stelle brillano, e quella stella, Quella stella.
>"[O what a wonderful night,
>What a beautiful night,
>The air is full of enchantment,
>The stars are twinkling, and that star, That star.]"

While I recited those lines, the other shepherds arrived on the scene. One said, "Look at that star!" And one shepherd said to me, "Look, the shepherds are bringing the baby Jesus gifts." Then it was time for me to wake up the sleeping angel and, oh, the people in the audience cried, honest to God. You can even ask Michelina Manfra or Ida Macchalone—they were in the play. All the others are dead now.

Paul Grande

"Come in, Taste It"

The milkman wouldn't want to make deliveries around Christmas or the holidays because every stop he'd make, they all tell him, "Come in and have a drink, have a piece of this, have a piece of that." My milkman said it was impossible to get home sober. Everybody used to make their homemade wine—they didn't buy wine in those days, they didn't believe in that. Every stop, you go through a building, six, seven tenants, there'd be six or seven stops, "Have a glass of wine, have a cookie." If they were eating, "Sit down and eat with us." They used to say, "Oh we hate holidays down there." I got people in this building here, they're living here two years, they don't know who their next-door neighbor is. In that sense, it has changed. Before, you'd go through a building and all the kitchen doors were open—you could smell the food right in the hallways, whatever they were cooking. And they'd all come in and they'd say, "Taste it, see what I'm cooking, look what I'm doing."

Mary Colantonio

After many years in the same apartment, Mary Colantonio faced eviction at age seventy. She remembered the old neighborhood's sense of community.

Exchanging Dishes at Christmastime

We were so poor in those days we could barely afford one thing. We were poor, but Christmas wasn't as commercialized as it is today. I remember my mother making all them cookies and giving them to everybody in our apartment house, and they would cook something special and give it to my mother. All the different—the Sicilians, the Neapolitans, the Romans—each one had their own traditional dish for Christmas. My mother's tradition was to make a spinach pie; it was Sicilian—she would make her own dough and put in olives and anchovies. And everyone in the building would wait for my mother to make that. And we'd wait for what the other people were doing—the Romans, the Neapolitans—they'd come and give us their goodies and my mother would share her goodies with them. And that was really, that was real Christmas. We used to look forward to those days. We didn't think of all these presents or material things. And whatever little thing we would get, maybe a little rag doll, we were four sisters and one would play with the little rag doll.

On Christmas Eve we'd go to Mass, come home, and we'd start to eat—wine, nuts, coffee—we'd stay up till two, three in the morning, play *à tombola*—it was like beano only in Italian. You had the little cards, and you called the numbers, and you put a penny there in the dish, and they'd be ten pennies in the dish, and we'd all want that and we'd all be waiting for our number to be called. Ten pennies was such a big deal to us, those days. The only Christmas thing we did was go to Mass; we'd visit each other for about a half hour, and then coming home from Mass we'd drop in there, wish them a merry Christmas, have a little cup of coffee, a little drink, or a little anisette. Then we'd go to our house where all our families would gather—each house had their own family, their daughters, and their children, their grandchildren.

Mary Molinari

Mary Molinari advocated for a senior citizen center for elders who needed a place to socialize.

"We Kissed Their Hands"

My parents were from Pratola Serra near Avellino. My father—we were all married—We'd wait for midnight. I don't know if it was the same bottle of whiskey, I don't know if he used to make it, it used to be the same bottle coming out every time. He would take it out at twelve o'clock and my mother used to make cream cheese pie and *'i struffoli*. Just at twelve o'clock, we'd get all around there and the first one would kiss my father. We had a habit—we didn't kiss him on the cheek, we kissed him on the hand. The old Italians would do it like that. And the same with my mother, too. And then we'd go around in circle, the other we'd kiss on the face, the other one we'd kiss on the cheek. It was something beautiful—it was a family tradition every year; we'd get together with my sisters and everybody and we'd do this every New Year's Eve [and] we'd have a nice time. We didn't want anything, but we wanted the family—we really had a nice time. It was beautiful.

Mary Pasquale   Mary Pasquale sang "La Novella di Natale" the same way her mother sang it at Christmas, accompanied by her uncle on guitar.

Singing at Christmas

And at Christmas time they'd all get together, they'd say, "Come on, let's all go up to Peter's house," which was my grandfather's house. Three rooms, you know, just three rooms. An uncle of mine had one of those things—it looked like a little guitar—put in his mouth and go bling-a-bling-a-bling! And another uncle of mine, Zi' Felice, buon anima [Uncle Felix, that good soul]! He used to play the harmonica so good, the type that you'd put a glass up on the side and give it a different tone. Well you should have heard my mother singing "La Novella di Natale," the Novena Prayers for Christmas. And after that would be a glass of wine, a glass of vermouth, and *le zeppole, le struffole*, and all these things. You know, it was togetherness.

Al Mostone

A North End Christmas in 1910

We were fifteen kids, I was the oldest, and we owned nothing here; we had to rent and we lived in a cold-water flat. I used to study by kerosene lamps—we had no gas—we had no hot water, and I had to sleep in the kitchen. Christmas didn't mean Christmas trees for us. We had nothing, and most of the Italian families here that came from Italy at that time lived the same way that we did. But there was one thing that I remember. And that was a bond that existed between the Italians. You were never alone, you always had friends, and I can emphasize that very strongly because as I grew older, I found that the same bond existed in the North End when I was much older, even today with the North End people—anything happened, you were sure you had enough of people to come to your house, bring their own food, do whatever they had to, give you whatever they could. They didn't have much, but what they had they gladly shared.

Helen Luongo

Helen Luongo was seventy-four at the time of our interview. As she described the many difficult times of her life, she paused in mid-sentence to ask if I wanted some ginger ale.

Zampognari, Christmas Trees, and the Infant Jesus

My husband used to start after Thanksgiving looking for the tree. "The tree, Angelo did you get the tree?" "No, everything I saw I didn't like. I didn't buy it." "But Angelo, what are they gonna make it grow for you?" He says, "You know, if I don't find the tree that I like I don't bring it in this house." He'd buy the tree, but the tree wouldn't go up until Christmas Eve. My father would start a month ahead of time. We didn't have ornaments on the tree. The best fruits—apples, grapes, pears—were hanging on the Christmas tree. My father used to make wine, and he'd keep the dried grapes and then tie them with red ribbons and tie it on the trees. These were the ornaments we had. And then we had candles with the clips, they had a clip like a clothespin and they had you put a candle in it and you'd put it on the tree. But of course, you'd light them only for a while, but then you'd put them out—you couldn't keep them on—before you went to bed.

Then underneath the tree you would have the crib, you'd have the Blessed Mother, the ox, the donkey, the sheep. But the infant Jesus (tapping on the table) couldn't go there until midnight—the infant Jesus isn't born, you don't put him there! He isn't born till midnight Christmas Eve. My father had a rubber doll, that was our infant Jesus, and he had just the diaper on him, he had the straw. Now everybody puts the Infant out before midnight but before anybody that had the crib, you didn't put the infant Jesus. The crib was there but the baby wasn't there because he wasn't born till midnight. Oh, Christmas was beautiful. The only thing is, my poor mother and father—God have mercy on their souls—they didn't have anything to give us, but what they gave us was love, was happiness.

The *zampognari* [singers with pastoral wind instruments]—the ones that play the bagpipes—they used to come in our house when I was a child for the Immaculate Conception for the eighth of December. We used to have them for eight days in the house every night and play and sing those hymns. The last night they'd come was on the Feast of the Immaculate Conception on the eighth of December. And we'd sing along with them and say the prayers, say the rosary. And then they'd come again for Christmas and we'd have them again for eight days.

There used to be four men who used to go house to house in the North End. One with the bagpipe, the other with the flute, and there was another one with another kind of an instrument. They'd sing all hymns in Italian, "Tu Scendi delle Stelle." It was so beautiful and I sang along with them! It was something. All our traditions are gone. It was so beautiful. We would have refreshments—wine, coffee, cookies, and all that there. Then the kids would follow them from house to house, the older people too. We would all follow them like a procession every house they'd go [to]. Of course, you had to hire them, but they didn't really do it for the money, they did it as a tradition. My mother would have to hold my hand.

Irish and Italians 23

> Prima che conosce una persona bisogna mangiare un sacco di sale
> (Before you really know someone, you have to eat a sack of salt).
> —MARY "CARMELLA" PAGLIUCA

In the 1860s, when the first Italians arrived in the North End, the Irish looked on them as barbarous, unclean, and inferior intruders, the same way nativist Anglo-Saxons had viewed the Irish decades earlier. Though the animosity between Irish and Italians often boiled over into bloody street fights, both groups had arrived from Europe with a similar past. Many were descendants of rural folk in Ireland or Italy who lived off the land as tenant and subsistence farmers. The deaths of millions of desperately poor Irish from the Potato Famine in counties like Galway and Donegal forced starving families to immigrate to Boston, crowding into neighborhoods like the North End.

Fifty years later Italians fleeing poverty and land deprivation arrived en masse with the same aspirations for a better life. Because the Irish and Italians had endured suffering, many chose to forget. Michael Moriarity, like many Italians, had been a tenant farmer from the village of Castlegregory in county Kerry and carried such bitter memories of the difficult life he had experienced that he refused to talk about Ireland with his children and never returned.

It was a warm Saturday in the North End, the only day of the week that the Louis and Merry Bakery on Prince Street featured brown bread and baked beans, a neighborhood favorite. Young Marguerite Carbone and her younger brother had just returned to their walk-up apartment on Charter Street with loaves of bread and ceramic pitchers filled with warm baked beans for the night's supper. As the family bowed their heads in prayer, angry voices of men cursing in Italian reverberated from the street. The Carbone family had grown accustomed to the nightly disturbances. One of the Irish gang's favorite tactics was setting up their slingshot squad, pelting Italians as they exited with pitchers of cold beer from the corner tavern. It was one of the many rough-and-tumble bars that served as headquarters for Irish gangs who controlled the movements of street corners and attacked anyone who looked suspicious.

Fisherman arriving after sunset slept on their boats, fearing the Irish gangs roving the Waterfront and never daring to cross Commercial Street to get to their homes on North Street. Mothers accompanied children to grammar schools to protect them from their Irish schoolmates.[1] Italians were easy targets in the early days, often walking the streets alone or in pairs, wearing country outfits, and speaking an undecipherable language. The Irish considered Italians unpatriotic because of their slowness to learn English and their habit of staying in American only long enough to earn enough money to permanently return home. The Irish also questioned the Italians' belief in the saints rather than the papacy or the authority of Irish priests, which alienated Italians from the Irish-dominated Catholic church. The spectacle of street theater in religious processions honoring statues further convinced Irish Catholics that Italians were unworthy pagans. Padrones won construction jobs with underpaid employees, which undercut the hourly wages of Irish workers, further alienating Italians.

By the late teens, Irish domination of the Commercial Street and Waterfront area began to wane as the Irish moved out and the numbers of Italians grew. Emboldened to fight back with their own gangs, some Italians became local heroes for their street-fighting ability. Some entered the ring as professional boxers, often changing their names to please Irish audiences and Irish officials who controlled the sport—Sabino Ferullo became Sammy Fuller, Tony Sciucco became Tony Shucco, and Alberto Delmonte became Al Delmont.

In the political arena, the Irish controlled the North End until the early 1930s, when people with names like Langone and Bacigalupo were elected to positions of power and some patronage jobs were handed out to Italians as the Irish had done for their countrymen for decades. However, most of the trade unions were dominated by the Irish, who also held a firm grip on City Hall and well-paying jobs.

Deeply ingrained in the social relationships between Italians and Irish were bitter memories of fighting, the competition for jobs, and mutual suspicion. The two worlds converged amid the music and dancing in "The Tent" in South Boston, Lyceum Hall in East Boston, and Roughan Hall in Charlestown when fair-skinned, sea green-eyed daughters of the Emerald Isle laid eyes on the dark-eyed, olive-skinned sons of the Mezzogiorno and Sicily. The two ethnicities began a new dance that often ended in marriage, forever binding two cultures that had traditionally been at war.

Giuseppe Freni

Giuseppe Freni and his wife owned Freni Bakery on 82 Endicott Street.

"You Couldn't Raise Your Head"

I first came to South Boston and then to the North End in 1922. I lived on 36 Cross Street before they knocked it down to make retail stores. At the time, work was scarce. A friend came to me and said, "Joe, do you want a job?" Yeah, I said. And I went to work, *al livello massimo* [all out], at a job doing hard labor laying and building roads in Lowell, Massachusetts. But in those days, you worked! It isn't like today. I knew how to work. I worked for eight hours a day, ten, twelve dollars a week, and we worked all out at hard labor, *al livello massimo*. We worked and worked. I had an Irish boss. You couldn't even raise your head while you were working for him. My friend [was] working with me, and he said, "Joe! But I just can't work like you!" I told him, "That's all right—when you see the boss, give him a hand, just do whatever he tells you to do." He said, "Joe, I just can't do it!" After two days, the boss fired him. Every day the boss fired people so he could get fresh hands. He worked people so hard because he was under contract and he got a bigger commission when he got the job done faster. I worked there for about a year and then I found work here in Boston.

Josie Zizza

"I'm Not a Guinea"

I worked with Irish and Jews at Columbia Packing. They always felt that the Italian was beneath them, you know? I used to argue with a lot of people on account of that, cause I always used to stick up for my nationality whether we were right or wrong. They called me Guinea. One day I had a fight with a big foreman. I wasn't afraid of him. He said, "Hey, you Guinea, get on the ball!" I said, "You're nothing but a big Irish, this and that," and we had it out. So I said, "Hey, you dirty Irishman, you don't talk to me like that. I am not a Guinea. I am an American like you are. I says your parents came from Ireland, my mother came from Italy. That doesn't make us any different than you." So he went and reported me to the big boss, and the big boss came up. He was nice because he could've fired me if he wanted to. But he said, "Josie, what's the story?" And I told him the story. And he let the foreman have it. I says, "I'm not a Guinea." I said, "I'm a human being like he is. And I'm an American of Italian descent. The way he's American of Irish descent." So since that time on that foreman respected me. We had it hard those days, believe me. Now everybody—you all have it a little easier. I had to work hard. And I sent all my boys to college, I made sure they received an education. I figured they needed it.

Dominic Rosso

Dominic described his life as a drummer: "As a boy of ten, I took a liking to drums because I heard a few bands that I liked. I had the beat the first day. I had the urge. I don't know, it just came to me because I heard it so much. I heard the best. And I was determined I'd make it."

"They Called Me Murphy"

The last job I had was with an Irish band, I never did it in my life before. The minute I played the first number they were all surprised—I was the only Italian in the place, the Shamrock Club in North Cambridge—they had their dances in the Veterans Hall. I pleased them so much that they started to call me Murphy (laughing). They couldn't get over how I got into that Irish swing right off, just like that. You know why? I was in the pit. I played every style. I learned all [the] vaudeville acts. In other words, it's like a doctor that knows you—your ears, your eyes, your body, your toes—same way with music. There's the kind that only sit in and play dance music—that's all they know. They don't even have to know music for that.

The real musician is the one that plays the shows, plays any style—French, Italian, German—that's a real musician. I played any of those styles, any type of vaudeville—they all have different music in vaudeville and if you're a musician they put the music in front of you and you play the show.

I played Italian shows here on Hanover Street in the Casino; they were closed some Sundays, some Sundays they were open. When they ran Italian shows the Casino Burlesque was on Hanover Street, at the beginning where Government Center is; it started way down and it was a very long street, like an avenue. There were no big Italian stars like Caruso or Mario Lanza, people like that. They had a lot of drama in between, but they overdid that drama stuff, like the half-Italian, half-American man would steal the wife of a typical Italian husband and they overdid that—it seemed like a repetition. And when they came out in the beginning, before they even performed, the Italian people, they were all applauding as though they were Caruso. They didn't do anything yet! You see they judged him from the previous performance and when they liked him they gave him a lot of courage—they wanted him to know that we were going to enjoy it anyway. I enjoyed every day of it in Scollay Square; when they changed it around to Government Center it broke everybody's heart.

Charlie Polcari

Charlie Polcari showed me the bed he invented for elders who are unable to fold their sheets down. At ninety-one he filed for a patent and was looking forward to marketing it.

"The Irish Got Hold"

At this time of the year, September, if you went over to North Square, you'd find four, five hundred Italian people waiting for jobs, to go out to work in the country. There used to be contractors—railroads, all different—and they used to take so many people and take them away with them; they worked for the whole summer. But you know what they used to say? You'll be surprised. They [the immigrants] used to say, "We stay here"—they were waiting for the election—"if the Republican comes in, we'll stay here, we'll get the work. But if a Democrat becomes president, we'll starve, so we'll go back to the old country." That's what they used to say. They wouldn't stay here if a Democrat was here. "If a Democrat becomes the president, we're gonna get outta here." This was in 1918 and even before that, too.

One of the earliest things I remember was when I went to school on North Square, and you know what this professor told us—because I was kid, what did I know? He called us, the fellas, he says "Do you know every Italian man that comes over here to this country is worth twenty thousand dollars to the

United States because they used to do all kinds of work." And another thing, the Italians found a lot of work, but there was a lot of smart people came from the old country, all over. They couldn't get a job over here, they didn't know. The Irish gotta hold of the whole goddamned thing, you know why? You'll never hear this. The Irish knew how to talk English. The Italians were smart people [but] they couldn't get a job because they couldn't talk English. The Irish got a hold on Massachusetts. We spoke broken English. That's why they were ahead of everything. Why do you think, because they're smart? Because they knew the language, see? If you didn't talk American, what the hell, they wouldn't give you no job.

Francesco Ventresca

Francesco Ventresca's nickname from Sulmona in Abruzzi was *Pastore* (Shepherd).

"They Thought We Were Talking against the County"

In 1922, I lived on 410 Hanover Street. The street was full of Italians but there were Irish too; they were tough like a son of a gun. In front of Burden's Pharmacy, the corner of Prince and Hanover Street, the Italians would gather and talk together. The police didn't want them on the corner; they didn't want you talking together—they figured they were talking about politics, doing something political and talking against the country. There was one young Italian guy, he was tough, about two hundred and seventy pounds, that seven or eight (Irish) policemen couldn't hold down. One day he had an argument with the cops on the corner and he threw two of the policemen into the street. They jailed him, he got a lawyer, and everybody helped him out. They freed him, and because the police had *legge a mano* [they had the law in their hands], the young man was afraid they might do something to him or shoot him the next time for what he had done to the two cops so he went to Canada. He became a police lieutenant.

Marguerite Locchiato

"Hi Mike"

My father came here from Italy when he was nine years old and he attended school here. He went to the Eliot School. And he had a few years of school [and] he had difficulty with the Irish. When he was nine years old, he had to go to school and there wasn't many Italians; they were mostly Irish there. And there was always one that would tease him about "Guinea, the spaghetti," and "Guinea eat the spaghetti." And after a while he couldn't tolerate it anymore, so he hit him. And the schoolroom he was in, as he says, he knew that he would be punished by the teacher, so he jumped out the window and went away.

His mother was a widow, and there was no means of welfare or anything where she had my father and a daughter and an older boy. So she had to go to work and she used to do housework, scrub floors and toilets in the North End, and that was her means of living. My father used to go shining shoes, and one day the truant officer saw him, that he was young, and asked him why he didn't go to school. And he told him what had happened, and my grandmother had no knowledge of that, and then she had to send him back to school. In the meantime, he did the few grades of school and then he went back to work.

One afternoon years later we were waiting for my father to come home from work; my mother was kinda worried [and] she said, "Gee, your father isn't home yet." So he came in a little later, so my mother said, "What's the matter?" So he said, "Nothing." She said, "Well, you're late you know, were you detained or something?" And she would talk to him naturally in Italian. So he said, "No I just came from the courthouse; it cost me seven dollars, but I don't care." So my mother said, "What happened?" He had a pushcart—it wasn't one of them small ones you see now, it was a box, it had a bar—and they would get in front of it and push. In the winter it would be a sled to come in the snow because after he'd sell, he'd have to deliver. Of course, the farmer wouldn't pay for that; the merchant, the buyer would pay for it, that was extra money for my father. So he happened to be on Richmond Street and this Irishman was on a horse on a team, and my father was in front of him, and he was telling my father to move where my father couldn't move. So he started calling my father a Guinea and he got in a fight with him. I don't know who got beat up but it cost my father that time seven dollars, but he didn't care.

Then a long, long time after my father came down with diabetes. So he was sitting near the door and there was this man—he was an Irishman that lived here—and every time he'd go by, he'd say, "Hi Mike," and my father would never answer him. So once, twice—one time I said to him, "Pa, gee, that man always says—he always talks to you and you never answer him. Why?" My father said, "That's none of your business." Now I was grown up, I asked my mother, "Gee, Ma, why is it that?" She said, "Gee, I don't know." And we got curious, every time he goes by, he says "Hi Mike." So one time I said to my father, "Gee, Pa, every time we go by that poor man, it's a shame." He said, "I hate that son of a bitch. He's the guy!" And he held a grudge against him. I said, "Is he the guy you pulled from the horse or at school?" He said, "In school!" Imagine that, he held that grudge against him. You would never think he would, but he did. He was a kid and it was in the back of his mind and he never, never forgave him. And my father was a forgiving man.

Fred Bourne

Roughan's Hall

There was a place in Charlestown called Roughan's Hall, a big yellow building as you come over the bridge. Every Saturday night all the North End guys went over there and they danced with the Irish broads from Charlestown and all the Irish guys were dancing with the girls from the North End. Then they'd go out the bridge and fight. No knives or guns. That was the "Saturday night special" when we were young, right at City Square. What do you think? That's how all the Italians married all the Irish broads. They were Charlestown girls. And all the Irish guys were marrying Italian girls years ago—I'll show you dozens of families where the mother is Irish, the father is Italian. Where'd they come from? Charlestown! Where did the wives come from? North End! You see a kid named Murphy and he's typical Italian-looking. You see another kid named Baciacolupo and he's got blue eyes and blond hair and looks like an Irishman!

Refugees in the North End

West Enders Tell Their Stories

24

> There's only one way to cure a place like the West End, and that is to wipe it out. It's a cancer in the long run to the community.
> —BOSTON BANKER, *In the Memory House* by Howard Mansfield

For years, Antonette Carrano and her husband, Matteo, ran Carrano's Market in New Haven's Wooster Square neighborhood. Like many established businesses in Italian American communities, Carrano's had evolved into a neighborhood landmark. More than just a place to buy fruits and vegetables, the store gained a reputation as an informal employment office where Antonette found work for newly arrived women from towns along the Amalfi coast. In the backroom kitchen of the store, Antonette negotiated for seamstress jobs with the local factory owner over his favorite dish of escarole and beans. Weekends drew *squillo-* (cigar-) smoking men who gathered around the only radio in the neighborhood to listen to broadcast boxing matches.

In 1949 Congress passed the Urban Renewal Act, which allocated federal money for slum renewal. In 1954 the Supreme Court granted legislatures the power of eminent domain, foreshadowing the demise of many self-contained ethnic neighborhoods like Wooster Square. City administrations formed advisory committees, combining "the political muscle of city hall with the corporate power of downtown boardrooms" to eradicate urban enclaves they deemed slums and often targeting working-class neighborhoods, which contributed modest revenues to city coffers in property taxes.[1]

In 1953 the John B. Hynes administration in Boston officially announced that the West End, which paid minimal property taxes to the city, would be redeveloped under federal guidelines. The project received the support of the media, the City Council, and the Catholic Church, though the actual "renewal" and the removal of West Enders did not begin until five years later. Jerome Rappaport, a former assistant to the mayor, transformed the West End into the fashionable Charles River Park, where the monthly rental of a studio in a luxury town house equaled the monthly rent of a six-room apartment in the old neighborhood. Even before the term *gentrification* was used to describe the process in the 1970s, well-to-do suburbanites replaced old residents and became the new West Enders, increasing the city's tax base. After mayors such as Richard C. Lee and John B. Hynes demolished closely knit, ethnic communities, no official reports could measure the human suffering caused by the loss of neighborhood.

When she was taken to live in a suburb with her children after the city's demolition of her house and store, a heartbroken Antonette Carrano left unannounced. When walking back to the old neighborhood to find her friends, she found sidewalks stripped of stately trees, piles of bricks and mortar where relatives and friends once lived, and old-time stores like Carrano's replaced by modern, industrial buildings.

As the city tore Wooster Square apart, Herbert Gans was conducting research in the West End for his book *The Urban Villagers*. While studying daily life in the narrow streets, tenement houses, and small businesses of an independent neighborhood of working-class, "poorly educated people without middle class aspirations," Gans found the West End "a good place to live."[2]

In April 1958, armed with the power of eminent domain, the city's bulldozers uprooted the West End's seven thousand residents from its twenty-eight hundred households. Although the Boston Redevelopment Authority (BRA) promised to rehouse every displaced family, community resettlement was not given a high priority and families had to rely on relatives and friends for relocation. In demolishing homes and businesses, the Boston Housing Authority's middle-class planners ignored the dynamics of the West End's strong social structure, which was based on family interrelationships. Gans described the social and psychological effects of community loss, reporting "a number of deaths attributed to the impact of the redevelopment decision," but stopped short of linking the cause to the loss of the neighborhood.[3]

Some displaced residents who wanted to replicate the closeness of the West End moved to the North End. Dorothy Mignoso, a West Ender for a half century, described the unreported consequences of neighborhood loss: "And a lot of people, a lot of the old-timers, as soon as they moved out of the

West End, then they died because they were heartbroken because they were brought up in the West End, because we were all like one happy family—we knew each other." Heartbreak was never listed on the death certificates of West Enders.

The aftershocks of the West End's destruction were felt in the nearby North End. Many feared the neighborhood would be the BRA's next target because of the lack of political leverage, the reluctance of bankers to grant loans to upgrade substandard housing, and the low property taxes that residents paid to the city. Lifelong North Enders like Emilia Dello Russo and her friends, who never intended to leave, began looking for apartments in other towns. Luckily for the North End, a young man working in the Department of Labor had been paying close attention to the events in the West End.

Alarmed by the imminent demise of his beloved community, Michael Nazzaro gave up a promising career in Washington, D.C., to return home and run for state representative. After two failed attempts and nearly losing his livelihood from many hours of campaigning, he won the seat. In a race against the wrecking balls, Nazzaro accomplished the near impossible: he convinced the legislature to pass a bill exempting the North End from eminent domain, thus stopping the city's ability to take properties for redevelopment.

When John Sheehan, a writer for the *Regional Review*, asked why Nazzaro fought for his neighborhood, he answered: "If I couldn't fight for my neighborhood, then there wasn't anything else worth fighting for." As a fearless neighborhood advocate who believed in the beneficial possibilities of politics, he never felt fatalistic in his battle against the powerful business and political interests of his times: "The only way we survived war and the Depression was that we stuck together as a neighborhood. We locked arms and tried to help. It was the neighborhood code during the Depression, and it carried over during the war. I never forgot that."

Phil D'Alessandro

"We Couldn't Go Back"

I lived in the West End when I first got married. It wasn't like the North End because it was beginning to—I mean lots of people in 1951, 1952, they were beginning to destroy the West End at the time and lots of people that had beautiful homes had to move out. I lived on Poplar Street; I had four rooms and I only paid thirty-five dollars a month. Then they kicked us out, and they were going to rebuild the West End and bring us back here and bring back the people that originally lived there. They took our name and addresses so we could go back. And then when they rebuilt the West End, you couldn't go back because you couldn't pay the enormous rents over there. Hynes was the mayor at the time, and they had a political deal with some people from New York that helped him to be reelected—he beat [James] Curley that year.

FIGURE 48. Dorothy Mignoso, 1980.

Dorothy Mignoso

"The West End Was One Happy Family"

It was one happy family. My parents were from Termini, [in] the province of Palermo in Sicily. My mother came to America when she was twelve years old and she stayed with her sister in Lawrence. My father came to Lawrence too, and they met each other. My mother worked in the woolen mill in Lawrence for a while. She was eighteen when she got married; she must have been nineteen when I was born in 1910, and I was the oldest of ten children. I lived on Hale Street, off from Green Street and South Margin Street, and of course right nearby is Bowdoin Square; there was a telephone company right near the square, Bowdoin Telephone Company, and there was Bowdoin Station. Oh, the West End! We had no trouble—we were all one happy family; everybody used to watch out for other people's kids because the streets weren't too long, it was small streets. There was no fights, no swearing, nothing. And then nighttime, in the summertime we'd sit outside until late, and whoever knew how to sing would sing, oh, and there was this young girl here, she used to know how to play the piano in her house and we could hear her play. And whoever knew what she was playing would sing along [with] her. But oh, it was real nice because those years when I was little girl there weren't too many cars, it was horses. On the corner of South Margin and Pitt Street there used to be a stable with horses and there was a great big fire and a lot [of] horses got burned to death. I was young girl around 1925.

I went to the Washington School on Norman Street, and my mother used to bake bread twice a week and we used to come for lunch; she used to make [us] find [surprise us with] those round buns with the Italian cheese and oil in between the bread—oh it was delicious. Then she used to make pizza too once in a while. My mother used to bake twice a week; those days it isn't like now. In the morning we hardly had cakes and pies—we used to cut the bread in pieces with milk and coffee in the bowl. But we were still happy. And then of course there was no washing machines. Ice box though. Wooden stove with the coal. I would have still been living in the West End if they didn't knock down all the buildings. Because they made that new Government Center there and all those new buildings. We were living there where all those new buildings are now. In 1960 I went to East Boston for a year, but as soon as I found a house with a toilet inside I moved to the North End.

Lucia Petringa was sixty-seven at the time of our interview.

Lucia Petringa

"Don't Throw Them Out"

I was born in the West End. I saw it all torn down—that was the worst thing. I go by there and look at all those tall buildings now and I could cry for how many people owned their little house and thought they were set for life and then they had to scatter like refugees. I met a woman on Salem Street that had been a neighbor—I lived on Ashmun Street [and] she owned a house on the corner; she was an elderly woman, a widow who thought she was all set, a four-family house, all she would do is collect the rents and live like that. Quiet lady I knew all my life—she was my mother's friend. That poor thing, they gave her a pittance for her money—she didn't know where to go. All her children were married. She landed over here on Salem Street, on the fifth-floor apartment.

The next time I saw her, that woman, it was the most pitiful sight you saw. She took a fall all the way down the stairs and was wearing one of these surgical collars, could hardly talk. You don't see these things in the paper, you don't read these things—nobody gives a damn. As long as they get their money and they build the Longfellow Towers and the Charles Street Complex [high-rises that replaced old apartment houses], they don't care. I felt like crying; I said to her, "Coraggio, che puo fa [Have courage, what can you do]?" She said, "Lucy, I can't even talk to you." I felt like crying—terrible way to end your life, poor thing with that straight [surgical] collar.

Eugene Bimonte

Eugene Bimonte was seventy-eight at the time of our interview.

From Calabria to Scollay Square

I was born in Calabria, where the *briganti* (guerrillas who fought against the northern army) were, near Cosenza. I was fourteen when I came here. My uncle sent me the tickets to come over here—that's why I come over to the West End. Michael LoPresti, [my uncle's] father, came from the West End too, right on the corner of Leverett and Prince Street. It was good. Today you can't even walk that way. People are afraid to walk in the street now. They knocked it all down. I've lived on 60 Prince Street for sixteen years in the North End and it's dead here now. Before it used to be like people dancing and you could have good time. Today you're afraid to go out the street. Didn't they just kill a kid here the other day down Hanover Street?

I had a good job at Scollay Square Theatre. Motion picture operator. I had the best job I ever had, three hundred and fifty a week. Doing nothing. Eight o'clock in the morning we used to go in there, get through at four o'clock in the afternoon, five days a week. Every other week we used to change, like the nights—that was delicious. Used to be good them days—it was the best. Used to have a five and ten there, a restaurant on the corner, the Howard Theatre, Scollay Square, Bowdoin Square, Olympic Theatre. I worked at the Olympic for sixteen years, then the union put me on Scollay Square. Three fifty a week, then they raised it to four hundred. Those were the days, thirty-nine years ago. But you know even [former mayor] John Collins said yesterday on television, "Them days are gone forever."

Joe Arigo and Joe Anastasi often met at their favorite hangout, Pal's Lunch, on Parmenter Street next to the North End Union.

Joe Arigo

"The Expressway Cut It Off"

All your big businesses, the North End used to be the candy center of the world. We had Schrafft's, we had Deran's, Touraine, we had' em all down here. All the people here worked in them. We had a big cracker factory, Loose-Wiles Biscuit; they had a cookie factory and a candy factory by the same name in the West End. All the shoe stores you find on Washington Street, they came from Cross Street—used to be the retail shoe center of the city, the state. There were more shoe stores—Sadler's—they all started on Cross Street. Jordan Marsh originated here on Hanover Street. In fact, they still owned the building; they just got rid of it only a couple a years ago—you know where the European restaurant is? The building aside [beside] the European, that used to be Jordan Marsh. They started their business in the North End, then they moved away. The highway cut it off. The North End, really now, is North Street, all of North Street, down to Commercial, up to Haverill Street. Haverill now, not the North Station—the street before North Station up to Cross Street and around there. That's all it is. And that's the North End. It's cut off by Government Center on one side, the expressway on the other side, and the Waterfront on the other side. Charleston on the other as far as sections go [before the expressway].

    We used to run all the way up to Scollay Square; we used to run all the way down to Causeway Street, all the way up Causeway Street, to Merrimac Street. Merrimac Street used to be the beginning of the West End; we used to run all the ways up to Merrimac Street. But no more now. It's shrinking. Now there's talk about urban renewal. You know what that means? They'll be like, uh, certain places, they'll be houses they'll [be] knocking down like what happened in the West End. That's the rumor for down here. I don't think it will happen [after that] mistake. Wait a minute, Joe, don't say that, they can clean out places like that—they can clean out anybody if they want to! But I mean what are they gonna do? Somebody has to stop at a point. You go down Haverill Street, like the factories down Medford Street, you build condominiums there or—urban renewal—you build high-rise offices. You're not replacing anybody; you're just replacing the businesses. As far as the residential, though, you're not replacing—you're bringing the value, they're bringing it in. Those factories there on Medford Street and all that, they're going one at a time anyway. They don't want to pay the city the taxes they pay, the prices they pay. Brandon, the candy place, then there's all them restaurant supply stores, then there's a big clothing factory where the Scotch & Sirloin (North Washington Street) is, the printing plant, there's a dressmaking shop—they'll make condominiums outta them!

Local Politics

25

> Senz 'a musica, non si fa a messa
> (Without music, the Mass is never said).
> —SOUTHERN ITALIAN PROVERB

> Addo cantano tanti galli, non fa mai iuòrno
> (When too many roosters crow, the day never comes).
> —AVELLINESE PROVERB

Michelina Manfra grew up farming in Parolise, near Avellino. When immigrating to the North End in the 1920s, she left a rural hamlet where outsiders were considered suspicious intruders and where officials who visited to collect taxes or issue draft notices treated the peasantry with disdain. In some towns, bondage in the southern caste system took the form of perpetual tithes levied by the church, the town, or the agents of absentee landowners who came to collect their share of crops at harvest time. Michelina's Irish neighbors in the North End had also been poor farmers, but though they were badly treated by the British, they benefited from the knowledge of England's republican government, whose parliament included elected representatives from Ireland. In contrast, landless southern Italians and those without professions or salaries were estranged under the regime of a reactionary monarchical government and had no representation. From centuries of living by the soil, the peasantry had been conditioned by the uncontrollable ability of nature to nurture or destroy, and many like Michelina abided by the southern code of behavior to accept *destino* (fate) with stoicism. In the peasant experience, institutions outside the family were incapable of changing life's trajectory, and the idea of government providing assistance was beyond their comprehension. Other than religious societies, Italians put their faith in self-reliance and family rather than government. Michelina's outlook reflected the ethos of the Italian immigrant's willingness to work and sacrifice for family survival without the help of politicians.

As the immigrants learned the rhythms of the new neighborhood, local politics seeped into daily life. Noisy street parades passing through the neighborhood gave them the first taste of American political campaigns. Perhaps Michelina had heard one of mayor John "Honey Fitz" Fitzgerald's fiery speeches on North Square when his political machine controlled the neighborhood from the Jefferson Club. Someone she knew may have received a food basket at Christmas from the "mayor of the poor," Michael Curley. She may have come to the door when one of Martin Lomasney's ward captains stopped by from the Hendricks Club to ask for her vote. She must have walked by the corner of Hanover and Prince Streets when large crowds gathered to hear political candidates deliver campaign speeches. However, because of his early death, Michelina never met George Scigliano, an early community advocate who dedicated his life to helping the neighborhood.

North Enders were slow to go to the ballot box, and as late as 1933, only small numbers of naturalized citizens had registered to vote. Italians never mustered a united force strong enough to figure into the larger political struggle between Protestant Yankees and Catholic Celts. Any hope of an independent Italian voting bloc had already disappeared in the early 1900s, when Italian-born *prominenti* [leaders] parted ways with American-born politicians, identifying as Republicans in part because of their distaste for the Irish Democrats, whom they believed were corrupt and lacking in manners and good taste.

Italian-born Republican leaders like Jerome Petitti, Vittorio Orlandini, and Salerio Romano gave way to second-generation politicians who put aside differences and allied themselves in the Roosevelt coalition with the Democratic Party, which was controlled by the Irish political machine. With the support of local religious, athletic, and social organizations, Italian American politicians such as Joseph Langone won elections to state senator seats, and Felix Forte, a Republican, and Vincent Brogna were appointed as Superior Court judges. Italian politicians convinced their followers to register as Democrats if they wished for any governmental assistance or municipal patronage jobs with benefits and monthly "kiss in the mail" paychecks. As the last great influx of immigrant groups to Boston, Italians were treated as newcomers to the political scene, and they would have to wait a century before Thomas Menino became mayor and they gained a voice.

In 1968, Mayor Kevin White's administration replaced the Celtic political machines of the Fitzgeralds, Curleys, and Lomasneys that controlled the North End. Keeping his campaign promise to assist Boston's neighborhoods, the new mayor created "little city halls," providing funds for police protection, transportation for the elderly, improved lighting, and urban forestry programs. The North End office, which coordinated Community Development Block Grant (CDBG) programs for neighborhood improvement, was staffed by White loyalists who acted as the eyes and ears of the mayor. By dangling funding grants to competing neighborhood organizations, the city maintained its control through divide-and-conquer tactics.

At election time, many North Enders were hired as foot soldiers for the mayor's reelection army. By 1980, Michelina Manfra had witnessed many political campaigns, and she viewed politicians with wariness, especially at election time. As the mayoral race heated up, the conversation between Michelina and her friends at the Prado (Paul Revere Park) quickly turned to politics. Rumors of the city's plan to convert their apartments into condominiums and fears of displacement unleashed a torrent of animated discussion. At the same time, a city hall worker was combing the neighborhood, checking the list of elders who had attended the past year's "Hoodsie ice cream lunches" sponsored by the mayor. It was time the elderly returned the favor and voted for him.

Richie Perez knew where to find the elderly on sunny days and met Michelina and her friends at the Prado to make sure of their vote. Fully aware of her voting rights, Michelina broke the Old-World code of treating officials with deference and responded to the worker with defiance: "Richie came up to me in the Prado, says to me, 'Who are you gonna vote for?' I says, 'I dunno, maybe *pe* [for] nobody.' He says, 'Aw no, you gotta vote a for Mayor White!' I say a to him, 'Maybe yeah, eh maybe no!' 'Oh no, you gotta do a for me,' he say. I says, 'Richie, I like a you'—I know Richie from when he was a small a boy, you know? 'I like a you—maybe I no gonna vote *pe* no one!' 'Oh you gotta gonna vote—for me.' 'Aggio ditto [all right],' I said, because he wanted me to go and vote *pe* Mayor White. I says, 'All right, don't worry, I go [to vote].' He says, 'I no make a you go over there, I commen a you house and you vote a you house.' I say, 'Oh no! I go to vote at the Michelangelo School.' He say, 'No, no, I bring a the paper [absentee voter form] home, eh you vote over there, cuz I make a sure you vote.' I say, 'Look a, Richie! *Se* [if] you say I gotta vote a for Mayor White, eh you gotta come make me vote in a my a house, I no vote a for no one!' He mad. He said, 'Michelina!—' I said, 'All right, I'm gonna vote a for Mayor White.' So when I gonna vote at the Michelangelo School, who do I find over there? Richie, like a this (frowns), with a long face, like a this! When I go in there nobody knows who I vote a for. I never tell who I vote a for. You know who I vote for? I voted for the one who comes out [wins the election]! He come out, I vote a for him. If he no come out, I no vote a for him, I voted for the other one. Is it his [Richie's] business who I vote for?"

Later that day Michelina went to the little city hall office on Parmenter Street to inquire about her water bill. Before she could talk with the clerk, the office manager intercepted her and called her over to his desk to remind her to vote for the mayor: "Then Charlie Falco, say to me, 'If you no go na vote a for the Mayor White, you no got a no favor over here. You come a to the [mayor's] parties and eat at the party over here.' I said, 'Yeah, when I come to the party, I'm a the last one to go [leave from] the parties, and when I go to those parties, if nobody no give me anything, I no get up! I no get up! What do you think, che ghi allo party morte di fame [that I go to the party starving]? Prima mi iénchia la pansa poi dopo vaco [First, I fill my stomach, then I go].' I say, 'Look, Charlie, you no do me never favor.'"[1] With a furtiveness reserved for outsiders, Michelina never divulged the candidate she voted for in the 1980 mayoral election.

Phil D'Alessandro

Phil D'Alessandro became a Grand Knight in the Knights of Columbus and the founder of the United Holy Name Society, an agency to unite the churches in the North End.

"We Created Little City Hall"

We used to have our own volunteer committees—this goes back to the 1950s—that dealt with issues like rubbish pickup; the streets we made one way, they used to be two-way; traffic up and down; we changed the name of streets. We took records of cars illegally parked, and we used to help the Italian-speaking people with their bills when they couldn't understand. I was one of the original community advocates to set in motion the rehabilitation program assigned to address community problems. We used to have meetings every Monday night and everybody brought their problems. Prior to Kevin White, we served on this council—Guy Beninati, Anthony Lombardozzi, Margaret Caruso—we met every Monday since the 1950s at the North End Union. It's not our generation anymore, although we tried to set a good example. And the whole idea of the little city hall evolved out of our work. We created the little city hall—the work we did at our expense, at our time and sacrifice, stuff we used to do for nothing, they're getting paid for, seven or eight people doing nothing, calling it a little city hall! When Kevin White took over here he began to build a political machine and these little city halls are nothing but a political machine. That was taken away from us.

Helen Luongo

Politics and the Feast of Saint Anthony

Now look at this trash he's [the mayor's] doing with the feasts we have. We didn't have this trash that we have now with the feasts. Are there North Enders at these feasts? Is there the tradition that we had? This is something that came in from our great-grandfathers—brought it over here (tapping the table). The Saint Anthony feast? Why, my father, my husband, they used to go crazy when the feasts came—oh it was a big deal! But it was a tradition; there was something behind it. But now, what is it? What do they have, all these trailers and pushcarts that come from all over, from Connecticut, from Rhode Island, from New York, from New Jersey. It's a racket, a racket. There's no more tradition behind it. Why? Why? Do you know why? It's Mayor White advertising it as "Summerthing." All right? Even that he took away from us down here. He advertises it as "Summerthing" on the radio, in the newspapers, on the television, and everything. And you got the swill. They don't know the meaning behind our feasts. Because they used to have it in Italy. It wasn't in my father's or my husband's hometown, but it was the suburban towns—Flumeri, Grottominarda, San Sossio Baronia—it was just like over here; everybody now that moved out of the North End they'd come down, but now they don't. There used to be people come from Philadelphia, Pennsylvania, from New Jersey, and New York down here for this day, for Saint Anthony. They don't come down anymore because they've seen the swill [that] goes on. The meaning of the day has gone out of it.

In Montefalcione, where they have the feast, they buy a baby pig—it belongs to the town—and that pig is taught that he goes door to door eating every day, everybody feeds him. Then on this day, on Saint Anthony's Day, they raffle it and get the money to have fireworks or whatever they have. See, and that's why they say, "'O porco di Sant Antonio," the pig of Saint Anthony. Yeah, "'O porco di Sant Antonio, you go eating from house to house." See that's the meaning, where it comes from, and as a child I couldn't understand it when my parents used to say, "Eh oggi si fa la festa dello porco di Sant Antonio [Today is the feast of the pig of Saint Anthony]." And then as I grew I saw the tradition that was behind it. And all the suburban towns around Avellino take part in it. In Italy the highest bidder carries the banner of Saint Anthony in the procession—it's an honor for you to carry the banner. Now over here what do they do? They make the money and they have it for the club to make themselves God knows how many barrels of wine and then they sell it all year round. What do they do with all that money? They [the society] used to make money before, but it was given for good purposes—they had scholarships, they used to give some to the church, they'd give some to different organizations like the Home for Italian Children, to MS [multiple sclerosis], to the cancer organizations. Now what do they do with all that money? It isn't the money they collect on Saint Anthony's, it's all that filth that they go in there and eat. I don't believe in it anymore.

Before they started "Summerthing," Saint Anthony wouldn't come by my door if I didn't give him money. Now since it's gone this way I don't give them a penny, to any of them. Because they could've stopped it, even though "Summerthing" advertised it and they used to send a band down to play. If they didn't want it, they could've stopped it. Let's keep our tradition! What is it, *Fiddler on the Roof*? Tradition! Oh, I think to the North End he's [the mayor's] done worse than the West End. At least those people, they knocked their houses down and they had to get away, but we have our houses standing over here and he's squeezing us out of our houses. This is it. We have no say. The only thing you can do is pack up and leave.

Fred Bourne

The Rise of the Italian Politician

The Irish were mostly politicians, including the president's [John F. Kennedy's] grandfather, John F. "Honey Fitz" Fitzgerald, who lived on North Square, and many other Irish families. You see, for years Ward 3 was dominated by the Irish even though in later years the Italians became the biggest percentage of the people living in Ward 3. It used to be George Lannigan, John F. Fitzgerald, the Lomasney brothers—what they used to do was put up nine Italian candidates, pay for their campaigns, and one Irishman, so that the Italian vote would be split up nine ways. And the Jewish and the Irish vote would elect the representative to the City Council because in those days they used to have city councilors from the wards, like Ward 3 they used to have George Lannigan. In fact, one time they even put up a Jewish dentist for representative—Doctor Finkelstein—and he got elected! (laughs) In an Italian district!

I'm going way back now. But then as they moved in and they had children and the children became Americanized, they wanted representation. In fact, the first one to run was Old Man Langone—Joe Langone became a state senator. He was the first Italian from the North End to achieve political prominence, and, of course, his sons inherited the mantle from the father because he became so well known, so Joe Langone got elected, then Gabe Piemonte got elected, then this one got elected. And this is the way it evolved—the Italians finally got representation. Of course, then they changed the elections to citywide elections—no more twenty-two councilors from twenty-two wards—it was a wide field. But you see, like the Jews, if they had money, they moved to Brookline or Newton. The Italians that had money suddenly moved to Medford, West Roxbury, and Roslindale so that we have a very large, predominately Italian population in Boston at one time and they still do, so they can elect one or two people to the city council where once it was a general election rather than by wards.

See, in numbers there is power, otherwise you have no power. The Jews, when they knocked down the West End to remodel it, which was Ward 3 the same as the North End, they moved to Brookline, Newton, the better areas. And the North End turned into a melting pot for the immigrants that came from Italy. And as the construction business progressed—these fellas were cement finishers and in different building trades and they started to make a lot of money. So they all started to buy their own houses, send their kids to college, something that had never been done prior.

Elvira DiMattia

"We Always Looked Out for Each Other"

My mom and dad always felt that if you could do any good to anyone or for anyone, you should. We always took an interest in what was going on about us in the neighborhood. We always looked out for each other. If we could say a word of encouragement or a word of some sort to enlighten people about things they don't know or maybe haven't heard, well why not do it? I was [a] member of the North End Community Action Program at the North End Union and I found at the time we had better community participation because everybody in this area participated. We used to meet every second Tuesday, and the people would take an interest in what was going on. And even if we didn't accomplish what we wanted to, at least the people in authority, like the mayor, the police commissioner, they at least knew what the people of the North End wanted. They should resurrect that—they should have people running for those positions; one person would take care of two or three streets and they would represent that area. Of course, we did all that without pay. It was a community thing that everybody enjoyed doing. Now we seem to be tossed out with the sewer water—I mean they don't give a darn about us anymore because we don't have any representation, I'm sorry to say.

We had people who spoke out for this area before. We used to have someone by the name of Principio Santosuosso—we used to call him "Princey." He had a newspaper he edited every week—it was called *The Italian News*—and he, along with the members of the Knights of Columbus, with Nick Scaramella who is gone now, we had a group very concerned with what was going on here in the North End. Let me tell you one thing. If they were living today there wouldn't be any drugs in [this] area. I remember when my oldest brothers were living. If they would see a child doing something that they shouldn't do they would just grab them by the neck and say, "Why did you do that? Don't you dare let me see you do that again, I'll tell your mother, I'll tell your father." To sort of scare them, to get them in line. We don't have that anymore. Princey would expose anybody through the means of his paper. If he had to write the president of the United States, he would to call certain attention. The Ausonia Council started here in the north of Boston because this is where the majority of Italian people lived.

Now these people in the so-called affluent society that live in the suburbs were all former North Enders. They either came from the North End, the West End, East Boston, or South Boston—none of them can lay claim to the fact that they were born in Belmont or Wellesley or Hyde Park—they all originated from here. So they formed the Ausonia Council, and now even if they moved out they stay active and were always coming. Now the people that are there now, all they are interested in is playing cards—they could care less about the North End. I'm sorry to say that as far as the Knights of Columbus are concerned, they are only interested in making money; they don't give a darn about this area whatsoever. I'm very disheartened—I never thought I would live to see the North End in the condition it is now.

Elvira DiMattia

Politics, Taxes, and Patronage

We don't have the immigration that came from Italy anymore that we had when I was a child, and so the people who came to live here in the North End wanted heated apartments, they wanted modern, up-to-date apartments, and some of them don't care how much they pay. Consequently, that has accounted for rents going up, and if people are willing to pay and you have the means to give it to them, why not? They can't keep their property vacant. They have bills to pay. But if they had left those people alone to live where they were we wouldn't have any need for that. And now a great many people who have bought property in the North End are not even residents—they are people who are buying for merely speculation purposes. They're out for the almighty dollar and they don't care who they rent to, and in a lot of instances they don't care to look into their background—so long as they repair the property to suit the needs and wishes of the people moving in, that's all they're interested in. And some of them are really getting the money they actually want at the expense of the ethnic population who live here. And I don't think that's fair. And how was that brought about? Politics. Right? It all goes back to that one particular word.

[James] Curley was the mayor when I was a very young child and I was old enough to hear his name mentioned. My dad used to always say, "Curley took from the rich and gave to the poor." But the person who has been in for the past twelve years has taken from the poor to give to the rich. Look at all these homes that have gone up along the West End. [Jerome] Rappaport owns so many buildings over there, and [the mayor] makes a deal with him. We should call this mayor [Kevin White] "Big Deal White." He gives them a special tax relief abatement, and who pays for the taxes? The poor, ethnic people. He goes out reassessing properties—it's really a shame—putting an additional three, four, five thousand additional assessment on. Because the people are not earning it. It's so unfair. It's too bad we have to be saddled with him for another three years, but I don't see any good that's going to come out of this administration, [which] I hope will be his last. A great many people—I think I can actually say the majority—they may have some member of the family he has given a job to. And I understand, everyone he has given a job to, when election time comes around, he makes it his business to contact them because I know some people that have been. And he has reminded them that their jobs are on the line. Well, naturally, if you have someone in your family who owes his job to the mayor, you're not going to vote for anybody else. And the people that don't are in the minority.

Elvira DiMattia

Elvira DiMattia was often called to speak as a community advocate at neighborhood meetings.

"Condos Should Be Out"

Condominiums should be absolutely out. I know people right on my own street [Snow Hill Street], nice Italian families that came to live there and now they're all looking for rooms to get out because they have to get out. The house was sold to a new landlord. And they're nice people. And when you start getting rid of the people like that, the North End changes. And that's exactly what the mayor wants—he wants to get the Italian element out! He's not making it easy for them to live here. And with the extraordinary expenses of the city—he's spending money like a drunken sailor. I tell them that [at community meetings] when they ask me to talk. When did you get a twenty thousand dollar raise? For me to get between three- and five-, ten-dollar, raise, I had to work for it.

Rose Giampaolo

Politicians and the Elderly

Some [politicians] are friends of the elderly and some are not and they pretend to be. And so while we know this sometimes, it's very aggravating. To see some of these politicians pretending they're your friends and you know they're not. I've come across a few. They pretend to do their jobs in office, but in fact I'm disappointed. I have learned more about politics in these last four years that I've been involved than ever before. I'm more aware of how these politicians work and I am disappointed in some—not all. Most of the elderly I don't think see the light. They're gullible. Yeah, I think most of them believe what they hear, but I for one do not. And it's very aggravating. I tell others because I think they should be made to know. And they shouldn't be fooled by the young politician into believing because they're looking for a vote. I happen to be the vice president of my group of seniors and I have many opportunities to get up and let them be aware. And I don't care if the politicians know about it. I'm a very independent person. I don't care if I make enemies because I don't need them. They need me for the votes.

Gangsters and Racketeers   26

> Caminà con un faccia pulita
> (Walk with a clean face
> [never dishonor your family's name]).
> —SOUTHERN ITALIAN PROVERB

At the turn of the century in the North End, the Black Hand, a loosely organized fraternity of extortionists, sent threatening letters with scrawled images of skulls and crossbones and crosses, warning of death if their victims failed to pay extortion money. Some, like Luigi Militante, refused, and his bullet-riddled body was found crumpled in an alleyway with Black Hand symbols chalked on the pavement beside him. Sensational headlines linking mysterious Black Hand murders to Italian surnames captured the public's imagination, and accounts of Italian gang members who practiced secret blood rites appeared in stirring newspaper articles. Italian-born North Enders sometimes resolved conflicts by the vendetta, settling an issue with a gun or knife rather than relying on the police. But most Italians believed in the aphorism for speaking in public about anything that brought dishonor to the family: "I panni sporchi si lava in famiglia" (Dirty clothes are washed at home). On August 4, 1901, the *Boston Globe* invited a panel of North Enders to answer the question, "Is the Italian More Prone to Violent Crime than Any Other Race?" George Scigliano's response, which future defenders would follow, cited statistics showing the low crime rate of Italian Americans and pointed to "one capital offense" and "comparatively few crimes of a violent nature" committed by North Enders since the beginning of Italian immigration.[1]

When the film *Little Caesar* debuted in December 1931, it marked an important turning point in movie history. Warner Brothers seized on a formula for commercial success portraying Italian American gangsters with never-before-seen violence that shocked and seduced the public. The brief triumph of the protagonist, "Rico" Bandello, over the inequalities of the capitalist system captured the imaginations of moviegoers mired in the Depression. As the thinly disguised character of Al Capone, "Rico" cries out in the last scene, "Mother of mercy, is this end of Rico?" Ironically, the death of the slick-talking, dandily dressed Italian American gave birth to a new film genre: mobster movies.

Although the final scene was meant to be a cautionary tale about the pitfalls of crime, it helped establish Italian Americans as synonymous with gangsters and organized crime. With flamboyant lifestyles and outlandish statements to the media, big-time mobsters like Al Capone were only too willing to reinforce the growing stereotype. The Italian American gangster depicted in *Little Caesar* appeared in real life during a brazen shootout in the North End. On December 22, 1931, an unseasonably warm afternoon attracted crowds of holiday shoppers on Hanover Street. At the same time, the reigning racket and bootlegging overlord of South Boston, Frank Wallace, was on his way to the office of "J.L." Lombardo to inform him that the North End was no longer his territory. Before getting into the car, Frank's brother had warned him against going to the North End, but to no avail. Gustin showed up at the Testa building on 317 Hanover Street and walked into "J.L."'s office on the third floor. Curses quickly led to bursts of gunfire, and when the smoke cleared, he and another member of the Gustin Gang lay dead. Before the shootout, newspapers had always printed hyperbolic accounts of North End murders, the headlines capped in bold print with Italian surnames. For most law-abiding North Enders, the gun battle was cause for shame. Some found the gangster's life of easy money, flashy clothes, and street respect irresistible and joined their ranks. Others with meager-paying jobs ran numbers in barber shops and grocery stores to make ends meet. North Enders with family members involved in illegal activities were well known and respected from a distance.

Unlike the disbanded Black Hand, which preyed on victims, the racket gangsters went about their daily business without bothering anyone outside their circle. Organized crime in the North End, like the criminal element run by the Irish in South Boston and the Jews in the West End, had long tentacles, from runners to bookmakers and from distillers to truck drivers hauling bootleg liquor, as well as corrupt politicians and policeman who were paid to look the other way.

After the kingpin of organized crime in New England, Charles "King" Solomon (described in William Whyte's *Street Corner Society*), was assassinated in 1933 and the Irish gangs of South Boston lost power, the North End took the lead in Boston as a neighborhood synonymous with organized crime. Tragically, one of the North End's most respected leaders, George Scigliano, whose eloquent voice and powerful pen would have challenged the growing stereotypes, had died decades before, at the age of thirty-one. A fearless politician and neighborhood defender, he was among the first to protect the reputation of the North End, whose residents were unjustly being depicted as criminals: "The majority of Italians, who, by their thrift, aptitude for all kinds of skillful work, assiduity in labor and respect for the law and its institutions, have secured or are on the way to secure that moral advancement which this country generously offers to all children of the earth—detest this class of criminals who disgrace the fatherland of Raphael and Dante and Galileo and Columbus."[2]

When *The Godfather* opened at movie theaters in 1972, the film's artistic and commercial success gave many Italian Americans cause to feel proud. Director Francis Ford Coppola expanded "Rico" Bandelli's family into a clan of likable criminals who acted like average Italian Americans, celebrating big family weddings and sharing homemade meals at long dinner tables. Some Italian Americans forgave Don Corleone's criminality because of his gravitas and the respect he commanded among his mobster peers. Others believed that organized crime brought disrepute to the Italian people and avoided the organization's existence as a topic of conversation. But many third- and fourth-generation Italian Americans forgot the lesson of *panni sporchi* (dirty clothes) and quoted lines from the movie, intimating their connections to organized crime to settle problems.

While non–Italian Americans outwardly supported their claims of real or imagined mob connections, they felt differently in the privacy of their living rooms, where they viewed Italian Americans as suspect. In 1984, after a job interview with the search committee that I thought had gone well, I waited three weeks for their decision. When I was finally hired as the director of the Council on Aging for the Town of Weymouth, I politely asked one of the committee members why the search had taken so long. Looking down when I asked the question, he slowly raised his eyes and answered, "Well, you're from the North End. We thought you might be in the Mafia."

Fred Bourne

When a friend paid Fred Bourne with a cab over a three-hundred-dollar bet, he began a business that lasted fifty-three years, during which he shuttled and befriended some of Boston's most powerful politicians and gangsters.

"The Racket Guys Kept Order"

I don't think the police or the politicians would like it, but one reason why the North End was the safest place in the city to live was because of the racketeers. Because as the racketeers evolved, they became the unofficial police force because they owned all the good Italian restaurants, whether it was Joe Lombardi's, Giro's, Stella's. The Vara Brothers, with Jerry and Humbie Vara, were racket guys—so that they kept the hoodlums in line. And when Henry Noyes [Henry Selvitella] said something—he used to just sit in Vara's, in the Florentine Restaurant. If you come to him with any beef, he used to get hold of the punks; even if they robbed your house, [they] hadda bring the stuff back or they'd wind up in the river. Now these kids aren't afraid of the cops, but not only did they idolize the racket guys because they dressed very well and drove Cadillac cars and threw money around like it was water, they all wanted to become part of the scene, so that they wouldn't cross Joe Lombardi. Because if he said you were dead, you were dead. The same thing with Henry Noyes [Henry Selvitella], you see?

So that these punks that are around now on junk—I remember them once going right into the Prado [Paul Revere Park] with baseball bats because Reverend Keller from the Old North Church went to Joe Lombardi—he didn't go to the cops because if the cops would run down Unity Street, they'd run out on Hanover, [and] if they came down Hanover, they'd run out—they were bothering visitors to the Old North Church, which gets a million and a half visitors a year. Now Reverend Keller went to "J.L." [Joe Lombardi] and complained these kids were bothering visitors who not only were interested in the North End but were spending their money in various restaurants, shops, curios, and everything else. So they sent up guys with baseball bats and they broke a few heads and told them, "You wanna be punks? Hang down the North Station! Stay the hell outta the Prado." So this in a way made the North End a very interesting place for people all over the world because actually, this is where the country began. Paul Revere House. That's in the North End section. Old North Church is in the North End section. This is where the country began, and right from the North End you can see the Bunker Hill Monument and Old Ironsides, so the influx of visitors, whether you believe it or not—if you took a count even today, there's over a million and a half a year that come just to see the things they read about when they were kids in school.

"They Never Bothered a Legitimate Person"

My house just got robbed Thursday and I know who did it. And I went to certain people. Anyway, he was grabbed before whoever I went to got to him. Now, in the old days you used to go out of your house, and I'm not giving you a word of exaggeration, leave your door unlocked or even wide open, and nobody as much stepped in your door because if you were a stranger, and you went into a house, people would say "Who do you want, who do you see?" Now they're so afraid of these kids throwing firebombs—the junkies in the house. Josie the baker [Josie D'Alessandro] saw them carrying out my television. She could have picked up the phone and called the cops and said they're robbing the apartments on Unity Street. Didn't even do it. They held her up with a gun. Took forty-eight dollars from her. She knew the kids who did it. But they said, "If you tell the cops on us we're gonna firebomb"—she owns three pieces of property there—so when the cops asked her, "You know who it is?" she said (faint voice), "No, I don't know, they only got forty-eight dollars." Because she just put four hundred in the safe.

You see I mixed with rough guys that were supposed to be killers, racketeers, tough tomatoes, and they never bothered a legitimate person. I drove "J.L." in a cab, Henry Noyes [Henry Selvitella] in a cab—always a gentleman with me. Punks try to pull things, see? Not the big shots. As long as you weren't involved with them. You double-crossed them in any way—they treated you like a lady and a gentleman. If you went into Giro's restaurant—in fact he [the owner, Joe Lombardi] used to tell the punks, "This is no hangout. And don't make any passes at any of the girls coming in here with people cuz I'll break your heads." And he ran one of the finest restaurants until the time he died. You wouldn't meet a finer gentleman.

See, the punks you gotta be afraid of. And another thing I have to emphasize to people that are not Italian don't know—dope was taboo. There were no Italian racketeers involved in narcotics or prostitution. No, believe me when I tell you. There were a few, there's always exceptions. There was Kid Morgan, he had a few girls, but he was one of the very few and they shot him I don't know how many times. He survived four bullets right here on this corner on Burden's Drugstore, right across the street. But the big shots—it was horses, dogs, baseball, football—any kind of gambling. And they talk about Raymond Patriarca, what a big shot he is. Had his telephone tapped. He went to the federal can. Joe

Lombardi was the don. And when Raymond Patriarca spoke to him at Jerry Vara's restaurant (the Florentine), Patriarca got up with his handkerchief, wipe his seat off, and say "Sit down, Joe." But Joe Lombardi was a gentleman. Never spoke on the telephone, even to his wife. In thirty years, the FBI couldn't get anything on him, and even if his restaurant lost money he made a hundred grand a year, and he lived in Medford in a hundred fifty thousand dollar home, and he had a yacht, and he had horses. And he paid his income taxes. What he got under the table they had no way of knowing. And in all the years they tried to get him he was never convicted of any crime.

Now he'd get into my cab, with some guy just probably came from the airport, and they'd take a cab to Nahant, and I'd park there, and they'd walk down the beach two or three miles—whatever conversation they had I didn't know because they didn't talk in the cab at all; they'd come back to the cab, I'd take them to the airport, take him back to Giro's. He'd throw me a fifty-dollar bill for a couple of hours. So you would have to say even though he was a racket guy (gambling)—very big—everybody paid him, including the Angiullos. See, he wasn't personally involved.

They had territories. He kept the peace, the territories. They had monthly meetings and was the chairman of the board. And you'd say, "You stole him from me." And he'd listen to the story like a judge, and he'd say, "You belong to him." In other words, if you want to write numbers, you are writing for him—you aren't writing for me [because] I stole you from him. You know what I mean? Adjudicated. Killings in most part of the North End, that there were quite a few killings in the old days, were retaliation. But then they got smart. They never shot anybody in the North End anymore. Some guy would end up in the pig farm and the pigs would eat him. Some guy just disappeared from the face of the earth. Nobody would know what happened to him. No corpus delicti, no crime.

Josie Picadacci

"They Killed amongst Themselves"

There was [a Mafia], oh yeah. Every now and then, you'd hear of somebody getting killed in a barber shop or getting killed in a doorway. But they would only kill amongst themselves, no one else. They wouldn't hurt anyone else. It was just amongst themselves. Yeah, they used to—like you hear stories like they'd be in a barber shop taking a shave or haircut or whatever, and they would just go in and shoot them. That's the way it used to be. Every now and then you would hear of somebody being found here, there, and everywhere.

Life in a Cold-Water Flat   27

> A Marònna mann 'o pane a chi nun tené i rientè
> (The Madonna sends bread to those without teeth).
> —SOUTHERN ITALIAN PROVERB

In the late 1970s, rows of tenements on picturesque streets with painted doors and worn staircases gave the North End the appearance of a charming old neighborhood. But behind the brick walls, North Enders, especially the elderly poor living on fixed incomes, found themselves in the midst of a housing crisis. As the value of real estate skyrocketed, some landlords sold properties to speculators for unheard-of prices. Other landlords raised rents or converted their properties to condominiums, forcing families to leave for the suburbs.

Struggling to get by on meager social security checks, elders were displaced from old apartments and moved into new, subsidized housing in the neighborhood. Others waited in the substandard cold-water flats where they had raised families decades earlier, which had not undergone any significant renovations during their lifetimes. When Jane Jacobs visited the North End in 1959, she discovered the reason why the North End's housing stock had not kept up with the times. Ever since the Depression, bankers had redlined the North End as a slum and refused loans for home improvements. By 1940, nearly 90 percent of the North End housing had no bathtubs and nine out of ten families shared hallway bathrooms.[1] By 1950, almost 92 percent of houses had no central heating.[2]

Compared to the West End, which had well-built structures, central heating, and large rooms, the North End's housing stock had been poorly constructed and repairs conducted with makeshift methods. Many old wooden buildings, some dating from colonial times, had been framed in brick to make them fire resistant. Peaked roofs were squared off to add another floor and had partially collapsed. For elders left behind in cold-water flats, living conditions were only slightly better than the hovels they had left in southern Italy.

Maria Chiucchiolo emigrated from a small town near Avellino and lived in a cold-water flat on Endicott Street. In 1980, her apartment showed some of the primitive conditions that immigrants had experienced at the turn of the century. On windy days, rotted windows let cold drafts enter in all directions. Cracked walls caused chunks of chalky plaster to fall on her bedspread and floors. An outdated gas stove served as the only heat source, with a small side fan blowing warm air. Constantly running, it provided some heat in the kitchen but barely reached the bedroom. Maria shared the hallway bathroom, which featured an antiquated pull-chain toilet, with other tenants. The constant cold from the dirt basement below worsened her arthritic condition and made walking painful. The threadbare linoleum had long ago lost its sheen from years of wear. A light bulb dangled on a long chord from the kitchen ceiling as the only source of light.

Maria's holy water bottle on the kitchen shelf protected her, a North End version of the ancient Roman belief in displaying statuettes and talismans in homes to ward off evil spirits. When Maria's name finally came up for an open apartment at the Casamaria Senior Home, her old friends were pleased to hear of her good fortune and told her, "Thank a God, che t'hai avuto la casa!" (you found a home). Hearing the good news, she spoke for many elders living in cold-water flats when she exclaimed, "Grazie signore! Che mi ha mandato questa casa! Si no, ieva a morì in questa casa di friddo" (Thank you, Lord! That you sent me this new house. If not, I would have died in this house of cold).

Rose Arigo Amato

Rose Arigo Amato volunteered at the North End Senior Center, answering the phone and coordinating programs.

Life in a Cold-Water Flat

The lock on my door is broken. My door is opened all night and I live on the street floor, two steps down, and I asked my landlord to fix it because I'm afraid someone might come in. I stay awake at night in the chair because

I might hear someone come in. Naturally, I'm alone and they can break in there, but she [the landlady] doesn't want to do it because she says we should fix things up. There's plenty of break-ins on Sheafe Street. [My] landlady, next door to me [she] rented rooms to the kids that hang in the Prado, five or six boys; they moved in Saturday. Them kids are the worst kids, and I told her, "Listen, Catherine, all the kids who moved next door, they're the worst kids in the North End, all junkies." I sleep sometimes on the chair because I'm afraid; I don't know what's going on there. I told her, "Catherine, I'm scared." She expects me to pay to fix the front door. What a nerve on her. Everything outside your apartment, it's up to the landlady to fix.

My apartment is very, very cold. I want to get out. There's no bath—I have to take baths at my daughter's at night. It's a good thing I stay with daughter a lot of times; I stay there to keep warm. My ceiling in the toilet is coming down, anytime the plaster—I wish it does and hits me; I bet I could sue her. And the toilet still has a pull chain, old-fashioned toilets! I'm seventy-two years old. I'm even ashamed to bring people in my house although it's spotless, that's one thing about me. My windows are broken, the ropes are all broken. The landlady says, "Well yous pay cheap rent, yous gotta do everything yourselves." The electrical lights are connected in the hallway and that's illegal.

When I say it's freezing, it's freezing. One time I had my granddaughter here to sleep in with me. The next day she said, "Grandma, please, don't ever ask me to sleep here anymore! Gram, I feel so bad for you." Do you know how many quilts on my bed beside my fur coat? That's how cold it is. Last year I got pneumonia so bad because of the cold flat, I got it there. When it's zero weather, my daughter won't let me stay here because of the time I got pneumonia. I had a health inspector down and he says, "Oh my God, this place is wicked!" He found more faults everywhere, but I haven't found housing yet. There's a lot of old people from Sheafe Street that didn't get in [to elderly housing]; they're on welfare too you know. It's a sin—it's a shame. I'm in the basement so I don't get any heat from below, I give it to the people upstairs. The floors are cold. I gotta put on woolen socks and wear them around the house, a long nightgown, pajamas. I don't know how many blankets I have to put on at night. My daughter just gave me two more blankets—she crochets them for me. Gotta lot of blankets, yeah. As I say, I don't mind it because I'm over my daughter's during the day. But if I had to go home and stay there I think I'd go nutty just to see the condition of that house—[though] the house is clean, don't get me wrong. The rent here is fifty dollars, but that's all it's worth.

I got three rooms, but one is dark, no window [so] it's only two rooms. And I still take care of the building. I listen for people in the hallway, I clean the stairways, I dust all the dirt. I can't even paint the windows because they are so bad. The bathroom walls are all cracked. I'm doing her [the landlady] a favor to live here. And she went to the rent control [office] to ask for more money! They told her I was doing her a favor to live here—they said she was lucky that people were living in the house. When someone comes in the building, the door gets stuck, stays open; everyone that comes out of the building I have to go after them, gotta go out and close it with my hands.

I live on top of a cold cellar, nobody underneath me to give me the heat—they get the heat from me [and] the other one gets the heat from the other one. I use the stove for heat—it's all gas. One side is the oven to cook, the top is the gas stove, and of course I have to leave it on high, a mile a minute—you want me to freeze to death if I didn't have it on? I put it on high but I don't feel anything. You can have it high as hell but you can't feel it. I had a

FIGURE 49. Tom Bardetti in his cold-water flat on Hanover Street, 1980.

plant on my bureau in my bedroom. Guess what? I noticed all the leaves were drooping—they were all full of ice! It died on me. Right in my bedroom on the table. See the heat don't go in the other rooms.

Tom Bardetti

Tom Bardetti was sixty-seven and alone in a starkly furnished, musty, cold-water flat. Two calendars hung on the bare kitchen wall, with each passing day marked with an X. Puffing on a cigarette, he explained in his gravelly voice, "My visiting nurse told me it's important you know the date. The calendars make the house look good—you gotta put calendars up. And the pictures on them make the house look like a house."

Living Alone in a Cold-Water Flat

I ain't got no phone. I don't want no phone. I don't get that many calls. I don't do that many calls. I ain't got many people to call. Nobody goes shopping for me when I'm sick. Nobody goes. I go. Well, when I'm sick and I can't do it, I got some stuff here to eat for a couple a days, and then I—I have to do it myself. If I get sick, well, I'm taking a chance. There's a family from East Boston, they come here once in a while—they ain't much help to me cause they're not here, they can't help me.

All the guys I grew up with, they all got married, they're all gone away—who's gone to New York, who's gone somewhere else—live in Somerville, Framingham, Worcester. Guys got married, bought houses, and moved away. There's very few people that I know now, see? Yeah—some of 'em died. And the new generation comes up and you don't know them. Well I know a few younger guys, but you can't depend on them now because there's too much money being given to them; you can't interest anybody. Like if I told a kid to come and wash my two widows, I'll give you ten bucks, they'd laugh at you. They want to go out in the street with those high stockings, those T shirts, go down the playground, play basketball. Everything is for the family here. Marriage and life is to have children. You can have fun, too, but—mostly the whole thing is based on the family. A job, intelligence, training, school, and everything—raising kids and it's all built around the family, see? If a guy ain't got no family, what has he got? What is he gonna work on? He ain't got nothin'. I woke up too late (laughs). I was asleep all that time like Rip Van Winkle—he slept for twenty years and I slept for forty! Yeah.

The Changing North End   28

> The Lord didn't tell the Italians, "The North End is yours forever."
> —MARY PULPI BENINATI

When Antonio Crugnale left Sulmona in 1938 to volunteer in Italy's war in Ethiopia, he stayed in uniform in Sicily during World War II. On being captured by American forces, he raised his hand when they asked for prisoners with carpentry skills and spent the rest of the war building barracks for American soldiers advancing across the island. After immigrating to the North End in 1954, he opened a cabinet shop on Salem Street and lived on Tileston Street among close-knit Abruzzese families, with mailboxes that displayed the surnames Federico, Cellurale, and DiCenso from the town of Sulmona. Antonio gauged changes in the 1970s by the growing number of unfamiliar faces who often greeted him and his wife, Philomena, when passing through Tileston Street. He recalled an earlier time when the street was full of *amici* (friends), *compagni belli* (close friends), and *compaesani* (fellow countrymen). Antonio had been raised with the Old-World tradition of respecting *stranieri* (strangers) and *forestieri* (outsiders), and he accepted the newcomers, albeit with some wariness:

> There's all new people now. They walk by me. They greet me. And first of all, I always respect all of them in return with great honor. Because the stranger, the person who is far from home, you should always respect them all the more. One of your *paesani* [friends from the same town], one of your *compagni belli* [close friends], yes, that's one thing, but the foreigner should be respected—well, at least that's the way I treat people.

I don't consider the newcomers good and I don't consider them bad either (chuckling). I respect them the way they respect me. But I don't know what intentions they have, what they have in mind.[1]

Al Mostone had been the sexton of the Old North Church and a well-known tour guide. He recalled parents who often asked him to find apartments for their transplanted children, saying, "We've heard so much about the North End that if I know my daughter was living there, we'd rest easy at home."

A lifelong North Ender who was proud of his community, Al tried to understand why so many outsiders "from the western part of the country, the central part, from New Jersey and New York, from all over the place" were so attracted to the North End. He said, "Take the new people that are moving here. Why? Why do they come here, they want to stay here? What's the reason? I've spoken to people here that are strangers, they say to me, 'Al, I love it here.' There must be something over here, something we can't see. It's like the old Irish used to say, 'I'm a dearo.' It means 'dear old North Ender.' They were very proud to say, 'I'm a dearo.'"

When the [John] Hynes administration modernized the city by attracting middle-class suburbanites to increase its tax base, parts of the South End, Brighton, and the entire West End were destroyed. Less than two decades later, the North End experienced the same reverse exodus of people returning to the city but without the destruction of buildings. The Boston Redevelopment Authority (BRA) plan to renew the Waterfront area into a separate neighborhood of expensive condominiums in the 1970s drove real estate values in the North End's core to unheard of levels. North Enders rented apartments to students and single young professionals at higher rents. Some treated them politely but kept a distance. Others treated them like their own children, sending food, caring for them when they were sick, and, especially for young women, making sure they returned safely at night. But by the early 1980s, when increasing numbers of elders had vacated old flats for subsidized housing, creating a vacuum, more landlords sold their multiunit apartments, which were converted to high-priced apartments and condominium complexes.

Some residents found the lifestyle of the new people odd, in part because they could afford expensive rent and condominiums yet had no families. North Enders also found it strange when a young, single person living next door with no relatives stayed inside rather than socialize outside with neighbors and came out only to walk a dog or go jogging alone. One North Ender compared the new people to the old neighborhood with classic North End humor: "The only time we used to see somebody in the neighborhood running was to get away from a cop."

By the early 1980s, more young professionals had discovered the neighborhood's allure: safe streets and personal security, workplaces within walkable distance to the financial district and Mass General Hospital, the pageantry of religious feasts, and the glorious Italian American cuisine, which many had never experienced. But what newcomers admired most about their new community was the humanity of Italian Americans, the affection they showed toward family and friends, how they cared for one another, and the pride they felt as North Enders, which they extended to them too.

Josie Piccadaci

Josie Piccadaci measured neighborhood change by the number of families left in its homes.

"They're Not Homes Anymore"

People started to make more money and it went to their heads, really. And then a lot of the old people died and all new people started coming in. Then all new people started coming in. Although some of the young people that are coming in now are friendly, because I have them around me, some live next door and two doors from me, a lot of strange girls, but they're very friendly. They say hi to us if we're outside when they go by. They're very friendly, but nothing like it used to be. A lot of families moved out—they wanted to better themselves, they wanted bigger houses, and of course their kids got older or some of them got married or whatever, and I don't know, they just disappeared, seems they just moved. There aren't homes in North End anymore—it's all single people—young girls, young fellas, whatever. There's no families; they're not giving the places to families anymore. They're not building—it's all apartments for young people. They're not homes.

Josephine Tranquillo

Josephine Tranquillo spoke about living in elderly housing compared to tenement living on North Margin Street: "Now they have to call you before they come to see you."

"No One Came By"

I live in Casa Maria [Endicott Street] now. But I used to live in an apartment house before. You'd go downstairs to see the neighbors standing in front of their doors. And they'd greet you. That meant a lot. Now, today, in my building, you don't see a soul. You push a button, get on the elevator, and there's nobody there. You could drop dead and nobody knows. The other day my daughter came to my place. So I was making toast and while we were talking, the toast burned, smoke all over the house. So I opened the door to let the smoke out. And nobody came out of their apartment. So I put the fan on, put on the air conditioner, and I finally got all the smoke out. Still and all, no one would come out and ask me what was the matter. I miss going up and down the stairs in my old building. I miss everything. I miss my rooms; I miss the whole building—I lived there for forty-two years. I had a beautiful flat. Now what do I see from my window? I don't see anything. Where I live now, all I see are rooftops. Who enjoys that? I see one of the eagles when they go by, an airplane when it goes by, that's all. What do I see? I see all antennas—all those building antennas.

Anita LaRocca

"The North End Is Going to Change"

I took care of my father when he was sick until 1991. So then we had to sell the building. The priests all knew me, the nuns all knew me; I lived on North Bennet Street since 1949 [and] they knew I had seven children. Every time they saw me, "Mrs. LaRocca, how are you? How are you doing today?" It was so unfortunate because I remember Father Francis at Columbus High School when my son Robert was going to school in the 1960s saying it was going to change. He said, "Mrs. LaRocca, do you see this piece of land right here? I'm gonna tell you now, this is gonna be worth so much money that you won't believe it; nobody will believe me." I said, "I know, Father, but I don't have the money to buy the land, so it's unfortunate," but his words came true. But he's the one—he just came up to me and he told me, he said, "I want to tell you something." It's almost like he wanted to tell me to buy something then because I would be sorry if I didn't. But we didn't have the money. We had seven kids. At thirty years old I had seven kids running around, one after the other. I says, "What the hell," what was I gonna do—we were lucky that we had food on the table and everything. But this is what he told me and [I] never forgot it in my life, I says, you know he was right. Property became prime. The school was sold. They made condominiums out of Saint Anthony's and Columbus High School. He knew, he even would say in the '60s, that the North End was going to change because of gentrification. He just knew.

Robert LaRocca

Robert LaRocca was a well-respected community leader and advocate who mentored many North Enders in youth programs.

"He Was So Right"

The handwriting was on the wall. If you were smart, had some background. I was a kid, I didn't know. I got a little angry from it. I took it almost—teenaged North Ender, come on, my community isn't going to change, the North End is not going to change. I thought he was being arrogant. It wasn't possible. My whole world and life living in the North End—I mean I worked for every agency in the North End and I knew thousands of people, practically all—what were there, thirty thousand at the time? We probably knew half of them. And I'll never forget—he was so right. Years later it started changing, and I said, he was so right. I was young and unaware. I didn't know communities could change like that. Although we did see it happen in the West End. We had some relatives there. My grandfather Antonio used to take me to see my mother's oldest brother who lived there, so we would walk from the North End into the West End—we'd go shopping, he'd take us to Morgan Memorial [Salvation Army], a huge warehouse with all kinds of things. It was just his way of getting away from work: "Come on Roberto, we go for a walk."

Frank Favazza

"Things Are Changing Too Fast"

I enjoyed my North End; I loved the North End. I was born here on North Street, and out of eleven children I'm the only one left in the North End; all the others are out of town. Most of them are in Gloucester. Now my children are all around, they're not here; being as I don't have a car, I depend on them when they come. They have their own families. They come, yes. With the coming of these condominiums—the other day sometimes you can live in a section and you don't go down that street and it's only a three-minute walk from here. The section I'm talking about is where Saint Stephen's Church is now; across the street I noticed the other day, condominiums. My God! I thought there wasn't such a thing as condominiums, and now I hear that they're making condos a stone's throw from where I'm living—on the corner of North Margin and Cooper Street they're renovating some buildings—eventually we'll have to be getting out.

They sell the buildings and what do they do? They convert them to condominiums. That's what I'm afraid of, that whatever few remain of the Italian population, about half of them, between dying and not being able to afford the rent—the children take them in and all that; it's tough, it's tough I tell you. I used to be a fisherman. I used to leave my house—I used to live where the post office is now on Hanover Street on that little alley there [Mechanic Court]; I'd go down to the wharf all the time—any hour because we had no set hours; it wasn't a factory, it didn't depend on any time. I'd go down there, Richmond Street, all the ways to the Waterfront—not to the [Waterfront] as it is now. I'd never been stopped once, not even somebody to ask me for a match. Now as soon as it gets dark, even on my own block, I don't go out anymore. I'm afraid. It's been done you know, but people don't talk about it. They shove you in a doorway and—or else—or else. They shove you in a doorway and what can you do?

My father was a fisherman, his father was a fisherman. There were two places on the Waterfront where we used to tie up the boats—one was named Packet Pier—and we had at least fifty, probably more, boats. There's not one left now. Things change for one reason or another; things change. Things are changing too fast. I cannot grasp all the changes in the last few years. And when I lost my old wharf where the new is now, that's where all the old-timers like me would congregate on sunny, nice days and talk, and I used to enjoy it. Now where am I gonna go?

Sam Perrelli

"We Don't Know Each Other"

I lived on Battery Street all my life, you know what I mean? My parents were from Avellino. They were happy because they were living near 'o mare [the sea]; it was nice here. They loved America. They were happy and they all died in America. There's no respect for old people. Used to get up, tip your hat to them; you'd go to church. You'd help them. They don't care—they have no manners. I don't throw everybody down. There's a few landlords left that ruined the North End, all right, they're in it for the money. They're chasing the old people out. I don't know why, but they're chasing them out and the people over here, they listen to a lot of baloney. I love the old people. And what are you gonna do? They can't live on what they get and they give them a hard time. They think if you get three hundred dollars [a month], they think you're giving them a lot with the social security, to live on. And I remember years ago when the happy days were here, way back, say forty-five years ago, we all knew one another.

But today we get up in the morning, we don't know each other. Now you come here, you live next door to me, I don't know who you are. You just come in. Say you're thirty-five. I don't know if you're a crook. Or you come from another city—I don't know what kind of a fella you are. I can't say, "Come in my house." They [the Italians] knew me from I was a little boy and they took you in. And even then you weren't even safe. You gotta be this way. As you grow up, we knew one another; we used to go to all these clubs here, like our mothers and fathers used to take us to these clubs [societies]: "I want you to meet him, meet so and so." Then when we grew up, we knew one another, they happen to know you. So, "This is my son, this is my daughter," and as you got older, people would say, "Well, I know the mother, I know the father." Now it's different.

All them buildings used to be all Italians, all the way down to the end. They're all foreign people here; now [the rent], three hundred, four-fifty.

What do they pay rent with? Three or four people live in one apartment. You know you can get four hundred so you can say, "Hey jeez, lady, I want you to get out." I remember when these rooms used to be seven dollars a month one time and they were looking for people at the time! "Eh I got *cinque stanze* [five rooms]! Hey come on." They used to come and grab ya. Well, see what I mean? A lotta changes. And that's it—the North End ain't like it used to be. See? Don't worry about the North End—this is gonna be like the West End.

Rose Pesce

"The Older Fellas Used to Hang on the Corners"

Believe me, the life years ago, I'm talking about right here in the North End compared to today, nothing like today. I used to go out, I'd think nothing of coming home one o'clock in the morning, two o'clock, walking the street, no being afraid. Because you didn't have no strangers here. We were all just the Italians, just us. It isn't like today now. They're from all different—I'm not saying they're bad people these people now; they work here and they get rooms here. I see them go by, I can see they're strange. But they live in the North End. But I know they weren't in the North End when I was here. These young people that work here, they'll get the rooms and all that. It was nothing like that. That's why I used to come home one in the morning, two o'clock, think nothing of it, leave my girlfriend's house.

And on our corners we had nice—the older fellas, they used to hang at the corner. Just talking, you know. I mean I'm not talking about like these kids of today. And they knew you lived here and they sort of—you didn't have to be afraid, how shall I say it? There was no fear in those days, no fear, believe me. Not like today. My corner, the two of us, going out, we'd just sit in our doorway—we'd think nothing of sitting down, talking, enjoying ourselves—we used to go down the North End Park. They used to have the piers at the time. Now they have the pool. At the time we had the piers and it was the water, the ocean itself. We'd go down there—we'd all congregate down there on the summer nights, beautiful. It was nothing, nothing like today. Today it's a different ball game, believe me. I go to my sister's down the street—she only lives down the street where the Old North Church is, she lives on Hull Street. When it reaches ten o'clock, I'll leave her house and I just have to walk up the street, up to my corner, cause I'm afraid now. You know there's nobody around. You see strange faces. You never know. You hear so many crazy things. We don't go out as much as we used to. There's too much crime in the streets—it might even be from our own area. There was a time when I'd come home at two in the morning. Now I wouldn't dare now unless my husband was with me.

Joe Anastasi

"Now It's a Town of Restaurants"

Then when I got married, I moved to Hanover Street and I've been living there since I'm married, thirty-eight years. It's not like it used to be at one time, but now, all outsiders now—I guess we got less than 50 percent now. It gets worse as it goes along. It turned out to be more a business section more than a residential. All businesses, restaurants. How many? Now it's a town of restaurants. Everybody comes to the North End for the Italian restaurants—we got about eighty of them in a little district like this. I would never leave. I for one, which I coulda left eighteen thousand times, I didn't want to leave. Why? What section is better than the North End? I mean you got a nice section here. People are nice. You can't find any more warmth than you can find in the North End. You go outta town, what are you gonna get? So I've never left it. I don't think I ever will.

Yes sir, I've gone all over—I mean I've seen the rest or most of the world, but the North End is still the North End. Compared to other sections [this] is still the best section there is. A lot of people say, "I'm born here, I lived here, and I'm gonna die here." That's right. I'm one of them. Gonna run into a little trouble because it's kinda heavy taking me down from the top floor. Let's hope it's a hundred years from now.

FIGURE 50. Saint Anthony's Playground, Prince Street, 1980.

Joe Anastasi and Joe Arigo

"They Will Not Stay Here"

I would never leave the North End, not if I could help it, unless I get pushed out. Which might be, you know? You see what's happening around here. First of all, whoever is moving in here, they're not family. You know what I mean? They're people that don't have families. They're all like professionals or businesspeople. And uh, you notice yourself, there aren't many kids—kids are starting to dwindle, you know? The people itself, that's what happened. We used to be a community of, how many, twenty-eight thousand? I mean a ward—there were twenty-eight thousand in this ward. Changing times. Progress. They cut through here, they brought the expressway through here; it was supposed to have been through Atlantic Avenue on the Waterfront, that was the original plan. To bring it down around along the avenue. There used to be the Elevated [Railway]; it stretched from where the molasses tank that blew up down on Atlantic Avenue. I was in the seventh grade. The people were more togetherness. Today they ain't worrying about togetherness, they're worrying about how much you can make, who can, well, who could uh—well, uh, I can't say, *cchiu malavagi* [too many bad people]. They don't help one another, that's false—I mean the people that are left.

Some do—I mean there are so few now that are willing to help out other people, all they think of is the almighty dollar anyway today. We used to have four churches down here. Four parishes. And those churches were jammed, always jammed. Now they can't even take care of one. I mean that doesn't hold them together either. If you had 'em you probably woulda held together the younger generation [and] they woulda grown up with the idea, you know? But they never had it to get together, so I guess—it's the fault of everybody. We didn't stick together. That's Roman Catholic churches, and then we had two other Protestant churches, the Baptist. We used to have eight, nine schools. Christopher Columbus, Cushman, Saint Mary's, Saint John's, Saint Anthony's. We had three or four of them knocked down. The only one left is Saint John's, the Christopher Columbus, that's all. And the Eliot, the Michelangelo. They knocked down one, the Eliot School, the original.

Mary Beninati

"They're Moving to Medford"

Well, families are all getting away. I speak to people in the [Beninati's] store, "I'm moving"—the family, the daughter—this week, they're moving to Medford because where they live they say there's condominiums. They can't afford to pay all that money. So they're moving; people are moving out. You hate to do it because, as I say, people come in, they're nice people, but you don't know them like you used to live with families all the time, you know? It's sad, it's sad. The people that are coming, they're a nice class of people, doctors, lawyers, people that work at City Hall, but it isn't as I told you, like when the families used to get together—you don't know hardly anybody now. They all love the North End. They're nice people, only they're individuals, they live alone. It isn't the family. One girl says to me "I'll never move unless I'm thrown out." They love the atmosphere, the people, I don't know, that's what they all say. How many people come in the store, "Do you know of any vacant rooms?"

Every day they come, every day! They love the North End. The rents are sky high, the people can't afford the rents, [the landlords] allow [tenants to do] remodeling, some of them are selling condominiums—they can't afford it. This mother and daughter are moving this week—they can't afford it. Over here before, fifteen, sixteen dollars, you have a flat. Of course, a cold-water flat—nobody had showers—but they were happy. But now everything is so high. But I enjoy my life; I like to clean, cook and that's all I want. That's what I live for, my family.

Frances Lauro

Frances Lauro recalled the Feast of the Madonna del Soccorso of an earlier time: "They used to make the boats, in the air, the angels. All the old-timers are all gone, honey, they're all dead. They used to put the pigeons in the boat and then when the Madonna used to come, they used to open them and birds all used to fly. It was beautiful years ago. They do it, but not like they used to."

"I Haven't Got Anything but I Like Where I Am"

My birthday is coming up on April fifteenth. I was born in 1902. I've lived in my apartment on 260 North Street for forty-seven years. I was born in the house. Today the houses are all remodeled. In those days we were born right in the house. We lived in old-fashioned houses. The people were all wonderful. We used to talk to each other: "Aye, what are you doing? You wanna come up for a cup of coffee?" Beautiful those days, please! Most are dead, most are moved out. The poor people, you know, they still want to come back to the North End. I always loved the North End. I could never depart it—I think I'll die if I had to go out of the North End. Truly. I was raised here; I know all my people, they're always good friends. How can you go outside and then be closed in and alone? I don't believe in that. It means a lot for me to live here, a lot. I spend my time, well, I do little errands in the morning, then I do a little housework, do the beds, clean up, and come over here a while [the senior center]; I see all my friends and we kill the time. I got a girlfriend—she always comes and sees me too. She lives across the street. I haven't got anything, but I like where I am. It doesn't bother me. My friends come and see me, they call me up.

I don't have neighbors like I used to, but I have one old-timer across the street from me, she stays with me; sometimes she comes after supper and we talk. And then, it's eleven and oh my God, you see the time it is! "Yeah!" I says, "Well you'll have to go across the street." And my son takes her across the street, that's all. But it's beautiful—I mean I like it. I live right across where they have the Feast of the Madonna del Soccorso; it's only a two-family. Well, honey, it's not like it used to be, say, like a Little Italy. We used to sit in the doorway, we used to sing, the kids used to play games. It was wonderful. Nobody used to get mad. We used to tell jokes. I like one-day vacations—I like to go for one day, but the weekends I don't like to leave my son, you know, like that—you know what I mean. The old people are always like that; they're more attached to the house. But now today, you can't say nothing. You bother them. They're all these outsiders around. They make these condominiums home and they're all for their own.

I'll tell you the truth, there isn't much of the young kids around anymore. These are all condominiums, homes, all young couples, but you don't know them. You don't mingle with people like that; they just come in. But they're having a ball too, they don't care. They come from all around cause they like the North End! They like it because it's more quiet, not much of these crimes around, you know? They like that. That's what it is. We're thrown out. [Just] like the Italians, they wanna take this building. Where you gonna go after? You gotta move out. They renovated the building and you have to go out, that's what it is.

More people coming in; in time they're gonna clean [out] that North End, they're gonna take all those homes. And they're making all condominiums—that's terrible. You can't even go anywhere. And not only that. They go fixing, and they raise it [rents] so high. Where you gonna get this money? It's really disgusting today. That's condominiums—they own each flat, their own flat. Like me, I'm paying rent but the other ones are condominiums. Right on Fulton Street, that's all they have. Oh boy, they're beautiful, but where can you get this money? Sometimes I wonder, how much money could you make? You think I wouldn't love to be in one of those? I couldn't afford it when my husband, poor guy, he used to work Depression time with five kids. How could you save money?

Josie Zizza

Crime

The biggest problem in the North End is crime. They're all breaking into homes and everything. We're afraid. This apartment on the first floor was so low people didn't want to live in it so they boarded them up because the kids used to go in there [and] they took a piece of the sink off. It's a big apartment. You know, we were never like that. Years ago, we'd go out ten, eleven o'clock—the stores were all open [so] if you needed a loaf of bread eleven o'clock at night, you'd get it. But now they close—they're afraid, they close early. Five or six o'clock, Salem Street is dead. Things are so different now. We've always slept with open doors and everything. Now even locked, you're afraid. You're afraid to say anything because they'll mark you. It's from outside.

I have a girl in my club and her husband has a drugstore and they went into his store. It was people from Charlestown and Cambridge, they had just got out of jail. And there's some, few kids here, their parents are more lenient. No, I never had my boys out in the street nine, ten o'clock nights. I definitely didn't, not that I want to brag, but my husband had a strap that big. My sons always tell me, "Ma, we had to be in bed at a certain time." Well, I say, "Look, now you have your own family, how is it?" They don't do it today though; their mothers aren't home themselves. It's hard. I had a family at the corner where I live just get robbed Friday afternoon, one o'clock in the afternoon. See what I mean? You're afraid.

I had a friend of mine went to Italy for a month; she celebrated her fiftieth wedding anniversary and her children gave her a trip to Italy. When she got home her house was robbed. Well first of all, I think there are kids on drugs and they need the money. And I don't know, second of all, if my sons took something home that didn't belong to them, I'd ask them where they got it. I think the parents should be notified. I spoke to Sal DiMasi. We had a little meeting. He is our representative. I think he should go in the schools and have a meeting and have the parents come. Because if the parents aren't home, the children aren't home either. I'm not blaming all the mothers. But if you're not home, how do you know where your children are? I knew where my children were. Cause I was determined. If I went out, my husband was home. If he went out, I was home. We didn't have all that drug thing. And then, mothers know—you can't approach a mother and say your children are—we see some kids getting the stuff [drugs] but you can't tell the parents. The mother gets mad.

FIGURE 51. Idolo Taglieri on Prince Street, 1981.

Idolo Taglieri

"You'd See Four Generations"

They're all gone; you have a few couples left, either the wife is dead, the husband. There was a lot of elderly people around here years ago. Now there's no more. Years ago, you used to see the grandfathers, the grandmothers sit down outside. They lived with their children. It was family—it was a real family affair. Grandchildren there, mothers and fathers. It's all gone. No more family. You used to find them outside at the feasts. You'd go four generations back—no kiddin'. Like on Hanover Street at the feasts, you'd see the grandfather, the great-grandfather, the father, and the kids, the grandchildren, and the great-great-grandchildren. There used to be a family down here, every time there was a feast they would congregate—there'd be about eighty of them in one family, from the great-grandfather down. They used to live in one building on 440 Hanover Street. There were all big families down there.

My mother's famous words: "Che crede che trova la? Che ci sta? Chella si trova. Niente. Niente. [What do you think you're going to find over there when it's over? What's there? Nothing, nothing.]" What's the name of that song? (singing) That's the end of the rainbow! Times. You can't hold the times back! That's been the way of life for centuries. Time goes on. Changes. Just like the weather changes. People change. Times change. It's a cycle anyhow, and it's going round and round; nothing changes, it just goes around in a cycle.

A Street Conversation between Two North End Tenants on Rising Rents

ELDERLY WOMAN: Sixty dollars more! Did your landlord raise you?

THERESA: Not yet. She'll raise it [rent] again, they always do—my landlord. My brother got raised twenty bucks.

ELDERLY WOMAN: Your brother?

THERESA: Yeah. My landlord. My brother just got raised twenty bucks. They're always doing it.

ELDERLY WOMAN: And they're supposed to be friends.

THERESA: I know, forget about friends. Friends are the worst ones.

ELDERLY WOMAN: Today for sure, especially, it's all money.

THERESA: It's all money, is right! Money, money, money.

THERESA: Money first, and then friends.

ELDERLY WOMAN: I know it.

THERESA: I guess I better go. Gotta go in town and do Christmas shopping.

Rose Giampaolo

New Landlords

We have many, many people from the suburbs moving into the North End, and it seems to me new landlords are buying all this property because property in the North End has been run down and hasn't been maintained over the years. Most of the apartments up to ten, fifteen years ago, many of them did not have bathrooms—they would have a toilet in the hallway which was shared sometimes by two families. And when I talk about a bathroom, I don't mean a bathroom, I mean a small area with a hopper—no sink, no shower, tub, just a hopper—and this hopper in the hallway would sometimes be shared, in some instances, by three families, and it wasn't the way to live. In the North End not many apartments were heated; they were all walk-up, cold-water flats, which in the winter makes it a very uncomfortable place to live. The rooms are cold. The hallways are not heated—they are cold.

The apartments in the North End are heated by oil stoves, and on the stove you heat your apartment and you also cook on the stove. So it serves two purposes. Today because the people are moving in, of course the landlords are buying all the property [and] they are renovating these old houses. But the old apartments as they were before, the rents would be sixty, seventy dollars a month, say, for three or four rooms. But when these apartment houses get bought over by a new landlord, the families are put out. They do renovate the apartments, they do put bathrooms in, steam heat, but then the rents will jump from [sixty], seventy dollars a month for that same apartment, up to two-fifty, three hundred dollars. They'll add a bathroom, put a little carpeting on the floor, perhaps panel a little bit, which makes them livable, but they are getting a big difference in rent.

The people in the neighborhood resent new landlords buying all the property and they do resent people coming in—strangers—because the North End has always been a very ethnic group. All Italians. Now that's changed. I don't think we have 50 percent Italians—I believe it's more 40 percent Italian, 60 percent other nationalities. In five or ten years the Italian people won't be able to live here because they cannot afford to pay the high rents, because the minute the new landlord buys the property—today some landlords are willing to sell their property because they can get a high price for it. But those old tenants have to go with the new landlord. And then of course these places [cold-water flats] get renovated and new tenants come in.

And so the new tenants, people that come from the suburbs, perhaps used to paying higher rents because they work in Boston, so they don't mind paying and they will stay. But it's the people that are used to paying their forty, fifty, sixty dollars a month's rent for that same apartment even though it wasn't renovated, they could afford those cheap rents but today they cannot. We haven't got enough elderly housing for these elderly people who are moving out of these apartments because they are being sold. Some of them are fortunate enough to get into elderly housing, but not many. We need many more elderly housing [apartments] for the elderly poor in the North End. The Ausonia Home is for the elderly but the Christopher Columbus Plaza is not. They only have a small percentage on fixed incomes—ones that are paying low rents—because there are low-, moderate-, and high-rent categories. We don't have too many low-income there even though the low- and moderate-[income apartments] are being subsidized.

Rose Giampaolo

"They Like the Feeling of Warmth in the North End"

I lived on the same street for seventy-one years in the North End; I love the neighborhood. From my bedroom window during the day there were many times when I spent watching the boats go by, especially the *Constitution*. I lived just a half a mile away from the *Constitution* where it's kept in Charlestown, so every year they would [have] that boat turn about and I would always, knowing the day it was, be at my window or on my rooftop to watch it turn about and go down and then back again. It was a thrill for me to watch it. When I leave the city, I enjoy the country—I think [it's] beautiful but I prefer the busy life of the city. I remember when times were hard when I was a little girl. We didn't have the luxuries that the youth of today have. There weren't many cars around in my day, very, very few.

Two years ago, I moved to the Christopher Columbus elderly housing on the Waterfront, and I feel within the last ten years there's been big changes in the North End. We're having many, many people from the suburbs coming back into the city because they feel that the North End of Boston is the place to be. I think they like the feeling of warmth in the North End. The North

End is a place where there is mostly Italian people, and I feel Italian people as a whole are very warm, hospitable people. They welcome strangers. They're not afraid of strangers; they trust people because they themselves trust one another. They care for one another in the neighborhood.

Mary Molinari

"Things Are Changing and I Don't Know Why"

This is our roots, where our parents came from in the 1900s, and we've been here from the originals, our parents. They landed here and we're gonna die here. They certainly worked hard to support a family of four, six—and low rent those days, and we enjoyed it. My mother and father made sure we had food on the table with a few pennies, a dollar. And we were happy. We were happy in our way. Today I don't know what happened. Everything sky high. We are—what are we doing? There's no harmony. I was evicted about a year ago. But I would never [have] moved out of the North End. I made it my business to stay in the North End because my parents came from the North End and I believe the people of the North End should be here. I have two sons and they live with me, and they know if I move out of town in the suburbs that I would take sick because I'm not used to the suburbs, I'm used to the North End. My sons bought the condominium, not me. I had to because I was evicted.

Where I was living, they renovated the place and the rent is four hundred dollars today. I was only paying a hundred fifty-five dollars. Look at how much they jacked it up! To have it renovated, to throw all of the people out of the North End. But I'm staying in the North End and I'm gonna die in the North End. Because we love the North End.

Our roots are from the North End. People are different today. I don't know what happened. Years ago we were just—one happy—we used to enjoy life. My mother, dad, and all their friends and sisters and brothers—but not today. I don't know what happened. It's changing very rapidly. When it's after four o'clock, people they're all in the house today. They're scared to go out. I heard last night that a friend of my friend was running down Commercial Street because three teenage boys were chasing her. She doesn't know [who they were] because she was so frightened that she screamed [and] the people from the Christopher Columbus Plaza all ran out to see who it was, who was chasing her. So you see, people are afraid to go out. Years ago we used to take those beautiful walks up the Common with my mother and father. Even when I was married, I used to go to Thompson's Spa—at night they used to have cakes at half price—we used to walk up Washington Street. Now you're afraid to walk through there, it's a combat zone, you're afraid to get hit there. See everything today is changed and I don't know why.

Viola Pettinelli

Viola Pettinelli felt like a prisoner of fear because her friends were afraid to go out, and she recalled the old neighborhood as vivacious because people used to go out and walk.

The New North End

Oh, I've seen a lot of changes, yes some for the good, and some not so good. This crime really is bad and it seems to be getting worse instead of better. But still, I like it here. When it gets dark, I can still run to the corner and get my paper, maybe because I'm so close, so close to the stores, to everything, and I've been here practically all my life. Even the new generation that I don't know, they know that I belong here and so I feel safe with them. The new people, well I don't know. It's hard to tell with them. They don't know me, I don't know them. They're just strangers. They might be better than me, I don't know, but I manage. Really, I'm not too scared. They [new people] don't talk too much aside from "How are you?" or exchanging greetings, that's it. Well, they're the new generation anyway. I would say they are the second generation according to my age, so you really haven't got much in common with them. And then they are mostly college graduates. I'm a grammar school graduate (chuckling) so that makes a difference too.

Frances Lauro

"We Can't Walk Anymore"

Sometimes I say, "Why don't we all go out together, three or four of us girls and go out? Why only go out when we have a feast? Why can't we go out and take a walk?" But nobody does it. And that's sad, that's very sad. I don't know—the new generation is missing a lot because they can't go out and walk. You know what I really miss? Before when it was safe, after you had your supper, you'd go out with a person—even alone—you take a walk around the block, we'd go up to Scollay Square [now Government Center]—that was supposed to have been a bad place [but] nobody ever harmed us. We went to Scollay Square every time we had fifteen cents, we'd go and buy an ice-cream soda. There was an ice-cream parlor with the old-fashioned chairs; you'd go up there, have your ice cream, and come back home. By ten o'clock you were home. It was nice.

   Today they say you can't even go up to Government Center unless there's a big shindig going on. And then they say, "Oh, it was bad there." I didn't think it [Scollay Square] was bad. There were bad people, but they didn't bother nice people. Nobody bothered nice people. I miss those days, just to go out some night. We'd have these hot nights, we'd have our supper, wash the dishes—it would be so nice to take a nice walk around the block or go up the street and down the street and then go home. But once it gets dark everybody is in their house.

The Old Waterfront and the New Boston   29

Chi chiàgne, chi rìre (Sometimes you laugh, sometimes you cry).
—NEAPOLITAN PROVERB

When the Boston Redevelopment Authority (BRA) and the city of Boston embarked on a plan to renovate the North End's Waterfront in the early 1970s, it signaled the end of a major industrialized port, which employed many North Enders in processing plants, warehouses and small businesses. Lifelong North Enders like Nunzio DiMarino had lived on Salem Street since 1919 and opened a wholesale tomato business on Commercial Street in 1947. He described working on the Waterfront:

> It wasn't big; everybody was in business. It was a tough struggle from the start, but after a while we were doing good. It was better back then than it is now, I tell you the truth. I had nice customers, I had good customers. There were a few, yes, but not all of them from the North End; most of the businesses were out-of-towners, from Medford, Melrose, and Cambridge. We had the Spenardi brothers that came from the West End, they were in the tomato business too, see? The tomatoes came from Florida, California, Mexico, Texas, and they're still coming from the same places, oh yeah. But it wasn't too bad. You don't make the money you're making now, because at that time you were working for 30, 35, 40 percent [profit], it was good money. But now they're working for 50 percent because everything is higher now. The most I paid when I had people working for me, I used to give them a hundred, a hundred twenty-five dollars a week, and that was good money at that time. And don't forget, we were working on a Sunday

too sometimes. We had to go in, what are you gonna do? You got a customer coming in, in the morning, Monday morning, they come in early—they come in from Worcester, Springfield—they're coming in, you hadda get the stuff ready. See, lotta time, I worked almost every other Sunday, I hadda go to work. Nights, get up at one o'clock in the morning. You had to. What are you gonna do? How many times—I had one customer from New Bedford, and he used to call up on a Saturday, and we were running short on tomatoes. So what did I hadda to do, I threw them in the car and I hadda bring them down. What are you gonna do? You hadda take care of them. Today they wouldn't do that anymore. Today they says, forget about it, come and get 'em. Because it cost too much money to handle that. The place was all right, you know, but you hadda work hard.

When the BRA took Nunzio's building by eminent domain in 1970, his only option was to move his business to the market in Chelsea, but at a cost of hundred thousand dollars, an investment well beyond his reach. The BRA offered him the chance to buy back the property but with stipulations to build residential housing according to their specifications, leaving Nunzio no choice but to leave: "So I figured out it woulda cost too much money, and I said, 'I don't want the building.' So they took it over. I was upset, but what could I do about it?"[1]

Few had the resources to buy their property back from the BRA. With the support of family, one of the luckier North Enders managed to hang on. Dr. Nicholas Dello Russo wisely borrowed from a family member to buy his property back from the BRA and built a home on Fulton Street, where he has lived since 1971. He observed the loss of the working class and the many commercial businesses that employed hundreds of North Enders: "The fishing industry was moved to Northern Avenue, the wholesale produce industry from Commercial and Fulton Streets and Faneuil Hall, to Chelsea, and the wholesale meat businesses moved to Newmarket Square and Widett Circle."

By the late 1970s, the city's conversion of old factories and warehouses into a separate, wealthy neighborhood in the "New Boston" was in full swing. On June 12, 1977, the *Boston Globe* reported an agreement between the owner of a meat-processing factory and a real estate developer to "recycle" the six-story site of the factory into an office and apartment complex. Word on the street reaffirmed the story that the abandoned Boston Sausage and Provision Company building on Commercial Street was being converted into a new condominium complex.

On a Sunday afternoon in late June, Mary Pagliuca and Nick Argiro met on Hanover Street and headed for the opening ceremony at their old workplace. Standing in the crowd, they watched as dignitaries cut the ribbon, proudly pointing to the building where Nick had been the night supervisor of hotdog skinners and meat processors from the North End. Mary Pagliuca had been one of his line workers from 1946, until she retired in the late 1960s. Now old friends, Mary had been Nick's most productive worker, who sometimes helped sleepy friends on the production line by handing them extra boxes of skinned hotdogs so they could produce the hundred pound an hour quota. When the ceremony ended and the crowd dispersed, the two stood gazing in wonder at the newly renovated structure. Peering into the gleaming office window for a glimpse of what had been the busy factory floor, they instead saw the reflection of two elderly North Enders from a bygone world.

FIGURE 52. The junction of Commercial Street, Atlantic Avenue, and North Street, 1900.

Al Mostone   Al Mostone recollected the vibrant Waterfront in its heyday.

On the Waterfront in 1915

At the age of seven I started to sell newspapers and shine shoes on Atlantic Avenue on the Waterfront. Atlantic Avenue was mostly stores; there were mostly fish markets on the wharf side of the avenue and on the opposite side there was the market, which doesn't exist today—most of it is gone. The Sicilian fishermen—most of the Sicilian people were in the fish business and they had their own private boats. They used to all come into Long Wharf, T Wharf, Eastern Packet Pier, and they all lived in the North End. And then the people, they'd sell the fish to stores and shops all the way along Atlantic Avenue on the wharf side. And there were barrooms over there, tobacco stores—they had everything at the time, all on that one side. All the farmers used to bring their produce to this market on North [and] South Market Street, and that's where they used to deliver, and that's where all the terminals were at that time.

When I started to sell papers I made a nice little group of businessmen as my permanent customers. I used to buy the papers from the *Boston American,* the *Herald,* the *Traveler,* the *Transcript,* the *Record,* and we used to pay for the *Globe* and *Herald* two for one penny and we sold it for a penny. Well I had about sixty, seventy customers starting from Battery Street and going up all the way to Rowe's Wharf. I'd stop in the stores and just leave them their papers—they would pay me by the week. Then I sold newspapers at the kiosk where the East Boston tunnel was. I used to sell anywhere from fifteen [hundred] to two thousand papers a night because at that time there were all the coffee shops where they used to roast the coffee, nuts and liquor warehouses, offices. The Custom House was there, and the people used to come down [to] that area because Rowe's Wharf used to have the ferry boats going to Revere and to Nantasket, and people used to come down there to State Street and go downstairs and take the streetcars to East Boston. And at the same time people would do shopping or whatever it was, they would come by State Street and buy whatever they want.

We had the Union Freight lines over there, and that brought in business. They used to transfer the freight cars all through Commercial Street all the way as far as South Station. They used to transfer the freight cars into the different wharves, like Union Wharf, Lewis Wharf, whatever. There were people who were working in these warehouses. We had the Carter & Meigs building at that time—that was a great office building right on the corner of State Street and Atlantic Avenue. We had a lot of warehouses and quite a few of these places where they used to roast coffee, peanuts, stuff of that nature in that State Street area all the way up to Washington Street—that was all businesses there. We had the Lincoln Powerhouse that used to supply the electric for the North End and part of Boston. We had the Elevated [Railway], which started at North Station—the shuttle elevated and ran all the way to South Station and then they would leave people off over there [and] they'd go down into South Station and take their trains to whatever towns they lived in.

Where everything was horses and wagons, oh, I'd say it was 99 percent horses and wagons—you see you had teamsters there and they would buy a paper, do whatever shopping they wanted. I was in the middle of everything. I used to board the ships—the *North Star*, the *Calvin Austin*. I was allowed to go on the ships and I'd leave papers to the captains, the mates, the crewmen,

FIGURE 53. The East Boston ferry coming into its berth in the North End, next to Lewis Wharf, 1900.

and as a matter of fact I used to have my suppers there onboard ship. I'd shine shoes for them and then if they had suits, I'd take it the tailor and then take them from the tailor and bring it back to them. We had a lot of cafes on the avenue, and in these cafes we had a lot of sporting women. Well, when they were broke and I'd be at the State Street entrance, they'd come to me and they'd say, "Al, I need twenty-five cents," so I'd give them twenty-five cents, and then when they'd come out with their gentlemen friends they'd always double whatever they gave me. So I was doing pretty good earning between five and six dollars a week—that was pretty good money in those days.

Charlie Polcari

"When Boston Was Sleeping, New York Was Awake"

That place was very good [in the mid-1920s] but the city of Boston was too goddamned lazy or too stingy. When they was running there used to be ships came from the Old Country—from Italy, France, all kinds of people—the ships used to land over here, the port of Charlestown, Chelsea. What happened? When Boston was sleeping, New York was awake. You know what they did? They built a big port in New York so the ships wouldn't come over here anymore. You had to see the people, all the stuff they used to buy—you know the Italian people when [they] go over to the Old Country, you ought to see all the stuff they used to buy—clothing, everything, they used to buy and bring it to the Old Country for presents. When the ships started to go to New York all the Jews that were around here went out of business. Can you beat that? When Boston was sleeping, New York was awake.

I used to see the ships when I just got to work in Chelsea; I had to go over the bridge, and you used to see the Italian ships, the French ships, all kinds of ships used to come in. After the Port of New York [was built] the people said, "Yeah, when Boston was sleeping, New York was awake." For twenty-five cents you could get twenty-five pounds of fish. The fishermen would go out in the morning, especially if it was a Wednesday or a Friday; they used to have a line of baskets—they used to put them in the baskets—for twenty-five cents you could get all the fish you want. One night I went over there [and] they [fishermen] gave me a bag [so] full I couldn't even carry it home. For twenty-five cents. Bananas. There was quite a few people—there used to be a man who'd come around to the store, on the corners, everywhere, and "Thirteen for ten a cents!" And he used to give you bananas that big. Today you gotta pay forty cents a pound. How many you get? You get one or two! And there used to be a lot of people, a lot of friends of mine used to work down there on the Waterfront. They used to pay thirty-five cents an hour. They used to unload when the boat used to come in. They used to go over there and lugging the bunches and carry them upstairs. You know how they used to carry them? There was maybe fifteen fellas, all line up—you hand it to me, I hand it to you—until you get [it] up the street. That's how they were getting the bananas out of the boat. Now they got the machines, they don't care. You know what they say? "Acqua passare non passano piu il mulino." You know what that means? "The water doesn't pass through the mill anymore." That's what the Old World's saying.

Marguerite Locchiato

Farmers, Market Men, and Pushcarts

Richmond Street and Fulton and Commercial Street was like a square and there were all stands. And different farmers would come in. And all along Fulton Street there were chicken houses. I remember some of the farmers—Benjamin and Moore, and Johnny Albert—in sheds, like, it would be all out in the open, winter and summer. The farmers would come in with either a horse and wagon, or maybe later on they had trucks. And these people would have to go in and load it all—whether they took lettuce, peppers, string beans, whatever it was—they'd have to unload them, stack them up, and then sell them out to the merchants and then deliver them wherever they wanted it to be delivered, whether it be around the North End, the West End, the South End—they would just have to hoof it and go. And that was for little money. Maybe fifty cents—they'd have to go all the way to the South End for it. And to push that load was something, especially like when the month of September would come along and they'd have the tomatoes, and the people would buy the tomatoes to make tomatoes [prepare them for sauce] and they'd have to push that along. Of course, that was extra money for them, and God knows how many loads they could make a day to make that extra money. They'd have to push it by foot. And I remember my father used to push it hard—he would probably have twenty, twenty-five bushels in the back of that boxcar and he'd be pushing it all alone—[and] that was really hard work, he really worked hard. All them market men worked hard. And it was long hours for them because that's when the farmers would go in. Of course the farmers then would leave around ten o'clock in the morning and the rest was left up to them. And the farmers would tell them, "Well, get rid of the stuff. If you can make a few cents for yourself, go ahead." Well if some guy came down and said, "Well this is fifty cents, if I can make a nickel on it, I'll make a nickel on it." [And he would say,] "Well, this is fifty-five cents, OK?" It's OK, the farmer wanted that price for it. As far as work was concerned, they'd have to do it winter and summer. The snow used to be high and we were kids. My father would get up in the morning, bank the stove up to make the house warm for us, and leave early in the morning. He used to come home in the afternoon—his mustache, he had all icicles, poor man. But he had to stay out in the cold because he had to make a living.

Elvira DiMattia

"People from the West End Came, Too"

We had salt water that flowed into that harbor there. And my mother used always take us down there, oh when we were tiny bits of babies, because the Italian people believed that the salt water was very beneficial. And another thing, too, they knew although they weren't any PhD graduates, but they knew that the salt water should dry on a person's skin to be beneficial to the person. So my mother used to bring us down, three, four of us. Of course, the older ones would probably be selling newspapers or shining shoes, but they used to go down afterwards just the same. And we had more fun when the water flowed into that bay there where the pool is. Then they decided the water was contaminated, but the tide flowed back and forth, and for so many years people went down there, we had people from the West End to use that beach. Then they decided it wasn't fit to go into anymore and they built the bowl. There were a great many factories there, stores, anything that you wanted to buy—if you had a boat and you needed rope or you needed outdoor paint for your boat—the finishing industry came up as far as Atlantic Avenue.

People that were shoemakers here would go there and buy their leather and anything they needed in that industry. It created jobs for people in this area. Even along Portland Street—anything you wanted to buy in the line of a curtain, a shade, paints, a bicycle, fixtures, carpets—anything you could possibly think of that you wanted to buy you would find right along Portland Street. Now if you don't have a car you're out of luck.

Leslie Surrette

From Nova Scotia to the Waterfront

My mother had seventeen children and she was hitting it rough, too, in Yarmouth, Nova Scotia. My father, John, was the only one workin'—we were kids, see? He was a carpenter—Christ, he could build you a house and he'd tell you how many nails and how many boards it'd take you to build it too! And God bless him, he's dead now, but he was good though! I lived with my aunt in Saugus and when I got a little older they took me back to Nova Scotia. They started hittin' it rough so I used to go out in the woods chopping wood, you know, just to make firewood for the house, and I worked on the farm too. I used to plow on the farm—it was kinda hard for me—I had four horses and I had a big plow. I used to dig the land for the summer with the manure. I did that for a long time. The grass would grow, then I'd go out and cut the grass and pile it up and throw it out in them there [a grass pile]. In Nova Scotia I used to play the harmonica on stage at the big barn dances, all cowboy music it was. Yeah, we used to go to the barn dances in Yarmouth, from my mother's house, maybe five minutes from my mother's house, you're there. Didn't cost you nothing. As long as you got something to make everybody happy. And the guy came with a guitar. I played the harmonica, he played the guitar. What a time we used to have. Didn't cost you nothing. It was nice. We used to have a good time. Lotta young people, that's all it was.

I learned all that music by myself. I like the Christmas songs; my wife likes them too. I played a long time, from when I was a kid. But my [mother] was living rough. She used to cook at nighttime and feed everybody in the daytime. So I says [to myself], I'm fourteen years old—I didn't tell her nuttin', I just put some clothes on—off I went. She was hittin' it rough—it was too much for her. I didn't want to hurt her too much. So I hitchhiked to Boston. It was rough. I was scared. You look at the woods. You don't know what's coming out. Tell you the truth, I was a scared. I'd get a ride so far and then after a while the guy would say, "This is a as far as I'm goin'." Then I start walkin' again. Then I start thumbing again. [The] guy says, "Where you goin'?" And

[I] says, "I'm goin' to Boston." And he says, "I'm going to Boston," and he picked me up. I says, "I got no money"; I says, "I can't pay you." He says, "Don't worry about it, you need anything to eat? I'll buy it for ya." Oh it was a long time getting into Boston. It was a long hike.

I worked on the Fish Pier, too! I was making cat food. I worked with my wife, Carmella, on the Fish Pier on the Waterfront. Big, big, big oven! I used to cook 'em. And I never got in no trouble. I had a thing this sharp, a needle that keeps moving, tells how much water, how hot you gotta have it. [That] was nice. I used to work in the daytime and then at nighttime sometimes they had fish [and] you [had] to do the fish right away because before all them bugs and ants would come—I couldn't do it alone! I was afraid. You'd see rats come out that big, honest to God. I was scared. I told the guy, I told the steward, I ain't workin no more nights! "Why?" "I gotta have a helper with me. Cause the rats are scaring me." I was even afraid to take a bath. The guy says, "Alright, tonight you'll have somebody with you." He gave me a helper.

We grind them—we had the machines to grind them, they got the big machines, they got the cans—they had a big machine with cans, the cans keep going around, and then the fish falls in the cans. Then it goes down again. Then they got a machine that puts the covers on. I used to do all that. I tell ya, it was rough. It used to be on T Wharf—now they have all the rooms [condos and apartments] on there now. Used to work there for a while too. Long time, too!

They moved out—they went to California or somewhere. The boss liked me—he wanted me [to] come with him when he moved. I says, "No, I can't come with you," because I was going with her [Carmella], see? I can't keep moving without her or she'd say, "The hell with him!" I got a good wife, thank God. Yeah. No, she's good. I met her at my sister's house in the West End. I met her and about a week later I went away. Went away for three years. Eighteen, nineteen years old. On the truck. Driving the truck, driving down the road. Never got in any trouble, never had any license neither, all over the country without a license. I never got stopped. I said to myself, I said, "Oh, she'll forget me anyway." No, no. She waited for me.

Joe Anastasi

Joe Anastasi was the owner of Anastasi Bros., a banana company in the North End.

The Banana Business on the Waterfront

My father came here from Messina, Sicily, in 1905. He came like everybody else who wanted to come over—to make a living. That's the reason. Well, like everything else, hardships. I guess in Italy, that's the only reason why they came over here, that's why 90 percent of them come here. A lot of them said how much they loved Italy, but they always were coming here for the simple reason for making a livelihood, make a living.

I've been here sixty-five years, that's all. Right around the corner, sixty-five years. You got up as a youngster, go to school, go to work when you come out of school—my father was in business all his life. Sell bananas! He's been selling 'em since 1905. You get outta school, you went to work in the store, work until seven o'clock, six o'clock, went home, had supper, do homework, and go to bed as a child. My two brothers and myself took the business. My father come over here and his brother-in-law [Arigo] was already in the banana business before when he came here from Italy. They were on Endicott Street when he first got here with his kids, thirty, forty years. They were all my uncles. Arigo was the original banana man; he's the one, not my father [Anastasi]. He was one of the first fruit peddlers around here. When my father came over, he used to come and live at his sister, Donna Maria, at her house on Endicott Street. He was [a] young single guy. My father used to go with his brother-in-law [Arigo], who taught him how to heat the bananas so they get ripe. Then they used to have Bunsen burners, gas burners—they were supposed to be at a certain temperature. [Arigo] started even before 1900. He must have been born in the 1860s; he came over here on a banana boat, like a freighter, forty-four days. And he landed in New York, not here.

Then nothing else. Now it's all apartments. Six hundred dollars and up. People started to move out because taxes, the city I suppose, they could find their businesses elsewhere cheaper; they moved out, [the buildings] were never reoccupied, and people started to build over again. Now they got all condominiums down along the wharves. You have two of [the] largest lobster companies on the East Coast down there—you got James Hook and Bay State. They're the two largest dealers of lobsters on the East Coast. It's a wonder they didn't lose it. This district here used to be busier than Washington

Street [downtown]. Salem Street at night, we used to do business till twelve o'clock at night. Today you walk by Salem Street at two o'clock on Saturday afternoons, you throw a rock through a window and nobody'd see you. That's changed too. Nothing down here anymore. Everybody's buying, everybody's fixing up, they're bringing outsiders in. Condominiums—it's all money, you know? They tell you it's progress. Could be, you know. Let's hope I'm not around when it really is [in] high gear.

Idolo Taglieri

"They'd Throw a Mackerel at You"

There is different type of people. Before you had people who were butchers, bakers, you know what I mean? Groceries. Today what have you got? You got all white-collar workers and you got restaurants. They're all middle-class people—they're not what you call tradespeople. It was nice, it really was. You needed corn beef hash or something, the freight cars were there—all you had to do was open up a freight car, get your corn beef hash. You wanted your ice, you went to the top, you took it out of the icebox. You wanted fruits, you went down Onion Alley over there; it was all you wanted. Onion Alley, used to be where all your fruit and produce was, you know, *la scarola* [the escarole] used to be there, spinach, cabbage, cauliflower. Yeah it was all there. Yeah, what the hell, they never missed it, so you'd go by and get a handful. If it was a nickel a bunch the guy used to throw it at you. You didn't have to steal nothing it was so cheap. Watermelons—they used to give away watermelons, fish, sure. That's a fact. How much fish they'd give away down the wharf over there! You hadda worry about fish? The fishermen used to call you, "Ayyee!" Throw a mackerel or a halibut at you. Give you all you wanted. Forget about price—they used to buy them two for a penny; now they want forty-five cents apiece for them, half a dollar. You know, the ones in the pushcart.

Rose Giampaolo

"They Wanted It Historical, but We Remembered the West End"

Before we got elderly housing I was one of the members on the committee for elderly housing that saw to it that we got elderly housing. We worked for almost two years trying to get elderly housing on the Waterfront because the people really didn't approve of it. They felt that Atlantic Avenue, Commercial Street, North Street, and Fulton should be historical areas. And it was supposed to have been a historical site named by Washington. And it was supposed to be kept in favor of the people. But of course the North End people fought it, and we didn't feel—living in the North End and being born here—we didn't feel there was anything historical about Atlantic Avenue or Fulton Street or North Street. It's just that they wanted to name it historical to keep it private so they could control that area. They were opposed to elderly housing on the Waterfront, what they considered historical. I don't know whether they didn't want the Italian people too close to them or whether they felt the Italian poor wouldn't be the kind of neighbors they would like. They wanted us to keep our distance. But of course, we saw the West End and how it came down.

Poor people had to sell their homes to make room for modern, updated apartments. Improvement as they call it, progressing. We saw those people—they were told they could come back once they had these new buildings up. But once those new buildings were up, the poor could not come back because they couldn't afford the rents. And it's the same way with the Waterfront. We were afraid that was going to happen like it did in the West End. So we fought a little harder. And we made sure it didn't happen. And that's why we got the first elderly housing, the Ausonia Home, that's for low-income elderly. and then we got the second site, the Christopher Columbus Plaza—this is on the Waterfront and it's a little different, and they had to make it for low-, moderate-, and high[-income] so we could get a mixture of tenants there. Now we're having Santa Maria elderly housing for the elderly poor on Endicott Street, and that should be in the month of May or June, and that's eighty apartments; the Christopher Columbus is one-fifty-one; the Ausonia is one hundred apartments for the elderly. Most of them are widows or widowers, there's not too many couples. At this age—you don't get husbands and wives healthy enough to live together at this age. Most of them are widows, not lucky enough to have their husbands.

Viola Pettinelli

Swimming at the North End Park

We had the North End Park there, the saltwater park—there was a little beach—that I enjoyed. I miss that a lot, right down here; now we have three tubs, three little pools, but then we had the water from the navy yard. We'd go there and swim and you could learn how to swim because the tide wasn't too high there, because when the tide rolled in, it wasn't like you'd get it in Revere or Nantasket—they'd come over your head—so it was kinda safe. My mother would take us—she wouldn't allow us to go alone because we were all small, you know. She would pack a lunch and take us down [to] the North End Park in the morning and in the afternoon we'd come home.

The piers down there extended out into the ocean, and the double piers, that's where all the good swimmers went. Not me—I'd just stay on shore and waddle in—then the good swimmers would go on the first pier, then the extra good swimmers would go on the top pier and they'd jump down. And they were only supposed to swim to a certain distance because the ships would be coming across there, and of course the good swimmers, they'd take that chance when the [Coast Guard ship] wasn't around, they'd swim beyond; but as soon as they see the Coast Guard ship coming, everybody would run back to the pier. It was nice, and that I miss a lot, and I miss that beach. They have these pools there, and I haven't been to a pool. I went by there, I looked at them; I didn't go into the pool, but I don't care for a pool. Then as we got older my mother took us to Revere, and the place got so polluted, I'll never forget it, that a couple of times we came home all full of grease. We didn't know that was pollution at the time, and you'd go home and have to wash up. It was really greasy, gunky, but we didn't care how gunky it was—my mother wanted to [keep] us out [the Revere], but we wanted to go there. But then it was closed off and we couldn't go anymore. So now we got the pools.

Frances Zanfani Corolla predicted that within five years "the North End will be gone."

Frances Zanfani Corolla

"We Were United"

I used to go down to the North End Park on the Waterfront—we used to have the salt water. I used to bring my children down there every day. People came from all over—we never had any problems. Jewish people came, Coloreds used to come, Italians used to come—we were all united. We used to have a good time at that park. The kids would always be around you—you'd sit with a certain group of friends, they'd wait for you. We used to have a floating hospital for sick children that would take them away for the day. We used to have fireworks. I don't like the change. I'd rather the old way. It was more homey.

Now it's more for the people who can afford it. It's people like us who can't afford it. The condominiums coming up and I think that's bad—they're moving us out. This is our home. They just want to push the Italian people out. I think it's sad. And to buy a condo? Why put yourself in debt? You're having a hard time just paying your rent now because they're going up, and every time you turn around, everything is going up. It's a beautiful place, yes, but I'd rather have the other place—we were more united, more close. This way, we're not close. Down there, they think they're better than you, which they're not, because we've all been born and brought up together.

Mary Molinari was a lifelong resident of the North End. Having been evicted by the city from her Richmond Street apartment after many years there, she was grateful to Jim Amalfitano of the North End Neighborhood Service Center, who helped find her another place to live.

Mary Molinari

The Waterfront's Effects on Small Stores

Faneuil Hall made the taxes go up. There's a lot of things going on there. A lot of those people, they come down [to] the North End and they do a lot of things and it's a disgrace. I don't say all, but a few of them, they get drunk, they sleep in doorways—it's disgusting. But they should put a stop to it. They should put a cop on foot to go around to protect there because a lot of people are getting hit and mugged and robbed. They should do something, and I don't know why [they don't]. Now they figure it's a rich residential section down there, they think everyone who lives on the Waterfront is rich, but they don't understand that a lot of the elderly had to vacate their apartments and were moved there, and they're living there by the skin of their teeth, let's put it that way. They're working hard, let's face it; they work day and night—those people had to leave where they lived. The elderly figured, if I have to pay three, four hundred dollars for rent I'll buy a place there. Taxes went up. Some of the little stores in the North End went out of business because of the big stores. And it's a shame. I won't go to the big stores. I'll be frank with you. I'd rather go to the little stores because those same people gave us a lot of happiness way back.

Why should I let them go out of business? Let the rich stay with the rich ones, let the big stores stay by themselves—they can afford it, but the little ones, they can't. Now since the Quincy Market, a lot of stores have gone out of business. They used to have the Christmas lights outside. No more! They can't afford it. I noticed right after Christmas three stores on Salem Street went out of business. They can't. They've been hitting them one after another because of the Quincy Market and big stores like the Stop & Shop. Now people leave the nutrition site [in the North End] and a bus takes them to Stop & Shop. And the poor people down here! Now I did all my shopping, I went down Salem Street—I knew the people; I bought all my stuff—let them live. It's a pity; I feel sorry for these little people. I had a little store of my own, a jewelry store in Needham about ten years ago. I know what it is.

Joise Zizza

"Now They Don't Know You"

It has affected me this way—There's a lot of people that have gone there to the Waterfront that lived around here. Now they don't know you when they—now we're trying to get a nursing home here and they're opposing it because they want it for parking space and all that. It has made them a little—I'm a leader of a small senior citizen club and I have—a lot of the girls that live down there are members. They're very nice to me, you know—they invite me to their homes on the Waterfront—but it's not the same, it's more tense; you see a lot of my old friends have gone away or have died. I don't have that—the new people come in and I don't feel as comfortable as I used to. I went in there [Christopher Columbus Plaza] one day to pay a visit and there was a nurse taking blood pressure. So she was there—she was the vice president, but they had the president there too. I said, "Can I have my blood pressure taken?" They said, "No, you don't live here." Years ago, when my mother was there—I came from a family of twelve children—so you see I had cousins, I had aunts all around me. I feel all alone now. See all my sisters, my brothers—I have seven sisters and four brothers—live out. The only sister I have is the one downstairs and a brother on the corner of Endicott Street. I know all their names, all their birthdays.

Poor Tenant, Poor Landlord   30

> Fa buone e scurdà, fa male e pensaci
> (Do good and forget, do bad and think about it).
> —SOUTHERN ITALIAN PROVERB

In the 1980s, when advertisements for condominiums appeared in storefront and apartment windows, North Enders blamed condo owners for rising property taxes and unaffordable rent hikes. Amid tensions between middle-class professionals and struggling North Enders, an unheralded story of goodwill was quietly playing out. Despite growing economic hardships, a few elderly landlords remained loyal to their old-time tenants, holding the line on rent increases and refusing to evict them to build condominiums.

For years, Helen Luongo's elderly tenant lived in the upstairs apartment of her building on Salem Street with minimal rent increases. As they were both widowed and had no immediate family nearby, the two women devised a daily routine to make sure they were safe. Signora Pagliarulo, an eighty-four-year-old widow, chose to remain in her Endicott Street apartment where she had lived for sixty-one years. She found the familiar surroundings of her outdated cold-water flat, which had no bathtub or central heat, more comfortable than the modern amenities of elderly housing. When her landlord suggested that the apartment reserved for her at the Casamaria would be better for her health, she vehemently disagreed, saying, "No, the only way I'll leave here is in a box."

Others, like eighty-three-year-old Marianna D'Antonio, who lived alone on the first floor of her small, three-room apartment on Unity Street, also refused a place at the Casamaria. Despite the constant pounding of renovation work to covert the upstairs apartments into condominiums and the landlord's offer to pay her to move, Marianna refused to leave. She told the landlord, "Chest è la casa mia!" (This is my house!). Work crews showed up early every morning, creating clouds of dust and soot that settled on her food, furniture, and clothes. When asked how she was getting by, she raised her voice indignantly, answering with classic southern Italian wit: "Eh, come faccio? E come puozzo fa? Chiano, chiano, facimmo tutta cosa. Come vuole dio! Eh allora, che ti credi? Chesta è la storia" (How do I do it? How can I do it? Nice and easy, we'll get everything done. Whatever God wants! What do you think? That's the story).

One morning, when the noise level became unbearable, she stepped outside to see what was happening upstairs. Looking up to the second floor, she lost her balance and fell to the sidewalk, breaking her hip. Marianna never returned, a casualty of the "New Boston" that never made the headlines.

Generosa "Josie" Zizza was born to immigrant parents from Guardia Lombardia in 1914. After her parents died, she took over the family homestead, which consisted of six apartments on Cleveland Place. Growing up in an Old-World culture that favored hard work over education, she had been denied high school in order to support her brothers' careers. Josie excelled in grammar school, and despite a cultural inheritance that favored males, her father chose his bright and quick-witted daughter as his translator and negotiator in business deals and transactions. Josie also became a community advocate in the tradition of Mike Nazzaro and George Scigliano, who delivered forceful speeches on behalf of the community. She joined the network of elderly landlords providing a safety net for their elderly tenants on fixed incomes who could not afford higher rents. Despite rising property taxes and the high cost of maintenance and insurance, they held on to their buildings, deciding not to take offers from speculators or go live with their children in the suburbs. Although Theresa D'Alelio's rental income barely covered the costs of building maintenance, she adhered to the southern Italian code of behavior, respecting her elderly tenants as her own family, explaining, "I wouldn't throw anybody out. Really. Because I wouldn't want my mother to be thrown out." Theresa adhered to the proverb she had heard many times: "Fa cose buone e scordatelo, ma fa male e pensaci" (Do good and forget, do bad and remember).

When Josie Zizza was asked about the difficulties of being a poor landlady, she described the compassion some landlords showed toward the less fortunate of the neighborhood. For them, the value of treating people with empathy outweighed the value of money. When asked how she would like to be remembered, a friend answered before she could respond: "She's a good Samaritan—she helps people." Josie smiled, and with typical North End humility said, "Well, it's not for me to judge, it's for other people to judge."

Lucia Petringa

"Tenants at Will"

When you're young, you're not afraid of anything, you can do anything. When you're older, whether you like it or not there's a limit to your capabilities. And then you don't know the language. And then they have all these cockamamie rulings like "tenant at will." What do these people know about tenant at will? They don't know. In my last apartment, my landlord withheld registering our rents at the rent board and registered the house under rehabilitation. He evicted everyone in our building and remodeled the apartments—got double the rents. You know where those old people ended up? Nursing homes. They lived a few years. Dead. All they needed was that last blow. And do you know how they evicted us even though we were under rent control? He [landlord] paid someone to take us off rent control. The story made the *Boston Globe* "Spotlight," his name and the guy he paid off. But the Italian people are a proud people. If a landlord says move, they move. Now you and I know there are laws here to protect us against landlords taking advantage, to stop them from doing it. All those elderly people, I used to say to them, "Come with me to the rent board, we'll all get together." "Oh, no, no, no, non mi sento buona. No, non vogghiu iri. A corte! Non sia mai! [Oh no, no, no, I'm not feeling well. No, I don't want to go. To a court! No way.]" All these old people are tenants at will—they have no leases. I don't know what's going to happen—they're all at [the landlords'] mercy, you see. These landlords just had a stroke of luck. How many people do you know where their area doesn't mean anything anymore, like Forrest Hills, Roxbury, and places where it's all dilapidated, abandoned. People that own property there, it's not worth anything. Over here they were lucky. It tripled, quadrupled and they're taking advantage.

   We lived here in the North End for thirty years, nobody bothered us and they were glad to have us as tenants. Now they take a chance on transients—people who work at Government Center, Massachusetts General Hospital, and don't need their cars to save gas. They don't even put up curtains, the new people. All kinds of guys come in to visit these single girls. And the landlords don't care. I don't object to anyone coming into the North End, but you don't throw out families just for the sake of the almighty dollar. All right, I want money too, but there should be a limit. There should be a way to stop these greedy people. I don't know how these people who don't know the language, I don't know how they do it, the poor things—and they're old. I look at these people who don't know the language and I say, boy, do they kick them around, raise their rents. Those people go hungry to pay their rents. And just for the sake of these transients.

Elvira DiMattia

Taxes

When I was a child the tax rate was much, much lower than it is now and the needs of the people were fewer. The thousands of people that lived here in those days, and everyone had large families—if someone had three or four children that was considered a small family. But everyone had five, six, seven, eight, nine, ten children. The DeAngelis family, there were nine sisters and four brothers in the family, there were thirteen children. People used to rent three rooms or four or five rooms and they were perfectly satisfied to use their kitchen stove to heat up those rooms. If they needed an extra stove they used to get one of those gas-fired parlor heaters, and loads of homes had them and they were perfectly happy with them. If they didn't have a modern up-to-date kitchen they didn't care so long as they had the water. And some had bathrooms and some didn't. I remember they even had to share a bath, but they didn't mind; they used to take a turn each doing the cleaning. One week one person would wash and scrub and clean [and] the following week the other person did.

And the landlords would paint the flats. Every summer my dad, he painted either one flat or another, whatever needed painting; he would take them in rotation that way. It was much more easier then. Now since the rent control came into effect it seems as though it has created a barrier between the landlord and the tenant, and that's something we never had. Years ago if the tax rate went up a few dollars, well, the people realized it—I remember all the people would ever be raised would be like two or three dollars a month, which was practically nothing. But now if you raise any rentals to anyone, why you just make an enemy out of them. The bills, oh, that comes under a different category. The water and sewer are out of the question. What we used to pay in a year in those days we're paying in a quarter now.

Now we're facing another tax increase; since Mayor [Kevin] White has been in, he has more than doubled the tax rate from the amount he found it. And he still wants to get more, and that's only to pay for the patronage jobs that he has handed out.

FIGURE 54. Theresa D'Alelio (left) and Josie Zizza (right).

Josie Zizza

"Who Wants a Mother-in-Law?"

I've lived in the North End for seventy years. I am the landlord and I have [two] tenants. I live on 14 Cleveland Place. People have asked if I want to sell my house. Some of them have offered me more money, but I haven't decided what to do yet. I did get a very good offer one night from this Jewish fella. He wanted the whole house for themselves. So we all had to get out, and that kinda of—and he offered me more money than anybody else. Well, within my heart—I have one tenant, that's my sister, she's a widow; she lives downstairs, she's on subsidized. I'm concerned about my sister. She's under the care of a social worker at the health center. She sees her every week. Me, I don't care where I go. If I sell the house I can go someplace and pay a little more money, but she can't. I could sell my house tomorrow, in fact, there's a couple of people says, "Anytime—" but then I say where am I gonna go? If I found someplace for me and my sister I think I would sell. It's getting me now—I'm tired of it. It's two flights up, I live on the top floor. Because I am a senior citizen.

Where will I go if I sell my house? And I can't get into elderly housing because I figure if I sold my house I'd have a lot of money. It's a three-apartment building. I live in one of them. In one of them I have a tenant, pays a hundred and seventy dollars for six room. I give heat, hot water, all ceramic tile bath, the rooms are all paneled. I have another one downstairs, she's subsidized because she's on SSI [Supplemental Security Income] and she's not quite sixty-two and on physical disability. I'm subsidized. I get two hundred for her. She gives me forty-seven and the Boston Housing Authority gives me one-fifty-eight. It comes to two hundred and five. I have a brand-new heating system, it's two years old. See, each one has their own thermostat. They put it on and take it off, put it on as high as they want. I pay for the hall lights—they put them on when they want and take them off when they want. And I don't feel I'm getting enough money. One tenant's been here for seventeen years, one for nine years.

And I've lived in that building all my life. The North End was nicer before. We had our own kind. The housing problems were not as bad as now. My mother used to live downstairs. She passed away and I lost my husband. I have a lot of memories in that house I'd like to get rid of too. I feel it's a lot for me now. I have six rooms and I'm alone. Six rooms is too much for me. Trouble is, how can I take care of anything now? I'm seventy years old. What can I do? When something is broken you have to call somebody and when they see a woman—then by the time you get a plumber, you get a carpenter, it isn't that easy! Really, let's face it. I heat up all these rooms. I want to move and I want to sell. If I would find a nice apartment, I would like to stay in the North End. Cause I don't drive. I have four sons—they all live out [of the North End], they have their own jobs, they have their own homes. None of my sons live in the North End. They all married girls out of town. They live there. Who wants a mother-in-law?

Santa and Bernadine Cacciola

Sisters Santa and Bernadine Cacciola were in their early seventies and lived with eight other families in an apartment house on Prince Street. They were all evicted so their building could be replaced with condominiums.

"Our Landlady Gets *Arragiata*"

We're both afraid. If we say one word out of the way to her [landlord], she'll kill me. She's taking care of the building for her brother-in-law; she lives there as though she is the landlord. She says, "I've been so good to you"—you know, the rents. She meant we don't pay enough. She always seems to pick on us. What happened was the upstairs tenant had her door open and she was saying, "Now that's a fine thing they're doing, what your brother-in-law did to us!" [serving eviction notices]. And that started it, and then I put my little two cents in too; I don't know what I said, but it must have been something that angered her because she started yelling. She's a funny girl. And yet every time she has trouble, she comes up [to] my house. When she has trouble, something goes wrong in her house, she calls me; she calls me to help her and I go down and do things for her, whatever it is.

Now the other day her refrigerator broke and she came up and asked me if she could put something in my freezer. I looked in my freezer to see, and you know I took all my stuff out of there so she could put all kinds of meat that she had in my freezer. I says to her, "Why don't you ask the lady next door to you?" She said, "No, no, I'm ashamed to go there." Once she locked herself out and she came in at seven in the morning and she stayed in my house for two hours. Every time she's got trouble, she calls me. But then she treats me like that—she picks on me. She doesn't bother anyone—I'm the one she bothers, I'm telling ya. She's a wild one; she's elderly, seventy. When she gets angry, like they say in Italian, *arragiata*, you know what I [mean]? Like a savage, like an animal, crazy like. She wants us out in five months—how can we get out in five months? We've been there eighteen years and we never thought—we even told him we'd give him a raise. He [the landlord] said, "No, no, no, I'll make about a hundred and fifty thousand dollars—why should I continue to give them that rent?"

Meglio Pane e Cipolla, e Sola   31

> Una mama campa cento figli, ma cento figli non campano una mama
> (A mother can take care of a hundred children, but a hundred children cannot take care of a mother).
> —ANONYMOUS

In the 1930s, successful business owners began moving to greener pastures in Medford, Melrose, Quincy, Braintree, Everett, and Revere, where they found spacious homes with adjacent lots where they could plant vegetable gardens and grow fruit trees. Others joined the movement to the suburbs. Upwardly mobile "college boys," those profiled in William Whyte's *Street Corner Society* as American-born North Enders, represented the first generation of educated professionals to attain homes outside the neighborhood. Many, like Mary, vowed to send their children to college. She explained: "I wanted to finish school, but my dad wouldn't let me. He felt I was the youngest and I had to help support—and I cried. And years later, and this I kept to myself. I said when I get married, and when I have children of my own—even if I have to scrub office floors, I'm going to send them to college. And I did."[1]

The trend continued into the 1960s and 1970s for those with college degrees, but the realization of the American dream often meant leaving the North End for professional careers. American-born children of the original immigrants like Mary Molinari—the elderly immigrants living in the 1970s and 1980s—strongly believed in the educational meritocracy to ensure a better life for their children.

Although few like Mary and her generation had the opportunity to get a high school education, they worked long hours to send their children to college. Consequently, by the late 1970s the days of multigenerational families living in the same tenements had mostly disappeared and fewer Anthonys ran home to waiting mothers on Wednesdays. Visits from sons and daughters outside the North End were often logistical nightmares, especially during the holiday seasons, when traffic and parking problems worsened. Frances Lauro described the trend of modern American families: "When you build up a tree, one side, you always like to stay there. When you get married and you start having children, you go away [from the North End]; that's a different story. And they don't want to come down to the city because it's too noisy to them. But to us it don't even bother us. I live right at the corner of Lewis and North Street, and what a mess they do with the cars and everything, yeah. But it doesn't bother me. The kids are all big. Most of them have little children. They're all married and they go away. They don't stay in the North End."[2]

In the early 1980s, elderly North End homeowners received repeated phone calls from lawyers and businesspeople offering considerable sums for their buildings. For some who had inherited properties, the thought of ending the constant worries over maintaining buildings and the lure of a sizable amount of money in one lump sum were too much to resist. Years later, when North End real estate prices skyrocketed into the millions, many regretted their decision to sell. Some business-minded landlords notified their longtime elderly tenants who were living alone as well as tenant families of their intention to convert their apartments into condominiums. When tenants failed to meet the steep price tag, eviction notices were slipped under their doors. Suddenly faced with evictions, bewildered elderly tenants with no understanding of the process or their legal rights had nowhere to turn.

Time ran out for some and they were forced to leave their beloved neighborhood, finishing their days with children. Other landlords, who had moved to the suburbs, renovated their buildings in the North End and jacked up the rents. The upheaval in the housing market severed many friendly relationships between tenants and landlords and community stability became a relic of the past.

In 1982, amid much fanfare and community support, the North End Nursing Home opened for elders who were too frail to live alone. The new institution kept many old-timers in the neighborhood but forever replaced the traditional Italian family, which had historically relied on children to care for aged family members at home. Elders who had taken care of their parents in old age and sent their children to college now carried on alone. Fearful of becoming burdens to children with busy, career-driven lifestyles, many decided to stay in the North End and often recited the proverb of the peasant who is resigned to a simple life of austerity and independence: "Meglio pane e cipolla, e sola" (Better to eat bread and onions, and alone).

Vladimir Ciani, an alert, well-spoken eighty-eight-year-old who immigrated from Mirabella in 1907, had witnessed the major Italian influx to the North End and the exodus of the Irish and Jews. He pondered the new wave of immigrants replacing Italian Americans and the inevitability of neighborhood change.

Eyes twinkling, he closed one chapter of North End history and opened another: "But then again, we should never lose sight of the fact that history for centuries has always repeated itself. In our case, it's happening exactly as history prescribes: ninety years ago, we, the Italians, especially from 1890 to 1914, came to Boston in huge quantities, with the net result that we displaced all the Irish and Jewish people from the North End and we made this little corner of Boston absolutely our own. Is it any wonder that we in turn should see this process duplicated?"[3]

FIGURE 55. Maria Virginio, 1980.

Maria Virginio

"Meglio Pane e Cipolla"

Tony, *figlio bello*, beautiful son—I'm talking to you like a mother to a son; I have no luck, I have nothing. I have nothing. What am I going to do? Whatever God wants I guess. I pay a hundred dollars a month for the rent. But I have to eat, I have to drink. I have to pay the electric bill. The electric bill two months ago was fifty dollars. They are charging me for two phones and I only have one. What do I have to do, rob somebody, kill somebody, so I can live? Last month I had to pay twenty-five dollars just to see the doctor and then thirty dollars for arthritis pills—how can I do it? I am a woman living alone with no help. Whatever God wants. My husband was a veteran and I had a lot of problems with his pension and all the doors are closed. I want to be honest and I don't want take from anyone. I was born in 1905 and I came here from Avellino in 1922. I got married in 1923 and I've lived on Prince Street for fifty-seven years in the same place. I'm a citizen. I always wanted to buy the house but with the bad luck I had, I never could save any money. My husband had an accident when he fell down the flight of stairs and broke his neck, and he was crippled and in a lot of pain, but we never sued the landlord and getting money, though everyone thought we were foolish for not doing so. We could have gotten a settlement but we were too good, we're not the kind of people to do that to the landlord, so we didn't. So we ended up, *figlio mio* [my son], like Christ on the Cross paying a lot of medical bills for eight years. And then I had to pay out of pocket a nurse for two years at home for my husband.

Now it's been two years he's passed away. Now I'm alone and full of bills I owe, and I don't know what to do. How am I supposed to live? Everyone who knew my husband knew how good he was to everyone. Now all the doors are closed *figlio mio*, when no one can help you. Sometimes I get light-headed and yesterday I fell. Would you like to come in for a cup of coffee? They're even charging me for two telephones and I only have one—everything is falling on me. What can I do? I only get a little veteran benefit and social security—I get four hundred dollars month. But I'm not like people who don't worry about things—they go out and have a good time eating and drinking. *Figlio mio*, I'd rather eat *pane e cipolla* [bread and onions (to live frugally)], while I pay my bills. La faccia deve stare pulita [my face has to be clean]—I

FIGURE 56. Antonia Tonzillo, 1981.

want to keep my name clean. I don't want people to say she has bills but she goes out and has a good time. But thank God, up till now nobody can say a bad word about me, that I took anything from them, that I was dishonest in any way. I have to see how I have to live now.

Honestly, like my mother in Italy used to say: "Poveri figli onorati, non macchiato la condotta, non stare carcerati [Poor, respectable children, don't stain your conduct and you'll never be in trouble]." I just turned seventy-five. What are you going to do? This is life. Chi chiagnà e chi rìre [sometimes you laugh, sometimes you cry]. I didn't have children. That ruined me. I am in the hands of God. It's tough when you have no one. *Translated from the dialect of Avellino.*

FIGURE 57. Josephine Bosco at her apartment on Prince Street, 1980.

Josephine Bosco

Despite her serious physical ailments and the fact that she was facing eviction, Josephine Bosco never lost her sense of humor. She said her children were planning to put sponges around her casket because she kept her apartment so clean.

"What's Going on in America?"

Pretty soon, they're gonna throw everybody out from the North End, they're gonna do just like they did to West End. And I keep it clean, and he [the landlord] knows it. I said to him, "Louie, I've been here for forty-two years." He said, "I know, you people have been good people in the building. But I want to make condominiums, so you'll have to get out." What could you say? What could you do? They're the owners. They make you so unhappy, so aggravated inside. If he wanted a little more money, all right, I'd give him a little more money but see, it's a standstill—we can't. He'd rather make condominiums, he'll make more money, so what could you say to them?

And I've been so used to it here, right across from the park here (the Gassy), when I don't go out I'll sit and watch the kids playing. I've been here forty-two years. I'm seventy-seven—I gotta go lookin' for rooms at my age? And I don't feel too hot—I've had two operations on my eye; they found a spot on my lung, then they took part of my lung out, but I'm OK, no cancer. I've got diabetes so that's why my son was here; I told him, "Stay with me, live with me son"—he's never married. He's a good son, he's not working right now. He said, "Ma you go over there, don't mind me." I said I want you with me because I need you at my age now, I need someone around me; I'm a widow, I've been a widow a long time. I've got no shower—if he [the landlord] puts [in] a shower he'll raise the rent. I've got a toilet in the house. It's my own heat; my stove heats here, [and] there's no steam heat. I pay my own electric, gas, everything—the only thing we pay the rent to the owner, ninety dollars a month.

My son paints, he wallpapers, we do everything, we don't bother him [the landlord]. Last Thursday he came here, he said "Mrs. Bosco, I've got to tell you something, I'm gonna make these houses condominiums, so if you want to stay and buy it, you could buy it but uh." He says the most it will be twenty-five or thirty thousand. He says ten thousand down and—he thinks they're like peanuts, the money comes like that, like he's got it. He's got loads of money. God bless him! But don't throw people out! For what? For that greenback, what they're doin' and putting the poor people out of—where am I gonna go looking for rooms? There's eight floors of us he's throwing out. The North End won't be the same Little Italy—they're bouncing them out one by one. And these poor people don't know where to go; I would really—I would swear he [landlord] would never do that. They fix a place over a little and they make their money, you see—that's what it is. Last night in bed I was thinking and thinking; I said, "What am I gonna do? Where am I gonna go?" I am so used to this house—this was my little castle, you know? Forty-two years I lived here; it's nothing for them to say go away now in my old age. Even my son is so downhearted for me. And I know I'll never find another apartment like this—it's airy, it's sunny, I like it here. I'm attached to it; I'm so attached to it because I don't think I'll find another place like this wherever I go now because I'm so used to this house.

We were Caterinari [Santa Caterina Villarmosa], from Caltanisetta in Sicily. I was born on Hanover Street—I'm so used to the North End. I had five children here. And now, in my old age, they're throwing me out. When he [the landlord] said it, I was stunned. See, I give myself the needle for diabetes every morning. I've got glaucoma—my son puts the drops in my eyes—there's a lot of tension in the back. I didn't sleep at all last night. For the owners, it's easy for them to say, "Go out." It seems like a dream—I think I'm dreaming, I don't think—I think it's a dream, all a dream. The other night I couldn't sleep—I slept maybe an hour or two, but last night I couldn't shut one eye. I feel lousy today on account of that. I got up twice and where I have diabetes, I took a piece of candy and put it in my mouth because I was nervous in bed, and I thought maybe the chocolate would let me fall asleep—but I couldn't sleep.

See, it's easy for these owners, it's easy. And they're making money too, on the poor people. It's a shame. It's a shame what's going—what's going on in life today. My days, it was so beautiful. There was respect for people, for your parents, there was respect. Everything was so lovely. Today, I dunno what's going on in America, it's not the same—it's not the same anymore. I'm sorry for my grandchildren and my great-grandchildren. Wouldn't you feel sorry for your mother too if they would do that to her (crying)?

During our conversation we heard someone call Helen from the stairway. Her tenant knocked and slowly opened the door to ask in Italian if she was all right. As her upstairs tenant left, Helen said to me, "She always does that, Anthony, just to make sure."

FIGURE 58. Helen Luongo and her tenant on Salem Street, 1980.

"Listen for My Radio"

Who takes care of me? You know how we do it between the two of us? The woman upstairs, between the two of us, we plan it. If she's away, I'm not away. Tuesday she had a tooth out, in fact it was a root, they had to open up her gum. But she's been home but—if it happens that I'm alone, eeehh, God, who you gonna call? (laughing) What are ya gonna do? You're alone! It isn't no joke to be living alone, don't you worry. It isn't a joke and especially when you're used to the family. And I have nine grandchildren, and you feel that here you are, you have such a big family and you're all alone. But, you just, uh—you just have to learn how to live with it, that's all, and just say dear God.

Now like her [the upstairs tenant], I have her key to her house, she has the key to my house, and we've told each other in the morning—now she knows the minute I get up. I even have a radio in bed with me, transistor radio all night, I have the radio going so that I feel there's somebody in the house. My radio or television is going all the time. My tenant is seventy (laughing), so we're both old ladies. So who's gonna take care of who? And I told her, if in the morning you get up, and you don't hear the radio going, come in and see that for sure that I'll be in bed—I'm dead! Call the undertaker, call my children! What are you gonna do, Anthony?

I don't want to live in with the children. I could live off the fat of the land living with my children and not have a worry in the world. But I want my own little hole in the wall. And now they tell me to get rid of it, get rid of my house! I couldn't get rid of it—where am I gonna go? Three or four people have suggested, "Why don't you sell your house, put it in your children's name, put your money away, and go to senior citizens home." I tell you the God's honest truth, I don't want them [the senior citizens home]. To me they remind me of an institution. Because when you go into those apartments, all you see is long hallways, doors on each side; everybody is with a key in their hand and they're going in.

Well that's what you see in an institution—the doors are all locked. You meet people in the elevator you don't know, you meet people in the hallways you don't know. You don't know who lives in the building. Maybe because I'm so used to livin'—maybe I'm old-fashioned, from the old school. Maybe I'm behind the times.

FIGURE 59. Rosa Birra at the time of her eviction, 1981.

Rosa Birra was eighty-one and living alone.

Rosa Birra

On Being Evicted

All my life—I've been here sixty-two years in the North End at the end of November. I was twenty years old when I came from the Old Country—all my life I spend over here in the North End. See how long I been here? Now the people [owners of the house] no need the house, they got a house—[so] they sell the house; they give the house to the children and they go to another house. They do, they do, they do—they got another house and I remain with—nothing. It doesn't matter what I do. "You don't leave me, please! Don't leave me! Remember to help me, all right?" "Yes, mama, please!" That's funny when you have nobody—don't you think so? I laugh but my heart a cry. Because that's funny, specially when I go to bring to her [the landlady], the hundred and fifty dollars. She says, "You find anything [rooms] when you [move out]? I can't fix the rooms downstairs unless it's empty." I said to her, "You're telling me that?" I told her, "What do you want me to do, throw

Meglio Pane e Cipolla, e Sola 369

me out into the street? No, I won't go. For you, I go in the street? I will not!" I says, "No! I know the laws. Make a believe I'm a born over here!" They [the owners] eight years ago come from—they gotta lot of money. They bought the old shack. And now they throw everybody out. They think they do what they want. You gotta wait till I'm ready. You don't have to throw me out. The law protect me, but every time I pay the rent they get me nervous. When they say, "When? When? When?" When a the time reach! That's the way I answer. I know what I gotta say to them—but—huuh—what am I gonna do?

I don't feel so good anyway. When I get nervous—the more nervous I get, the more bother me, my breathing—because I suffer with my heart. And the high blood pressure bother me. That's all. The nervous go together and make a me feel—bad. I'm eighty-one years old and I go eighty-two next October. I'm an old person, my dear child, see? Look, I gotta see what I gotta do. If I move from my house, I don't want to move anymore. Then I'm gonna move when God a move me. That's all I wanna do. I try to do my best. So thank God, still I try to help a myself. I have no one near. They're not in Boston. But they know. I just talked now to my brother. I have three applications [for housing], all my receipts in order, my doctor appointments. I sit down and I choose all cards that belong to any housing applications and I try to put them all together.

My God, I'm sick and tired of doing things because I'm a person alone; I'm old, I'm tired to do these things; see, you're tired when you read and write, and you do things like that you're tired. Lot a times I'm tired just the same to do little things. I can't do more than that. Sometimes I think, and I feel so tired. I don't have to think too much. I go to bed many times and I can't even sleep. I say to myself, what a terrible I have in my life. Sleep? How can I? How many times I say, I no wanna take that stuff [Valium], I no wanna ruin my life, I wanna try to do my best. And sometimes—you can't help it. When you have trouble, you take it. But I understand my situation and I think I'm in trouble that way. I don't know what God give to me.

"If I *Alliet* My Mind, I'll Be All Right."

I need to take the pills for the pressure, for the heart—those I need and that's it. If I don't have those for my heart, I can't breathe. And the blood, it gotta help to keep the heart. But the other things, I try not to take them, so those other pills [Valium] are no good—I don't take them. The doctor told me if you're really—in case you're in trouble and you really can't stand it—you can have one. But I never take them, very seldom. I cut them in half. I never take them because I know they're no good. I understand everything. I'm not a person to be really stupid. (laughs) I try not to stay home all the time because when you have time to think, I do something with my hands so that when you do something *allieta*—you understand Italiano? *Allieta, contenta* [happy, content], you know? Allietare in Italiano, vuol dire, è una parola grande [*Allietare* in Italian is a great word, it means to make someone happy]: Allietare la mente [to make your mind happy]. I read. I try to do my best. That's what I can do. I want to try to keep my mind *allietata*. No, if I *alliet* my mind, I'll be all right. I don't even know another place. (whispering) I don't want to go out of the North End.

Grace Pinelli

"I Pray God Takes Me Quickly"

I live alone. I realized that's the best thing, Anthony. Unless you're an invalid, you can't help yourself. And I hope and pray to God that He takes me quickly so I won't be a burden. And I don't like nursing homes—I don't want to wind up there either. And I think the children should lead their own lives; I led my life—I lived along with my husband and my children. I think a third person changes your life. It's not the same, it isn't. It isn't, your wife and yourself—you don't have the privacy you deserve, and instead of drawing closer together you draw apart. Cause you feel you can't talk to her the way you should cause there's a third party there. And that third party might interfere. It's no good. I don't want to live with anyone—I want to live by myself. And I've built a new life for myself, I try. I have friends—they've been wonderful. And that's my life, my friends—they came with me last week to look for an all-weather coat and then we wind up at the Santa Maria House; we went there for coffee. I didn't get back till five-thirty; I said I should go home, they says, "Why? Who's waiting there?" (laughing) And it's fun. I came home happy. You just make a new life for yourself. And your friends have the same problem. You're not alone—they're all widows. We have something in common—we understand one another. Their children, my children, wouldn't understand because they're young. They haven't been through it, so they don't know what it's all about, see?

Teresa Costanzo

"I Pray the Saints Don't Forget Me"

I worked in a factory making *mandasini* [aprons] on Congress Street until I was sixty-three at thirty-five cents an hour. Yes, I'm telling you, Anthony, What can I tell you *a matri*? See what kind of life I had? This is my story. I would like to be young again and go back to work and not be like this, like a dog. Every once in a while, you know who comes and sees me? That girl—she is a good woman. She always comes to see me, that kid; even if I have a little headache, she calls me whether it's day or night. When I don't know other families around me, I get scared, I'm not happy within myself. Nun praticu cu nuddu [I don't associate with anyone anymore]. I'm not like a lot of other people. I don't understand anything anymore, Anthony! I don't know anybody; I only know God, *a matri*, that's all. I never really learned how to get around places and now I don't understand anything. I can only scribble a few words. I only went up to the second grade in elementary school in Italy. I can write only a few words. Sicily is always Sicily.

In Rome they speak Italian well. I speak it *strozza*—I mean I speak Italian with difficulty. I speak real Sicilian, plain and simple. In the cities everyone speaks Italian well. This is what I'm telling you *a matri*. What can I tell you? Don't you respect your mother? Don't you call her? To see how she is? You don't call? The phone! It means if you don't call me, I could be dead. But I don't say anything to him, my son. What can you do? I say "pensa alla saluta [think of your health]," take care of yourself. Does my son, da facci bedda [that pretty face], think of his father, that good soul? My children in Italy think of him. They have a Mass said for him every year in Riposto for his good soul, and this is the fourteenth year, going on fifteen. See? They have a Mass for him and my daughter Maria, that good soul who died here in Boston during the Spanish flu. I thank God and I pray to all the saints not to forget me and that they wait for me to come to heaven. Who will take care of me if I get sick? My son? *Translated from the Sicilian dialect of Riposto.*

Frances Lauro

"Frances, Let Me Die under the Stove"

I keep myself—not that I keep myself, only God keeps us up—but I went through a lot. My mother-in-law was very sick—she was confined in bed. And I had three children and one was coming and I had to take care of her. We had no washing machine in those days; I had the big tub, wash the clothes, hang 'em up, take care of her—poor soul! I was so busy I didn't know who my neighbors were. They used to say, "Why don't you put her in the home?" "No! While I can do it, I'll do it." I couldn't see that. And she used to tell me, you know the old people used to say, she used to love me: "Frances, put me under the stove, don't take me away from here." I said, "Don't worry—as long as I'm living, I'll take care of you." And really, until the last minute—she was passing away—she called me, and I was right there with her. In Italy, the same thing, honey, with my grandmother, I took care of her, too. And when I came over here, my father had gotten remarried and my stepmother had her mother and I had to take care of her, too. I've been taking care of these old ladies like that.

And that's my life—I took care of the old people. And still, I had my neighbor, Mary, she had heart trouble, she had this, she had that. We had the windows like this, "Frances, come over." I used to go up there, "What's the matter Mary?" "I don't feel good," I used to take care of her, I used to stay in the house until her husband came home—I didn't want to leave her all alone, see? We used to take little walks, you know, when the weather was nice, yeah, "Mary, come on, let's take a walk." We used to go, easy, easy, we used to take a walk; she used to get tired: "Mary, do you want to sit down?" We'd sit on some doorstep. So we used to come home, she'd rest, I used to cook for her husband, and when her husband used to come home I'd go away. I lost her, too. I don't know—this is my life. My heart is too soft with anybody; I feel bad for everybody but I don't know if anybody feels bad for me. (laughs) My kids say, "Ma, when something's wrong with you who's gonna take care of you?" I said, there's God—in three days I'd like to go away. If I get sick, and I'm gonna go, in three days, I always pray for that. Three days I'd like to die. It's suffering—you suffer and I gotta suffer.

Viola Pettinelli

Viola Pettinelli never left the house without checking with her Italian-speaking neighbor across the hall, who was in poor health and had failing eyesight. Viola brought her anything she needed from the store.

"Do Good and God Will Always Find Someone to Help You"

How many times did my upstairs neighbors, he and his wife, have to come downstairs and help me pick up my mother because her legs weren't too good. My mother always used to say when they asked how she was doing, "How are you Teresa?" "My legs a good, my bod-ee no good." That was my mother, all the time. So sometimes she was kinda stubborn—she insisted that she had to walk even if I wasn't there. When I would put her to bed, I'd say, "Ma, I'm going out for a couple of hours"—you know, you have to go out and do something. "Now don't get up. Stay in bed or stay in the chair." No. As soon as I go out, my mother would try to get to the bathroom. One thing, you got to give her credit though, she had to make it to that bathroom by herself. Well a lot of times the woman couldn't make it. And sometimes at night—she was stubborn also—she would get up and she had to go to the bathroom and she'd fall. Well, she was three times my size, so I would have to call the neighbors, so either the man upstairs or the lady downstairs. The people downstairs, if they heard a big bash, they always ran up. One time at two in the morning they heard a big bash, [and] the whole family from downstairs came up in their pajamas to help my mother up.

So that's the way it was living over here. Today, well, I don't know, if they heard a big bash, if anybody's gonna come up and pick me up! But my mother says, "Yes, you do good and God will always find someone to help you." And you know? She was right! Too bad the young people don't believe too much in God, because I'm not what you call a God person. But I do believe in a hereafter and I do believe in a supreme being—what it is I don't know, but I always think there's somebody somewhere that's looking after us. And when I think of the things that my mother used to tell me. My mother was always saying to me before she passed away, "You know, in every family there's always one person that's going to be left alone." So she used to say this a lot of times. So I said, "Mom, I don't want to wish you any harm, but I hope that you go before me because if I go before you, you're gonna be all alone and what are you gonna do, because with your legs, you can't do too much, just sit down.' And she said to me, "It doesn't make any difference—God will take care of me if I'm alone."

And do you know, she was right, because now I have all these nice people [neighbors], that when I need help, before I open my mouth, I get the help. So that's why there must be somebody someplace, whether it's upstairs or what, that looks after us. And too bad that the younger people don't want to see it that way. Like I say, it doesn't have to be a man, it doesn't have to be a woman, it doesn't have to be a certain color, but there's something somewhere. Would you call that a philosophy? Well, that's the way I look at it. Well, I think if that if you look at something like that you have more to live for, more to fight for. This way if you think there's nothing, you say, "Oh there's nothing," and you just let go, right? That's the way I feel. I'm not going to let go, not if I can help it. But I would like to go kinda fast. Because I've seen lingering death in my family and some bad, very painful—and I don't think I would want that and I don't think I would want it for anybody else.

"Let Me Go Quickly"

They got some kind of an injection for elderly people so they won't get pneumonia. Well, I think pneumonia is a beautiful death for elderly people. They go fast. See, because all my grandparents lived to be old, except my father's father. He got pneumonia and went fast. The others, all from pneumonia, but later, when they were old, eighty, ninety years old. And the same way with my mother and my father. He was eighty-seven, [and] my mother was ninety-two. They both got pneumonia. That's a good way to go. Then the younger members of my family, they went young, they got the darn cancer, and oh, that's no good.

So if I gotta get an injection not to get pneumonia and get something else, I'd rather have pneumonia. Inside of nine days, you're gone! I wonder if I'm selfish when I say this, but I've seen pain, bad pain, and I hope to God that nobody would get that pain—it's no good, no good. But today, then they get you better, then you get it again, then they get you better, and you get it again. That's not helping you. Like at my age now, if I get pneumonia, then they let me come back. Well, [if] I get better, I'm not gonna feel half as good as I am now. That takes a lot out of you. So then I get it again and they're gonna do something else to me and I come back. And then I'm gonna feel even a little lower. Well, that's not living. They say, "Yeah, we want people to live long."

Yes, providing you can get around. I don't mean that you have to go around and do a day's work or scrub a floor, but take care of yourself, do your own cooking, be able to make up your own bed. If you can't do these things I don't think you'd want to live. How young people feel, I don't know. That's the way I feel at my age. I'll be seventy-five pretty soon, so if I get something, oh God, I just want to go (laughs).

Look it, we all have to go. If you're born, anything that's born, anything that breathes has to die, huh? Even a plant—has to die—so—we die. And as my father used to say (laughing), you know how he would say it in Italian? They used to have the funniest saying, oh what a humor, huh? Although we're beginning to get crowded as it is. "Eh come ci capimmo, se nessuno muore, come ci capimmo qua—we can't even stand up [Well if nobody dies, how would we fit in the world]?" And sometimes he would say, "Well, if people don't die, Lu cimitero come addà' riempi, con ò capo d'ò ciuccio?" That means, "If nobody dies and everyone lived, how would we fill up the cemeteries? With donkey heads?" (laughing) It was fun living with them [my parents].

FIGURE 60. North End, 1980.

Vladimir Ciani presided over his men's club, where he often made pizza while his friends played cards. Grinning, he said, "Pensa a mangiare bene" (one has to think about eating well).

Vladimir Ciani

"Soon the North End Will Be a Memory"

As I say, a good part of the old imprint, of this nucleus which represents, so to speak, a part of our old country transplanted in a typical American city such as Boston, is fast fading and will soon disappear in its entirety. When you walk through Hull Street and North Street, Sheafe Street and Salem Street and Hanover Street—and instead of seeing Italian names on doors, you begin to notice instead the Ryans, McGraths, and Russells, and so forth, and other typical American names, you can't help but put two and two together. "What's happening?" one would ask. It's not so hard to figure out. The Italian landlords are remodeling at a fast pace, all the old buildings and shacks, making them very habitable and very attractive. But after these embellishments, these rents, naturally enough, jump to two hundred, three hundred and even four hundred a month! Result: the Italians as a rule are not able to pay these exorbitant rents and have to make an exit to other towns where rents still remain relatively cheap. The net result of all this is that within a decade our old North End will disappear as a symbol of our Italianity. It will only remain as a memory of what it once was. But then again, we should never lose sight of the fact that history for centuries has always repeated itself.

In our case, it's happening exactly as history prescribes: ninety years ago, we, the Italians, especially from 1890 to 1914, came to Boston in huge quantities, with the net result that we displaced all the Irish and Jewish people from the North End and we made this little corner of Boston absolutely our own. Is it any wonder that we in turn should see this process duplicated?

FIGURE 61. North End, 2017.

Epilogue

Anthony's Gift to Us

JAMES S. PASTO

The North End that Anthony visited some forty years ago has changed. We no longer hear the cacophony of dialects intermixed with the Italianized English spoken by North Enders—"the North End Accent." We no longer see old men playing cards in the Prado, meet old ladies on their way to Mass, or run into "characters" on every corner. And we no longer smell the aromas of Italian foods wafting from numerous apartment windows out onto the streets. Things are different. Yet not all is gone—there are remainders. The "sidewalk ballet" that Jane Jacobs described and which Anthony documented with his photographs continues, as many of the newcomers have adopted North End patterns of socialization and networking, while there are enough old-timers to show them how it is done. Moreover, one can still hear Italian spoken, catch a few words of North End English, and most definitely encounter Italian scents from the Italian restaurants, many of them owned and run by the same families who sat with seven, eight, nine, or more in the old apartments.

So the North End today is not a dim reflection the North End of old: it is an ongoing story in which Italians still figure large in its telling. I want to focus on that ongoing story. I cannot tell the whole of the story, for that would take another book of photographs and oral histories. And I cannot presume to speak for the people who live there today since I have not lived in the North End since the 1990s. What I will do, instead, is to share some thoughts, reflections, and even stories of my own, told through the lens of before-and-after photographs that Anthony has chosen. If the result is

FIGURE E.1. J & N Meat Market with Danny Lorusso and Angelina Raffa.

FIGURE E.2. Monica's Mercato and Salumeria.

somewhat *'ntrasatta* (off the top of my head), it is nevertheless also *di cuore* (from the heart). I will, however, leave important space after this to say something about Anthony's book as a gift he is offering to us and those who come after us.

Figure E.1 is the *J & N Meat Market* at 130 Salem Street, which closed in the late 1980s. The owners, Joe Lorusso and Nick Di Bisceglia, are visible inside, along with one of Nick's sons and some customers. Outside, Joe's son Danny is standing at the door, while sitting next to him is Angelina Raffa. J & N was one of perhaps a dozen butcher shops in the North End that were part of the North End's ethnic "enclave economy," that economy in which businesses specialize in goods or services primarily intended for the ethnic group that makes up the majority of its clientele and labor force. New immigrants to America could live in the North End and find work in this economy, giving them time to gradually habituate and assimilate to the wider American society. Businesses like J & N were family owned, and each had some special characteristic or character that made them special. The smell of Nick's cigar, whose smoke is visible in the image, was one characteristic of the store that I remember, for the smoke would mingle with the smells of sawdust and raw meat in a way that seemed not only pleasant but almost essential. Nick was more outgoing than Joe, who was rather quiet, but both were truly sweet men. They would always ask me how school was going or how my grandfather was feeling or mention that they had seen my Aunt Sylvia and comment on how beautiful she was. They would cut the meats on the counter, wrap them in paper with the price written on it, and record the amount on a list they kept behind the counter for my mother to pay the next time she stopped by. Angelina Raffa, who did not speak English, sat outside the shop at all times of the year. She lived on the fifth floor of a building on Prince Street and she knew a place somewhere outside the North End that had delicious wild mushrooms. When they were in season, she would often come back with a bag full of them. From what I understand, that place remains a secret that she never revealed.

Figure E.2 shows what stands in the same location, *Monica's Mercato and Salumeria*, one of several businesses owned by the Mendoza brothers, Jorge, Patrick, and Frank. You cannot see any of the brothers in this image, though one or more of them are never far from the store. I did not know them growing up in the North End as I am older, but I met Frank and Patrick one night through my good friend and *cumpare* Tommy Damigella—or *Passannànze* ("Go-Getter") as Anthony calls him. The Mendoza brothers immigrated to the North End in 1984 with their parents and other siblings. They found work in the enclave economy, where they learned enough of the restaurant business to open *Monica's Bar and Grill* in 1995 and then *Monica's Mercato* in 1997. Both are named after their mother, who grew up in northern Italy and who cooked for the family of seven in their small North End apartment. They told me that they learned to cook by watching their mother cook and eating her food; many of her recipes give their food its special quality. The *Mercato* began as a local market, not too different in its first incarnation from those you see in Anthony's photos. It was a place where one could buy domestic and imported Italian ingredients for dinner. They began selling subs by popular demand, as locals would ask them to add their freshly sliced cold cuts to their fresh baked breads. There is no smell of sawdust, raw meat, and cigar smoke inside but rather the aromas of cured meats, cheeses, olives, peppers, breads, and pizza. The people you see walking outside the store in the photograph are worlds away from Danny and Angelina, but the employees, many of them new immigrants from Central and South America, would have meshed well with them.

The transition from *J & N* to *Monica's* speaks to the paradoxical nature of gentrification in the North End. One the one hand, it has reduced the presence of butcher shops and similar local businesses, such as cobblers, tailors, and grocery stores. Many of the younger generation did not want to continue in the trades of their fathers, mothers, or grandparents. In addition, when many of the aging buildings were sold, the new owners increased the rents according to the market rate, which made it hard for the businesses to remain, and then made use of the space for apartments. In addition, the incoming non-Italian and more affluent residents cooked less and ate out more. This stimulated a demand for restaurants—not just any restaurants, but Italian restaurants, because the gentrifiers were coming to the North End to live in an Italian neighborhood, and they associated the word "Italian" primarily with food and wine. The Boston Bicentennial also increased tourism, with a corresponding increase in the demand for food venues. North Enders met the demand by opening restaurants, small food shops, or *salumerie*. Some of these North Enders were of the second and even third generations, but others were recent immigrants like the Mendozas. In fact, the latter were part of that second wave of post–World War II immigrants from Italy and South America who moved to the North End in the 1960s, 1970s, and 1980s. These immigrants helped keep the neighborhood Italian and give it that "Old World" ambience, which it retains today, even if it is small. They did this through their restaurants and by taking advantage, in the best way, of

FIGURE E.3. NU 5 & 10, "Willy's" (interior).

FIGURE E.4. NU 5 & 10, "Willy's" (exterior).

FIGURE E.5. Locale Restaurant.

gentrification. Thus, they not only found their America, they made it themselves in the North End. We must thank them.

Figure E.3 is the *NU 5 & 10* cents store at 352 Hanover Street. Bobby Chiota, the owner, is in front, standing next to the two women. We called the store "Willie's," the name of Bobby's father (we think). Bobby's wife, Angie, and a woman named Anty worked there. Willie's sold cookware, lamps, outdoor items, puzzles, toys, and other things like that. If you did not see what you wanted in the aisles, they probably had it in the cellar. I think many North End kids have fond memories of that store. Bobby had nicknames for everyone, and his wife, Angie, was angelic. My mother took me there when she went shopping. While she would browse or chat, I would wander about in the aisles. Figure E.4 shows you what the store was like inside. For me it seemed like a labyrinth in which there was always some new item to discover. Inevitably I would end up at the toy section. There is a huge space in my memory about this store, which is probably why I often have dreams that I am back there. When I do dream of being there, it is a very happy visit. I see the many-colored items standing out amid the darker recesses of the store and my mother is nearby. I feel very safe, and there is a sense of permanence.

Figure E.5 is what stands at the site today: *Locale*, an Italian restaurant and pizzeria, which is owned by North Ender Jennifer Pittore. Before *Locale*, which opened in 2013, she owned a pizzeria on Prince Street called *Mineo*, which became a restaurant called *Sage*. Anthony took the photo at a quiet time of day, probably the morning, and happened to catch a North End woman, Rosa Fierro, passing in front of the restaurant. She is looking at Anthony and giving him a very "North End" look, something like: "Wha'da you doin', you?" It's classic. *Locale* is a very different venue from Willie's but maintains something essential of both Hanover Street and the North End. It is a "modern" restaurant, with a menu that includes a pesto ricotta, burrata with capers, and pizza with Brussel sprouts. Yet at the same time, *Locale* has something of the "old-style" North End restaurants, by which I mean places like *the Blue Front*. These were family-owned and -run venues with limited menus of homemade dishes at low cost. They were neighborhood places where locals and "outsiders" gathered, and they were as much a space for socialization as a place to eat. That is what *Locale* feels like inside and what Jennifer thinks of as characteristic of her restaurant. When I asked her if restaurants like *Locale* helped keep the North End Italian, she replied, "I don't think the restaurant makes the North End survive as an Italian neighborhood, but I do think it helps us remain a neighborhood. I love that I can talk to and feed people I have known my entire life, and I love that I have met so many great new neighbors because of *Locale*."

Thus, like the *Mercato* on Salem Street, *Locale* remains a place of continuity between old and new made possible through the agency of people like Jennifer, who are willing to put in the hard work to create a business in the wake of changes brought through gentrification.

There is something else I want to mention. Jennifer stands in a long line of women owning and running restaurants (and other businesses, as described later) in the North End, while also cooking at home for their families as wives and mothers. There was no contradiction between the two: both were woven into the wider social fabric and both activities accorded value and prestige. Keep in mind that food production was central to Italian and Italian American women in the North End. As Thomas Belmonte said of women in Naples, they were "the living center of a tight-bonded human group" and "guardians of the hearth." They gathered the family resources and then redistributed them in the form of that "most highly valued resource: palatable food."[1] The same applied regarding the women of the North End. Our food speaks for us, and it does so now in and through the restaurants of the North End and the many women who own and run them.

I can't speak of food without mentioning my mother. She did not own a restaurant but she cooked for six during the week: me, my sister, my father, my grandfather, and Aunt Sylvia. We ate her food at my grandfather's home, a block away from our apartment, where my Aunt Sylvia also lived. Since she worked full time on Broad Street, my mother would cook for all of us and we would eat there together. The meals had a pattern: Monday was an old-style Italian dish for my grandfather, which my sister and I did not always like, so there was also a homemade soup or casserole for us; Tuesdays and Thursdays were macaroni (penne, rigatoni, etc.) or spaghetti; Wednesday was usually American night, with steak, meatloaf, or something like that. But every night we also had an early appetizer, maybe fried peppers or a frittata; we always had a cooked vegetable, like broccoli or rapini (rabbis); and we always finished the meal with a salad of lettuce, cucumber, and tomato dressed with oil, vinegar, salt, pepper, and oregano. Fridays was either fish night or pizza—even when it was not Lent. The meat and fish were always fresh, from J & N's, along with fresh bread from Boschetto Bakery. My grandfather made wine down the cellar of his building, so we had some with every meal, in small glasses. He also grew tomatoes and peppers on the roof or fire escape. It really was just like what you read about in Anthony's book.

FIGURE E.6. Burden's Drug Store and "Coco."

FIGURE E.7. Burden's owner, Louis Spagnuolo.

FIGURE E.8. Rita and Tommy Damigella (sitting).

Figure E.6 is *Burden's Drugs* at 308 Hanover Street which was located where Hanover and Prince Streets meet. This is pretty much the main intersection of the North End and is in fact one of the busiest corners, both past and present (though you would not guess that from the photo). The man sitting on the car was nicknamed "Coco" because his last name was Cuocco. He hung out at Bee Gees, a social club a few doors away. He lived in Medford and was a relative of Joyce Cuocco, the famous ballerina who appeared on the *Ed Sullivan Show*. *Burden's* filled prescriptions, sold and developed film, and provided a small stock of greeting cards and similar items. It was one of a half-dozen family-owned pharmacies or drug stores in the neighborhood. There was a family coat of arms above the pharmacy counter and two phone booths beside it. To the left there was a soda counter where you could get ice cream and tamarindo—an exotic mix of sugar, water, and tamarind. You can see the counter in Figure E.7, along with the owner, Louis Spagnuolo.

Burden's was around the corner from St. Anthony's School and across the street from Martini's store (which is still there). I would stop at Martini's every day after school to buy the Italian newspaper *Il Progresso* for my grandfather and then stop at Burden's for a soda or ice cream. Sometimes I would see some of the nuns who taught at the school there, most often Sister Rosaria. She went there to purchase the chocolates that she used as prizes in the raffles she ran in the classroom, raising money for orphanages. We nicknamed her "Raffling Rosie." Burden's is another place I often visit in my dreams. It is always evening and there are always many sounds coming in the store from Hanover Street—cars, voices, music. The store was usually busy and the corner was a popular one, which was active late into the night, especially as it was a few doors down from several cafes and restaurants. It made an impression on me and I'm happy to go back there once in a while, even if it is in a dream.

Figure E.8 is *Caffé Dello Sport*, which now stands in place of *Burden's*. It is one of three "Italian cafes" in North End, if we do not count the pastry shops or the *gelateria* that also serve coffee. *Dello Sport* is a popular spot for both Italian Americans and Italians and also for other locals and tourists, and it is yet another North End business that owes its existence to post–World War II immigrants: Angelo Cattaneo, who came to the North End from Bergamo, Italy, by way of Argentina (and New York) in 1962. He opened the cafe in 1989 across the street but moved to 308 Hanover in 1992, where it has remained since and is now run by his grandson, Mivan Spencer. Mivan has kept it a traditional Italian café, a place to get espresso and watch soccer. However, he has also modernized it with new TV screens and multimedia technology. It is busy during the day and evening and there are plenty of characters inside and about. The handsome couple you see sitting in the photo of *Dello Sport* are Rita and Tommy (*Passannànze*) Damigella. I could tell you stories about them (all good), such as their legendary Carnevale family dinner. I wish I had the space here to do so because it is something to tell. As for the man walking past them—he is a North Ender but I will not tell you his name. Instead, I'll give you the "North End test": if you know who he is, then you are a North Ender. *Dello Sport*, incidentally, is right across the street from St. Leonard's Peace Garden and St. Leonard's Church. There are restaurants running up and down Hanover Street all around. I remember sitting in the upper Church of St. Leonard's in May 2011, at the Mass celebrating the fiftieth anniversary of my uncle, Father Claude Scrima. The doors of the church were open and Hanover Street was busy with its huge dinner crowd. I could hear it all outside, but even more I could smell it—garlic, olive oil, spices, meats, fish, cheeses, sauces, all wafting into the church and filling the space. I knew at that moment what heaven would smell like. People sometimes ask how long the North End can remain an "Italian neighborhood." My answer is this: as long as it still smells Italian.

FIGURE E.9. "The Saint's Store."

FIGURE E.10. Helen D'Alessandro.

FIGURE E.11. Core Properties.

Figure E.9 is *D'Alessandro's Religious Goods Store* at 44 North Bennet Street. It was right across from the North Bennet Street Industrial School and close to the once very active corner of Salem and Sheafe Streets. We called *D'Alessandro's* the "Saints' Store," for reasons you can guess by looking at the image. It opened in 1927 and was owned and run by "Nonna" Lucia D'Alessandro. It specialized in religious goods, statues, bilingual bibles, chalices, crucifixes, and other items (and a small selection of toys). In addition to supplying religious items to the churches and religious societies, the store also collected clothes and money annually for the Franciscan Mission in Tegucigalpa, Honduras, which was founded and led Nonna Lucia's brother, Bishop Bernardine Mazzarella, OFM, who was the first principal of Christopher Columbus High School. In addition, Nonna Lucia provided free translations of bills and government documents and wrote and translated letters to and from Italy for residents corresponding with their families in Italy. When Lucia died in 1961, her daughter Helen ran the store until it closed in 1999. You can see Helen in Figure E.10.

I used to go by the store every day on my way to or from St. Anthony's school. I went in often, alone or with my friends, to look at the model airplanes and ships and to look at the statues of the saints and read their stories. The store itself felt like it was a kind of sacred space, and a very safe and protective one. I can explain this better if you know what the saints were to us. First, they were our superheroes: powerful beings we could call on for aid with any problem from serious illness to lost objects. We usually did so through someone who had a special connection to the saint. For my family, that person was Aunt Connie. If you lost an important item and needed to find it, you asked Aunt Connie to say a prayer to Saint Anthony. Once she did, you knew the object would turn up—it always did. Of course, we understood that it was the power of God who was revealing the object. The saint simply gave our request a jump up to the ear of God, while my Aunt Connie was there to pass it to the saint. It was all about connections. As for the image of the saint, we saw it a as symbol, like the photograph of a relative—an ever-comforting reminder, tangible and accessible, of the protection of the saint. This was especially important for people like us who really had little actual power of our own as weighed against forces of the world.

Second, the saints were "characters," individuals marked by certain idiosyncratic features, larger-than-life personality, a certain look, a remarkable life story, or all these factors together. Characters, as Brian Culkin says, give "an extra sense of life" to local life "through their simple, but remarkable, presence." Characters signify as an individual "what the neighborhood socially produced." Characters are therefore inseparable from the neighborhood as a whole: its location, history, ethnic makeup, and social organization.

The saints were remarkable presences to us by virtue of their miraculous deeds but also because of their remarkable lives and personalities, which included the kinds of faults, quirks, and struggles that we knew in ourselves. Their lives were inseparable from our own, and we celebrated them not only in private devotion and calls for help but also in our feasts, processions, and saints' day celebrations. Foremost among them was our Blessed Mother, Queen of the Saints, whose visitation in Fatima we watched at the annual screening of *Our Lady of Fatima* in the auditorium of the Michelangelo School. There we were, more than a hundred strong, children and adults, from infants to seniors, crowded together in that hall, intimate and intergenerational: individuals all, but all sharing a deep communal bond. Just like the saints in the window of the store. We also had living superheroes. They were not Superman or Wonder Woman but rather our parents and grandparents, our coaches and community leaders, a fantastic ball player or street fighter, an incredibly kind woman—or an incredibly beautiful one, a renowned lover, a talented singer. Their fame did not go much beyond the neighborhood, but that was enough. The neighborhood was where it mattered. We knew who they were.

We also had characters—plenty of them. I can tell you about one of them. My cousin Johnny was a character. Some people called him Giovanni or Gio; others called him "Barabbas" because in the 1960s and 1970s he had long hair and a beard and took part in the protests of that generation. He got into the hippie movement when he lived in New York, and ended up marrying Barbara, from Long Island, with whom he moved to the North End in 1970. Their daughter, my cousin Ali—Alessandra—grew up in the neighborhood. By the early 1990s, Johnny had shaved his beard, cut his hair, and begun to sport a mustache, making him look like the spitting image of Saddam Hussein, which earned him the new nickname of "Saddam."

Johnny would give you the shirt off his back and have your back in any conflict. But he loved to gamble too—numbers, cards, and 'the dogs.' He borrowed money from friends and family and also from local lenders. Sometimes when we went out together we would have to avoid certain streets to avoid some of those lenders. It was not matter of fear but rather of respect. He would pay them as soon as he got the money and he always did so. He knew it and they knew it. In the meantime, it would have been disrespectful to walk past them until he had paid. That was the way it was.

When Johnny was in New York City he did some acting. He had told us that he knew Martin Scorsese. We had been a little skeptical, but a few years ago my friend Nicky Savino confirmed it. He had visited Johnny in New York, where he met Scorsese too. Here is how Nicky described the meeting:

> One day we're in Central Park with a lot of his [Johnny's] new friends and we got to meet—I think he knew him but it was my first time and only time that I met Martin Scorsese—this guy, after seeing his movies in the years later, like we related to so many things, like Doo-Wop music was one of them, that the music playing in his movies were things that I— I can't believe that this guy likes the same music as me. Dion and the Belmonts or the Dubs or the Crests. I couldn't believe [this was] a New York guy; I realized that yeah, Italians from New York are a lot like the Italians of Boston in the North End.

A few years later, Scorsese was going to give Johnny a role in the film *Taxi Driver*. He would have got the part but something happened. This was typical of poor Johnny's luck. But that is a story for another time.

Now let's return to our photos. Figure E.10 is of *Core Properties*, the business that occupies the same space as the Saints' Store. On first glance, and even after multiple glances, *Core* seems to be realms away from *D'Alessandro's*. There are no saints crowded in the windows and it is hard to see heroes or characters in the advertisements, ordered in rows and separated by borders, which are anonymous and indistinguishable from a distance. So it seems like we might have a rupture with the past here, one not only brought on by gentrification but directly signifying it: a real estate office. In an early draft of this chapter, I described *Core Properties* as just such a rupture. However, as it seemed wrong not to at least speak to the owner of the business, I decided to find out who it was and found his name on the company's website: Giancarlo Tiberi. That sounded Italian. So I checked with a cousin in real estate: he told me that Giancarlo's family was from the North End and that he was "a good guy." I emailed Giancarlo and we spoke by phone. I'm glad I did.

Talk about connections—it turns out that Giancarlo's father emigrated from Italy in 1969, followed by his grandparents in 1970–1971. His mother's parents emigrated around the same time. They lived in the North End initially, but Giancarlo grew up in Dedham because his father moved there after marriage, while his grandparents remained in the North End on Hanover Street. That is why Giancarlo spent a good part of his youth hanging out in the North End and then living there with his grandparents during part of his

FIGURE E.12. Carmine Tiberi.

schooling at Boston University. As far as he is concerned, he grew up in the North End and regards it as his first home. His brother Massimo owns *Aria* restaurant. When Giancarlo moved his real estate business into 44 North Bennet, he gave D'Alessandro family a tour of the newly renovated building. The family appreciated it and there is "good energy" between them, Giancarlo told me. Giancarlo also told me that he tells clients who want to live in the North End that they are coming to a "real neighborhood" where they will soon find themselves woven into a web of communal familiarity. It is the old North Enders and the restaurants that create this fabric, and it is all but impossible not to be drawn into that web.

It also turns out that Giancarlo's grandfather Carmine appears twice in Anthony's previous book, *From Italy to the North End*. In one image, Carmine Tiberi is pictured with Massimo in his arms; in another, he is tasting wine with Libby Federico in a cellar. Giancarlo is good friends with Libby's grandson. The handsome Carmine Tiberi, now deceased, is in Figure E.12. Thus, here again in these images we find a connection between past and present. You can't get away from it in the North End.

I have to say one more thing before I conclude. The apartments advertised from companies like *Core* are quite elegant and they are like castles compared to our old apartments. Nevertheless, I can tell you that have no "space envy" when I look at them. The apartment I grew up in was about 600 square feet; it was divided into five rooms, with no doors between rooms and a bathroom outside in the hallway. Well, it was not quite a bathroom but rather a toilet bowl in an unheated cubicle with neither bath, shower, nor sink. You washed your hands in the kitchen sink when you came out. To bathe we took sponge baths when we were young and went to the public "Bath House" as adults. The apartment was in a three-story building, also unheated, while the heat in the apartment came from old steam radiators, all of which worked except for one in "the back room" (as we called it), which came on sometimes but not always. We spent most of our waking time in the kitchen. It was a small kitchen, bursting with pans and dishes and cups and food; three of the other rooms served as bedrooms, while the fifth was the "parlor," where we kept the television and the record player. The apartment was old but it was also clean, like the building's hallways, which my mother swept, scrubbed, and mopped. I loved our apartment—we called it "the house." I miss it. I still have dreams that I am back there. In the dreams, someone else owns the apartment but these owners are not living there and we have sneaked back inside, residing there in secret and hoping nobody hears us so we don't have to leave.

I wish we had more before-and-after photographs so I could continue to describe the connections and continuities that characterize the North End today, making it an ongoing story and ensuring that this epilogue is not an epitaph. Of course, I could not do this if we did not have Anthony's book. So I want to take some time and space to talk about the importance of his work. In my foreword to his previous book, I described his photographs as "remembrances of the past and cultural treasures for the future."[3] I wrote that the images could tell us—we who grew up in the North End—how we came to be, and that the images of the people he preserved were images of our ancestors and founders, our elders and wise folk, who traveled a perilous route to find a new life in a faraway land. They wanted to make a place for us here, and they succeeded in doing that. In Anthony's new book, which you hold in your hands, we can read what their journey was like in their own words. We can hear in their own words about the places they came from and why they left. We hear them speak about their early days in the North End, their struggles and hardships, and their perseverance and achievements. We hear of the changes to the North End and how it affected their lives, and we hear of the joy they felt in achieving what they came for: a better life for their children. It is the archetypal Italian immigrant story.

Currently we live in a time when this Italian "immigrant story" is caught between those who want to reduce it to a teleological descent into whiteness and privilege and those who want to keep it shackled to a Columbian story of original innocence and moral superiority. Neither one of these narratives does any justice to the actual history of these people in southern Italy or honors the truth of their story in America. The fact is that they always saw their own progress as part of an upward climb that they believed was due to everyone. They never felt their lives were particularly advantaged, and if we can now see "racial" privileges that gave their children access to spaces closed to others, we should not forget that the North End in which they lived was a redlined neighborhood into the 1970s, an "urban village" of old and crowded tenements, persistent poverty and unemployment, youth drug addiction and drug violence, and growing traumas of assimilation and gentrification that were real and palpable. This part of the "twilight" story remains untold. The fact that many of their children took some control of the gentrification though creating businesses that have helped them prosper is not something to decry but rather to see as a model for other people in other neighborhoods facing similar conditions. I have not even spoken of the efforts that were made to create housing, health, and nursing facilities for North Enders by North Enders to keep our elders and even a future generation in the North End. That is a story that still needs to be told. In any case, North Enders of every generation have nothing to feel ashamed of and everything to take pride in.

Anthony's new book, then, is a book of honor because it honors the people who made the North End the place that we all loved so much and tells "outsiders" how it came to be and what it was like for those who lived there. These stories and photographs speak for themselves and for a truth that political narratives can never obscure or deny. Anthony is thus a life giver, because he gives life to the people who are passed and past through these photos and stories and because these in turn enliven us in the present—for a present without a past is a dead present. And indeed, the North End is a present and living place, where the past lives not just as memory but as ongoing life established by its founders—our ancestors, our people. Anthony became part of that story and he remains a part of it. He is a North Ender as far as I am concerned. His book is a gift to us, a Derridean gift that "irrupts" into the circle of historical exchange. As such, it cannot be returned but only lived forward. Forward to what and for whom? There is an Italian saying to the effect that "those who leave an old way for a new way know what they are leaving behind but not what they will find" (*chi lascia la via vecchia per la nuova, sa quel che perde ma non sa quel che trova*). If we Italians in America are going to maintain a sense of shared identity in the future—and by "we" I mean those of us who have been here for a while and those new Italians coming today—then this identity needs to be formed in a new way because the old ways of pre–World War II Italy and of "classical" Italian America have all but passed. At the same time, we cannot abjure those old ways completely. Nor forget them. As "old ways" they must be remembered. They must be integrated into the Italian America to come, perhaps with the above saying modified to remind us that "those who forge a new way while forgetting the old, know neither what they will find or what they left behind." This is a task for the next generation, and here I mean mainly those new Italians coming to America. They must come to know and understand the old Italians in America. They can start at our beginning, with Anthony's book, with the stories, memories, poems, and the pleas of our founders and our ancestors. Ours are yours too. If you too come to know them. If you accept Anthony's gift to you—his gift to all of us.

FIGURE E.13. Nick Argiro (center) and Family, 1980.

Notes

Chapter One. Life in Southern Italy at the Turn of the Century

1. Clotilde DeFilippo, *La guerra delle sanniti* (Benevento: Edimedia, 2011), 27–28, cites the diary of a Piedmontese soldier, Carlo Margolfo, who documented the indiscriminate shootings and cries of the townspeople being burned alive in Pontelandolfo. Memories of the brigands were still vivid in 1935 when Carlo Levi was exiled to Gagliano and wrote, in *Christ Stopped at Eboli*, "When I talked to the peasants I could be sure that, whatever was the subject of our conversation, we should in one way or another, slip into mention the brigands. Their traces are everywhere; there is not a mountain, gully, wood, fountain, cave or stone that is not linked to their adventures or did not serve them as a refuge or hideout" (reprint; New York: Farrar, Straus and Giroux, 2000).

2. DeFelippo, *La guerra delle sanniti*, 100. See also Harry Hearder, *Italy in the Age of the Risorgimento, 1790–1870* (London: Longman, 1983), 241. Hearder reported the brigands' tactics of operating on horseback, sweeping down on villages to kill officials of the new regime, and destroying title deeds in town archives that had been stolen from common ownership.

3. Hearder, *Italy in the Age of the Risorgimento*, 7.

4. Antonio Ciano, *I Savoia e il massacro del sud* (Rome: Grandemelò, 1996), 14–17. Ciano also cites the thriving tourist industry due to the discoveries of Pompeii and the burgeoning flour mills and hundreds of oil presses and bakeries that supplied the South. For a detailed contrast between the culture of the Piedmont territory and the Kingdom of Two Sicilies, see Nicola Zitara, *L'invenzione del Mezzogiorno* (Milano: Jaca Book, 2011), 8–14.

5. Zitara, *L'invenzione del Mezzogiorno*, 44.

6. Loreto Giovannone and Miriam Campagnino, *Italiani Deportati 1863* (Cosenza: Falco Editore, 2018), 97. The authors specify Il Gorgona as the island for forced labor in the fields, Il Giglio for women and children, Capraia for cammoristi and those

who had committed crimes or engaged in bad behavior during their internment, and L'Elba for forced labor in the mines and fields (98).

7. Romano Canosa, *Storia del brigantaggio in Abruzzo dopo l'unità* (Ortona: Menabò, 2001), 101–102.

8. Giovannone and Compagnino, *I Deportati*; Ciano, *I Savoia e il massacro del Sud*; Zitara, *L'invenzione del Mezzogiorno*.

Chapter Two. Leaving Italy for the Promise of America

1. William M. DeMarco, *Ethnics and Enclaves* (Ann Arbor: UMI Research Press, 1981), 11.

2. Nathan Glazer and Daniel P. Moynihan, *Beyond the Melting Pot* (Cambridge, MA: MIT Press, 1963), 182.

3. Sari Roboff, *The North End, Boston 200 Neighborhood Series* (Boston: Boston 200, 1975), interview with Pietrina Maravigna. Pietrina's father was a laborer at the Filene's construction site in downtown Boston. He told his family that some mornings they found workers who had slipped and fallen to their deaths the day before.

4. Constantine Maria Panunzio, *The Soul of an Immigrant* (New York: MacMillan, 1922), 77. Panunzio described farmers as farm laborers closely resembling serfs who worked on the estates of large landowners. He also described archaic farming methods from biblical times, with laborers still using a *zappa* (a wide mattock), an ax, and a wooden plow.

5. DeMarco, *Ethnics and Enclaves*.

6. Mark Weyman, *Round-Trip to America* (Ithaca: Cornell University Press, 1993), 134. Weyman documents the rise of land ownership, especially in Sicily, due to returning immigrants and American money used to purchase land. See also Carlo Levi, *Christ Stopped at Eboli* (New York: Farrar, Straus and Company, 1947), 43. Levi noted the houses of the Americans in the town of Aliano, which were distinguished from the peasant shacks by second stories, balconies, and brass doorknobs. See also Glazer and Moynihan, *Beyond the Melting Pot*, 184. From 1899 to 1910, 1.9 million southern Italians immigrated to the United States. Of these, 77 percent were farm workers or laborers without skills and the remainder worked in skilled occupations.

Chapter Three. The Journey to Boston

1. Jerry Mangione and Ben Morreale, *La Storia* (New York: Harper Perennial, 1993), 103.

2. Edwin J. Clapp, *The Port of Boston* (New Haven: Yale University Press, 1916), 6. Clapp estimated that eight thousand people were employed in the business of handling ships.

3. Clapp, *The Port of Boston*, 139.

4. City of Boston, Boston Landmark Commission, Environment Department, "East Boston Immigration Station Study Report," as amended July 13, 2010, 8. The East Boston Immigration Station replaced the Immigration Station on Long Wharf in 1920.

5. Mark Weyman, *Round-Trip to America* (Ithaca: Cornell University Press, 1993), 85.

Chapter Four. A New Life in the North End

1. American patriots chose to hang two lanterns on the bell tower of the Old North Church because it was the highest standing building. Though it was Loyalist at the time, the church became a symbol of American freedom after Henry Wadsworth Longfellow's poem "The Midnight Ride of Paul Revere" was published in 1860.

2. William M. DeMarco, *Ethnics and Enclaves* (Ann Arbor: UMI Research Press, 1981). Marriage records from Saint Leonard's Church and Sacred Heart Church show marriage records not only from southern Italy but also from Milan, Piacenza, Savona, Vicenza, and Bologna.

3. Constantine Maria Panunzio, *The Soul of an Immigrant* (New York: MacMillan, 1922), 228.

4. Anna Maria Martellone, *Una Little Italy nell'Atene d'America* (Napoli: Guida Editori, 1973), 382. In March 1904, George Scigliano addressed over a thousand Italian workers in support of the Unione generale dei lavoratori. The *Boston Traveller* reported another meeting on April 7, 1904, at the Paul Revere Hall on Snow Hill Street, attended by over a thousand Italian workers interested in joining the American Federation of Labor. George Scigliano also delivered a speech in Italian and translated the speeches of the Central Labor Union president, Dennis Driscoll, and New England union organizer Frank McCarthy. In recognition of Scigliano's work in the North End, Italy's King Emanuele III knighted him a Cavaliere della Corona d' Italia on January 21, 1906.

5. Memoir of Josephine Amarù Mirabelli: *Growing Up in Boston, Malden, Palermo & Lexington* (self-published, 2003), 4.

Chapter Five. Becoming an American Citizen

1. Author's interview with Betty Panza, January 9, 2020.

2. In *The Value of Worthless Lives*, Ilaria Serra used the phrase "from voice to pen" to describe the changing consciousness of Italian immigrants when autobiography became a new form of expression (New York: Fordham University Press, 2007). Here the term is used to describe the transition from the oral culture of Italian immigrants to the acquisition of basic writing skills (pen) to become citizens.

Chapter Six. The Italian Mother

1. Author's interview with Al Mostone, October 30, 1981.

Chapter Seven. The Italian Father

1. Constantine Maria Panunzio, *The Soul of an Immigrant* (New York: MacMillan, 1922), 238.

2. William M. DeMarco, *Ethnics and Enclave* (Ann Arbor: UMI Research Press, 1981). Marriage records from Saint Leonard's Church and Sacred Heart Church also show marriages of couples from Como, Milan, Piacenza, Savona, Vicenza, and

Bologna. See Anna Maria Martellone, *Una Little Italy nell'Atene d'America* (Napoli: Guida Editori, 1973). There were also stonemasons, cabinet makers, tanners, street vendors, and sculptors from Lombardy and Piedmont and stone cutters, statue sculptors, fruit vendors, and factory workers from Tuscany (204–205).

3. Richard Gambino, *Blood of My Blood* (Garden City: Doubleday, 1974), 117–120. Gambino expands on the idea of manliness in the chapter, "L'Uomo di Pazienza—The Ideal of Manliness."

4. Author's interview with Helen Luongo, 1979.

Chapter Nine. Italy and the North End in World War I

1. Cesare Donnaruma modified Henry Cabot Lodge's views of immigration restriction and five prominenti defended Italians as prone to violence in a *Boston Daily Globe* forum on August 4, 1901.

2. Christopher M. Sterba, *Good Americans* (New York: Oxford University Press, 2003), 4.

3. Author's interview with Francesco Ventresca, December 2, 1980.

4. Ventresca interview.

5. *Boston Daily Globe*, April 22, 1918.

6. Salvatore J. LaGumina, Frank J. Cavaioli, Salvatore Primeggia, and Joseph A. Varacalli, *The Italian American Experience: An Encyclopedia* (New York: Garland Publishing, 2000), 671.

Chapter Ten. Garlic Necklaces, Camphor Bags, and Shots of Anisette

1. *East Boston Times–Free Press*, December 18, 1918, 5. See also Mark Honigsbaum, *A History of the Great Influenza Pandemics* (London: Tauris, 2014), 181.

2. Alfred W. Crosby Jr., *Epidemic and Peace, 1918* (Westport: Greenwood Press, 1976), 206.

3. Crosby, *Epidemic and Peace*, 228.

4. Author's interview with Rose Amato, May 25, 1980.

Chapter Eleven. The Molasses Explosion

1. Author's interview with Marguerite Locchiato, December 4, 1980.

2. Italian American Street Life

1. Jane Jacobs, *The Death and Life of Great American Cities* (New York: Random House, 1961), 9.

2. Author's interview with Mary Arigo Ventola, February 12, 1979.

Chapter Thirteen. Going to School

1. Antonio Ciano, *I Savoia e il massacro del sud* (Rome: Grandemelò, 1996), 8–39.

2. Author's interview with Theresa D'Alelio, 1980.

3. Author's interview with Theresa D'Alelio, March 13, 1981.

4. D'Alelio interview, 1980.

5. William F. Whyte, *Street Corner Society* (Chicago: University of Chicago Press, 1943; reprint, 1981), 99. See also Paula J. Todisco, *Boston's First Neighborhood: The North End* (Boston: Boston Public Library, 1975), 39. Girls were taught sewing, cooking, and decorating.

6. *Boston Daily Globe*, October 6, 1917.

7. Author's interview with Thomas Damigella, February 7, 2020.

Chapter Fourteen. Justice Denied

1. Patrick Selmi, "Social Work and the Campaign to Save Sacco and Vanzetti," *Social Service Review* 75, no. 1 (March 2001): 118. The quote describes the issue raised by Paul Kellogg, editor-in-chief of *Survey*, who wrote many thoughtful articles during the trial of Sacco and Vanzetti.

2. Benedicte Deschamps and Stefano Luconi, "The Publisher of the Foreign-Language Press as an Ethnic Leader? The Case of James V. Donnaruma and Boston's Italian-American Community in the Interwar Years," *Historical Journal of Massachusetts* 30, no. 2 (Summer 2002).

3. Israel Shenker, "Sacco-Vanzetti Case Evoking Passions 50 Years after Deaths," *New York Times*, August 23, 1977, 74.

4. Michael Dukakis, proclamation declaring the date Nicola Sacco and Bartolomeo Vanzetti Memorial Day, August 23, 1977.

5. "Sacco & Vanzetti: Proclamation," *Mass.gov*, April 30, 2018, https://www.mass.gov/info-details/sacco-vanzetti-proclamation.

Chapter Fifteen. The Depression in the North End

1. Author's interview with Josie Piccadaci, 1979.

2. Charles H. Trout, *Boston, the Great Depression, and the New Deal* (New York: Oxford University Press, 1977), 177.

3. Trout, *Boston, the Great Depression, and the New Deal*, 253.

4. Author's interview with Marguerite Carbone, October 29, 1980.

5. William F. Whyte, *Street Corner Society*, 3rd ed. (Chicago: University of Chicago Press, 1981), 106–107.

6. Piccadaci interview.

Chapter Sixteen. Seamstresses and Factory Workers

1. William M. DeMarco, *Ethnics and Enclaves* (Ann Arbor: UMI Research Press, 1981), 85–86.

2. Author's interview with Francesca Corrao, September 8, 1980.

Chapter Seventeen. Making It in the North End

1. Stephan Thernstrom, *The Other Bostonians* (Cambridge, MA: Harvard University Press, 1973), 135.

2. Anna Maria Martellone, *Una Little Italy nell'Atene d'America* (Napoli: Guida Editori, 1973), 246. North End shoemakers went to Haverill, Lynn, Brockton, and East Weymouth; stonemasons to Quincy, Milford, Bay View, and North Adams; granite quarrymen to Lowell and Fall River; and garment workers to Lawrence.

3. Giancinto Spagnoletti, ed., *Conversazioni con Danilo Dolci* (Milan: Gruppo Editoriale GEM, 2013).

4. Author's interview with Angelo Santomaggio, February 1, 2020.

5. Pietro DiDonato, *Christ in Concrete* (New York: New American Library, 1939), 13.

6. Author's interview with Dr. Nicholas Dello Russo, February 25, 2020.

7. Jane Jacobs, *The Death and Life of Great American Cities* (New York: Random House, 1961), 10–11.

Chapter Eighteen. Making Wine, Drinking Wine

1. Author's interview with Pasquale Capone, October 7, 1980.

Chapter Nineteen. Life in the Tenements

1. Guild Nichols, "North End History—The Italians," Northendboston.com, accessed January 27, 2022, https://www.northendboston.com/north-end-history-volume-5/#:~:text=%E2%80%9CNowhere%20in%20Boston%20has%20Father,of%20garlic%20are%20sufficiently%20convincing.

2. Anna Maria Martellone, *Una Little Italy nell'Atene d'America* (Napoli: Guida Editori, 1973), 238.

3. Martellone, *Una Little Italy*, 242.

4. Martellone, *Una Little Italy*, 238.

5. Herbert J. Gans, *The Urban Villagers* (New York: Free Press, 1962), 21–27.

Chapter Twenty. Sicilian Fishermen in the North End

1. Giovanni Verga, *I Malavoglia* (Milan: Francesco Libri, 2010).

2. Frank Viviano, *Blood Washes Blood* (New York: Washington Square Press, 2001), 53.

3. Author's interview with Antonia Luzzo, September 8, 1980.

4. Charles H. Trout, *Boston, the Great Depression, and the New Deal* (New York: Oxford University Press, 1977), 6.

5. Author's interview with Dr. Nicholas Dello Russo, March 8, 2020.

6. Author's interview with Keith Favazza, March 11, 2020.

7. Author's interview with Mariano Penissi, June 22, 1981.

8. Dello Russo interview.

9. Keith Favazza, *Captain Storm*, self-published, 2000.

Chapter Twenty Two. Christmas in the North End

1. Author's interview with Mary Ventola, February 12, 1979.

Chapter Twenty Three. Irish and Italians

1. William Foote Whyte, "Race Conflicts in the North End of Boston," *New England Quarterly* 12, no. 4 (December 1939), 626.

Chapter Twenty Four. Refugees in the North End

1. Thomas H. O'Connor, *Building a New Boston* (Boston: Northeastern University Press, 1993), 74. Besides Boston and New Haven, Pittsburgh, Philadelphia, Baltimore, and Albany launched similar programs.

2. Herbert J. Gans, *The Urban Villagers* (New York: Free Press, 1962), 16.

3. Gans, *The Urban Villagers*, 362. For studies on grief over neighborhood loss, see Marc Fried. "Grieving for a Lost Home," in *The Urban Condition*, ed. Leonard J. Duhl, 151–171 (United States: Hassell Street Press, 2021).

Chapter Twenty Five. Local Politics

1. Author's interview with Michelina Manfra, October 22, 1980.

Chapter Twenty Six. Gangsters and Racketeers

1. Badaracco Da Rieti, Giuseppe De Marco, Joseph Santosuosso, and George Scigliano, "Is the Italian More Prone to Violent Crime Than Any Other Race?" *Boston Sunday Globe*, August 4, 1901, 30.

2. Da Rieto, De Marco, Santosiosso, and Scigliano, "Is the Italian More Prone."

Chapter Twenty Seven. Life in a Cold-Water Flat

1. Anna Maria Martellone, *Una Little Italy nell'Atene d'America* (Napoli: Guida Editori, 1973), 237.

2. Robert John Frasca, "The Renewal of the North End of Boston," MA thesis, MIT, 1959, 14.

Chapter Twenty Eight. The Changing North End

1. Author's interview with Antonio Crugnale, September 8, 1981.

Chapter Twenty Nine. The Old Waterfront and the New Boston
1. Author's interview with Nunzio DiMarino, April 13, 1981.

Chapter Thirty One. Meglio Pane e Cipolla, e Sola
1. Author's interview with Mary Molinari, September 9, 1980.
2. Author's interview with Frances Lauro, November 4, 1980.
3. Author's interview with Vladimir Ciani, May 29, 1980.

Epilogue. Anthony's Gift to Us
1. Thomas Belmonte, The Broken Fountain (New York: Columbia University Press, 1979), 87, 88.
2. Anthony Riccio, *From Italy to the North End: Photographs, 1972–1982* (Albany: State University of New York Press, 2017), 87 (with Massimo), 123 (with Federico).
3. James Pasto, Foreword, in Riccio, *From Italy to the North End*, xi.

Index

NOTE: Names ending with *f* denote figures.

Albanese, Lena, 53–54, 91–92, 141–143, 153, 155–156, 188–190, 249
Albanese, Louie, 141
Albert, Johnny, 339
Amalfitano, Jim, 347
Amaru, Maria, 44
Amaru, Placido, 43–44
Amata, Giovanni, 115
Amato, Rose Arigo, 47, 114, 116, 121, 125, 146–148, 230–231, 306–309
Anastasi, Joe, 285, 319, 320–321, 343–344
Anastasi, Marie, 56
Anastasi, Mary, 259f
Antoinette (Mary Pasquale's mother), 77
Argiro, Nicola (Nick), 4–6, 4f, 196, 335, 398f
Argiro family, 398f
Arigo, Annie, 263
Arigo, Donna Maria, 47, 55–56, 120, 343
Arigo, Joe, xix, 285–286, 320
Arigo, Mary, 120
Arigo, Rose, 120
Arigo family, 143, 343

Badaracco, Louise, 181
Baldassare, Ursula, 249–250, 251
Baldwin, Roger, 163
Bardetti, Tom, 13, 52, 85, 212–213, 218–219, 308f, 309

Belmonte, Thomas, 385
Beninati, Guy, 291
Beninati, Mary, 158, 321–322
Beninati, Mary Pulp, 311
Benjamin (farmer), 339
Bernardo, Salvatore, 8f, 9, 37
Bianco, Luigi Del, 165
Bibby, Miss, 159
Bigelow, Miss, 153, 154, 155–156
Bimonte, Eugene, 284–285
Birra, Rosa, 369–371, 369f
Bloom, Mrs., 265
Borglum, Gutzon, 165
Bosco, Josephine, 364f, 365–366, 368
Bossio, Josephine (Josie), 250, 261–262
Bourne, Fred, 90–91, 163–164, 165–166, 172, 206, 219, 278, 293–294, 302–304
Bradenese, Rose, 139
Brogna, Vincent, 123, 288
Brovaco, Jimmy, 250–251, 258
Brovaco, Tommasina, 250, 260–261
Brovaco family, 260

Cacciola, Bernadine, 357
Cacciola, Santa, 357
Caffarelli, Anna, 39–40, 246–248
Capone, Al, 300
Capone, Pasquale, 28, 30, 217–218, 222–223

Capones family, 27, 28
Carbone, Marguerite, 107, 170, 271
Carbone, Marguerite (aunt of), 181
Carrano, Antonette, 279, 280
Carrano, Matteo, 279
Carrao, Francesca, 181–183
Caruso, 273
Caruso, Margaret, 291
Casalino, Barone, 5
Cataldo, Angelo, 183
Cataloni, Joe, 120, 123
Cattaneo, Angelo, 388
Cellurale surname, 311
Chiarenza, Maria, 264f, 265–266
Chiota, Angie, 384
Chiota, Bobby, 383f, 384
Chiucchiolo, Maria, 306
Ciani, Vladimir, 59–60, 361, 377
Ciano, Antonio, 2
Ciardi, John, 44, 226
Clayman, Mister, 141
Colantonio, Mary, 266–267
Collarton, Miss, 158
Collins, John, 285
Columbus, 43, 301
Compagnino, Miriam, 2
Coppola, Francis Ford, 301
Corolla, Frances Zanfani, 78–79, 80–81, 235, 347
Corolla, Frances Zanfani (mother of), 227
Corolla, Frank, 176, 176f
Costanzo, Angelo, 117, 243
Costanzo, Jenna, 30
Costanzo, Maria, 30, 117, 372
Costanzo, Mario, 30
Costanzo, Teresa, 29f, 30, 117–118, 240f, 241–243, 372
Crugnale, Antonio, 13–14, 220–221, 220f, 311
Crugnale, Philomena, 220–221, 220f, 311
Cuocco, "Coco," 386f, 388
Cuocco, Joyce, 388
Curley, James, 144, 206, 282, 296
Curley, Michael, 288
Curleys, 289
Cutillo, Vincent J., 109

D'Alelio, Signora, 151–152
D'Alelio, Theresa, 152, 153, 187, 352, 355f

D'Alelio family, 151
D'Alessandro, Helen, 390f, 391
D'Alessandro, Josie, 303
D'Alessandro, Lucia, 391
D'Alessandro, Phil, 281–282, 290–291
D'Alessandro family, 395
D'Allesandro, Phil, 166
Damigella, Rita, 387f, 389
Damigella, Thomas, 44
Damigella, Thomas (Tommy), 381, 387f, 389
D'Antonio, Marianna, 351–352
DeAngelis family, 354
Della Russo, Nicholas, xv
Dello Russo, Carmela, 201
Dello Russo, Emilia, 281
Dello Russo, Nicholas M., xxii, 200, 201, 226, 334
Delmont, Al, 272
Delmonte, Alberto, 272
DeMarco, Tony, 44
Di Bisceglia, Nick, 380f, 381
Di Sessa, Pietro, 256
DiCenso, Giuseppe (Joe), 11–12, 175
DiCenso surname, 311
DiDonato, Pietro, 200
DiMarino, Nunzio, 1, 204f, 205–206, 333–334
DiMasi, Sal, 324
DiMattia, Elvira, 88–89, 209–210, 294–296, 340–341, 354–355
Distasio, Maria, 121
Doak, Miss, 153
Dolci, Danilo, 200
Donnaruma, James, 43
Donnaruma, James V., 164
Drake, Samuel Adam, 226
Dukakis, Michael, 165
Dunn, Mrs., 138
Dunovan, Miss, 75, 93

Faavaloro, Leonardo, 238
Falco, Charlie, 290
Favazza, Frank, 12, 110–111, 127, 129, 138, 237, 238, 239, 241, 242f, 243–245, 246f, 316–317
Favazza, Joseph (Joe), 245, 246f
Federico, Libby, 395
Federico surname, 311
Felicani, Aldino, 164
Ferullo, Sabino, 272

Fierro, Rosa, 384f, 385
Finkelstein, Doctor, 293
Finnochietti, Rosa Maria, 43
Fitzgerald, John F. "Honey Fitz," 60, 288, 293
Fitzgeralds, 289
Forte, Felix, 288
Francis, Father, 314–315
Frederico, Gabriele, 32
Freni, Giuseppe (Joe), 35, 37, 111–112, 111f, 273
Fried, Marc, 130
Fuller, Governor, 166
Fuller, Sammy, 272

Galleani, Luigi, 164
Ganger, Mr., 93
Gans, Herbert, 226, 280
Giamba, Concetta, 256
Giampaolo, Rose, 52–53, 149, 297, 327–329, 345
Ginnetti, Mr., 65
Giovannone, Loreto, 2
Grande, Dominic, 60–61, 67f
Grande, Gaetano, 67f
Grande, Paul, 60–61, 63–64, 67–68, 67f, 248, 266
Guarino, Joe, 253
Guidi, Ubaldo, 115
Gustin, Frank, 300

Hynes, John B., 280, 282, 312

Iantosca, Pasquale, 121

J. Alfred Prufrock, 217–218
Jacobs, Jane, 129–130, 201, 305, 379
Jannini, Rose, 181
Jell, Arthur, 120

Keith, Sally, 129
Kellard, Father, 88
Keller, Reverend, 302
Kennedy, John F., 60, 293

Langone, Freddy, 166
Langone, Joseph (Joe), 288, 293
Langone, William, 165
Lannigan, George, 293
Lanza, Mario, 273
LaRocca, Anita, 90, 314–315

LaRocca, Antonio, 315
LaRocca, Charlie, 90
LaRocca, Robert, 90, 314, 315
Lauro, Frances, 10f, 11, 57, 59, 132, 177–179, 322–323, 331, 360, 373
Lee, Joseph, xix
Lee, Richard C., 225, 280
Leveroni, Elvira, 181
Leveroni, Luisa, 181
Levi, Carlo, xvi, xvii
Liotta, Leonardo. *See* DeMarco, Tony
Locchiato, Esther, 126
Locchiato, Joe, 126
Locchiato, Marguerite, 12, 69, 117, 119, 126–127, 157–158, 171, 184–185, 277–278, 339–340
Locchiato, Peter, 126
Lochiatto, Carmella, 120, 121
Lodge, Henry Cabot, xix, 83, 107
Lodge family, 164
Logue, Ed, 225
Lomasney, Martin, 288
Lomasneys, 289
Lomazney brothers, 293
Lombardi, Joe, 302, 303–304
Lombardo, "J. L.," 300
Lombardozzi, Anthony, 291
Longorini, Graziano, 109, 153
LoPresti, Alfonsa Emilia Mazzarino, 153
LoPresti, Emanuel, 43, 109, 115
LoPresti, Laura, 109
Lorusso, Danny, 380f, 381, 382
Lorusso, Joe, 380f, 381
Luongo, Angelo, 84–85, 263
Luongo, Helen, 59, 73, 75, 119, 121, 125–126, 210, 269–270, 291–292, 351, 366–368, 367f
Luongo family, 121
Luzzo, Antonia, 237

Macchalone, Ida, 266
Macri, capomastro, 21–22
Malavoglia family, 237
Manaro, Alessandrina, 61–62
Manfra, Michelina, 7, 9, 14–15, 179, 197, 266, 287–288, 289–290
Mann, Thomas, 152
Mansfield (lawyer), 206
Mansfield, Howard, 279

Marinella, Angie, 123–125
Marino, Eddie, 100, 251f, 252–253
Marrotta, Louis, 135
Mazzarella, Bernardine, 391
Mazzarino, Ann, 44
Mazzotta, Antoinette Tommasi, 181
McGrath, John F., 152
Mendoza, Frank, 381
Mendoza, Jorge, 381
Mendoza, Patrick, 381
Menino, Thomas, 165, 289
Miceli, Saruzzu, 30
Mignoso, Dorothy, 280–281, 282–283, 282f
Militante, Luigi, 299
Missiano, Maria, 95–96, 99f, 100–103
Molinari, Louis, 228f
Molinari, Mary, 114, 115, 228–229, 228f, 267, 329–330, 347–348, 359
Moore (farmer), 339
Morgan, Kid, 303
Moriarity, Michael, 271
Mostone, Al (Louie), 46–47, 71–72, 88, 134, 202f, 203, 231, 235, 268, 312, 336–338
Mostone family, 71–72
Mussolini, Benito, xvi, 69

Nastasi, Mary, 250, 258–260
Natale, Sam, 264
Nazzaro, Michael, 281
Nazzaro, Michael (Mike), 352
Nichols, Malcolm, 205
Noyes, Henry, 302, 303
Ntoni (patriarach of the Malavoglia family), 237
'Ntoni, Master, 84

Onesti, Alessandro, xviii
Orlandini, Vittorio, 288

Paglia, Giuseppe Luigi, 256
Paglia, Theresa, 81–82
Pagliarulo, Signora, 351
Pagliuca, Arpito, 132–133
Pagliuca, Linda, 173
Pagliuca, Mary "Carmela," 24f, 25, 95, 98, 100, 173–174, 185–186, 194–196, 195f, 271, 335
Palmerozzo, Salvatore, 211f, 212

Palumbo, Ralph, 109, 119
Panunzio, Constantine Maria, 27, 28, 35, 41, 42, 83
Papa, Helen, 85
Papa, R. P., 84–85
Parziale, Giuseppe, 43
Pasquale, Antonetta, 48
Pasquale, Mary, 48, 68–69, 74–75, 74f, 77, 93, 94, 181–183, 186, 268
Pasto, James S., 379
Patriarca, Raymond, 303, 304
Pelaggi, Mastro Bruon, 100
Pennisi, Mariano, 238
Perez, Richie, 197, 289–290
Perrelli, Sam, 317–318
Pesce, Rose, 79, 191–192, 318–319
Petitti, Jerome, 115, 288
Petriglia, Monsignor, 256
Petringa, Joe, 89–90, 139, 141, 214–215
Petringa, Lucia, 283–284, 353–354
Pettinelli, Viola, 45, 75, 77, 149, 159–161, 233, 235, 330, 346, 374–376
Picadacci, Diego, 36, 38–39
Picadacci, Josie, 79, 103–105, 169, 170–171, 193–194, 230, 304, 313
Piemonte, Gabe, 263, 293
Pietrangelo, Cosimo, 62–63
Pinelli, Grace, 87, 371
Pinelli family, 86f, 122f
Pittore, Jennifer, 385
Polcari, Charlie, 41, 43, 44, 49, 51, 206–209, 207f, 275–276, 338–339
Ponzi, Charles, 42, 58f, 200
Prezzolini, Giuseppe, 95

Raffa, Angelina, 380f, 381, 382
Rappaport, Jerome, 280, 296
Revere, Paul, xix
Ricci, Rolando, 164
Riccio, Anthony, xxi–xxii
Riccio, Joseph, 217
Riccio, Lena, 71, 96, 97f, 263
"Rico" Bandello, 300, 301
Romano, Gabriele, 119
Romano, Salerio, 288
Rosaria, Sister ("Raffling Rosie"), 388
Rossi, Adolfo, 35
Rosso, Dominic, 129, 274–275

Sacco, Nicola, 163, 164, 165, 166
Santacqua, Elizabeth, 65, 66
Santacqua, Frank, 65
Santacqua, Jenny, 65
Santacqua, Maria Grazia, 65–66, 151
Santomaggio, Angelo, 200
Santosuosso, Principio, 294
Santosuosso, Principio (Princey), 295
Sardo, Angelo, 16f, 17–22, 167
Savino, Nicky, 393
Savo, Louise Bombace, 169
Scapicchio, Sebastiano, 256
Scarmella, Nick, 294
Scigliano, George, 42, 288, 299, 301, 352
Sciucco, Tony. See Shucco, Tony
Scorsese, Martin, 393
Scrima, Father Claude, 389
Selvitella, Henry. See Noyes, Henry
Shaw, Pauline Aggiz, 152
Sheehan, John, 281
Shucco, Tony, 272
Sinopoli, Vita Orlando, 225
Snow, Frank, 63
Solari, Arthur J., 109
Solomon, Charles "King," 301
Sorrentino, Alberto, 50f, 51
Sousa, Father Antonio, 115
Spagnuolo, Louis, 387f, 388
Spenardi brothers, 333
Spencer, Mivan, 388
Summa, Crocefissa, 36
Surrette, Carmella, 342
Surrette, John, 341
Surrette, Leslie, 341–342
Sutera, Anna, 252

Taglieri, Idolo, 149–150, 325–326, 325f, 344
Tarantino, Antonio, 254–257

Tarantino, Carlo, 256
Thayer, Webster, 164
Tiberi, Carmine, 394f, 395
Tiberi, Giancarlo, 393
Tiberi, Massimo, 395
Tonzillo, Antonia, 41, 363f
"Tough Tony," 206
Tranquillo, Josephine (Josie), 23, 37f, 38, 109–110, 184, 188, 314
Troisi, Joe, 145–146, 145f
Tupper, Earl, 44

Vanelli, Ester, 163
Vanzetti, Bartolomeo, 163, 164, 165, 166
Vara, Humbie, 302
Vara, Jerry, 302, 304
Ventola, Mary Arigo, 144, 263
Ventolo, Mary Arigo, 54f, 55–56, 130, 190–191
Ventresca, Anna, 31f, 32
Ventresca, Francesco, 31f, 32–33, 107–108, 276
Ventresca, Giovanni, 107
Verga, Giovanni, 84
Virginio, Maria, 361f, 362, 364
Vittorio Emanuelle III, 4

Welch, William Henry, 114
White, Kevin, 289, 291, 296, 355
Whyte, William F., 170, 301, 359
Woods, Robert, 152

Zachero (tavern owner), 201
Zitara, Nicola, 2
Zizza, Generosa (Josie), 78, 79, 80, 86, 92–93, 113, 116, 136f, 137–138, 153–155, 172–173, 192–193, 273–274, 324–325, 348–349, 352–353, 355–356, 355f

www.ingramcontent.com/pod-product-compliance
Lightning Source LLC
Chambersburg PA
CBHW060333010526
44117CB00017B/2818